Graphic Design
Learn It, Do It

T0266731

Graphic Design
Learn It, Do It

Katherine A. Hughes

CRC Press
Taylor & Francis Group
Boca Raton London New York

CRC Press is an imprint of the
Taylor & Francis Group, an **informa** business

CRC Press
Taylor & Francis Group
6000 Broken Sound Parkway NW, Suite 300
Boca Raton, FL 33487-2742

International Standard Book Number-13: 978-0-367-07536-1 (Hardback)
978-0-367-07534-7 (Paperback)

Visit the Taylor & Francis Web site at
http://www.taylorandfrancis.com

and the CRC Press Web site at
http://www.crcpress.com

Contents

Acknowledgments

This book is dedicated to my parents, Paul and Betsy Hughes. Thank you for your constant support and encouragement, and access to your traveling writing station.

The author would also like to thank her students, from whom she has learned so much.

Author

Katherine A. Hughes, PhD, is an educator, a traveler and a photographer. Katherine began her career as a multimedia producer and project manager for a series of dot com companies. After earning her doctoral degree in mass communications from the S.I. Newhouse School of Public Communications at Syracuse University, she returned to the university classroom teaching communication courses in graphic design, digital photography and online content development. When not in the classroom, Katherine is likely on the road exploring the national parks or planning her next study abroad program.

Introduction

Graphic Design: Learn It, Do It is an introduction to the fundamentals of graphic design and the software applications used to put these concepts into practice, specifically Adobe Photoshop CC, Illustrator CC and InDesign CC. This book is intended for production-oriented audiences, those interested in the what, why and how of graphic design.

The "what" is effective graphic design—using the elements of design and design principles to create a visual solution (an image) that stands out in a crowded marketplace. This discussion includes color theory, typography and page layout.

Focus on the "why" of design begins with the reasons why we communicate; attention is paid to the motivation behind the visual solution, as well as to its audiences. The rationale is revisited throughout the design process, including reviews of output options (print vs. onscreen) and their related properties, including resolution, color mode and file format.

The "how" of design addresses the stages of production and the use of select Adobe Creative Cloud applications (i.e., Photoshop, Illustrator and InDesign) to translate an idea into a visual solution. Following an overview of each application and its uses, exercises are presented to foster familiarity with each application's workspace and the capabilities of its tools while featuring specific design concepts.

This book is based on the approach of *learning*, then *doing*, and thus the title, *Graphic Design: Learn It, Do It*. In a production-oriented environment, this approach translates to discussing the fundamental design principles, then experimenting with these concepts in the Adobe applications. Guided exercises are included to get the designer working in the applications; they are intended to serve as a jumping-off point, from which the designer is encouraged to continue exploring the Adobe applications and their capabilities.

The application portions of this book refer to the 2019 release of the Adobe Creative Cloud running on the macOS. These chapters include Mac-based screen captures of application interfaces and step-by-step instructions through specific tasks. Designers using other versions of the applications or a different platform may notice minor differences between their workspaces and those represented in this book; however, the underlying concepts and basic practices should be consistent.

Look for references to this book's companion website throughout the text: http://www.crcpress.com/9780367075347. The files available for download from this site are provided to support the *learn it, do it* approach.

Let's get started.

Breaking Down Design

Graphic design surrounds us. We engage graphic design both passively and actively. We experience images passively in the forms of banner ads or targeted advertisements displayed along the sides of a Web browser or in an app when we post a status update. Similarly, think about the signs passed traveling to school or work, roadside billboards and storefront signs. Against this background of visual noise, there are images that we actively seek. Consider the day's news headlines or results from a recent sporting event; the type, photos and layouts used to present this information are components of graphic design. When a weather radar map is checked to track a band of approaching rain or snow, the colors used to represent the passing weather system have meaning; this too is a form of graphic design. Finally, think about the photos that are shared or viewed on social media. These photos reflect decisions made about the framing (what to include and exclude); the use of filters, lenses or emojis; and whether to include a text caption or a hashtag. These choices represent graphic design in action, decisions made to create an image that informs, inquires, persuades or merely entertains. These actions are at the core of why we communicate.

Why We Communicate

- *To Inform:* We communicate in order to share messages or data with others. Our purpose is to educate or simply tell.
- *To Inquire:* We communicate to solicit input from others. Our purpose is to gain knowledge and foster interactions.
- *To Persuade:* We communicate to change or support a point of view. Our purpose is to sell an idea, product or service.
- *To Entertain:* We communicate to provide a distraction or fill time. The bulk of mass media falls under this umbrella.

A single image or piece of media may satisfy multiple reasons why we communicate. Watching a DIY (do-it-yourself) video may initially serve "to entertain." However, when a viewer is inspired to try a technique demonstrated on the program or to purchase a featured product, the additional reasons "to inform," "to inquire" and "to persuade" become involved.

First Lines, Then Shapes

As consumers, we are presented with images; as designers we have the potential to create images. In this book, we discuss how to plan for and create effective graphic design. Let's begin with one of the most basic elements of design, the line. A line can possess meaning and can communicate its meaning to an audience. Take a look at the horizontal line in Figure 1.1. What could it represent? Perhaps

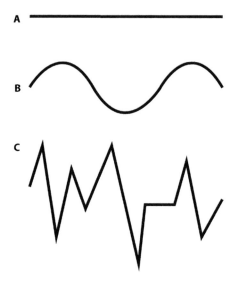

Figure 1.1

Lines: (A) horizontal line, (B) wavy line, (C) jagged line.

Graphic Design: Learn It, Do It

a road… a snake… a division between sections in a document? There are many potential meanings of this line.

What happens when a few curves are introduced into the line? What could this line represent? Maybe hills… rolling waves… the profile of a guitar?

Finally, convert the curves into sharp elbows. What could the jagged line represent? Perhaps a reading from an EKG (heart) monitor… the stock market… a jagged mountain range?

How these lines are interpreted and what is "seen" in each line is influenced by our personal experiences, background and context. The people, places and things that we have each been exposed to serve as a mental reference when we attempt to apply meaning to new experiences or, in this case, a series of lines. As consumers and designers, we regularly draw on what we know to provide context or meaning to an image.

Lines and Strokes

When a line is used to outline a shape or an object, it is referred to as a *stroke*. A stroke possesses multiple properties that can be adjusted to alter a line's appearance, including length, weight (thickness), color and type (e.g., solid, dashed, wavy).

From basic lines, we progress to shapes. What happens to the meaning of the original horizontal line when its ends are connected and a circle is created (refer to Figure 1.2)? What could this shape represent? Is it a ball… the full moon… a scoop of ice cream?

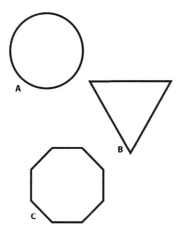

Figure 1.2

Shapes: (A) circle, (B) triangle, (C) octagon.

Let's try this with another shape—a triangle. What could it signify? Perhaps a yield sign… a slice of pizza… a cone for the scoop of ice cream?

Once more, this time let's use an octagon. Other than a stop sign, what could this eight-sided shape represent?

Symbols, Logos and Signatures

Building on a basic shape, let's see what else it can communicate with a few minor adjustments. Beginning with a blue circle, what happens when four more circles (black, red, yellow and green) are added and positioned so a total of three circles are on a top row and two circles are staggered below so they appear to be overlapping and interlocking? What is the result? The Olympic rings (see Figure 1.3).

In another example, beginning with a circle that has a red stroke, let's increase the weight (thickness) of the stroke and then add a smaller filled red circle inside the original circle. Do you recognize the symbol for a major department store? It is the symbol for Target, specifically, the Target Bullseye (Figure 1.3).

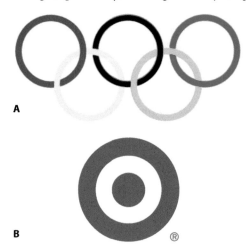

A

B

Figure 1.3

Symbols: (A) Olympic rings, (B) Target Bullseye.

As these examples illustrate, shapes have the potential to possess a broad range of meanings. Shapes that convey meanings are *symbols*. The Canadian road sign in Figure 1.4 presents a series of symbols. Can you determine their intended meanings?

Humans have used symbols to communicate and record their histories for centuries. Examples of this include rock art, petroglyphs and pictographs found around the globe with the exception of Antarctica. A *petroglyph* is a motif that has been pecked or scratched into the rock surface, such as those shown in Figure 1.5. These petroglyphs were found in present-day Arches National Park, Utah, and are attributed to the Ute people. These designs were created after the mid-1600s when

Figure 1.4

Canadian road sign, symbolic meanings from upper-left to lower-right: fuel, food, picnic area, winery, museum, golf, information, internet access.

Figure 1.5

Petroglyphs at Arches National Park, Utah (Wolfe Ranch panel) depicting bighorn sheep and riders on horseback.

horses were acquired from the Spanish (Aches National Park 2018). A *pictograph* is a painting or drawing on the rock surface using mineral pigments and plant dyes. Cave paintings in Lascaux, France, are among the earliest known examples of prehistoric art dating back 20,000 years (Bradshaw Foundation 2011).

In the current media-saturated landscape, companies use symbols to *brand* themselves and their services to target a particular market. Branding aims to promote a business's name, encouraging recall and recognition. Ideally, this recognition will attract a consumer's attention when a choice between products is available. Think of the branding images that accompany such classic choices as Coke vs. Pepsi and Mac vs. PC.

Take a moment to look for examples of branding around you. Look at your clothing and footwear, what symbols are emblazoned there? Next, look at your electronic devices. See any symbols?

In this search, you may notice that some brands rely on text and not symbols to promote their presence. This use of text is referred to as a *logo*. Logos use a combination of font, color, size and style to create impact. The terms *symbol* and *logo* are often used interchangeably; however, we make a point to be specific about our use of these terms.

When a symbol and logo are used together, this is referred to as a *signature* or a *combination mark*. Notice the differences among the three types of marketing tools presented in Figure 1.6—symbols, logos and signatures. What would you add to this collection?

Figure 1.6

Examples of symbols, logos and signatures: (A) symbols: Nike, Apple, McDonald's, Under Armour; (B) logos: CNN, Disney, Campbell's; and (C) signatures: The North Face, Pepsi, Dunkin' Donuts, and Adidas.

Figure 1.7

Hidden messages: FedEx, Baskin-Robbins, Amazon, and Toblerone.

In addition to promoting a company's name, logos and signatures sometimes contain a hidden message. Can you spot an additional meaning in each of the examples presented in Figure 1.7?

In the FedEx design, look for an arrow pointing forward between the "E" and "x." This shape is created in the negative space between the two letters. The Baskin-Robbins ice cream chain is known for its "31" flavors of ice cream. So, look for this significant number, presented in a contrasting color in the letters "BR." In Amazon, the arrow that points from "A" to "Z" provides a subtle reminder that the company sells "everything from A to Z." The arrow also doubles as a smile, which is used on much of Amazon's packaging. In the Toblerone design, look for a standing bear in the Matterhorn, a mountain in the Alps. The bear pays homage to the Swiss town of Bern, which is known as the "city of bears" and is where the famous chocolate was created.

Brand Evolution

Branding is an element of marketing that may remain consistent across a company's history or may change as a company grows and reinvents itself. International beverage maker Coca-Cola has used the same basic logo, shown in Figure 1.9, to represent its brand since the design's creation in 1886. The Spencerian script used in the original "Coca-Cola" has seen minor refinements over time, but some elements remain, including the white "wave" below the type added in 1969.

At the other end of the revision spectrum is the Seattle-based coffee chain Starbucks. A company familiar with change, the Starbucks logo has experienced

Test Your Knowledge

Want to test your knowledge and recognition of company brands? Check out Joey Katzen's *Retail Alphabet Game*™ (http://www.joeykatzen.com/alpha/) (Figure 1.8). Access the most recent game online. How many companies can you identify based on a single letter of a company's name? Notice how the font and use of color help identify a company.

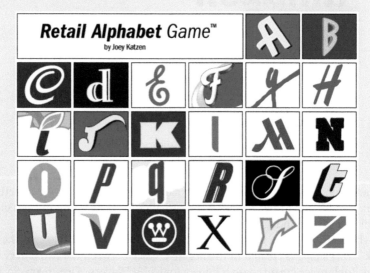

Figure 1.8

Joey Katzen's *Retail Alphabet Game* (version 5).
(Printed with permission from Joey Katzen.)

several iterations across its history (Figure 1.9). To commemorate its 40th anniversary, Starbucks revealed a change to its logo in 2011, dropping its name "Starbucks Coffee" and increasing the size of the siren (mermaid) in the design. Starbucks presented this change as an opportunity to expand its product range beyond coffee-based items.

Looking Ahead

From a simple line to evolving logos that contribute to company branding, we begin to recognize the role and importance of graphic design in communicating a message. In the next chapter, we look at the elements and principles of graphic design that contribute to effective communication.

Figure 1.9

Brand evolution, Coca-Cola logo and Starbucks logos (from left to right: 1971, 1987, 1992, and 2011).

Discussions

Discussion 1.1: Reason(s) You Communicate

Think about your typical day. When and how do you communicate? Now think about *why* and *with whom* you communicate. Are you informing someone about a recent decision or activity? Are you asking a question? Are you trying to persuade someone to join you for a meal? Are you simply trying to entertain someone via social media?

Is there another reason you communicate beyond to inform, to inquire, to persuade or to entertain? What reason would you add to this list, and how is it different from the existing actions?

To network (to connect with others) is often offered in response to this question. Explain how the rationale behind "to network" is similar to or different than "to inform," "to inquire," "to persuade" and "to entertain."

Discussion 1.2: Everyday Symbols

Let's connect symbols to things many of us use on a regular basis, emojis. What do the emojis in Figure 1.10 mean? We use such symbols in messages assuming that the message recipient will understand their intended meanings. As new emojis are added to the lexicon, have there been any emojis that you did not fully

Figure 1.10

Example emojis for *Discussion 1.2: Everyday symbols.*
(Adapted from Apple Color Emoji font accessed in Adobe Photoshop.)

understand when they first appeared? How did you learn their meanings, formal and informal?

What symbols would you like to add to your emoji library? What meanings or messages do you want to send in this format?

Activities

Activity 1.1: A Page of Circles

Exercise file(s): **Ch01-Ex01.pdf** (Refer to Figure 1.11)

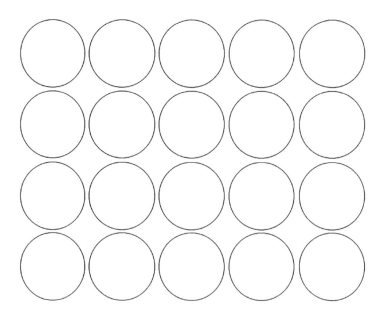

Figure 1.11

Page of circles used in *Activity 1.1: A Page of Circles.*

Use the page of equally sized circles, available on the book's companion website, and give meaning to these circles. For example, try adding a face to one of the circles or creating a peace symbol within another. Set a timer for 3 minutes and see how many circles you can use. When time is up, take a look at your work. What did you create using this simple shape?

Now is a good time to allay any concerns that you may have about the perception that one needs to be able to draw in order to be a graphic designer.

Can't draw? Don't worry. Let the tools work for you.
Can draw? Great, use the tools to enhance your work.
Find yourself somewhere in between? That is where most of us start.

As you begin designing, focus on capturing your ideas on paper and then use the Adobe applications to implement these designs.

Activity 1.2: Change of Face

Select one of the logos from Figure 1.12 that relies on a distinctive font, and using a word processing application, type the logo text at least six times, each time changing the font face used. What is the impact of these changes? How do the changes influence the tone of the brand? Do you prefer one of your examples to the original? If so, why?

Figure 1.12

Logos for *Activity 1.2: Change of Face.*

Exercise File(s) Available on the Companion Website, URL

Ch01-Ex01.pdf | *Activity 1.1* file, A page of circles.

URL: http://www.crcpress.com/9780367075347

External Links Mentioned in the Chapter

Joey Katzen's "Retail Alphabet Game™" | http://www.joeykatzen.com/alpha/

2

The Elements and Principles of Design

Graphic design is created and assessed based on a recognized series of elements and principles of design. These concepts provide terminology to use when discussing an image, as well as assessment measures to use when analyzing or comparing images. The *elements of design* make up an image, and the *principles of design* describe how these elements are used. Application of the design principles determines the overall success of a design.

Elements of Design

There are six elements of design: *line, shape, direction, size, texture* and *color*. As designers, these elements are used to translate an idea into an image, whether electronically or on paper.

1. *Line:* A line refers to the linear marks made with a brush or pen (Figure 2.1).
2. *Shape:* A shape is a self-contained defined area of a geometric (e.g., circle, square) or organic (e.g., natural) form (Figure 2.2).

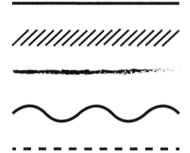

Figure 2.1

Elements of design, line.

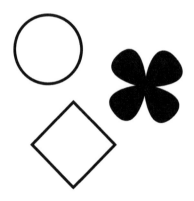

Figure 2.2

Elements of design, shape.

3. *Direction:* All lines have direction, whether horizontal, vertical or oblique (a.k.a. angled) (Figure 2.3):
   - A *horizontal line* (–) suggests calmness, stability and tranquility.
   - A *vertical line* (|) gives a feeling of balance, formality and alertness.
   - An *oblique* or *angled line* (/ \) suggests movement and action.
4. *Size:* Size is the relationship of the area occupied by one shape compared to that of another (Figure 2.4).
5. *Texture:* Texture refers to the surface quality of an object, for example, rough, smooth or glossy. In two-dimensional designs, patterns are often used to communicate textures, refer to Figure 2.5.

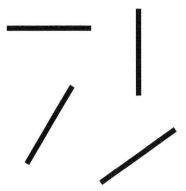

Figure 2.3

Elements of design, direction.

Figure 2.4

Elements of design, size.

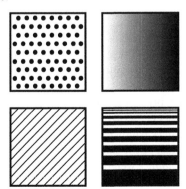

Figure 2.5

Elements of design, texture.

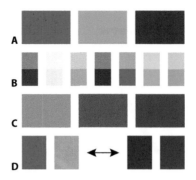

Figure 2.6

Elements of design, temperature: (A) hue, (B) saturation, (C) value, and (D) temperature.

6. *Color:* Color is light reflected from objects. Color has four main characteristics, which are represented in Figure 2.6:
   - *Hue* is synonymous for "color" or the name of a color (e.g., red, green, blue).
   - *Saturation* refers to the intensity or purity of a color.
   - *Value* describes the lightness or darkness of a color. Brightness is a synonym for value.
   - *Temperature* addresses the perceived warmth or coolness of a color.
   Note: Color is discussed in greater detail in *Chapter 3: Color in Design.*

Let's take a moment to identify the presence of the elements of design in the study abroad promotional flyer, shown in Figure 2.7.* How is each one of the six elements being used in the design of the flyer? Which element is used the most?

Principles of Design

There are six fundamental principles of design: *balance, alignment, repetition, contrast, proximity* and *space.* These principles use the previously described elements of design to achieve particular effects in a finished image.

1. *Balance:* Balance provides stability and structure to a design. The placement of objects within an image creates weight that can be distributed to achieve balance (Figure 2.8). *Note:* Balance does not mean that the objects must be the same size or possess the same characteristics.
   - *Symmetrical balance* weights objects evenly on all sides of a design.
   - *Asymmetrical balance* uses contrast to even out objects in a design.

---

* This flyer is available as a printable PDF file (Ch02-Ex01.pdf) available for download on the book's companion website. Use this page as reference throughout this chapter.

Graphic Design: Learn It, Do It

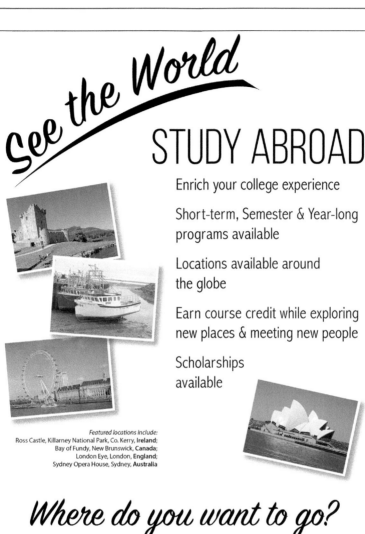

Featured locations include:
Ross Castle, Killarney National Park, Co. Kerry, **Ireland**;
Bay of Fundy, New Brunswick, **Canada**;
London Eye, London, **England**;
Sydney Opera House, Sydney, **Australia**

Figure 2.7

Promotional flyer.

2. *Alignment:* Alignment creates order and organization in an image. Aligning objects allows them to create a visual connection with each other, as shown in Figure 2.9.

3. *Repetition:* Repetition creates consistency and supports organization in an image; it can be expressed through a variety of properties, such as font, line, color or size (Figure 2.10). Repetition can unify individual objects, strengthening the overall design with a sense of unity.

Figure 2.8

Principles of design, balance.

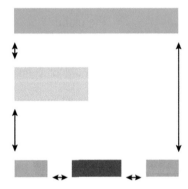

Figure 2.9

Principles of design, alignment.

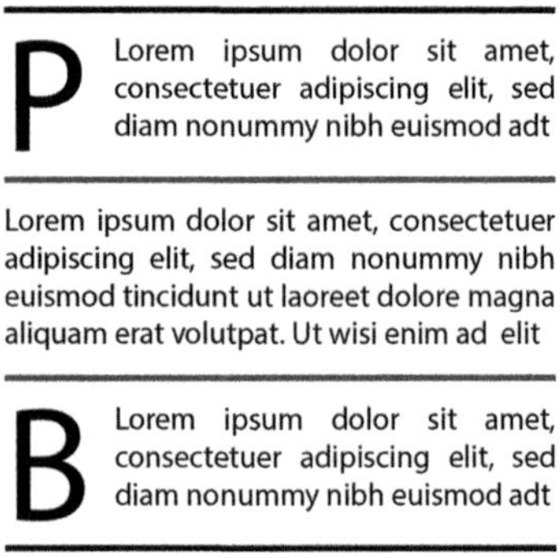

P Lorem ipsum dolor sit amet, consectetuer adipiscing elit, sed diam nonummy nibh euismod adt

Lorem ipsum dolor sit amet, consectetuer adipiscing elit, sed diam nonummy nibh euismod tincidunt ut laoreet dolore magna aliquam erat volutpat. Ut wisi enim ad elit

B Lorem ipsum dolor sit amet, consectetuer adipiscing elit, sed diam nonummy nibh euismod adt

Figure 2.10

Principles of design, repetition.

4. *Contrast:* Contrast can be used to highlight or emphasize specific objects in a design. Contrast is the juxtaposition of opposing elements (e.g., *value:* light vs. dark; *direction:* horizontal vs. vertical; *size:* large vs. small) (Figure 2.11). The differences attract attention, guiding the viewer's eye to the most important parts of an image and helping to organize the design.
5. *Proximity:* Proximity creates a relationship between objects; it provides a focal point in a design. Proximity does not mean that objects have to be grouped together; instead, they should be visually connected in some way (Figure 2.12).
6. *Space:* Space can help a designer avoid clutter and confusion. Space in an image refers to the area between, around or within objects (Figure 2.13). Both positive and negative spaces are important factors to be considered in every image.

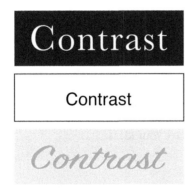

Figure 2.11

Principles of design, contrast.

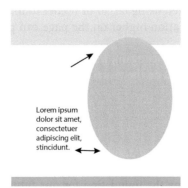

Figure 2.12

Principles of design, proximity.

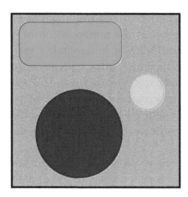

Figure 2.13

Principles of design, space.

In any design, we should be able to locate the six design principles. That said, the strength or impact of each principle may vary in an image. Let's return to Figure 2.7. Describe how each design principle is used in the promotional flyer. Which principles are most dominant in the flyer? How would you strengthen this design? *Note:* You will have the opportunity to redesign this flyer in *Chapter 15: InDesign Continued*, so save your ideas.

Visual Hierarchy

When used together, design principles can create a *visual hierarchy* or a sense of order within a design. This hierarchy aids in identifying what is more important in the image. As designers, we want to make sure that we are giving extra weight or visual significance to the most important message. Order and dominance can be created using larger or bolder fonts. Similarly, placing the most important information higher on the page can provide prominence to the focal point.

Referring to Figure 2.7 once again, what is the most important message being presented in the flyer based on the visual hierarchy of the design? Which design principles support this idea?

Looking Ahead

The use of design elements and design principles contributes to the success of visual hierarchy within an image. These concepts are revisited throughout this book and should serve as the foundation for our future designs. In the next chapter, we dive deeper into color, discussing its characteristics, symbolism and the steps involved with selecting a color palette for a project.

Graphic Design: Learn It, Do It

Positive and Negative Spaces

Looking at an image, it is important to see not only what is there, but also what is not there. *Positive space* contains content, areas filled with colors, text or images. *Negative space* surrounds the content; it provides the *ground* to the positive space's *figure*. This negative space can create shapes and highlight important information in the image.

The interplay between positive and negative spaces is often used to create symbols, logos and optical illusions. The Bronx Zoo signature, shown in Figure 2.14, creatively uses the combination of positive and negative spaces in its design. Look for the city skyscrapers created in the negative spaces among the giraffes' legs.

Figure 2.14

Negative and positive spaces, Bronx Zoo signature.

Discussions

Discussion 2.1: A Choice among Elements of Design

You are challenged to use only three of the six elements of design (line, shape, direction, size, texture and color) in an ad that will run in the local or campus newspaper. Which design elements would you choose to use, and why? How would your limited set of design elements impact the design principles?

Discussion 2.2: Design Principles in Action

Select a magazine cover, and describe how each of the design principles (balance, alignment, repetition, contrast, proximity, space) is being used in the layout. Which of the design principles are being used the most in the cover design? If presented with the opportunity, what changes would you make to strengthen the cover design? Explain your rationale behind these changes.

Note: If you do not have access to a magazine, use an online search engine, specifically searching "Images," to locate a magazine cover for the purposes of this discussion.

Activity

Activity 2.1: Design Elements at Work

Design a one-page flyer for a local charity bake sale using at least four of the six design principles. Sketch your ideas for this flyer on paper. On the back of the page, list the design principles that you chose to employ in the design.

The flyer must include the following information:

Semiannual Bake Sale
All proceeds benefit the local area food bank.
When: Next Friday, 10 a.m.–1 p.m.
Where: Library patio

Feel free to include additional information in the flyer.

Exercise File(s) Available on the Companion Website, URL

Ch02-Ex01.pdf | *Exercise 1* file, Promotional flyer.

URL: http://www.crcpress.com/9780367075347

3

Color in Design

Just as we are surrounded by graphic design, a similar statement holds true for the following discussion of color. Colors have the ability to influence moods and emotions, take on cultural and personal meanings, and attract attention. As designers, our challenge is to balance these complex roles that color plays in order to produce an effective design.

Colors have the ability to communicate; we receive information from the language of color. The colors on a stoplight have meaning: go, caution, stop. The colors (and patterns) of awareness ribbons are used to promote specific causes and thus have meaning. What causes do the ribbons in Figure 3.1 represent? Be aware that some colors are used by multiple causes.

During elections in the United States, political pundits describe the country as a patchwork of red and blue states, representing the Republican and Democratic parties, respectively.* In this context, what does a "purple state" represent? Purple unofficially represents a "swing state," a state frequently contested between the Republican and Democratic parties.

---

* Consistent use of the red and blue representational colors has been in place since the 2000 U.S. presidential election (*George W. Bush* [R] vs. Al Gore [D]) (Elving 2014).

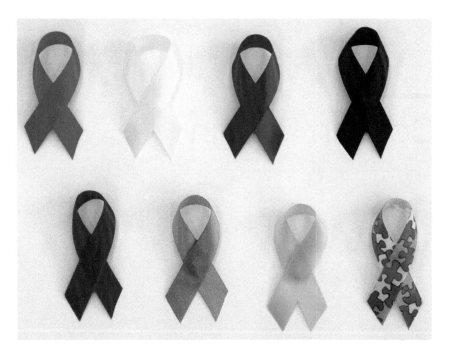

Figure 3.1

Awareness ribbons, represented causes include the following: *red:* AIDS/HIV, substance abuse, *yellow:* support our military, hope, *dark blue:* child abuse prevention, colon cancer, *black:* POW-MIA, mourning, *purple:* Alzheimer's disease, domestic violence, *green:* organ donor, leukemia, *pink:* breast cancer, *jigsaw puzzle:* autism.

When creating a *color palette*, a group of colors used in a single project, the designer needs to be aware of color symbolism in relation to the design's context and its intended audience(s). As part of any conversation about color and audience, it is important to mention that 8% of the male population and 0.5% of the female population have some sort of color blindness (van Beveren 2012). Color blindness affects a person's ability to clearly distinguish between different colors; instead colors are seen in a limited range. An awareness of color contrast and avoiding certain combinations can help members of this audience experience the visual hierarchy of a design as intended. For more information about color blindness and ways to design for this audience, refer to the reference included at the end of this chapter (see *External Links Mentioned in the Chapter*).

The Color Wheel

Let's now focus on some fundamentals of color theory, beginning with the traditional color wheel, shown in Figure 3.2. The *color wheel* is a useful tool for painters and designers; it helps in the understanding of relationships among

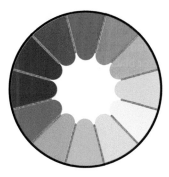

Figure 3.2

The color wheel.

colors and how colors can be mixed. Mixing colors on the color wheel can be likened to mixing finger paints. For example, when red and yellow finger paints are combined, orange is created; the same is true for colors on the color wheel.

Colors on the color wheel are grouped into three levels: *primary colors* (red, yellow and blue), secondary colors, and tertiary colors (Figure 3.3). When the primary colors are mixed, red and yellow, yellow and blue, blue and red, three *secondary colors* are created, orange, green and violet, respectively. Similarly, when the primary and secondary colors are mixed, six *tertiary colors* are created; these colors include red-orange, yellow-orange, yellow-green, blue-green, blue-violet and red-violet.

The 12 colors on the color wheel provide the basis for the broader spectrum of colors with which we will be working. To expand this palette of available colors, varying amounts of white and black can be added to the original hues to create tints and shades. Also, properties such as saturation and value can be used. Let's review these terms before continuing. *Note:* Some of these terms will be familiar from *Chapter 2: The Elements and Principles of Design*, while others will be new.

- *Hue:* Hue is synonymous with "color" or the name of a color. Traditionally, hue refers to one of the 12 colors on the color wheel.
- *Tint:* A tint is a hue lightened with white.

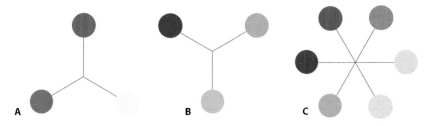

Figure 3.3

Colors: (A) primary colors, (B) secondary colors, and (C) tertiary colors.

- *Shade:* A shade is a hue darkened with black.
- *Saturation:* Saturation refers to the intensity or purity of a color. Each primary, secondary and tertiary hue is at a level of *full saturation,* which means that no white or black has been added. The closer a hue approaches to gray, the more *desaturated* it is.
- *Value:* Value refers to the lightness or darkness of a color. *Brightness* is a synonym for value.

The Color Pyramid

Refer to the *color pyramid* in **Figure 3.4** for an illustration of how hue, saturation and value relate to one another. The color at the top of the pyramid is the fully saturated *hue* from the color wheel. As black and white are added to this original color, the *saturation* of the resulting shades and tints decreases along the vertical axis of the pyramid. The colors' *values* span from the darkest shade to the lightest tint along the horizontal axis of the pyramid.

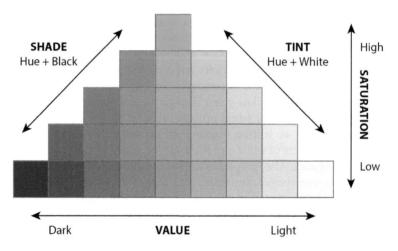

Figure 3.4

The color pyramid.

Color Temperature

Color temperature refers to the perceived warmth or coolness of a color (Figure 3.5). *Warm colors* include red, orange and yellow, and variations of these colors. These are the colors of fire, fall leaves, sunsets and sunrises, and they are generally considered energizing and positive. Warm colors are used in design to represent passion, happiness and energy. *Cool colors* include green,

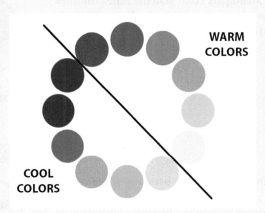

Figure 3.5

Color temperature, warm and cool colors.

blue and purple; these colors are often more subdued than warm colors. They are the colors of night, water and nature, and they are considered calming, relaxing and somewhat reserved. Cool colors are often used in design to provide a sense of calm or professionalism. *Note:* White, gray and black are considered neutral colors that take on the properties of the surrounding colors.

Color Schemes

The visible color spectrum contains millions of colors, so selecting a color palette for a project can feel like a daunting task. To alleviate some of the pressure, let's review the classic palettes based on the color wheel that could be used to create balanced and visually pleasing *or* high-contrast and striking images. These color palettes or *color harmonies* consist of two or more colors with a fixed relationship on the color wheel.

Complementary: A complementary color scheme features opposites on the color wheel, such as red/green or blue/orange (Figure 3.6). Complementary colors are high-contrast and high-intensity colors, but they can be difficult to apply in a balanced, harmonious way (especially in their purest form, when they can easily clash in a design).

Figure 3.6

Complementary color scheme.

Analogous: An analogous color scheme relies on hues that are side-by-side on the color wheel, or close to it (Figure 3.7). This type of color scheme is versatile and easy to apply.

ANALOGOUS

Figure 3.7

Analogous color scheme.

Triadic: A triadic color scheme uses any three colors that are evenly spaced on the color wheel (Figure 3.8). This scheme features trios of the primary, secondary or tertiary colors.

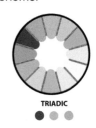

TRIADIC

Figure 3.8

Triadic color scheme.

Split-complementary: A split-complementary color scheme is a variation of the complementary color scheme. In addition to the main color, split-complementary uses the two colors adjacent to the main color's complement (Figure 3.9). This scheme still has strong visual contrast but is less jarring than a complementary color combination.

SPLIT-COMPLEMENTARY

Figure 3.9

Split-complementary color scheme.

Tetradic (rectangle): The tetradic or rectangular color scheme uses four colors arranged into two complementary pairs, meaning the four hues are not equally placed around the color wheel (Figure 3.10). This scheme works best if one color is dominant.

TETRADIC (RECTANGULAR)

Figure 3.10

Tetradic (rectangular) color scheme.

Graphic Design: Learn It, Do It

Square: The square color scheme is similar to the tetradic (rectangle) color scheme; however, for the square, the four colors are evenly spaced around the color wheel (Figure 3.11).

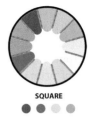

SQUARE

Figure 3.11

Square color scheme.

The following color schemes rely on a combination of tints and shades to produce a cohesive design.

Monochromatic: A monochromatic color scheme uses various tints or shades of one color, for example, a range of blues varying from light to dark (Figure 3.12). This type of color scheme can be considered subtle and conservative.

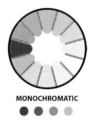

MONOCHROMATIC

Figure 3.12

Monochromatic color scheme.

Achromatic: An achromatic color scheme relies on only blacks, whites and shades of gray (Figure 3.13).

ACHROMATIC

Figure 3.13

Achromatic color scheme.

Color schemes can also be based on a particular color quality, such as *temperature:* warm or cool colors; *saturation:* vivid colors often look youthful, while faded ones look vintage; *mood:* bright and fun, dark and serious; or *theme:* location, season, holiday. To explore different color schemes, access one of the available color-picking tools online, such as Adobe Color CC (https://color.adobe.com) or Paletton (http://paletton.com). These tools allow the designer to easily preview color schemes and to record the selected colors' values for the color model (e.g., CMYK, RGB) relevant to the design's intended output. A *color model* is a system for creating a range of colors from a small set of primary colors. Refer to *Chapter 4: Defining the Project* for additional information about color models.

The 60-30-10 Rule

Typically, a color scheme will need to be split into a dominant color and one or more accent colors. A color would be considered dominant based on either how much of it appears in a design, or how it stands out in comparison to the other colors. When using a three-color palette (e.g., triadic or split-complementary color scheme), the *60-30-10 Rule* can be a useful guide. According to this guideline, the dominant color should account for 60% of the color in the design and the two accent colors the remaining 30% and 10%.

Color Symbolism

The meaning and symbolism associated with colors are influenced by the cultural and societal groups with which we identify. Let's take a look at some common meanings associated with colors in Western culture.

- *Red:* Red is a color that can communicate many different ideas depending on its context. Because red is associated with fire, it can represent warmth or danger. Red is also the color of blood, so it is considered an energetic, lively color. It is also associated with matters of the heart, and sometimes violence.
  In branding: Red often communicates strength, confidence and power; it is a highly visible color.
- *Orange:* Orange is also a fiery color, combining the warmth of red with the cheerfulness of yellow for a hue that communicates activity, energy and optimism. It is also associated with the autumn season.
  In branding: Orange often represents youthfulness and creativity.
- *Yellow:* As the color of sunshine, yellow often communicates happiness and cheerfulness. It can also signal warning or caution in certain contexts. *Gold*, which is a type of orange or yellow depending on its hue, is a symbol of luxury or high quality.
  In branding: Bright yellow easily attracts attention. However, it can be hard to see if not used carefully; avoid placing yellow text against a white background or vice versa due to the lack of contrast between the colors.

- *Green:* Green is the color of nature, plant life and growth. As such, it often communicates health, freshness or an "all-natural" quality. *Dark green* can represent money, wealth or stability.
  In branding: Companies or brands that want to be perceived as "green," in the sense of natural, environmentally friendly, healthy or organic, often use nature-inspired colors such as green and brown.
- *Blue:* The color of the sea and sky, blue often communicates peaceful, clean qualities. As opposed to more energetic, warmer coolers, blue is seen as calming. In some contexts, blue can represent sadness or depression. *Dark blue* is a popular choice for corporate contexts; it is perceived to have serious, conservative and professional qualities.
  In branding: Blue is widely used and one of the most versatile colors. It is generally used to communicate trustworthiness, security and stability.
- *Violet/purple:* Purple is traditionally associated with royalty. It can also have spiritual, mystical or religious connotations.
  In branding: Darker shades of purple symbolize luxury or opulence, while brighter shades can come across as childish.
- *Black:* Like red, black has many and sometimes opposing meanings. It can represent power, sophistication and exclusivity. In other instances, black can symbolize death or mystery.
  In branding: Black is so widely used that it is almost a neutral, though it can still communicate the previously mentioned meanings depending on context. Colors look brighter and more intense against black. Some designs are presented in black and white or grayscale, based either on designer preference or a decision made to reduce printing costs.
- *White:* As the color of snow and light, white regularly represents purity, innocence or goodness; however, it can also come across as stark or sterile.
  In branding: White often communicates simplicity or a clean, modern quality. Designers seeking a minimalist aesthetic will frequently use a lot of white in their work.

Selecting a Project's Color Palette

When selecting colors for a design, it is important to consider the following steps:

1. Clearly identify the desired results you want to achieve with color. Then, make a connection between these intended results and the "Reasons We Communicate" (see *Chapter 1: Breaking Down Design*). This connection will help clarify the overall purpose of the design, which can help direct the overall tone and therefore the color palette.
2. Select a main color that reflects the needs of the project.
3. Select a color scheme based on the central color.
4. Refine the color choices based on the particular project, its context and its intended audience(s).

A Color's Surroundings

Take a look at Figure 3.14. Are the green squares the same color? Yes, they are. Any perceived differences in color are an optical illusion based on the colors surrounding the green squares. In each instance, the green square takes on the properties of its surrounding color, and in certain combinations, this appears to create a new hue. For the designer, it is important to look for unintended color shifts in order to resolve the situation by adjusting the color or position of the object (e.g., green square) or the object's surroundings.

Figure 3.14
Surrounding colors.

In addition to these basic steps, the designer should be prepared to answer the following questions:

- Is the client or product that you are working with associated with a particular color? If so, how will this color be incorporated into the color palette? Brand recognition is tied strongly to color. Think of UPS, Facebook or Starbucks. What colors are associated with these brands? It is important that the colors you choose support the brand and fit its personality and market context.
- What is the competition doing? It is important to have an awareness of the competition's palette in order to distinguish your design from theirs and to avoid duplication. Think of how Coca-Cola and Pepsi successfully distinguish their brands through the use of color, red vs. blue, respectively.
- Finally, what is your budget, both in terms of finances and time? If the design is to be printed, are funds available for four-color printing or black-and-white printing (see *Chapter 5: File Properties* for more about print options)? This information can dramatically limit or expand your color palette and your approach to the design. Similarly, if the client can pay you for 3 hours of work, any time spent beyond that is time (and money) lost. Financially, it is important to value your time and understand your time constraints before beginning work on a project.

Looking Ahead

This introduction to color, its meaning and symbolism highlights the importance of knowing your audience and the context of your design. These are the topics that we explore in the next chapter along with the stages of production.

Discussions

Discussion 3.1: Mass Media's Use of Color Symbolism

Think of examples of color symbolism in mass media—books, TV shows or movies. How was color used in F. Scott Fitzgerald's novel, *The Great Gatsby* (1925) or the movie *The Wizard of Oz* (1939)? What about in *Star Trek*? Whether on television or the big screen, the crew members' shirt colors represent different work specialties. Trekkies recognize that those wearing red shirts are often the first to die when the away team is in danger. Next, look to the *Star Wars* franchise where the color of a lightsaber is used to distinguish between the Dark Side (red) and the Light (blue, green). Then, there is the exception, the purple lightsaber of Mace Windu (portrayed by Samuel L. Jackson) as first seen in *Attack of the Clones* (2002). The actor wanted to easily spot himself in scenes, particularly, the large arena battle scene, so his Jedi weapon was purple (Giles 2013). What examples of color symbolism in mass media can you think of? What do the colors represent?

Discussion 3.2: Color Comparison

Take a look at the images in Figure 3.15. The same photograph is used in each image; however, the color palette has been altered. First, describe the use of saturation and value in each image. Next, describe your initial reaction to each image. Which is your favorite? Which is your least favorite? *Note:* There is no right or wrong answer, you are being asked for your opinion. Describe a scenario in which each image might be used, explaining why the respective color palette would be appropriate for that outlet.

Activities

Activity 3.1: The Pantone Color of the Year

Pantone LLC, a self-described "authority on color," annually selects a *Color of the Year*. This color becomes a part of the visual landscape, used in design, clothing and home décor accents. The choice has been described by Pantone, as "A symbolic color selection; a color snapshot of what we see taking place in our global culture that serves as an expression of a mood and an attitude" (*Pantone* 2017).

Visit the Pantone website (http://www.pantone.com) and identify the current PANTONE *Color of the Year.** With the color as reference, locate at least three

---

* The "Color of the Year" may be more than one hue; in 2016, Rose Quartz (13-1520) and Serenity (15-3919) were both selected. For an explanation of this choice, visit the Pantone website.

Figure 3.15

Color comparisons: (A) original photograph, (B) saturation high, (C) saturation low, (D) desaturated (a.k.a. grayscale), and (E) desaturated with accent color. Peggy's Point Lighthouse, Peggy's Cove, Nova Scotia, Canada.

examples of the color in use on commercial websites. Having difficulty finding examples? How would you use the color? Brainstorm three scenarios in which the color would be appropriate (e.g., clothing, home décor, media campaigns).

Activity 3.2: Create a Color Wheel

Take a series of photos that represent the hues contained in the color wheel. Target at least three objects per hue. *Tip:* Start with one object per color and expand this collection as you find additional examples of the color.

Alternative 1: If you do not have access to a camera, download images from the Web that reflect the hues contained in the color wheel. Keep track of the source and its Web address (URL) for each image.

If you are in a position to print your photos, do so. Then, affix these images to a sheet of paper or poster board positioning the objects in their relative positions around the color wheel. As needed, refer to Figure 3.2 for reference when arranging the objects. Post your color wheel in your workspace to use as a reference when designing and creating.

Alternative 2: If you possess the necessary Adobe skills, use Photoshop or InDesign to create a digital color wheel using your photos. When complete, print a color version of this image to use as a reference in your workspace.

External Links Mentioned in the Chapter

Colorblindness
We Are Colorblind | http://wearecolorblind.com

Online color-picking tools
Adobe Color CC | https://color.adobe.com

Paletton | http://paletton.com

PANTONE Color of the Year
PANTONE Color | http://www.pantone.com

4

Defining the Project

Defining a project *before* any design work begins is an important task for the designer. Through this step, the scope of the project is outlined, the stakeholders (client, audience) are identified and the project's timeline is established. During the definition process, the image's purpose and intended output are also identified, along with the tools and resources that will be used to create the image. The Kipling method,* also known as the 5W1H method, is a useful technique to begin information gathering. This method asks the following questions: who, what, where, when, why and how. Or, if listed in the order in which each question is introduced in this chapter, what, why, who, where, how and when.

Kipling's Questions

Let's address each of these questions in the context of a design project that has tasked the designer with creating an image, specifically, a visual solution to a defined set of project constraints.

---

* The *Kipling method* is drawn from a Rudyard Kipling poem, which accompanies "The Elephant's Child" part of the *Just So Stories* (1902). Kipling's short poem outlines a powerful set of questions, "I keep six honest serving men, (they taught me all I knew); I call them what and where and when, and how and why and who" ("Poems—Six Honest Serving Men" n.d.).

What? What is being designed? A visual solution is being created in response to a presented opportunity. The solution should be clear and accessible to ensure that the target audience comprehends the visual hierarchy in the image and the intended message. Ineffective communication can lead to a misunderstanding of information.

Why? Why is the image being created? What is the purpose behind the design? A visual solution can be most successful when the designer clearly understands the purpose of the project. Think about the reasons why we communicate (refer to *Chapter 1: Breaking Down Design*). Which role will the image fill: to inform, to inquire, to persuade or to entertain? Will the image multitask and serve more than one role? *Tip:* It is a useful practice to revisit the project's purpose throughout the development process in order to keep the project on track and focused on its intended goal.

Who? Who encompasses several parties connected to the project, including the client, the audience and the designer:

- Who is the client for this project? Who has requested the visual solution? If the client is represented by several people, who is the designer's main point of contact? Identifying this contact before work begins facilitates communication.
- Who is the intended audience for the visual solution? Identifying the audience and understanding its needs are vital to creating an effective image. Designers address their audiences through the use of color, font, layout and overall style. Developing an overview of the audience's demographics (e.g., age, background) can serve as useful reference when answering the question, what will attract and hold *this* audience's attention? Is there more than one audience for the design, a primary and secondary audience? If so, how will the image address each of these audiences?
- Finally, who will create the design? The designer may be working alone or as part of a team. It is not uncommon for multiple designers to work on a single project owing to the scope of the project or its timeline. Additional resources may be employed if they possess areas of expertise relevant to the project, such as a vector artist or photographer.

Designing for Accessibility

Creating work that is accessible to a broad audience is an important focus for media creators, including graphic designers. Accessibility implies universal design, design for all. In the United States, *Section 508 of the U.S. Code* requires that all government-sponsored website content and all attached files be accessible to people with disabilities. Web content created by federal agencies and their contractors must adhere to a minimal level of accessibility. Some nonfederal companies, while not legally required to be "508 compliant," may also request that a project meet these guidelines, especially if the company provides public services or its target market includes people with disabilities.

Section 508 has three main requirements:

1. *Technical:* Make sure the coding of a product (i.e., website, software, operating system) is compatible with assistive technologies.*
2. *Functional:* Ensure that in addition to the technical coding, the entire system is usable by someone with a disability.
3. *Support:* Make sure that supporting documents and alternative information are also accessible by people with disabilities.

If a project does not meet all three of these requirements, then it is not legally compliant (Horner 2013).

Designers who create images for the Web are likely to encounter Section 508 requirements. In general, increased attention should be paid when planning website navigation and Web graphics that include text or limited color contrast. Be prepared to work with Web developers providing the necessary descriptive text, which describes the contents of an image for use by an assistive technology. For more information about Section 508 and ways to plan for accessibility, refer to the references included at the end of this chapter (see *External Links Mentioned in the Chapter*).

---

* The Assistive Technology Industry Association describes assistive technology as "any item, piece of equipment, software program, or product system that is used to increase, maintain, or improve the functional capabilities of persons with disabilities" ("What is AT?" 2017).

Where? Where will the design be presented (and in what format)? Knowing whether the visual solution will be presented as an onscreen or print solution allows the designer to set up the working file correctly. Similarly, identifying the project's output allows the designer to select the appropriate resolution, color model and file type, properties that will be discussed in the next chapter (refer to *Chapter 5: File Properties*).

How? How will the design be created? Which application(s) will be used to create the visual solution? Each application in the Adobe Creative Cloud has its own purpose and can be used individually or in conjunction with the other applications for more complex solutions. *Photoshop* is used for image editing, working with digital photographs or scanned images; *Illustrator* is used to create scalable vector images; and *InDesign* is used for page layout, often incorporating images created in the other two applications into a single or multipage document.

When? When is the design needed? This information allows you to begin planning the project's timeline, outlining the stages of development. In this process, the project is translated into actionable steps for *both* the designer and the client. For example, when will a draft of the visual solution be submitted to the client for review? When will the client's feedback on the draft be received by the designer? Related to these milestones are the logistics of how information will be relayed between the designer and the client, including delivery of the completed visual solution. Clearly defining the channels of communication early in a project facilitates the smooth transmission of information between parties.

Stages of Development

The development process of most media-based projects, including graphic design, can be divided into three stages: pre-production, production and post-production. For small projects, the designer may move quickly from one stage into the next; however, regardless of a project's size, it is important to complete each stage in order. The organization and structure of each stage help to keep the project on track.

Pre-Production

The pre-production stage is focused on planning and idea generation. Pre-production is an opportunity to gather additional information about the project. Use this time to talk to the project's *stakeholders*, the people who have a vested interest in the project or are affected by its outcome either directly or indirectly. Discuss any ideas that have already been generated about the project. Find out if the visual solution will be part of a larger context or campaign and if so, what guidelines are available to foster consistency among the

Pre-Production Tasks

- Research the visual solution
- Collect project materials from the client (as applicable)
- Generate ideas and translate these into visuals
- Solicit client feedback on initial ideas
- Receive client approval on the preliminary sketch (e.g., thumbnail sketch, storyboard, wireframe)

elements. If the visual solution includes an organization's brand, a style guide or style manual may be provided for the designer's reference. A *style guide* is a set of design standards developed to ensure uniformity in style and formatting wherever an organization's brand is used.

During the pre-production stage, gather any available materials from the client (e.g., the company logo, articles written for a newsletter). When available, collect high-resolution images and electronic files for text (to avoid retyping). Inventory any materials received so they can be returned at the project's conclusion.

Capturing Ideas

Brainstorming is one process for conceiving creative ideas and solutions either individually or when working on a team. During this process, consider all ideas, no matter how seemingly random or offbeat; stray ideas often spark unexpected solutions. Do not criticize any ideas while brainstorming, just capture the ideas on paper; analysis and evaluation will follow. Some techniques that can help jump-start the brainstorming process include free association, mind mapping and doodling. For more information about these practices, refer to *Activity 4.1: Brainstorming Techniques* at the end of this chapter.

Translating Ideas into Images

With ideas generated, the next step is to translate these ideas into a sharable, visual depiction of the design. Depending on the project's intended output, the format of these representations will vary. Most projects begin with *thumbnail sketches*, simple line drawings that represent elements of the potential solution (Figure 4.1). For animation and video projects, a *storyboard* is developed, which

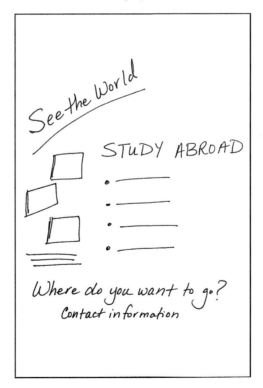

Figure 4.1

Thumbnail sketch.

Figure 4.2

Storyboard.

features a series of thumbnail sketches outlining the changes that will occur on screen (Figure 4.2). A site map and wireframe are the planning tools most frequently used for web design. A *site map* is a kind of flowchart representing how pages within a website are interconnected (Figure 4.3). A *wireframe* is a mockup of an individual page illustrating the navigation and page content (Figure 4.4).

Soliciting Feedback

As ideas are translated into visual depictions, it is a good practice to produce variations of an idea; aim for three options. When ideas are shared with the client, having multiple sketches on paper allows for comparison and serves as a useful basis of conversation. What works? What would the client change? Are there elements of one option that the client would like to see applied to another? Based on the client's

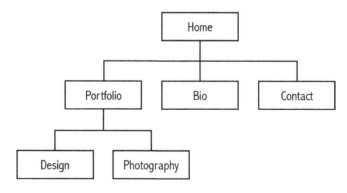

Figure 4.3

Site map.

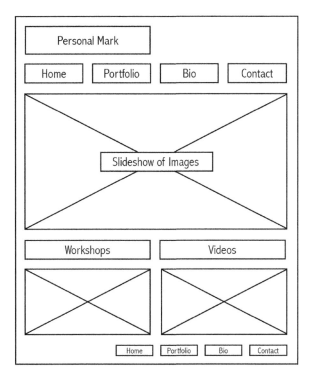

Figure 4.4

Wireframe.

review of these ideas, the designer may need to rework their sketch to incorporate the provided feedback. Revision is a regular step in the pre-production process. Securing the client's buy-in or agreement on initial ideas for the visual solution is important, and it should help to avoid major changes later in the development process.

Production

The production stage is the creation stage, producing a visual solution based on the agreed-upon sketch (e.g., thumbnail sketch, storyboard, wireframe). An Adobe application, or a combination of applications, will be used to create the visual solution. Later chapters introduce the Adobe Creative Cloud and how to use these applications to translate ideas and sketches into a realized design.

Production Tasks

- Create a visual solution that fulfills the stated purpose
  - Assess design for content and purpose
- Submit for client review
- Update design based on client feedback
- Deliver completed visual solution to the client
- Return any project materials to the client (as applicable)

The Feedback Loop

The production stage is cyclical. As illustrated in Figure 4.5, the designer creates an image and submits it to the client for review. Following this review, one of two things happens: either the client approves the image with no changes suggested and work on the project continues, or the image is *not* approved as is and the client requests changes, providing feedback to the designer. The designer then reviews the client's feedback and either accepts or challenges the requested changes. If accepted, the designer incorporates the changes and submits an updated image

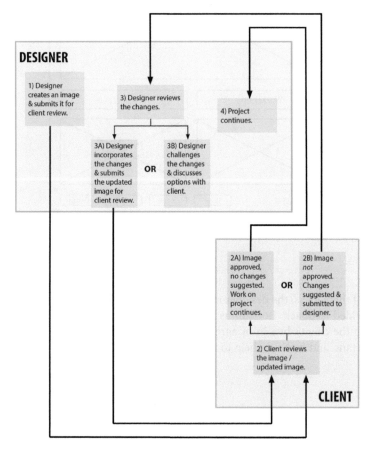

Figure 4.5

The feedback loop. (1) Designer creates an image and submits it for client review. (2) Client reviews the image/updated image. (2A) Image approved, no changes suggested. Work on project continues. *Or* (2B) Image not approved. Changes suggested and submitted to designer. (3) Designer reviews the changes. (3A) Designer incorporates the changes and submits the updated image for client review. *Or* (3B) Designer challenges the changes and discusses options with client. (4) Project continues.

to the client, for approval of the changes. The client's review of the updated image can result in the changes being approved or rejected. If approved, work on the project continues. If rejected, the client provides feedback to the designer and the revision cycle continues. At any point during the review cycles, if the designer challenges the client's feedback, then a conversation is held between the parties to discuss options and hopefully arrive at consensus.

It is vital to define feedback loops in the project's timeline, including the frequency and duration of feedback cycles. Otherwise, the feedback loop can become an endless cycle, a costly black hole of feedback and updates.

Review Your Work

A valuable step during the production stage is reviewing the visual solution for content. A simple step like *Check Spelling*, a tool available in the Adobe Creative Cloud applications, can prevent the embarrassment felt when the client highlights a typo during their review of the image. For the designer, reviewing a design for content is also an opportunity to revisit the "why" of the project definition, the project's stated purpose. Does the work-in-progress meet the project's specifications? Critically assess use of the elements of design and the design principles (refer to *Chapter 2: The Elements and Principles of Design*). Does the solution use these concepts effectively? Does their use contribute to the realization of the stated purpose? If so, continue working. If not, use this opportunity to correct course and get back on track.

Delivery

The production phase concludes with the delivery of the completed visual solution. The manner and method of delivery should have been identified and agreed to during the project definition phase. Once the final image has been delivered, make a point to return any materials that the client supplied.

Post-Production

The post-production stage is dedicated to reflecting on the development process, including the completed visual solution and archiving work. This stage is often skipped in the rush to declare a project finished and move on to the next project. However, it is important to make time for post-production, as valuable information is collected that can be applied to future projects.

Post-Production Tasks

- Conduct "lessons learned" session
- Archive project files and notes
- Follow up with the client
- Look ahead to the next project

Lessons Learned

A "lessons learned" session provides the designer and other members of the design team an opportunity to conduct self-assessment about the project. Questions asked during this session might include the following: What worked well on the project? What could be done differently next time? Did the designer or team of designers possess the necessary skills to complete the project? Document and review the collected responses.

Project Archive

Next, gather all of the resources that were created or used during the development process, including original sketches, early versions of working files, the completed visual solution and project notes. If possible, the designer will archive these files in a space separate from their working computer (e.g., external drive, on the cloud, burned to a CD/DVD). This practice provides a backup that is accessible for future reference and security should the designer's computer be damaged.

Follow Up and Look Ahead

Finally, follow up with the client, ask for feedback on this project, the completed visual solution *and* the production process. Also, inquire about future opportunities. Are there upcoming assignments for which you might be suited? Much of the designer's time is spent seeking work. Developing repeat clients and identifying continuing projects will help maximize time spent creating.

Looking Ahead

With the project defined and an overview of the development process completed, we next review the file properties that correspond to the intended output of the visual solution.

Discussions

Discussion 4.1: Know Your Audience: Audience Demographics

Identify a group of people to which you belong, this could be an interest group, a club/organization or a team. Outline the general demographics of the group, details that would be useful to know if you were hired to design a brochure promoting the group's upcoming events and activities. The brochure will be distributed to group members and will also be made available to prospective members.

Begin with the following demographic topics, adding to or removing items from the list as you deem them relevant or irrelevant to the group.

- Age
- Gender
- Education
- Community (e.g., urban, suburban, rural)

How will such demographic information help you design an effective brochure? How might the average age of the group's members be considered for the design? Think about the font size and colors use in the design. How might these be adjusted to benefit members of the group?

Discussion 4.2: Challenges of the Feedback Loop

Review the *Feedback Loop* in Figure 4.5. What challenges does this cyclical loop present to the designer *and* the client? What could be done to mitigate these challenges and their potential impact on the project timeline?

Activities

Activity 4.1: Brainstorming Techniques

Read the descriptions of the following associative brainstorming techniques and then give them a try. When brainstorming, it is natural to come up with the most obvious ideas first. Employing associative techniques pushes our ideas beyond the obvious to more complex ideas. Each of the following techniques is intended to encourage the free flow of ideas and spark creativity:

- *Free association:* This is a text-based means for capturing ideas.
  How to: Begin with a blank page (or word processing document) and begin writing (or typing). Capture every word and thought that comes to mind. Do not worry about spelling, grammar or punctuation, just write. Consider this process a proverbial brain dump. *Need more structure?* Set a timer for 3 minutes, and write for the duration. When time is up, review what has been written, circling or highlighting ideas that resonate. *Note:* If you typed your ideas, print them out for review.
- *Mind mapping:* This is a visual way to organize ideas and information.
  How to: Start with a blank piece of paper, and write down a single idea in the center of the page. Working out from this central idea, like a tree, draw a limb (a line) that ends in a related idea. From this idea, additional branches and related ideas can be added to the page.
- *Doodling:* This is an informal way to capture ideas that encourages jotting down ideas and sketches.
  How to: Start with a blank page of paper. Think about the project that you are about to undertake, and begin jotting down ideas that come to mind. This process is less structured than mind mapping. Connective links may not exist between your ideas, just keep moving your pencil or pen.

Activity 4.2: Brainstorm a Solution

Scenario: You have been hired to design a multipage booklet that will accompany a wildlife photography exhibit at the local nature center.

Select one of the techniques introduced in *Activity 4.1: Brainstorming Techniques* and generate ideas about the information to include in the booklet.

Unsure where to begin? What information would you expect to find in an exhibit booklet? Start with your response to this question, and build your ideas from there.

External Links Mentioned in the Chapter

Assistive Technologies

Assistive Technology Industry Association | https://www.atia.org

WebAIM: Web Accessibility in Mind | http://webaim.org

Section 508 of the U.S. Code

U.S. Access Board: Advancing Full Access and Inclusion for All | https://www.access-board.gov

U.S. Department of Health and Human Services | https://www.hhs.gov/web/section-508

5

File Properties

When it is time to begin production, there are several file properties that must be defined before work in the chosen Adobe application can begin. The intended output for the design, onscreen or print, dictates many of these file properties. The informed designer will make a point to correctly define these properties when creating a new file in order to avoid potential conflicts later. Let's begin with the basics, pixels and resolution.

Resolution

A *pixel* (from the term, *picture element*) is the smallest unit on screen that can be edited. Looking at the photo of fuchsia in Figure 5.1, the natural shapes of the blooms are curved; however, when we zoom in on the photo, we can see the square pixels that make up the blooms and the overall image. At this level of magnification (3200%) the rectangular grid or *raster* that contains the rows and columns of pixels in the image is visible. In Photoshop, the designer has the ability to change the appearance of an image one pixel at a time, though it is more typical to alter many pixels at once.

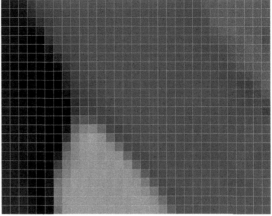

Figure 5.1

Close-up of pixels that compose a photo of fuchsia, Kilkenny Castle, County Kilkenny, Ireland.

Resolution is a measurement of an image's output quality that can be expressed in pixels, dots or lines. The unit of measure varies according to the intended output device. *Pixels per inch* (PPI) refers to the actual image resolution and is used for onscreen resolution; *dots per inch* (DPI) is used for imaging device output including desktop printers; and *lines per inch* (LPI) is used for commercial (generally offset) printing with halftone screens.

Images can be described as either low resolution (low-res) or high resolution (hi-res). Similar to unit of measure, a file's resolution is dependent on where the image will be displayed. Onscreen images use a low resolution of 100 ppi (pixels per inch) or less to facilitate fast loading of images. Web graphics are traditionally created using a resolution of 72 ppi. High resolution applies to images that will be printed, generally using a resolution of 300 ppi or higher. The higher an image's resolution, the greater the image's quality (i.e., more detail and clarity) and the larger is the corresponding file size.

A file's resolution can be changed, which indicates that pixels can vary in size. Figure 5.2 presents a series of images labeled A, B and C, each measuring 1 square inch in size; however, each image illustrates a different resolution. The first image (A) has the lowest resolution (4 ppi) and displays the least amount of detail when compared to the other images. The second image (B) with a resolution of 16 ppi shows more detail than A, yet less than the third image. With a resolution of 64 ppi, the third image (C) allows for a finer level of granularity than that of the other images. However, remember that this increased detail comes at the cost of a larger file size.

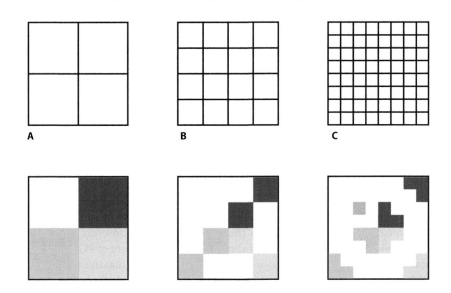

Figure 5.2

Resolution examples: (A) 4 ppi, (B) 16 ppi, and (C) 64 ppi.

Resampling and Interpolation

Situations may arise in which the designer needs to change the resolution of an image file. *Resampling* occurs when a file's resolution is reduced, for example, from 300 to 150 ppi. In this process, data is discarded from the file. When this happens, quality is lost, and the file's dimensions (width and height) are reduced.

When a file's resolution is increased, let's say from 72 to 150 ppi, *interpolation* takes place. No new content is created. Instead the existing context is divided into smaller units; additional details are not added to the image. The designer simply has more pixels with which to work. This process can produce the appearance of jagged or pixelated edges around a shape, particularly on curves or angles.

Neither option is ideal for the sake of an image's clarity, but sometimes changing a file's resolution is necessary. The preferred action is to correctly define the resolution when creating a new document file based on its intended output.

Color Models

Another decision that needs to be made is the file's color model. A *color model* is a system for creating a full range of colors from a small set of primary colors. The two most common color models that the designer is likely to use are the RGB color model for onscreen displays and the CMYK color model for printing. *Note:* The RGB and CMYK color models are not related to the color wheel discussed in *Chapter 3: Color in Design*. Instead, they pertain to how colors are created for their respective output.

RGB Color Model

In the *RGB color model*, also known as the *additive color model* (Figure 5.3), red, green and blue light are added together in various combinations to produce a broad spectrum of colors. The RGB color model contains over 16 million colors. This color model is used for images that will be displayed onscreen, including mobile devices. Each device has the ability to control the amount of RGB light that is visible in every pixel. When an area onscreen displays the maximum intensity of red, green and blue, the color white is visible. Conversely, the lack of intensity among red, green and blue (a.k.a. the absence of light) produces black. Adobe Photoshop uses the RGB color model as its default.

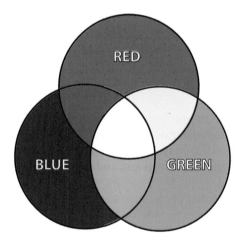

Figure 5.3

RGB color model.

CMYK Color Model

The *CMYK color model* is described as a *subtractive color model* because the printed ink combinations of cyan, magenta, yellow and key* (black) subtract the

---

* The "K" in CMYK stands for *key*, because in four-color printing, cyan, magenta and yellow printing plates are carefully keyed, or aligned, with a black key plate.

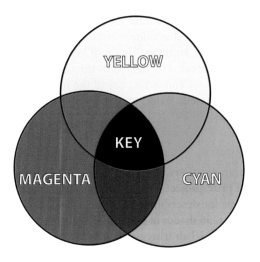

Figure 5.4

CMYK color model.

brightness that is normally reflected from the page (Figure 5.4). This model is also referred to as the *four-color process* because the offset printing process uses four printing plates, one for each color. When the colors are combined on paper, the final full color image is visible. In the CMYK color model, the color white represents a lack of ink or color on the page. In contrast, to create the color black, cyan, magenta and yellow are combined, at least in theory; however, in actuality, when these colors are combined as inks, a muddy brown is produced, thus the inclusion of key as a primary color to provide a pure black color. Adobe Illustrator and InDesign use the CMYK color model as their defaults.

Changing a File's Color Model

A file's color model can be changed at any point in the design process. Depending on the direction of the conversion, the change will be less or more noticeable. Converting an image's color model from CMYK to RGB (from print to screen) should go unnoticed, as this is essentially a one-to-one translation of colors. However, when converting a color model from RGB to CMYK (from screen to print), a shift in colors, particularly among bright colors, may be noticed. The reason for this shift is the relative difference in the sizes between the RGB and CMYK color palettes; the RGB color palette (based on light) is larger than the CMYK color palette (based on ink).

Color gamut refers to the range of colors that a specific device is capable of producing. Since the RGB color model contains more colors than the CMYK color model, some RGB colors may be considered *out of gamut*, unavailable in the new CMYK color model. Put another way, a color that may be displayed on a computer screen in RGB may not be printable in the gamut of a CMYK printer.

In this situation, the application looks for the *nearest neighbor,* the color closest to the original color, and assigns this value to the out of gamut color.

When a project involves an image that will be used for both onscreen and print output, it is recommended to start with the CMYK model and design all of the print assets first. Then, convert a copy of the image file to the RGB model and design the onscreen assets. Working in this order will produce a closer color match across the images.

Adobe's Color Modes

Within the Adobe applications, the *color mode* determines the color model used to display and print project files. The applications base their color modes on established models for describing and reproducing color, including bitmap (two colors), grayscale (256 shades of gray), RGB (red, green, blue), CMYK (cyan, magenta, yellow, key) and Lab (three-axis color system; "L" for lightness and "a" and "b" for the color dimensions: green-red and blue-yellow). In addition to determining the number of colors that can be displayed in an image, the color

Available Color Modes

Photoshop provides the designer with the following choices of color mode when creating a new file: Bitmap, Grayscale, RGB Color, CMYK Color and Lab Color. Instances of the same photo illustrate the different color modes (Figure 5.5).

Figure 5.5

Different color modes: (A) RGB Color (millions of colors); (B) CMYK Color (four-printed colors); (C) Lab Color (based on human perception); (D) Grayscale (256 grays); (E) Bitmap (two colors). Fence-line flowers, Lititz, Pennsylvania.

mode affects the number of channels* and the file size of an image. The intended output dictates which color mode should be used for a project file. The majority of our work will utilize the RGB and CMYK color modes.

Types of Images

The design solution is created using one of two types of images, a bitmap or a vector image. This is one decision that has more to do with style and the appearance of the created design than the file's output.

Bitmap Image

A *bitmap image* (also known as a *raster graphic*) is composed of a series of pixels, each assigned a color and then arranged in a pattern to form an image (refer to Figure 5.1). Bitmap images are *resolution dependent* and contain a fixed number of pixels per inch. Digital photographs and scanned images are bitmap images as they are composed of pixels. As previously discussed, image resolution corresponds to the overall quality and file size of the image.

Vector Image

In contrast, a *vector image* uses a series of mathematical formulas to define objects in an image. A combination of paths and anchor points forms editable shapes that can be filled with or outlined in color. Vector images are *resolution independent*, which means that pixels are not used to create the image. Another significant difference between vectors and bitmaps is a vector's ability to be scaled in size from very small to very large without losing image clarity or quality. This quality is extremely convenient for marketing purposes; the same vector image could be used to print business cards and to create a roadside billboard. This flexibility makes vectors a popular choice among clients.

At this point, the question is often asked, "Why not work with vectors exclusively?" To help answer this question, take a look at the two images presented in Figure 5.6. The first is a bitmap image, and the second is a vector image based on the same content. Notice the stylistic differences between the images, particularly in the sky and sand. When compared to the details visible in the bitmap image, the vector image resembles a paint-by-number painting that uses areas of color to create an image. The choice between using a bitmap or vector often depends on the desired style and appearance of the design.

File Formats

The final choice to make is what file format will be used for the project. Throughout this book, we will be creating and editing a variety of file formats including several of the following.

---

* Photoshop uses channels to store color information about an image. The image's color mode determines the number of color channels created: *RGB*, three channels (red, green, blue); and *CMYK*, four channels (cyan, magenta, yellow, key).

Figure 5.6

Bitmap image vs. vector image. Lifeguard tower, Jensen Beach, Florida.

JPEG/JPG | Joint Photographic Experts Group | .jpg File Extension

The JPEG file format compresses the image data within a file, which results in a relatively small file size. Digital cameras use the JPEG file format since photos can be saved with small file sizes, allowing for more files on the camera's memory card. JPEGs use *lossy compression*; *lossy* means "with losses to quality." Each time a JPEG is saved, some of the image details are discarded during the compression process; the image loses quality with each save. JPEGs are not good for images containing text, line drawings or logos. These subjects tend to become pixelated during the compression process.

Uses: Photos on the Web, sharable images (e.g., sent via email)

GIF | Graphic Interchange Format | .gif File Extension

The GIF [*pronounced:* jif] file format is used for Web images that contain a limited color palette, no more than 256 colors (Indexed color mode). GIFs are good for line art and logos; however, since GIFs possess a limited palette, they are not suitable for photos. GIFs use *lossless compression*, a process in which no image details are discarded during the compression process; however, because no information is lost, the file size cannot be as small as a JPEG. A GIF can contain transparency, allowing the viewer to look through the transparent sections of a GIF to the image or background placed behind the GIF. They can also be used for animations.

Uses: Web images with limited colors; supports transparency and animation

PNG | Portable Network Graphic | .png File Extension

The PNG file format was created as an alternate to GIF. PNGs can display more than 256 colors and have better compression. A PNG also contains transparency.
  Uses: Web images; supports transparency

TIFF/TIF | Tagged Image File Format | .tif File Extension

The TIFF file format is used for high-resolution graphics. TIFFs use lossless compression, so they contain a lot of image data, which translates to large file sizes. TIFF files support a variety of color formats (e.g., grayscale, CMYK, RGB) and content including layers and image tags.
  Uses: Photo editing and page layout

PSD | Photoshop Document | .psd File Extension

The PSD file format is the native Photoshop file format. PSD files contain layers and allow the designer to work with an image's layers across work sessions. The layers can be flattened and the image converted into a JPG, GIF or TIFF, so it can be shared. *Tip:* Always save the PSD file with its layers intact before converting the file format. Be careful not to overwrite the file during the conversion.
  Uses: Multilayer images

AI | Adobe Illustrator | .ai File Extension

The AI file format is the native Illustrator file. AI files are used to create vector images, which were introduced earlier in this chapter.
  Uses: Vector images

INDD | InDesign Document | .indd File Extension

The INDD file format is the principal document type in InDesign. INDD files contain formatting and linked files. They are used for desktop publishing to create single- or multipage documents, such as flyers, magazines or newspapers.
  Uses: Single- or multi-page documents

SVG | Scalable Vector Graphics | .svg File Extension

The SVG file format is used for vector images online.
  Uses: Web graphics

EPS | Encapsulated PostScript | .eps File Extension

The EPS file format is a vector format used to print to PostScript printers and imagesetters. It is the best choice for high-resolution printing of illustrations. EPS files are created and edited in Illustrator.
  Uses: High-resolution illustrations

PDF | Portable Document Format | .pdf File Extension

The PDF file format is generally associated with desktop publishing; however, it can also be used to share images and layout designs across platforms. PDF files can be created (i.e., saved, exported) from each of the applications in the Adobe Creative *Cloud* and many other applications. The PDF format can be used to share designs with audiences that do not have access to the Adobe applications and therefore cannot open the applications' native file formats (i.e., PSD, AI and INDD). PDF files can be read in multiple applications, including Adobe Acrobat Reader* and any Web browser.

Uses: Sharing formatted documents across platforms

Raw Images

Raw files contain a lot of data that is uncompressed, which translates to very large image file sizes. These files usually come straight from a digital camera and have not yet been processed, so they cannot be edited or printed. There are many different raw formats; each major camera company has its own proprietary format. Raw files are usually converted to TIFF before image editing begins.

Uses: Capturing details in a photograph

Looking Ahead

This chapter described the connection between intended output of a design and its file properties. As we begin working in the Adobe applications, think about how the selected file properties and file formats support the image's presentation onscreen or in print. Next up, an introduction to Adobe Photoshop, its workspace and tools, is provided.

Discussions

Discussion 5.1: Corresponding File Properties

Scenario: You have volunteered to create a series of graphics for a community clean-up event. The graphics will be used across several media platforms in order to broadly promote the event.

This list describes the graphics and where each will be used:

1. *Graphic 1:* A scalable logo for the event that will be printed on T-shirts for volunteers and will also be on display on a local billboard, a space that has been donated to support the event.

---

* Adobe Acrobat Reader is a free software application that allows the viewer to view, print, sign and annotate PDF files; for more information about this application, visit http://acrobat.adobe.com

2. *Graphic 2:* A graphic that will be included in a mass email sent to community members. The graphic needs to include photos from last year's event and text announcing this year's dates.
3. *Graphic 3:* A graphic that will be printed in color in the local newspaper. The graphic's content will match that of *Graphic 2*, it will just be larger.

For each of these graphics, indicate which image type (bitmap, vector), color mode (RGB, CMYK) and resolution (72, 150, 300 ppi) you would recommend using, and why.

Discussion 5.2: A Stylistic Choice: Bitmap vs. Vector

Consider the stylistic differences between bitmap and vector images; refer to Figure 5.6 for reference. Identify a scenario when each of these styles would be well suited. Determine what is included in each design solution (e.g., photo, text or symbols). How does the selected image type best support your design?

Activities

Activity 5.1: Change the Color Mode

Exercise file: **Ch05-Ex01-photo.jpg** (Refer to Figure 5.7)
If you are familiar with Photoshop, complete the following activity that tasks you with changing the color mode of the provided image, Ch05-Ex01-photo.jpg.

Note: If you are not familiar with Photoshop, proceed to *Chapter 6: Getting Started in Photoshop*, and then return to this activity once you are comfortable navigating the Photoshop workspace.

Figure 5.7

Activity file (Activities 5.1 and 5.2). Mountain goats in Glacier National Park, Montana.

Changing the Color Mode

Step 1: Open the provided file (**Ch05-Ex01-photo.jpg**) in Photoshop.

- From the *File menu*, select the *Open... menu command* [File menu > Open... | ⌘O].
- In the *Open dialog box*, navigate to the downloaded image file.
- Click *Open* to launch the file.

Step 2: Take note of the file's current color mode, which is shown in the Document window tab. In this tab the file name, the current magnification, the color mode and the bit depth are listed.

Step 3: Change the current RGB Color to CMYK Color.

- From the *Image menu*, position the cursor over the *Mode menu command* to view the available options.
- Select *CMYK Color* from the list, clicking on the option.
- This action launches an alert window; click *OK* to close the Photoshop message.

Did you notice any change of color within the photo when the CMYK color mode was applied?

Step 4 (Optional): Use the Undo and Redo menu commands to look for a shift in colors.

- Select the *Undo menu command* from the *Edit menu*, looking for a change in the image colors [Edit menu > Undo | ⌘Z].
- To redo the action, return to the *Edit menu*, and select the *Redo menu command* [Edit menu > Undo | ⌘Z].

Changing an image's color mode is just that straightforward. Remember to consider the image's intended output when selecting a color mode.

Activity 5.2: Changing the Resolution

Exercise file: **Ch05-Ex01-photo.jpg** (Refer to Figure 5.7)

If you are familiar with Photoshop, complete the following activity, which tasks you with changing the resolution of the provided image.

Note: If you are not familiar with Photoshop, continue to *Chapter 6: Getting Started in Photoshop*, then return to this activity once you are comfortable navigating the Photoshop workspace.

Changing the Resolution

Step 1: Open the provided file (**Ch05-Ex01-photo.jpg**) in Photoshop.

- From the *File menu*, select the *Open... menu command* [File menu > Open... | ⌘O].
- In the *Open dialog box*, navigate to the downloaded image file.
- Click *Open* to launch the file.

Step 2: Take note of the file's current resolution.

- From the *Image menu*, select the *Image Size... menu command* [Image menu > Image Size...].
- The *Image Size dialog box* lists the image dimensions, resolution and file size (Figure 5.8).

Figure 5.8

Image size dialog box (Photoshop), Image menu > Image size....

Step 3: Reduce the file's resolution (150 ppi) to 72 ppi in the Image Size dialog box.

- In the *Image Size dialog box*, select the current resolution value and enter the new resolution.
- Make sure that the interpolation method (*Resample*) is set to its default "Automatic" option.
- Look for the updated *Image Size* shown in the top row of the dialog box. This value should be less than the original Image Size listed in parentheses "was ##."
- Click *OK* to perform the conversion.

Step 4: Save the adjusted image, adding "-72" to the end of the file name [File menu > Save As…]. *Note:* Do not include the quotation marks in the file name addendum.

- Select *Save As…* from the *File menu* [File menu > Save As… | ⇧⌘S].
- In the *Save As dialog box*, add -72 to the file name, before the punctuation and file extension (**Ch05-Ex01-photo-72.jpg**).

Step 5: Reopen the provided file (**Ch05-Ex01-photo.jpg**) in Photoshop.

Step 6: Increase the file's resolution (150 ppi) to 300 ppi.

- Again, notice the new Image Size value. It should be larger than the previous value.

Step 7: Save the adjusted image, adding "-300" to the end of the file name.

Step 8: Open all three files in Photoshop in order to compare their dimensions and image quality. *Note:* Use the same magnification for each file. Use the Zoom Tool as needed to adjust these values [View menu > Zoom In (⌘+); View menu > Zoom Out (⌘−)].

What differences do you notice across the three files? In your opinion, is the difference in file size worth the change? Again, think about the image's intended output when assigning resolution.

Exercise File(s) Available on the Companion Website, URL

Ch05-Ex01-photo.jpg | *Activity file (Activities 5.1 and 5.2).* Mountain goats in Glacier National Park, Montana.

URL: http://www.crcpress.com/9780367075347

External Links Mentioned in the Chapter

Adobe Acrobat Reader | http://acrobat.adobe.com

6

Getting Started in Photoshop

We begin our discussion with the obvious question, why use Adobe Photoshop? Adobe Photoshop is the industry standard for professional photo editing, graphic design and digital imaging. Digital imaging involves the process of acquiring or importing images from scanners, digital cameras or other devices into a computer. Using Photoshop, designers can manipulate, enhance and apply effects to selected parts of an image or to an entire image. Photoshop can also be used to create images from scratch. Originally intended for simple digital photo editing, Photoshop's functionality has greatly expanded over time to be used by graphic designers, publishers and photographers.

Photoshop Overview

This chapter begins with a high-level overview of Photoshop, outlining how to create and save an image file, then shifting attention to the application workspace and tools. This knowledge is put into practice through *Exercise 6.1* in which you will be tasked with creating an image file, adding content to the image using selected tools and saving the file.

Photoshop provides an extensive collection of tools; however, most designers rely on a subset of these tools for the bulk of their projects. We follow suit, beginning with a limited number of tools. This chapter introduces and utilizes a subset of the available tools, tools selected to get you quickly creating in Photoshop. When you are ready to expand your personal toolset, access the *Photoshop Online Help* resource, which is always available via the *Help menu* [Help menu > Photoshop Help...].

Notes to the Reader

- This chapter is most effective when you have the Photoshop application open in front of you while reading. This allows you to *learn* and then *do*, navigating the interface and utilizing the tools.
  - If you do not have access to the application, the included screen captures serve as visual references for much of the content.
- Throughout this chapter, you are directed to perform specific actions. A path listing the related menu and menu command is provided to help you navigate the task.
  - For example, when instructed to apply the Mosaic filter to an image, you are directed to click on the *Filter menu*, then select the *Pixelate menu command* and finally select *Mosaic*; the accompanying path reads [Filter menu > Pixelate > Mosaic].
- Keyboard shortcut commands are also listed for frequently used tasks. Refer to Figure 6.1 for a guide to frequently used keyboard keys and their corresponding symbols.
  - For example, to save a file you can either access the *File menu* and select *Save* or press the following combination of keys on the keyboard, *Command + S* (macOS); *Control + S* (Windows) [File menu > Save | ⌘S].

SYMBOL	KEY ON KEYBOARD
⌘	Command (or Cmd) on Mac OS | Control key on Windows
⌥	Option on Mac | Alt on Windows
⇧	Shift key
^	Control (Control–click = Right click)

Figure 6.1

Symbols and corresponding keyboard keys.

- If you are just beginning in Photoshop, first get to know the menus and their respective menu commands. Then, once you are comfortable with the interface, gradually incorporate keyboard shortcut commands into your workflow. With repeated use, these shortcuts will become second nature.

Creating an Image File

When Photoshop opens, a *Home Screen** appears welcoming the designer to the application (Figure 6.2). In this dialog box, select either the "Create New…" or "Open…" button located along the left side of the window to get started. Let's choose "Create New…," which launches the *New Document dialog box*.

In the *New Document dialog box*, Photoshop provides a series of preset values based on the project type and expected output (Figure 6.3); these sets include Photo, Print, Art & Illustration, Web, Mobile, and Film & Video. Once a blank document preset has been selected, the following preset properties can be reviewed and modified as needed to accommodate a project.

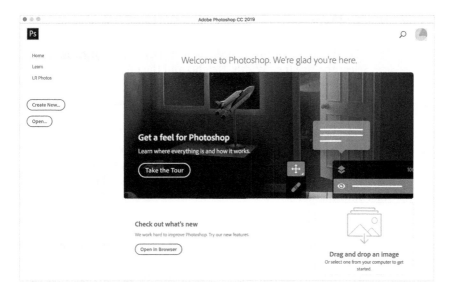

Figure 6.2

Home Screen dialog box.

---

* To disable the *Home Screen*, go to the *Photoshop CC menu*, access Preferences > General…, select "*Disable the Home Screen*" and click OK [Photoshop CC menu > Preferences > General…].

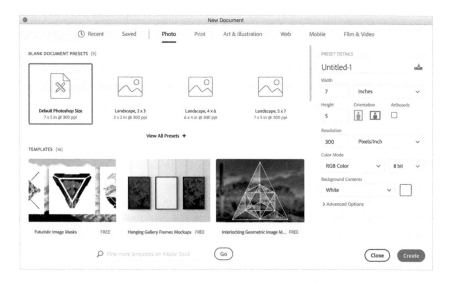

Figure 6.3

New Document dialog box, File menu > New....

Preset Details (descriptions drawn from *Photoshop Online Help*)

- *Name*: Set the name for this new document (*Default:* Untitled-1).
- *Size*: Select the size (i.e., Width, Height) and the unit of measure for the new document.
- *Orientation*: Portrait (vertical), Landscape (horizontal).
- *Artboards*: Toggles the Artboards option* on, off.
- *Resolution*: Set the resolution for the new document.
- *Color Mode*: Set the color mode for the new document.
- *Bit Depth* (located to the right of *Color Mode*): Specify the bit depth, a.k.a. the maximum number of colors that can be used (see box, "Bit Depth: Color Information").
- *Background Contents*: Set the initial background contents for the new document.
- *Advanced Options/Color Profile*: Specify a color profile for color management.
- *Advanced Options/Pixel Aspect Ratio*: Set the pixel aspect ratio for the new document.

---

* In Photoshop, *artboards* are useful when creating multiple instances of the same design, particularly for websites or apps, which are prepared for multiple devices. Behaving like a special type of layer group, artboards provide an infinite canvas. For more information about artboards, access the *Photoshop Online Help*.

To proceed, select a set; let's choose the *Photo set*. Then, from the available *Blank Document Presets* select *Default Photoshop Size* (7 × 5 in. @ 300 ppi). The file properties associated with this selection are listed along the right side of the dialog box. Click the *Create button* and the resulting image file appears in the workspace.

Bit Depth: Color Information

Bit depth refers to the color information stored in an image file. The higher the bit depth of an image, the more colors it can store. The simplest image, a 1-bit image, can show only two colors, black and white. This is because the 1-bit can store only one of two values, 1 (black) and 0 (white). An 8-bit image can store 256 possible colors, while a 24-bit image can display approximately 16 million colors.

Along with an image's resolution, its bit depth contributes to the file size of the image. As the bit depth goes up, the file size of the image also increases, because more color information has to be stored for each pixel in the image.

Saving an Image File

It is a good habit to save a new image file *before* creating content in the image. This practice can help the designer avoid losing work should the application or computer freeze and need to be restarted while working. Throughout this book, you are encouraged to save your work, early and often.

To save a new file, access the *File menu* and select the *Save As... menu command* [File menu > Save As... | ⇧⌘S]. *Note:* Once this initial *Save As* has been completed and content added to the file, the *Save menu command* will be available under the File menu [File menu > Save | ⌘S].

The *Save As dialog box* is presented in Figure 6.4. Here the file can be named, if this was not done when creating the image file (in the *New Document dialog box*). *Tip:* When naming a file, be careful to not overwrite the provided file extension, which is included in the *Save As field*. The native Photoshop file is a *Photoshop Document*, which uses the (.psd) file extension. The provided file extension matches the current file format (shown in the *Format dropdown menu*). If the file format needs to be changed, do so via the *Format dropdown menu*, selecting the desired file type. *Do not* type the desired file extension into the file name field (*Save As field*) and assume the file type will be changed; this technique *will not* work and can prevent the file from opening in the future due to the disconnect between the listed file extension and the actual file format.

Finally, before saving the file, know *where* the image file will be saved. When in doubt, select the computer's desktop for easy file retrieval. Select an appropriate

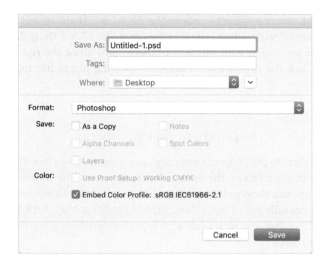

Figure 6.4

Save As dialog box, File menu > Save As....

location,* and then click the *Save button. Note:* If the computer is connected to the internet, options may be available to save an image file on a cloud drive (e.g., iCloud Drive, Creative Cloud Files).

File Naming

When naming files, avoid using special characters (e.g., @, #, $, %, *). Similarly, do not use spaces, as some software will not recognize file names that contain spaces. In lieu of a space, consider using a hyphen (-) or an underscore (_). Or, try using *Camel Caps*, a technique in which the first letter of each word in a file name is capitalized, such as UsingCamelCaps. psd. Finally, try not to make file names too long as lengthy file names do not work well with all software and across all platforms.

Photoshop Workspace Introduction

The Photoshop workspace is presented in Figure 6.5; the workspace is composed of the following labeled elements. These descriptions are drawn from the *Photoshop Online Help.*

A. The *Photoshop menu bar*, also referred to as the *menu bar*, provides access to the application's menus and menu commands.

---

* *Tip*: For designers using the macOS, pressing the down arrow located to the right of the *Where field* provides additional options for navigating to a specific location on the computer.

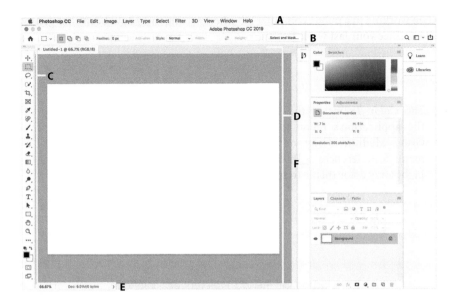

Figure 6.5

Photoshop workspace: (A) Photoshop/application menu bar, (B) Options bar, (C) Tools panel, (D) Document window, (E) Status bar and (F) Panels.

B. The *Options bar* displays options for the currently selected tool.

C. The *Tools panel* contains tools for creating and editing images.

D. The *document window* displays the image file.
- The working area is referred to as the *canvas*; this is where the image will be created.
- If more than one file is open at a time, document windows can be tabbed and, in certain cases, grouped and docked.

E. The *status bar* is part of the document window; information about the image file is displayed here, including the image's current zoom level or magnification.

F. *Panels* help you monitor and modify your work.

Adobe provides the ability to reset the Photoshop workspace to the *default workspace* when opening the application. Resetting the workspace returns the tools and panels to their default settings. This option is useful while getting to know the workspace as you experiment with tools and their settings. To reset the workspace, hold down the following keyboard keys when starting Photoshop: *Option + Command + Shift* (macOS); *Alt + Control + Shift* (Windows). Release the keys when the application prompt, *Delete the Adobe Photoshop Settings File?* appears on screen. Click *Yes* in response to the prompt to complete the reset process. *Tip:* Resetting the workspace at the start of a work session is a good habit when working in a public computer lab where settings may have been changed by others since your last work session.

Application Tip: Interface Appearance

The *Color Theme* of the Photoshop interface can be changed under the application's menu to one of the following colors: Black, Dark Gray, Medium Gray or Light Gray (Figure 6.6) [Photoshop CC menu > Preferences > Interface…]. Screen captures in this book use the Light Gray color theme to increase readability within the images.

Figure 6.6

Color theme, Photoshop CC menu > Preferences > Interface….

The Photoshop Menu Bar

Located along the top of the application window, the *Photoshop menu bar* consists of a series of menus, including Photoshop CC, File, Edit, Image, Layer, Type, Select, Filter, 3D, View, Window and Help. Clicking on a menu's name presents a list of related menu commands. As shown in Figure 6.7, some menu commands are followed by ellipses (…), such as the *New…* and *Open… menu commands*. The ellipses indicate that the menu command is augmented by a dialog box where additional settings can be entered. Other menu commands are followed by a right-pointing arrow, which indicates a submenu of related commands. Notice that many menu commands are followed by keyboard command shortcuts, which are provided to facilitate your use of the application.

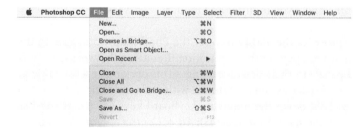

Figure 6.7

Photoshop menu bar, File menu selected and related menu commands shown.

The Options Bar

Below the Photoshop menu in its default location is the *Options bar*, which is *context sensitive*; its content changes when different tools are selected. Figure 6.8 presents multiple instances of the Options bar, illustrating its appearance when three different tools are selected (i.e., Lasso Tool [L], Brush Tool [B] and Paint Bucket Tool [G]). Some tool properties available in the Options bar (e.g., Opacity and Painting Modes) are common to several tools, while others are specific to a particular tool. The Options bar can be moved from its default location to anywhere in the work area using the *gripper bar** located along the left edge of the Options bar.

 Tip: If the Options bar is not visible in the workspace, access: Window menu > Options.

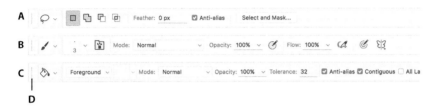

Figure 6.8

Multiple instances of the Options bar showing different tools selected: (A) Lasso Tool (L) options, (B) Brush Tool (B) options and (C) Paint Bucket Tool (G) options, (D) Gripper bar.

The Tools Panel

Generally located along the left side of the application's workspace, the *Tools panel* provides the designer with an extensive collection of tools with which to create. The *Photoshop CC 2019 Tools Panel Overview* presented in Figure 6.9 and continued in Figure 6.10 lists all of the Photoshop tools organized by the following broad function-based categories: Selection, Crop and Slice, Measuring, Retouching, Painting, Drawing and Type, Navigation. This guide is also available as a printable PDF file on the book's companion website. *Tip:* This is a useful reference to have available when learning the tools, their names and their locations. A brief description of each tool's functionality is available via the *Photoshop Online Help.*

 Tip: If the Tools panel is not visible in the workspace, access: Window menu > Tools.

 When interacting with the Tools panel, if the cursor hovers over a tool icon, a *Rich Tooltip†* may appear below the cursor's pointer presenting a simple animation

---

* A similar *gripper bar* is available on other windows and panels with the same purpose, to move objects within the application's workspace.
† Rich Tooltips can be turned off in the application's preferences [Photoshop CC menu > Preferences > Tools > Use Rich Tooltips].

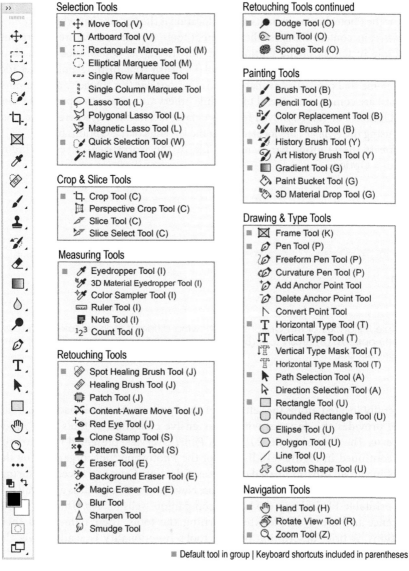

Selection Tools

- ◼ ✛ Move Tool (V)
-    ◻ Artboard Tool (V)
- ◼ ⬚ Rectangular Marquee Tool (M)
-    ◯ Elliptical Marquee Tool (M)
-    ⋯ Single Row Marquee Tool
-    ⋮ Single Column Marquee Tool
- ◼ ◯ Lasso Tool (L)
-    ⬠ Polygonal Lasso Tool (L)
-    ⬡ Magnetic Lasso Tool (L)
- ◼ ◌ Quick Selection Tool (W)
-    ◢ Magic Wand Tool (W)

Crop & Slice Tools

- ◼ ⌐ Crop Tool (C)
-    ▦ Perspective Crop Tool (C)
-    ◢ Slice Tool (C)
-    ◩ Slice Select Tool (C)

Measuring Tools

- ◼ ◢ Eyedropper Tool (I)
-    ◢ 3D Material Eyedropper Tool (I)
-    ◢ Color Sampler Tool (I)
-    ▭ Ruler Tool (I)
-    ▤ Note Tool (I)
-    $1_2{}^3$ Count Tool (I)

Retouching Tools

- ◼ ◈ Spot Healing Brush Tool (J)
-    ◈ Healing Brush Tool (J)
-    ⬡ Patch Tool (J)
-    ✂ Content-Aware Move Tool (J)
-    ⊕ Red Eye Tool (J)
- ◼ ♁ Clone Stamp Tool (S)
-    ♁ Pattern Stamp Tool (S)
- ◼ ◢ Eraser Tool (E)
-    ◈ Background Eraser Tool (E)
-    ◈ Magic Eraser Tool (E)
- ◼ ◊ Blur Tool
-    △ Sharpen Tool
-    ◊ Smudge Tool

Retouching Tools continued

- ◼ ◢ Dodge Tool (O)
-    ◔ Burn Tool (O)
-    ◉ Sponge Tool (O)

Painting Tools

- ◼ ◢ Brush Tool (B)
-    ◢ Pencil Tool (B)
-    ◢ Color Replacement Tool (B)
-    ◢ Mixer Brush Tool (B)
- ◼ ◢ History Brush Tool (Y)
-    ◢ Art History Brush Tool (Y)
- ◼ ▣ Gradient Tool (G)
-    ◢ Paint Bucket Tool (G)
-    ◢ 3D Material Drop Tool (G)

Drawing & Type Tools

- ◼ ⊠ Frame Tool (K)
- ◼ ✎ Pen Tool (P)
-    ✎ Freeform Pen Tool (P)
-    ✎ Curvature Pen Tool (P)
-    ✎ Add Anchor Point Tool
-    ✎ Delete Anchor Point Tool
-    ⌐ Convert Point Tool
- ◼ T Horizontal Type Tool (T)
-    ⥮T Vertical Type Tool (T)
-    ⥮T Vertical Type Mask Tool (T)
-    T Horizontal Type Mask Tool (T)
- ◼ ▶ Path Selection Tool (A)
-    ▷ Direction Selection Tool (A)
- ◼ ▢ Rectangle Tool (U)
-    ◻ Rounded Rectangle Tool (U)
-    ◯ Ellipse Tool (U)
-    ◯ Polygon Tool (U)
-    / Line Tool (U)
-    ⬠ Custom Shape Tool (U)

Navigation Tools

- ◼ ✋ Hand Tool (H)
-    ◈ Rotate View Tool (R)
- ◼ ◯ Zoom Tool (Z)

◼ Default tool in group | Keyboard shortcuts included in parentheses

Figure 6.9

Photoshop CC 2019 Tools Panel Overview.

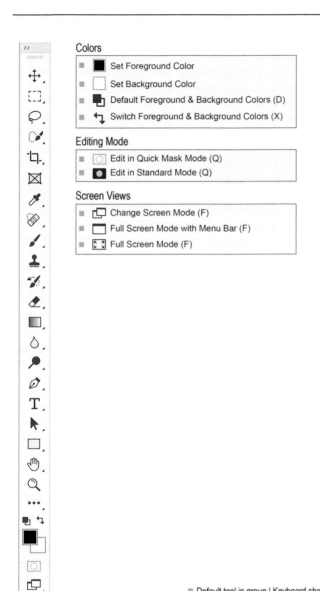

Colors

- ■ ■ Set Foreground Color
- ■ ☐ Set Background Color
- ■ ⬛ Default Foreground & Background Colors (D)
- ■ ↰ Switch Foreground & Background Colors (X)

Editing Mode

- ■ ◯ Edit in Quick Mask Mode (Q)
- ■ ⬤ Edit in Standard Mode (Q)

Screen Views

- ■ ⬜ Change Screen Mode (F)
- ■ ☐ Full Screen Mode with Menu Bar (F)
- ■ ⬚ Full Screen Mode (F)

■ Default tool in group | Keyboard shortcuts included in parentheses

Figure 6.10

Photoshop CC 2019 Tools Panel Overview continued.

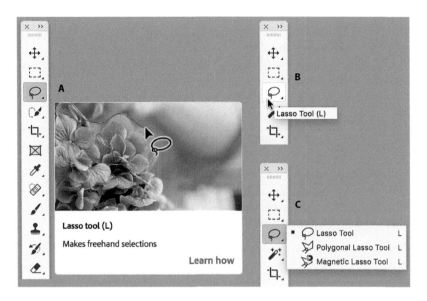

Figure 6.11

Tools panels: (A) Lasso Tool's *Rich Tooltip* and associated keyboard shortcut; (B) Lasso Tool's *Tooltip* and associated keyboard shortcut; and (C) Lasso Tool selected, *hidden tools* visible.

of the tool in use along with the tool name. A simplified version of the *Tooltip** is also available, which only presents the tool name. As shown in Figure 6.11, when available, a *keyboard shortcut* is listed to the right of the tool name. Keyboard shortcuts can be used to select tools in the Tools panel, allowing the designer to remain focused on an image. Using these keyboard shortcuts, the designer can avoid shifting their attention between the canvas and the Tools panel.

Looking at the Tools panel in Figure 6.9, only a portion of the available tools is currently visible. Notice that a majority of the tool icons display a small triangle in their lower-right corner; this triangle indicates that *hidden tools* are present, tools that share space with other tools. Refer to Figure 6.11 to see the Lasso Tool's hidden tools: Polygonal Lasso Tool (L) and Magnetic Lasso Tool (L). To access a hidden tool, position the cursor over the visible tool icon, then hold down the mouse button and from the resulting list of tools, select the desired tool. Keyboard shortcuts can be used to select *some*, but not all, hidden tools. To select a hidden tool using its keyboard shortcut, first, select the visible tool that shares space with the hidden tool, then hold down the *Shift key* while pressing the hidden tool's associated shortcut key. Press the shortcut key until the desired tool is visible in the Tools panel. When the hidden tool is visible in the Tools panel, it is available for use.

---

* Tooltips are labels or short descriptions displayed when you hover the cursor over a tool or property. This feature is available across all Adobe applications. *Note*: Tooltips can be turned off in the application's preferences [Photoshop CC menu > Preferences > Tools > Show Tooltips].

Application Tip: Tools Panel

The *Tools panel* can be displayed in one or two columns, as shown in Figure 6.12. The choice between these options is based on personal preference and available screen space. To change the Tools panel from the default single-column display to two columns, click the >> icon in the upper-left corner of the Tools panel. Clicking the << icon returns the two-column display to a single column.

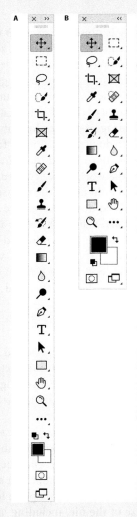

Figure 6.12

Tools panel: (A) single-column display and (B) two-column display.

Figure 6.13

Document window tabs.

The Document Window

By default, a *document window* is presented as a *tab* within the workspace. As shown in Figure 6.13 the tab contains the file name, zoom level (e.g., 100%, the current degree of magnification), color mode and bit depth. When more than one file is open, the document windows are presented in a group of tabs docked below the Options bar. To select a specific file, click on its tab, and the corresponding document window appears in front of the other tabs, its canvas visible.

Tabs can be rearranged by dragging a window tab to a new location within the group. To undock or float a document window from a group of windows, click and hold down the mouse button and then drag the window tab out of the group and release it over the workspace. To return an undocked window to a docked position, click and hold down the mouse button along the top of the file. While continuing to hold down the mouse button, move the cursor toward the other docked file tabs. When a blue bar appears above the docked file tabs, release the mouse button; the undocked window should now be docked. *Tip:* If an open file is "misplaced" or not visible in the workspace, click on the *Window menu* and look to the bottom of this menu for a list of open files. Select the name of the desired file, and it will be brought to the forefront of all open files.

The Status Bar

The *status bar* is available for each image file. Located in the lower-left corner of the document window, the status bar displays the active image's zoom level or current degree of magnification (e.g., 66.67%) (see Figure 6.5). To display other types of information in this bar, click the right arrow (>) in the status bar, and select one of the options presented in this menu.

Document Sizes is a useful option to display in the status bar; this feature can help the designer keep track of the file's size. Photoshop presents two numbers to approximate the size of the image. The first number (left) represents the size of the file if the file were to be flattened, combining any individual layers into one and saving the file in the native Photoshop file format (PSD). The second number (right) shows the size of the file, including layers, channels and other components. Accordingly, the second number is generally larger than the first. For information about the other options available in the status bar, refer to the *Photoshop Online Help.*

Panels

In addition to being accessed from the Options bar, tool properties can be accessed from individual *panels*. Panels help the designer monitor and modify images and their elements. The list of available panels is accessible from the *Window menu*. When a panel name is selected in the list, the associated panel is displayed in the workspace. A checkmark located to the left of the panel's name means that the panel is open in the workspace.

Tip: An open panel can be hidden behind other panels. If an open panel (indicated by the checkmark shown in the Window menu) is not visible in the workspace, try closing and reopening the panel. To do so, close the panel by first selecting the panel from the *Window menu*, then reopen the panel by selecting it again from the *Window menu*. Once reopened, the panel should be visible in front of other open panels.

A *dock* is a collection of panels or panel groups displayed together, generally in a vertical orientation. Panels can be docked and undocked by moving them into and out of a dock. To dock a panel, drag its tab into the dock, at the top, bottom or in between other panels. To dock a panel group, drag its title bar (the solid empty bar above the tabs) into the dock. To remove a panel or panel group, drag it out of the dock by its tab or title bar. This panel or panel group can be dragged into another dock or left free floating. A floating panel can be positioned anywhere in the workspace.

Panels can also be collapsed to icons to reduce clutter on the workspace. Our first view of the default workspace in Figure 6.5 included panel icons (i.e., Color, Properties and Layers). For more information about managing panels, visit the *Photoshop Online Help*.

A Subset of Tools

The following subset of tools is selected from the Tools panel. Accompanying the selected tools are each tool's keyboard shortcut command, if available, and the tool's respective description drawn from the *Photoshop Online Help*. As you read these descriptions, locate the tools in the Tools panel and refer to the *Photoshop CC 2019 Tools Panel Overview* (see Figure 6.9). Remember that some of these tools may be hidden.

Selection Tools

- The *Move Tool* (V) moves selections, layers and guides.
- The *Marquee Tools* (M) make rectangular, elliptical, single-row and single-column selections.
- The *Lasso Tools* (L) make freehand, polygonal (straight-edged) and magnetic (snap-to) selections.
- The *Quick Selection Tool* (W) lets you quickly "paint" a selection using an adjustable round brush tip.
- The *Magic Wand Tool* (W) selects similarly colored areas.

Measuring Tools

- The *Eyedropper Tool* (I) samples colors in an image.

Retouching Tools

- The *Eraser Tools* (E) erase pixels and areas of an image to a previously saved state or to transparency.

Painting Tools

- The *Brush Tool* (B) paints brush strokes.
- The *Paint Bucket Tool* (G) fills similarly colored areas with the foreground color.

Drawing & Type Tools

- The *Type Tools* (T) create type in an image.

Navigation Tools

- The *Hand Tool* (H) moves an image within its window.
- The *Zoom Tool* (Z) magnifies and reduces the view of an image.

The lower portion of the Tools panel contains several useful features shown in Figure 6.14.

Colors

- The *Foreground* and *Background Colors* set foreground color and background color.

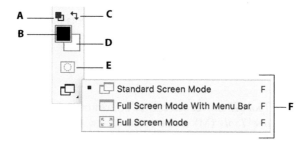

Figure 6.14

Tools panel, Colors, Quick Mask, and Screen Modes: A: Default Foreground and Background Colors (D), B: Foreground Color, C: Switch Foreground and Background Colors (X), D: Background Color, E: Edit in Quick Mask Mode (Q), and F: Change Screen Mode (F).

Graphic Design: Learn It, Do It

- *Default* Foreground and Background Colors (D).
- *Switch* Foreground and Background Colors (X).

Screen Views

- Standard Screen Mode (F)
- Full Screen Mode With Menu Bar (F)
- Full Screen Mode (F)

Note: Additional tools will be introduced in *Chapter 7: Photoshop Continued* and *Chapter 9: Photo Editing in Photoshop*.

It is time to put this information into practice. *Exercise 6.1* is designed to help you explore the Photoshop workspace and become familiar with the processes of creating and saving an image file. If needed during the exercise, refer to the earlier explanations of the workspace components, processes and tool descriptions.

Exercise 6.1: Create, Save and Add Content to an Image File

Exercise brief: Create and save an image file, then use the following tools to add content to the file: Brush Tool (B), Marquee Tools (M), Lasso Tool (L) and Paint Bucket Tool (G).

Step 1: Create a new image file using Photoshop's Document Type presets, specifically the Default Photoshop Size, which is available under the Photo set.

- Begin at the *File menu* and select the *New... menu command* [File menu > New... | ⌘N].
- In the *New Document dialog box* look for the *Photo header,* and from the *Blank Document Presets* select *Default Photoshop Size* (7 × 5 in. @ 300 ppi).
  - Take a moment to review the *Preset Details,* the file properties associated with this selection: *Width,* 7 in.; *Height,* 5 in.; *Orientation,* Landscape; *Resolution,* 300 pixels/in.; *Color Mode,* RGB Color; *Bit Depth,* 8 bit; and *Background Contents,* White.
- Click *Create* to generate the image file.

Step 2: Save the new image file as a Photoshop Document. Use *Ch06-Ex01* for the file name, *Photoshop* for the file format and select an appropriate location for the file (Ch06-Ex01.psd).

- With the new image file open in the workspace, access the *File menu* and select *Save As...* [File menu > Save As... | ⇧⌘S].
- In the *Save As dialog box,* enter the file name, *Ch06-Ex01,* verify the *File Format* (Photoshop) and navigate to an appropriate location.
- Click *Save* to save the image file.

Step 3: Add content to the image file using the Brush Tool (B).

- Select the *Brush Tool* (B) in the Tools panel and then position the cursor over the canvas.
- Hold down the mouse button while "painting" on the canvas to create a mark.
  - The color being used by the *Brush Tool* (B) is the current *Foreground Color*, which is visible in the lower portion of the *Tools panel* (see Figure 6.12).
- *Tip:* Until another tool is selected, in the *Tools panel* or using a *keyboard shortcut*, the cursor will remain a brush.
- Try changing the appearance of the brush (e.g., brush, size and hardness) and paint some more.
  - Look to the *Options bar* while the *Brush Tool* (B) is selected, to see the brush properties that can be adjusted (Figure 6.15). Photoshop provides an assortment of brushes via the *Brushes Preset picker*. Once selected, each of these brushes can be modified.
  - Additional brush options and property controls can be found in the *Brush panel*. To access this panel, go to the *Window menu* and select the *Brush menu command* [Window menu > Brush]. *Tip:* Be careful not to get distracted by the variety of available brushes; try a few and then move on.

Changing Values

There are multiple ways to change a property's value in the Options bar or in a panel; these labeled options are shown in Figure 6.15.

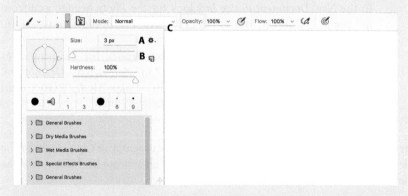

Figure 6.15

Options bar, Brush Tool selected, Brush Preset visible. Three ways to change values, (A) enter value; (B) slider bar; (C) side-to-side "scrub" over the property name.

A. Highlight the current value and type a new value.
B. Use the available slider, dragging the slider to increase or decrease the value.
C. Position the cursor on top of the value's name (the cursor's appearance will change to a *scrubby cursor*), then click and drag the cursor side to side to "scrub" to a larger or smaller value.

Step 4: Change the color used for the Brush Tool (B) and add additional content to the image file.

- Click once on the *Foreground Color chip* in the Tools panel, and the *Color Picker (Foreground Color) dialog box* will open (Figure 6.16).
  - The *Color Picker dialog box* presents multiple methods for representing a color (i.e., HSB, RGB, #: Hexadecimal, Lab, CMYK). Refer to *Chapter 3: Color in Design* for a review of the different color modes.
- Click anywhere within the gradient located on the left side of the Color Picker dialog box to select a *new* foreground color.
  - To change the range of available colors within the gradient, click on the desired hue in the spectrum of colors located to the right of the gradient.
- The selected "new" color will be shown as a chip above the "current" color chip located near the center of the Color Picker dialog box.
- Click *OK* to change the foreground color.

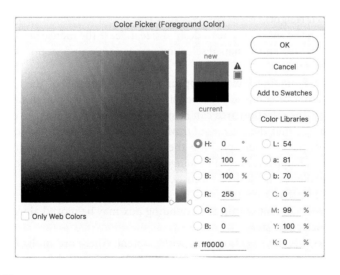

Figure 6.16

Color Picker dialog box.

Note: To change the *Background Color,* use the same process: First click on the *Background Color chip* in the *Tools panel.* This action launches the *Color Picker (Background Color) dialog box.* A new color can also be selected using either the *Color panel* or the *Swatches panel.* Access to these panels is available from the *Window menu* [Window menu > Color | Swatches].

Step 5 (Optional): Clear the canvas. If you would like to remove all content from the canvas before moving forward, do so now. If not, move ahead to Step 6.

- Go to the *File menu* and choose the *Revert menu command* [File menu > Revert].
  - The *Revert menu command* returns an image file to its last saved state, which in this exercise occurred when the newly created image file was saved in Step 2.

Step 6: Add content to the image file using the Marquee Tools (M) in conjunction with the Fill menu command and then the Paint Bucket Tool (G). A selection area will first be created, and then it will be filled with color.

- Select the *Rectangular Marquee Tool* (M) in the Tools panel and then position the cursor over the canvas.
- Click and hold down the mouse button while moving the cursor diagonally away from its starting point.
  - A tooltip will appear during this step below the cursor pointer listing the dimensions of the shape being created (i.e., W: Width and H: Height).
- When the shape reaches a desired size, release the mouse button.
  - The rectangle-shaped selection area is empty; it does not contain any content.
  - A *bounding box* will appear along the borders of the shape; this animated outline of dashed lines is referred to as "marching ants."
- *Note:* The selection area can be moved around the canvas. To do so, first confirm that the *Rectangular Marquee Tool* (M) is still selected in the Tools panel. Then, position the cursor within the selection area (the cursor's appearance will change), and click and drag the rectangular selection to the desired location.
  - *Tip:* If you try to move the selection area using the *Move Tool* (V), any content within the bounding box may be moved along with the selection area.
- Next, fill the selection area with content. There are multiple ways to complete this task; here are two options to try.
- *Option 1:* Use the *Fill... menu command* to fill a selection area with content.

- Begin at the *Edit menu* and select the *Fill...* menu command [Edit menu > Fill...].
- In the *Fill dialog box,** select the fill contents from the *Contents dropdown menu* (i.e., Foreground Color, Background Color, Color..., Content-Aware, Pattern, History, Black, 50% Gray, White).
- Blending options are available (i.e., Mode and Opacity) to alter the appearance of the fill.
- Click *OK* to apply the fill.
- *Option 2:* Use the *Paint Bucket Tool* (G) to fill a selection area with content. By default, the *Foreground Color* in the Tools panel is used as the source of the fill.
  - Select the *Paint Bucket Tool* (G) in the Tools panel.
  - Review the properties presented in the *Options bar* and make any adjustments *before* using the tool (e.g., source for fill area, fill mode and opacity).
  - Position the cursor *within* the selection area, and click once to apply the fill. *Note:* Additional clicks repeat the fill layering content within the selection area.

Application Tip: When an area on the canvas is selected, *only* that selection area can be modified. For example, if you try clicking outside of the selection area with the Paint Bucket Tool (G), no color will be applied.

Tool Tip: Marquee Tools

By default, the *Marquee Tools* (M) create rectangles and ellipses. However, these tools can also create squares and circles, respectively. To do so, hold down the *Shift key* on the keyboard while drawing the shape. *Tip:* Release the mouse button *before* the Shift key in order to preserve the shape.

Shapes created using the *Marquee Tools* (M) can be created from the center point of the shape outward. *Tip:* Turn on the document grid before attempting this technique [View menu > Show > Grid | ⌘']. Use an intersection of guidelines as the center point for a shape, growing the shape out from that point. Place the cursor at one of these intersection points and then hold down the *Option key* while drawing the shape outward from the center point.

To create a circle using this method, hold down *both* the *Shift* and *Option keys* before or while using the *Elliptical Marquee Tool* (M) to draw the circle. Release the mouse button first, then the keyboard keys to preserve the shape.

---

* Once a selection has been made, pressing the keyboard's *Delete key* will also launch the *Fill dialog box.*

Step 7: Save and close the file and then quit Photoshop.

- Return to the *File menu* and select *Save,* or try the following keyboard shortcut command: Command + S (macOS); Control + S (Windows) [File menu > Save | ⌘S].
- To close the image file, go to the *File menu* and select *Close* [File menu > Close | ⌘W].
  - This step will close the *document window* but will leave the Photoshop application open.
- Finally, to end the work session, quit Photoshop by going to the *Photoshop CC menu* and selecting *Quit Photoshop CC* [Photoshop CC menu > Quit Photoshop CC | ⌘Q].

Congratulations, you have completed your first exercise, and you have created a Photoshop image composed of lines and shapes. While perhaps not a masterpiece, it is a start, and hopefully, you are becoming familiar with the Photoshop workspace. Before proceeding, let's discuss some important nuggets of information that will facilitate your work in Photoshop. These topics are called *Need to Know Fundamentals,* a label that will surface in the application-based chapters.

Need to Know Fundamentals

Undoing Your Work

When you perform a task, it is helpful to know how to undo that task. Under the *Edit menu,* the *Undo menu command* allows the most recent operation to be undone [Edit menu > Undo | ⌘Z]. Photoshop supports multiple levels of undo.*
Another way to undo and redo multiple operations is to use the *History panel.*

Note: If an operation cannot be undone, the menu command is dimmed and changes to *Can't Undo.*

Using the History Panel

The *History panel* allows the designer to jump to any recent state of the image created during the *current* working session.† To access the History panel, go to the *Window menu* and select the *History menu command* [Window menu > History].

---

* Photoshop CC 2019 is the first version of the application to support multiple levels of undo. For designers using earlier versions of the application, to undo multiple operations, return to the *Edit menu* and select *Step Backward* [Edit menu > Step Backward]. Notice that there is also a menu command for *Step Forward,* in case you undo one too many steps [Edit menu > Step Forward]. These steps are comparable to using the *History panel,* which can also be used to undo and redo multiple operations.

† When a file is closed, the current work session for that document is concluded, and information pertaining to the session is discarded (e.g., iterative states in the History panel and data copied to the clipboard).

Tip: The History panel is a useful panel to keep docked along the right side of the application window for easy access.

Each time a change is made to an image, the new *image state* is added to the History panel as the bottommost entry. For example, if the designer makes a selection and fills it with color, then rotates the selection, each of these steps is a separate image state in the History panel. When one of the earlier states is selected, the image reverts to how it looked when that change was first applied. Work can then proceed from that state, recognizing that subsequent changes will be deleted.

The History panel can also be used to delete image states and, in Photoshop, to create a document from an image state or snapshot.* For more information about these options, access the *Photoshop Online Help.*

Selection Options

Once a selection area has been created and filled, it would be helpful to view the canvas without the marching ants outlining the selection. To deselect an area, go to the *Select menu* and choose the *Deselect menu command* [Select menu > Deselect | ⌘D]. Within the *Select menu*, menu commands are available to select: *All* [⌘A], *Reselect* [⇧⌘D] and *Inverse*, the opposite of the current selection [⇧⌘I].

Image Size, Color Mode and Canvas Size

When beginning a design project that involves acquired or provided images, it is a good practice to review the properties of the assets before working with them. This step allows you to make any necessary changes in an effort to standardize image properties (e.g., dimensions, resolution and color mode). Certain file properties are listed in the *Properties panel*, which can be accessed from the Window menu [Window menu > Properties].

Image Size

An image's dimensions and resolution can be accessed via the *Image menu* and the *Image Size… menu command*, which opens the *Image Size dialog box* (Figure 6.17) [Image menu > Image Size… | ⌥⌘I]. First, review the *Dimensions* fields and confirm the unit of measure used for Width, Height, and then look to the *Resolution* field.

If you need to adjust the image's dimensions, make sure the *link icon* is selected to preserve the image's proportions. With this option enabled, when the width is changed, the height will automatically be updated to an appropriate size.

Note: If a file contains content on multiple layers, when an image is resized, content on each layer will be affected.

If you need to adjust a file's resolution, refer to *Chapter 5: File Properties,* "Resampling and Interpolation," for a refresher on the challenges of resampling

---

* The *Snapshot* command (available from the History panel menu) lets you make a temporary copy of any state of the image. Snapshots are only available while the document is open; they are not saved with the image.

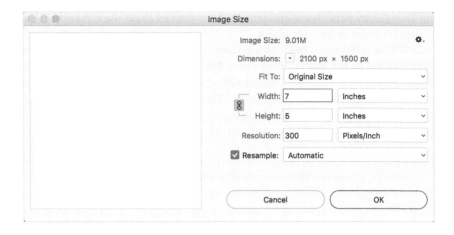

Figure 6.17

Image Size dialog box, Image menu > Image Size.

(reducing resolution) and interpolation (increasing resolution). Based on this information, we know that increasing an image's size can result in the image becoming pixelated. Accordingly, it is better to reduce the size of an image, reducing its dimensions or resolution. When you change the resolution, the image's dimensions (and file size) will be altered accordingly; if the resolution is increased, the dimensions will increase, as will the file size, conversely, if the resolution is decreased, the dimensions and file size will decrease.

Color Mode

Earlier in this chapter, you learned that the color mode and bit depth of a file are listed in the document window tab. If either of these values needs to be adjusted, access the *Image menu* and select *Mode* [Image menu > Mode]. Refer to *Chapter 5: File Properties* for possible rationales for such a change. The submenu provides the following options, for color mode: Bitmap, Grayscale, Duotone, Indexed Color…, RGB Color, CMYK Color, Lab Color and Multichannel; and these for bit depth: 8 Bits/Channel, 16 Bits/Channel and 32 Bits/Channel.

Note: Not all Photoshop functions (e.g., filters) work in all color modes. If the application prevents you from making a change or a menu command is grayed out, you may need to change the color mode, generally to RGB Color, to complete the change; when finished with adjustments, return the color mode to the desired option.

Canvas Size

There will come a time when you need additional room to work in a file, a.k.a. additional canvas space. To increase the canvas, access the *Image menu* and select *Canvas Size…*, which launches the *Canvas Size dialog box* (Figure 6.18) [Image menu > Canvas Size… | ⌥⌘C].

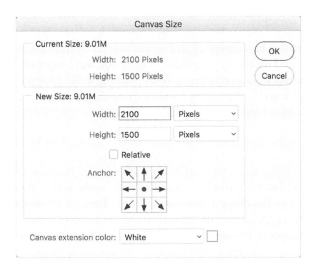

Figure 6.18

Canvas Size dialog box, Image menu > Canvas Size.

Canvas Size is most often used to extend the canvas, increasing the image work area. To do so, first enter new values for the *Width* and *Height*, always double-checking the unit of measure. Unlike changing the *Image Size*, *Canvas Size* does not offer a proportional setting, so you need to enter values for both settings, as applicable. *Relative* indicates whether the new size dimensions are absolute or relative. *Tip:* If in doubt about how large to make the canvas, give yourself plenty of room to work and double the existing dimensions. You can always trim any unnecessary areas using the Crop Tool, which is introduced in *Chapter 9: Photo Editing in Photoshop.*

Next, determine on which side or sides you would like the canvas extension(s) applied. The *Anchor* indicates where the new size will take effect. In its default position, the center square, the *anchor point* distributes space evenly on all sides. If additional space is only needed along the right and bottom sides of the image, relocate the anchor point by clicking once on the upper-left corner box and notice the directional arrows that indicate where the canvas extensions will be applied.

Finally, select the *Canvas extension color* from the provided dropdown menu (i.e., Foreground, Background, White, Black, Gray, Other... [Color Picker]). *Note:* If the image file does not contain a Background layer, the canvas extension will be transparent; information on layers is presented in *Chapter 7: Photoshop Continued.*

When *Canvas Size* is used to *decrease* the image work area, the following Photoshop alert is presented, *The new canvas is smaller than the current canvas size; some clipping will occur.* In this scenario, clipping is the process of deleting content around the edges of the image on one, two, three or four sides. Click *Proceed* to accept the clipping; click *Cancel* to dismiss the change.

Looking Ahead

A lot of information has been presented in this chapter. Spend time experimenting with the tools and repeating the processes until you feel comfortable navigating the Photoshop workspace, creating a file and saving a file. *Chapter 7: Photoshop Continued* builds on the Photoshop basics, expanding your use of the application. The fundamentals of layers and type are presented.

Staying Current with Software Updates and New Tools

Software updates routinely introduce new tools and capabilities to Photoshop and the other Adobe applications. These new features expand the respective application's functionality and the designer's ability to create. When updates are released, access the online *Adobe Photoshop Learn & Support* resource for information about changes made to the application. In the *User Guide* section, the designer will find answers to questions and guided instructions for completing specific tasks. In the *Tutorials* section, the designer will find tutorials from novice to expert intended to expand their application knowledge and skills. These online tools can provide just-in-time solutions, answers to questions while the designer is working in the application. To access these resources, go to the *Help menu* and select the *Photoshop Online Help... menu command*, which will launch the Adobe website [Help menu > Photoshop Online Help...].

Discussion

Discussion 6.1: Photoshop the Verb

In recent years, the term *photoshop* has been used as a verb to describe altering the contents of a photo, image edits that may or may not be performed in Adobe Photoshop CC, for example, in the following statements:

- It's okay, I will just *photoshop* their head from another photo in which their eyes are open.
- Yes, I can *photoshop* the power line out of the photo to remove the distracting line.

What verb is *photoshop* replacing in these statements? Are you familiar with, or have you used this terminology yourself? How does use of this term enter our lexicon?

Activity

Activity 6.1: "Learn & Support" Tutorials

Access the *Photoshop Online Help* and watch one of the available tutorial videos (Tutorials) [Help menu > Photoshop Online Help...]. Once on the *Adobe Photoshop Learn & Support* website, click on *Tutorials* to find a collection of tutorials organized by experience level. Select a topic that is of interest to you and that reflects your experience level with the application.

   Tip: Bookmark this site for easy access in the future, https://helpx.adobe.com/photoshop/tutorials.html.

Exercise File(s) Available on the Companion Website, URL

Ch06-Photoshop-CC-2019-Tools-Overview.pdf | *Photoshop CC 2019 Tools Panel Overview*

URL: http://www.crcpress.com/9780367075347

External Links Mentioned in the Chapter

Photoshop Resources

Adobe Photoshop Learn & Support | https://helpx.adobe.com/photoshop/tutorials.html

Photoshop Online Help | https://helpx.adobe.com/photoshop

Photoshop Tool Galleries (Photoshop User Guide > Workspace > Tool Galleries) | https://helpx.adobe.com/photoshop/using/tools.html

7

Photoshop Continued

Building on the Photoshop fundamentals presented in the previous chapter, this chapter introduces layers and the roles that layers play in adding graphic elements, text and text effects to an image. *Exercise 7.1* presents an opportunity to use layers to enhance an image file. Then, attention shifts to creating text in Photoshop and the associated type properties; *Exercise 7.2* provides practice in using these tools and processes. Following each exercise, *Need to Know Fundamentals* contribute enriching nuggets of information about the application, its tools and its capabilities.

Understanding Layers in Photoshop

Layers are a key component to the designer's ability to create and edit an image in Photoshop. Think of layers like a stack of overhead transparencies, clear sheets of acetate. You can see through transparent areas of a layer to the layers below, just like you can see through the stack of transparencies to content on the bottommost sheet.

Every image file contains at least one layer. Each time content is pasted into an image file, a layer is created; when type is created, a layer is created. These are just two ways that layers can be added to an image. The number of layers and layer effects added to an image are limited only by the computer's memory.

The Layers Panel

The *Layers panel*, shown in Figure 7.1, is accessible from the *Window menu* [Window menu > Layers]. In this panel all of the layers, layer groups and layer styles in an image file are listed whether seen in the image or not. The Layers panel can be used to show and hide layers (a.k.a. turning the *visibility* of layers on and off), lock layers, create new layers, delete layers and work with groups of layers. Additional commands and options can be accessed via the *Layers panel menu*, available in the upper-right corner of the panel. Many of these commands are also available from the *Layer menu* in the Photoshop/application menu bar.

Application Tip: In order to edit content in an image, the content's respective layer must be selected in the *Layers panel*. If the correct layer is not selected, the edit could be performed on the wrong content or the following Photoshop alert will appear, *Could not use the [selected tool] because no layers are selected.* In this situation, click *OK* to dismiss the alert, then select the correct layer in the Layers panel and complete the edit.

Renaming, Managing, Deleting and Grouping Layers

Layers can be renamed, reordered, deleted and organized in the Layers panel. When a new layer is created, it is named *Layer #*; "#" is an incremental value (e.g., Layer 1, Layer 2, …). To change a layer name, double-click on the current

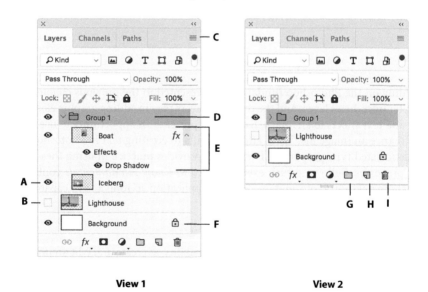

View 1   **View 2**

Figure 7.1

Window menu > Layers panel. *View 1*: Layer group expanded, (A) Visibility toggle (eye icon); (B) Hidden layer (no eye icon); (C) Layers panel menu; (D) Layer group; (E) Layer with layer style applied; and (F) Locked layer. *View 2*: Layer group collapsed, (G) Create a new group; (H) Create a new layer; and (I) Delete layer.

name in the *Layers panel* and when the layer name is highlighted, enter a new name. When finished, press the *Return/Enter key* on the keyboard to commit the change. A layer can also be renamed via the *Layer menu* by selecting the *Rename Layer... menu command*, which highlights the layer name in the *Layers panel* [Layer menu > Rename Layer...]. *Tip:* Unlike a file name, spaces can be used in a layer name without causing potential conflict.

The order in which layers are presented in the Layers panel, the *stacking order*, affects the presentation of layered content in an image. The topmost layer in the Layers panel is closest to the viewer. The stacking order can be changed by clicking on a layer name and while holding down the mouse button, dragging the layer up or down within the Layers panel. A highlight line appears where the layer will be inserted when the mouse button is released. The order of layers can also be adjusted via the *Layer menu* using the *Arrange menu command* (i.e., Bring to Front ⇧⌘] | Bring Forward ⌘] | Send Backward ⌘[| Send to Back ⇧⌘[) [Layer menu > Arrange]. If content onscreen is "missing" after layers have been reordered, the content is likely hidden behind another layer's content. To resolve this issue, return to the Layers panel and adjust the stacking order.

Deleting a layer will delete any content that the layer contains from the image. This action is as straightforward as selecting the layer to be deleted in the *Layers panel*, then clicking on the *Delete layer icon* (trashcan icon) located along the bottom edge of the panel. Deleting a layer can also be completed via the *Layers panel menu* and the *Layer menu* [Layer menu > Delete Layer].

A *layer group* serves to organize layers in the Layers panel. There are multiple ways to create and utilize a layer group; here are two options.

- *Option 1:* Create the layer group first, and then move the layers into the layer group.
    - Create the *layer group* by clicking on the *Layer Group icon* (folder icon) along the bottom edge of the *Layers panel*. Or, from the *Layers panel menu*, select *New Group....*
        - The new layer group is named *Group 1*.
        - Layer groups use an incremental numbering system in their naming (e.g., Group 1, Group 2, ...), similar to layer names.
    - Click once on the layer that will be moved into the layer group; this action selects the layer.
    - Then, click and hold down the mouse button over the layer name and drag the layer *over* the layer group (Group 1).
        - An outline appears around the layer group when the cursor is in position over the layer.
    - When the outline appears around the layer group, release the mouse button. This action moves the selected layer into the layer group.
        - Layers within a layer group appear indented beneath the layer group name.

- – *Note:* When a layer group is collapsed, layers within the layer group are not visible in the Layers panel (see Figure 7.1, View 2). In this example, the *Boat* and *Iceberg layers* are no longer visible.
- – To view the layers within the layer group, expand the group by clicking on the *disclosure triangle* (>) located to the left of the group name (Group 1).
- • *Option 2:* Select the layers to be grouped, and then create the layer group.
  - • Select the layers that will be grouped. *Note:* Layers can be moved one at a time or in groups. To select more than one layer, try the following methods.
    - – If the layers are located next to one another in the Layers panel, within this group of layers, click on the topmost layer, then while holding down the *Shift key* on the keyboard, click on the bottommost layer. All of the layers in between should be selected. Release the Shift key.
    - – To select multiple layers that are scattered throughout the Layers panel, use the Command key on the keyboard. Click on one layer, then press and hold down the *Command key* while clicking on the other layers. When all of the layers have been selected, release the Command key.
  - • With the layer(s) selected and the cursor positioned over a selected layer, hold down the mouse button and drag the layers over the *Layer Group icon* located along the bottom edge of the *Layers panel*.
    - – Notice that the cursor icon changes to a closed fist during this process.
  - • Release the mouse button over the *Layer Group icon*; this action creates the new layer group (Group #).
    - – To view the layers within the layer group, expand the group by clicking on the *disclosure triangle* (>) located to the left of the group name (Group #).

Rename the layer group by double-clicking on the provided name (Group #) and entering a new name.

The Background Layer

When a new image file is created, the designer is presented with a choice of *Background Contents* for the image (i.e., White, Black, Background Color, Transparent and Custom). If a color option is chosen, the bottommost layer in the *Layers panel* is defined as the *Background*. *Note:* An image file can have only one background layer. By default, the *Background* possesses certain limitations: the stacking order of the background layer is always the bottommost layer in the Layers panel, and the blending mode or opacity of the background layer cannot be changed. However, the Background can be *unlocked* and converted into a *regular layer*, allowing its stacking order to be changed and its attributes to be adjusted. To initiate this change, click once on the *lock icon* located to the right of the background layer name; this action converts the *Background* to *Layer 0*, an editable layer.

During the file creation process, if the designer chooses *Transparent* for the *Background Contents*, the image file will not contain a background layer. Instead, a transparent layer is created in the Layers panel and used as the basis of the image. This layer is not constrained like a background layer; its stacking order can be changed, and its opacity and blending mode can be adjusted.

Layer-Friendly File Types

Only certain file types support layers, meaning these file types preserve layer information and make the layers available across work sessions. The *Photoshop Document* (PSD) is one such file type; a PSD does not flatten an image file's layers, discarding layer information when saving the file.

Another file type that supports layers is the *Tagged-Image File Format* (TIFF; TIF). Photoshop can save layers in a TIFF file; however, if the TIFF file is opened in another application, such as Preview, only a flattened image (without layers) is opened.

When the time comes to save an image file, if the file contains layers, be sure to select a file type that supports layers, in case the file needs to be edited at a later date. This sounds obvious, but when forgotten creates unnecessary work for the designer. Without editable layers, making changes to an image can be time-consuming and can sometimes necessitate re-creating the image.

Once an image file has been saved with its layers preserved, it is normal to save another instance of the image to share with others who do not have access to Photoshop. This second file differs from the Photoshop Document because it is *flat*; it does not contain layer information. For more information on file formats and their capacities, refer to *Chapter 5: File Properties*, "File Formats."

Let's put this information into practice with an exercise that involves creating new layers in an image file and then using these layers to affect content in the image. First, review the exercise brief and then get started.

Exercise 7.1: Working with Layers

Exercise brief: Using the provided image file, a photograph taken at the annual Albuquerque International Balloon Fiesta,* add additional hot air balloons to the

---

* The Albuquerque International Balloon Fiesta is a 9-day event held each October in Albuquerque, New Mexico. The event attracts hot air balloonists, fans and photographers from around the world. For more information, visit http://www.balloonfiesta.com.

image. Content will be selected and then duplicated using the Copy and Paste menu commands, a process that will produce a new layer each time it is used. Use the Move Tool (V) to reposition and resize the new hot air balloons.

Exercise file: **Ch07-Ex01-photo.jpg** (Figure 7.2)

Figure 7.2

Exercise 7.1 file. Ascension, Albuquerque International Balloon Fiesta, Albuquerque, New Mexico.

Step 1: Open the provided image file (Ch07-Ex01-photo.jpg) in Photoshop.

- Begin at the *File menu* and select the *Open... menu command* [File menu > Open... | ⌘O].
- In the *Open dialog box*, navigate to the photograph.
- Then, click *Open* to open the image file in the workspace.

Step 2: Identify which hot air balloon will be copied (your choice), then zoom in on this area of the canvas to make the selection area larger and easier to see.

- Select the *Zoom Tool* (Z) in the Tools panel.
  - In the *Options bar,* confirm that the tool is set to *Zoom In* (+).
- Zoom in on the selected hot air balloon.
  - Using the *Zoom Tool* (Z), click once on the image over the selection area. *Note:* Each click enlarges the image magnification to the next preset percentage and centers the display on the point clicked.
  - Or, click and hold down the mouse button while dragging the *Zoom Tool* (Z) over the selection area. Then, release the mouse button.
- Try using the keyboard shortcut commands for *Zoom In* (⌘+) and *Zoom Out* (⌘−).

- *Tip:* A related command, *Fit on Screen* (⌘0, Command+Zero), shows the entire canvas, zooming in or out as needed to fit the image to the display screen.
- These menu commands are available from the *View menu* [View menu > Zoom In (⌘+) | Zoom Out (⌘−) | Fit on Screen (⌘0)].
- The current zoom level is listed in two easy-to-spot locations within the Photoshop workspace.
  - One instance is in the *document window tab*, located between the file name and the color mode and bit depth (e.g., Ch07-Ex01-photo.jpg @ 214% (RGB/8)).
  - Another instance is in the *Status bar*, located along the lower-left edge of the document window. This instance can be selected and a new zoom level entered. Give this a try; change the degree of magnification to 300%.
- As needed, use the *Hand Tool* (H) to move the viewable area of the image. Center the selected hot air balloon on the canvas.
  - *Note:* The *Navigator panel* can also be used to move and change the magnification of the visible area of the image [Window menu > Navigator].

Step 3: Use the Lasso Tool (L) to select the hot air balloon.

- Select the *Lasso Tool* (L) in the Tools panel and then position the cursor over the canvas.
- Hold down the mouse button while drawing a selection area around the chosen hot air balloon.
- *Tip:* The application will close a selection area using a straight line to connect the start and end points of a selection. So, return the cursor to the starting point (or close to it) *before* releasing the mouse button.
  - When the mouse button is released, the selection area is outlined in marching ants (Figure 7.3, View 1).

Making an onscreen selection takes practice, so be patient. Here are a few tips that may help:

- Need to start the selection again? Remember that any selection can be deselected via the *Select menu* using the *Deselect menu command* [Select menu > Deselect | ⌘D].
- Need to add to the selection? Perhaps the entire hot air balloon was not included in the selection when the mouse button was released, as shown in Figure 7.3, View 2. In this situation, to add to a selection, hold down the *Shift key* on the keyboard while using the *Lasso Tool* (L) to select the missing area(s).

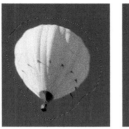  

View 1   View 2   View 3

Figure 7.3

Exercise 7.1, selection areas. *View 1:* Selection complete; *View 2:* Selection incomplete, too small; *View 3:* Selection too large.

- Need to remove content from the selection? Perhaps the selection area was too large when the mouse button was released, as shown in Figure 7.3, View 3. To subtract or take away content from a selection, hold down the *Option key* on the keyboard while selecting the area(s) that should be removed.

This method of adding to and subtracting from a selection can be used with most selection tools or a combination of tools. For example, if the original selection area was created using the *Lasso Tool* (L), a *Marquee Tool* (M) can be used to add or subtract from this selection area.

Default vs. Precise Pointer

How did you know where the Lasso Tool (L) would make its selection? Each default pointer has a different hotspot, where an effect or action in the image begins. With most tools, the designer can switch to a *precise pointer*, which appears as crosshairs centered on the hotspot. To activate the precise pointer, turn on the *Caps Lock* feature on the keyboard by pressing the *Caps Lock key*. To return to the default pointer, turn off Caps Lock.

Step 4: Duplicate the selection using the Copy and Paste menu commands to add a hot air balloon (and a layer) to the image.

- With the selection made (marching ants should be visible around the selected hot air balloon), go to the *Edit menu* and select the *Copy menu command* [Edit menu > Copy | ⌘C].
  - The copied data has been placed in the computer's clipboard.*

---

* The *clipboard* is a temporary storage area for data that the designer wants to copy from one place or file to another.

- Now, return to the *Edit menu* and select the *Paste menu command* [Edit menu > Paste | ⌘V].
  - The action of pasting data in the file creates a new layer in the Layers panel for this content.
  - The copy of the hot air balloon (Balloon #1) has been pasted into the original selection area, *on top* of the original selection. The new hot air balloon is currently not distinguishable from the original photo.
  - In contrast, if the *Deselect menu command* had been used between copying the selection and pasting the selection, Balloon #1 would have been pasted into the center of the viewable canvas [Select menu > Deselect | ⌘D].

Tool Tip: When the *Move Tool* (V) is selected, look to the *Options bar* and turn on the *Auto-Select: Layer* option. This option automatically selects the appropriate layer when the designer clicks on a layer's content in the document window. Similar to using keyboard shortcut commands, this feature saves time and attention, reducing the number of moves between the canvas and the Layers panel. If you elect not to use this feature, confirm that the correct layer is selected in the Layers panel *before* performing an edit.

Step 5: Move Balloon #1 to a different location within the image.

- Select the *Move Tool* (V) in the Tools panel and position the cursor over Balloon #1 on the canvas.
- Click once on Balloon #1 to select the layer in the Layers panel (Balloon 1). *Note:* If the *Auto-Select: Layer* option was not activated, select the Balloon 1 layer in the Layers panel.
- Click and hold down the mouse button and drag Balloon #1 to a new location.
  - If a blue halo around the hot air balloon is visible, do not worry, this is sky that was included in the original selection of the hot air balloon. The halo may be visible in the new location against a different shade of blue or another hot air balloon. This extraneous content is addressed in an upcoming step (Step 13).

By default, the layer name is Layer 1 ["Layer #" (# is an incremental value in sequence)]; this name can be easily changed by double-clicking on Layer 1 and entering a new value.

Step 6: Rename the new layer (Balloon 1).

- In the *Layers panel*, double-click on the new layer name (Layer 1) to select the layer name.
- While the layer name is selected, enter *Balloon 1* as the new layer name.

- The layer name could also be changed via the *Layer menu* and the *Rename Layer... menu command* [Layer menu > Rename Layer...].

Step 7: Save the image. *Note:* The original image file was a JPEG file, a format that does not support layers, so the file format will need to be changed.

- From the *File menu*, select the *Save menu command* [File menu > Save | ⌘S].
  - Notice that this action launches the *Save As dialog box*. Photoshop recognizes that the *file format* needs to be changed in order to support layers and so the *Save As dialog box* is opened.
- In the *Save As dialog box*, confirm that the *Format dropdown menu* lists "*Photoshop.*"
  - The application has defaulted to its native Photoshop Document (PSD), which supports layers; use this file format.
  - Below the Format dropdown, look for the *Layers checkbox* and confirm it is checked in order to preserve layers in the file.
  - Review the file name located in the *Save As field*, it should also reflect the Photoshop Document; the file name should include the PSD file extension, Ch07-Ex01-photo.psd.
- Click *Save* to save the image file (and its layers).

The computer's *clipboard* retains the copied content (Balloon #1), until another selection is copied or the clipboard is cleared. So, to add another instance of the hot air balloon to the image, the hot air balloon does not need to be reselected and copied again. Instead, the contents of the clipboard can simply be pasted into the image file and a second instance of the balloon will be added to the image.

Step 8: Add a second instance of the copied selection (Balloon #1) to the image.

- Return to the *Edit menu* and select *Paste* [Edit menu > Paste | ⌘V].
  - Balloon #2 (a duplicate of Balloon #1) is added to the image, and another layer (Layer 2) is created in the Layers panel.
  - Since there was no active selection area (no marching ants) onscreen when the second instance was pasted, Balloon #2 is pasted into the center of the viewable canvas.

Step 9: Rename the new layer (Balloon 2).

- In the *Layers panel*, double-click on the new layer (Layer 2) to select the layer name.
- While the layer name is selected, enter *Balloon 2* as the new layer name (Figure 7.4, View 1).

A   B   C   D   E   F   G
View 1   View 2

Figure 7.4

Exercise 7.1, Window menu > Layers panel. *View 1*: (A) Link layers; (B) Add a layer style; (C) Add a layer mask; (D) Create new fill or adjustment layer; (E) Create a new group; (F) Create a new layer; and (G) Delete layer. *View 2*: Group layer visibility.

Transparency

Transparent areas of an image file appear as a gray and white checkerboard pattern (Figure 7.5). These areas do not contain content. *Note:* The final image will *not* display the gray and white checkerboard pattern.

Figure 7.5

Transparency example.

Certain file types support transparency, including the Photoshop Document (PSD) and certain Web graphics (i.e., GIF: Graphics Interchange Format; PNG: Portable Network Graphic). When used on a website, these images let the viewer see through transparent areas of the image to the Web page content, generally, a background color or pattern. If an image containing transparency is saved using a file format that does not support transparency (e.g., JPEG: Joint Photographic Experts Group), the transparent areas will be filled with white in the final image.

Step 10: Organize the layers using a layer group in the Layers panel.

- In the Layers panel, use the *Move Tool* (V) and click once on the topmost layer to ensure that the layer group will be added *above* all other content in the Layers panel.
- Still in the Layers panel, click the *Create a new group icon* located along with bottom edge of the panel.
  - By default, the new layer group is named *Group 1*.
- Move the two balloon layers (Balloon 1, Balloon 2) into Group 1.
  - Click and hold down the mouse button on the Balloon 1 layer and drag the layer over Group 1.
  - When the group name is outlined, release the mouse button; this action moves the layer into the layer group.
  - The Balloon 1 layer is now indented beneath Group 1.
  - Repeat the process for the Balloon 2 layer.
- Try turning off the visibility of Group 1. This action should hide both balloons (Balloon #1 and Balloon #2) in the image.
  - Toggle the visibility of Group 1 and its layers off and on by clicking the *eye icon* located to the left of the layer group name (see Figure 7.4, View 2).
  - Turn the visibility of Group 1 back on.
- *Optional:* Rename Group 1.
  - The process for renaming a layer group is similar to renaming a layer. Double-click on the layer group name and while the name is selected, enter a new name. Press the *Return/Enter key* on the keyboard to complete the change.

Step 11: Resize the second hot air balloon (Balloon #2).

- First, zoom out on the canvas to provide enough viewable canvas to complete the next step [View menu > Zoom Out | ⌘−].
- Select the *Move Tool* (V) in the Tools panel and click once on Balloon #2.
  - This action should select the Balloon 2 layer in the Layers panel, which will allow the layer content to be edited.

- From the *Edit menu,* select the *Transform menu command* and then the *Scale command* [Edit menu > Transform > Scale].
  - A bounding box with handles should appear around the selection.
- Select one of the corner handles of the bounding box, then click and hold down the mouse button and drag the handle to increase or decrease the size of the selection (Balloon #2).
  - Starting in Photoshop CC 2019, scaling occurs proportionally, changing the width and height of an object at the same time.
  - For designers using earlier versions of the application, holding down the *Shift key* on the keyboard while scaling an object ensures that the object scales proportionally. Release the mouse button *before* the Shift key to preserve the proportional scale and to avoid distorting the shape of the hot air balloon.
- When satisfied with the hot air balloon's new size, release the mouse. Press the *Return/Enter key* on the keyboard or click the *Commit button* ✓ in the *Options bar* to confirm the transformation.
  - To cancel this transformation, press the *ESC key* on the keyboard or click the *Cancel button* ⊘ in the Options bar.

Step 12: Reposition the balloons so they overlap; move Balloon #2, so it slightly overlaps Balloon #1.

- Select the *Move Tool* (V) in the Tools panel, and use the tool to reposition Balloon #2 so it overlaps Balloon #1.
- Do you notice a blue halo around the edge of Balloon #2? If so, do not worry, this halo of blue pixels was created in the selection of the first hot air balloon (Step 3). It is time to remove this extraneous content.

Step 13 (Optional): Clean up the edges of the selections.

There are several ways that this halo of pixels can be removed; one of the easiest methods involves the *Magic Wand Tool* (W), a tool that selects similarly colored pixels. *Note:* The *Magic Wand Tool* (W) is a hidden tool, sharing space with the *Quick Selection Tool* (W), so double-check that you have the correct tool selected before proceeding.

- First, turn off the *visibility* of the *Background* in the Layers panel to make the blue halo easier to see.
  - Click on the *eye icon* located to the left of the background layer name to toggle off the visibility of the layer.
- Select the *Move Tool* (V) in the Tools panel and use this tool to select Balloon #2 in the image (and its layer, Balloon 2 in the Layers panel), allowing the layer content to be edited.
- Return to the Tools panel and select the *Magic Wand Tool* (W); position the cursor over the canvas.

- Click once anywhere in the blue halo that surrounds Balloon #2 and a selection area indicated by marching ants encircles the halo.
  - If the entire halo is not selected, remember that holding down the *Shift key* on the keyboard while clicking with the *Magic Wand Tool* (W) in an unselected area of blue will expand the selection.
- With the blue halo selected, go to the *Edit menu* and choose the *Clear menu command* to delete the selected pixels [Edit menu > Clear].
  - *Note:* The *Delete key* on the keyboard can also be used to eliminate the selected content.
- Repeated this process as needed for Balloon #1.
- When these edits are complete, turn on the visibility of the Background in the Layers panel.
  - Click on the *eye icon* located to the left of the background layer name to toggle on the visibility of the layer.

Step 14: Save the file.

- Return to the *File menu* and select the *Save menu command* [File menu > Save | ⌘S].

Well done, you have successfully altered a photograph adding content and layers to an image file. Before moving on, here are some *Need to Know Fundamentals* that pertain to the exercise.

Need to Know Fundamentals

Show Transform Controls

The basic transformation commands used to alter an object are available from the *Edit menu* and the *Transform menu command* [Edit menu > Transform]. These commands include Scale, Rotate, Skew, Distort, Perspective, Warp and Flip.

Photoshop provides an option that makes these commands readily available in the workspace. To activate this feature, select the *Move Tool* (V) and look to the *Options bar* and turn on the *Show Transform Controls* option. This feature displays a bounding box around a selected object, which allows the designer to use the handles of the bounding box to transform the object (e.g., scale, stretch and flip).

Magic Wand Tool vs. Quick Selection Tool

The more time spent working in Photoshop, the more recognizable the subtle and not so subtle differences between related tools will become. In *Exercise 7.1* (Step 13), the *Magic Wand Tool* (W) was used to select content, specifically, the blue halo surrounding a hot air balloon. This tool works well when selecting semi-flat colors* that may or may not be connected (contiguous). However, if the object

---

* Flat colors exclude gradients, textures and shadows.

to be selected contains many colors and tones, the *Quick Selection Tool* (W) is preferable. When the *Quick Selection Tool* (W) is moved over an object, Photoshop continuously samples the surrounding area, doing its best to create a seamless selection. Give this tool a try. Reopen the original photograph (Ch07-Ex01-photo.jpg) and use the *Quick Selection Tool* (W) to select one of the hot air balloons. Try selecting the black hot air balloon with the colorful accents near the center of the photo, and this will demonstrate the tool's ability to select multiple colors.

The Eraser Tools

Another way to remove the blue halo around the hot air balloon would have been to use one of the three *Eraser Tools* (E). The following descriptions drawn from the *Photoshop Online Help* highlight the subtle differences between the three tools:

- The *Eraser Tool* (E) erases pixels and restores parts of an image to a previously saved state.
- The *Background Eraser Tool* (E) erases areas to transparency.
- The *Magic Eraser Tool* (E) erases solid-colored areas to transparency with a single click.

Let's give these tools a try, comparing their capabilities first-hand.

Practice 1: Using the Eraser Tools

Practice brief: Save a copy of the completed *Exercise 7.1* image file, then experiment with the *Eraser Tools* (E) in this file copy.

Step 1: Save a copy of the completed *Exercise 7.1* image file (Ch07-Ex01-photo.psd).
- Open the file in Photoshop.
  - From the *File menu,* select the *Open... menu command* [File menu > Open... | ⌘O].
  - Navigate to the file (Ch07-Ex01-photo.psd).
  - Click *Open* to open the file in the workspace.
- Return to the *File menu* and select the *Save As... menu command* [File menu > Save As... | ⇧⌘S].
- In the *Save As dialog box,* check the *Save: As a Copy checkbox.* This action should append "copy" to the file name in the *Save As* field (Ch07-Ex01-photo copy.psd).
  - Notice that a space was inserted in the file name. Consider changing the space to a hyphen or underscore to further the practice of good file naming (Ch07-Ex01-photo-copy.psd).
- Select an appropriate location to save the file copy, and then click *Save.*
- *Tip:* The copy of the file just created is *not open* in Photoshop. Check the *document window tab* and notice that the open file is the original version of the file that was created (Ch07-Ex01-photo.psd).

- From the *File menu,* select the *Open... menu command* and navigate to the newly created copy of the file (Ch07-Ex01-photo-copy.psd) [File menu > Open... | ⌘O].
- Click *Open* to open the file in the workspace.

Step 2: Experiment with each of the eraser tools (i.e., Eraser Tool [E], Background Eraser Tool [E], Magic Eraser Tool [E]).

- With the file copy open, select the Balloon 2 layer in the Layers panel so the contents of this layer can be edited.
- Select the *Eraser Tool* (E) in the Tools panel.
  - Notice the properties that can be adjusted in the *Options bar* including the *Mode* of the eraser (i.e., Brush, Pencil and Block).
  - Select a mode of your choice and adjust the size of the eraser as needed.
- Click and drag the *Eraser Tool* (E) over Balloon #2 in the canvas.
  - As the cursor is dragged over content, the content is erased, making the Background behind the hot air balloon visible.
  - *Tip:* The *Eraser Tool* (E) only impacts content on the *selected layer* in the Layers panel. When the *Eraser Tool* (E) is used on the *Background layer,* erased areas are filled with the current *Background Color* shown in the Tools panel.
- Select the *Background* in the Layers panel, then choose the *Background Eraser Tool* (E) in the Tools panel and try erasing content on the Background.
  - The *Background Eraser Tool* (E) allows the designer to erase the background layer, introducing areas of transparency into the image.
  - Notice that use of the *Background Eraser Tool* (E) changes the nature of the *Background* to a *regular layer* and in the process renames the layer, *Layer 0.*
- Now, use the *Background Eraser Tool* (E) on Balloon #1, the contents of the Balloon 1 layer. *Tip:* Remember to first select the appropriate layer before beginning the edit.
  - When used on the Balloon 1 layer, the *Background Eraser Tool* (E) behaves like the traditional *Eraser Tool* (E).
- Select the *Magic Eraser Tool* (E) in the Tools panel. This tool allows solid-colored areas to be erased with a single click.
  - Give this tool a try by erasing content on the former background layer (now, *Layer 0*).
- Continue to experiment with the *Eraser Tools* (E), then save or revert the file to its previously saved state [File menu > Save | ⌘S; File menu > Revert].

Tool Tip: The *Eraser Tools* (E) do not work on an *editable type layer* (the next topic to be introduced). If attempted, the cursor changes to a *Cancel symbol* indicating that the tool will not work on the current layer. A type layer would need to be *rasterized* before the eraser tools could be used to edit the text. *Note:*

Rasterizing and the steps involved with rasterizing type are presented later in this chapter; see "Rasterizing Type Layers."

Using the Type Tool

Type in Photoshop consists of vector-based type outlines, mathematically defined shapes that describe the letters, numbers and symbols of a *typeface*. Typography is discussed in detail in *Chapter 10: Typography in Design*. So, for now we stick with the basics and review the three ways that type can be created in Photoshop, at a point, inside a paragraph and along a path. These three methods are illustrated in Figure 7.6.

A. *Point type* is a horizontal or vertical line of text that begins where the cursor is clicked in the image.
 - Entering text at a point is a useful way to add a few words to an image.
 - When point type is created, each line of type is independent, the line expands or collapses as the content is edited, but it does not wrap to the next line.

B. *Paragraph type* uses boundaries to control the flow of characters, either horizontally or vertically.
 - This method is a useful way to create one or more lines or paragraphs.
 - When paragraph type is created, the lines of type wrap to fit the dimensions of the bounding box. The *bounding box* can be resized, causing the type to reflow within the adjusted rectangle. The bounding box can also be used to rotate, scale and skew type.

C. *Type on a path* flows along the edge of an open or a closed path. A *path* consists of one or more straight or curved segments. *Note:* Paths will be presented in detail in *Chapter 11: Getting Started with Illustrator*.
 - Paths are generally created using the *Pen Tool* (P) or a *Shape Tool* (U).

Save Your Work, Early and Often.

A

This practice will help you avoid losing work should the application or computer freeze and need to be restarted while you are working. Throughout the book, you will be encouraged to save your work, early and often.

B

C

Figure 7.6

Examples of the three methods used for creating type in Photoshop: (A) point type, (B) paragraph type, and (C) type on a path. *Typeface:* Myriad Pro.

When finished entering the text, the designer must signal the end of the text entry; any of the following actions can be used to indicate the end of the text entry.

- Click elsewhere on the canvas with the *Type Tool* (T).
- Click the *Commit button* in the *Options bar*.
- Select another tool in the *Tools panel*.

A new *type layer* is added to the Layers panel when type is created. Once created, type can be edited and its appearance adjusted using a variety of properties. Another way to affect type appearances is to apply a layer style to the type layer. A *layer style* is a nondestructive way to add an effect, such as a drop shadow or stroke, to the contents of a layer.

Converting between Point Type and Paragraph Type

Type can be converted from *point type* to *paragraph type* in order to adjust the flow of characters within a bounding box. Similarly, *paragraph type* can be converted to *point type* to make each text line flow independently from the others. To convert the type, first select the type layer in the *Layers* panel. Then, from the *Type menu*, select either the *Convert to Paragraph Type* or the *Convert to Point Type menu command* [Type menu > Convert to Paragraph Type | Convert to Point Type].

When paragraph type is converted to point type, a carriage return is added at the end of each line of type (except the last line). Be aware that during the conversion process, all characters that overflow the bounding box are deleted. *Tip:* To avoid losing text, adjust the bounding box so that all type is visible *before* the conversion.

As with other tools, when the *Type Tool* (T) is selected in the Tools panel, the *Options bar* displays the properties available for adjustment (Figure 7.7). These options include the following labeled properties (from left to right):

A. Toggle text orientation (i.e., Horizontal, Vertical)
B. Search for and select fonts
C. Set the font style (e.g., Regular, Italic, Bold)
D. Set the font size
E. Set the anti-aliasing* method (i.e., None, Sharp, Crisp, Strong, Smooth)
F. Align text (i.e., Left, Center, Right)
G. Select the text color (opens the Color Picker)

---

* *Anti-aliasing* produces smooth-edged type by partially filling the edge pixels. As a result, the edges of the type blend into the background.

Graphic Design: Learn It, Do It

A	B	C	D	E	F	G H	I

Figure 7.7

Options bar, Type Tool options: (A) Toggle text orientation; (B) Search for and select fonts; (C) Set the font style; (D) Set the font size; (E) Set the anti-aliasing method; (F) Align text; (G) Select the text color; (H) Create warped text; and (I) Toggle the Character and Paragraph panels.

H. Create warped text*

I. Toggle the Character and Paragraph panels

The Character panel and Paragraph panel, shown in Figure 7.8, provide additional properties and formatting options for adjusting type. The *Character panel* provides options for formatting characters and letterforms. Use the *Paragraph panel* to change the formatting of columns and paragraphs. Both panels are accessible via the *Window menu* or the toggle button on the *Options bar* [Window menu > Character | Paragraph].

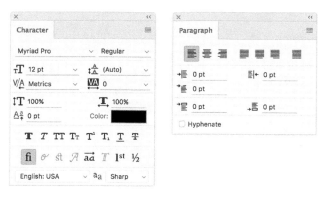

Figure 7.8

Window menu > Character | Paragraph.

Rasterizing Type Layers

Certain commands and tools (e.g., filter effects and painting tools) cannot be applied to type or shape layers in their original state. The content on these layers must first be *rasterized* before it can be affected. The process of rasterizing converts a type layer into a regular layer making its contents uneditable as text, using the *Type Tool* (T); however, the layer content can be edited as a pixel-based bitmap image.

---

† *Warped text* conforms to a variety of shapes, such as Arc, Bulge, Flag and Rise.

To rasterize a type layer, first, select the type layer in the *Layers panel*. From the *Layer menu*, choose the *Rasterize menu command* and then the *Type command* [Layer menu > Rasterize > Type]. *Note:* The selected type layer can also be rasterized via the *Type menu*, selecting the *Rasterize Type Layer menu command* [Type menu > Rasterize Type Layer].

Let's use this information in *Exercise 7.2* to add text to an image and then stylize the text. Review the exercise brief and get started.

Exercise 7.2: Working with Type

Exercise brief: Add type to an image and then apply a layer style to the type. Use the image file created in *Exercise 7.1* (or use the provided image file, Ch07-Ex02. psd) for this exercise.
　　Exercise file: **Ch07-Ex02.psd** (Figure 7.9)

Figure 7.9

Exercise 7.2 file. Ascension, Albuquerque International Balloon Fiesta, Albuquerque, New Mexico.

Step 1: Open the image file that will be used in this exercise.

Step 2: Create a line of text (point type) in the image promoting the "Albuquerque International Balloon Fiesta."

- Select the *Type Tool* (T) in the Tools panel and position the cursor over the canvas.
- Click once on the canvas to create *point type* and begin typing.

- When finished entering the text, click elsewhere on the canvas with the *Type Tool* (T) to signal the end of the text entry.
  - The text will be placed on its *own layer* in the *Layers panel*.
  - By default, the *name* of the *type layer* is based on the text that was entered.
  - The name of the type layer can be changed by double-clicking on the layer name and entering a new value. *Note:* Changing the name of the type layer will *not* affect the onscreen text.
- Use the properties available in the *Options bar* or the *Character* or *Paragraph panels* to alter the appearance of the type (e.g., font, size and color). *Note:* The type must be selected *before* its properties can be changed.
  - Select the text using the *Type Tool* (T) and then adjust the desired properties.
  - *Tip:* Some transformations require the designer to *Cancel* or *Commit* the change(s) before work on the image file can continue. In this situation, look to the *Options bar* for the *Cancel button* (*Alternative: Escape key* on the keyboard) and the *Commit button* (*Alternative: Return/Enter key* on the keyboard).

Step 3: Apply a layer style to the line of type.

- Use the *Move Tool* (V) to select the line of type on the canvas (and its associated layer in the *Layers panel*).
- In the *Layers panel*, click on the *Add a layer style icon* located along the bottom edge of the panel; the icon is highlighted in Figure 7.10. This action opens a menu of layer styles that can be applied to the selected layer and its content.
  - The menu of layer styles can also be accessed from the *Layer menu* [Layer menu > Layer Style].
- Select *Drop Shadow...* from the menu of layer styles.
  - This action opens the *Layer Style dialog box* (Figure 7.11). Here the properties associated with the selected layer style (Drop Shadow) can be modified (e.g., *opacity* of the shadow, *angle* of the shadow and *distance* of the shadow from the object).
  - *Note:* Confirm that the *Preview checkbox* is checked in the dialog box; this feature allows the designer to view the layer style being applied to the onscreen text as adjustments are being made.
- When satisfied with the drop shadow, click *OK*.
  - Notice that the *layer style* is listed in the *Layers panel* below the layer to which it is applied.
  - The visibility of the layer style can be turned off and on just like the visibility of a layer or layer group. Click on the *eye icon* to toggle the layer style off and on.

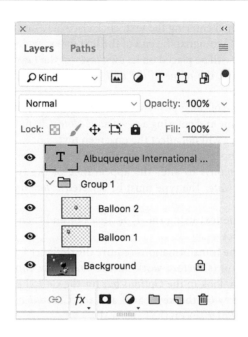

Figure 7.10

Exercise 7.2, Window menu > Layers panel. Add a layer style icon highlighted.

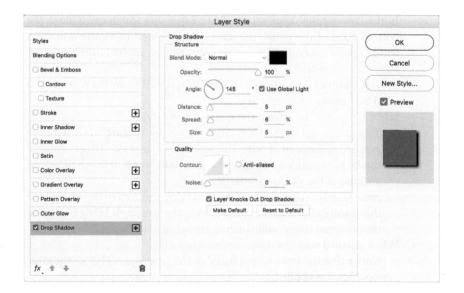

Figure 7.11

Layer Style dialog box, Layers panel > Layer Style.

Multiple layer styles can be applied to a single layer. However, make sure that the layer styles do not distract from the text and its message.

Step 4: Save the file and view the image in Full Screen Mode (F).

- Return to the *File menu* and select the *Save menu command* [File menu > Save | ⌘S].
- Compare the workspace's appearance in each of the screen modes.
  - In the lower portion of the *Tools panel*, click and hold down the mouse button on the *Change Screen Mode icon* to see the available options (i.e., Standard Screen Mode, Full Screen Mode with Menu Bar and Full Screen Mode).
  - The screen mode can also be changed via the *View menu* and the *Screen Mode menu command* [View menu > Screen Mode].
- View the completed image in the *Full Screen Mode* (F).
  - When the *Full Screen Mode* (F) is selected, the following Photoshop alert appears. *In Full Screen Mode, panels are hidden. They can be accessed on the sides of the screen or revealed by pressing Tab. While in Full Screen Mode, you can return to Standard Screen Mode by pressing "F" or Esc.*
  - Select *Full Screen Mode* (F) to fill the screen with the image.
  - To exit *Full Screen Mode* (F) and return to *Standard Screen Mode* (F), press the *ESC key* on the keyboard, or the letter "F."

Well done. You have completed *Exercise 7.2.* You should be feeling familiar with the Photoshop workspace and comfortable adding text to an image file. Before continuing, here are some additional *Need to Know Fundamentals* related to the tools and processes used in *Exercise 7.2.*

Need to Know Fundamentals

Creating Warped Type

Another way to alter the appearance of text, aside from layer styles, is to create warped text. Examples shown in Figure 7.12 illustrate the variety of effects available to the designer. The *warp style* is an attribute of the *type layer*. It can be changed at any time to alter the overall shape of the warp. Warping options allow for precise control over the orientation and perspective of the warp effect.

To create warped text, try the following steps:

- Use the *Type Tool* (T) to create a line of type (point or paragraph type).
- Activate the text frame by clicking *in* the text frame using the *Type Tool* (T).
- In the *Options bar,* click on the *Create warped text icon.* Or, in the *Type menu,* select the *Warp Text... menu command* [Type menu > Warp Text…]. Both actions launch the *Warp Text dialog box.*
  - In the *Warp Text dialog box,* select a warp style.

Figure 7.12

Warped text. *Typeface:* Minion Pro.

- Experiment with the *orientation* (i.e., Horizontal, Vertical), *bend* and *distortion* options.
- Click *OK* to apply the warp or *Cancel* to discard the warp.
- Now, click elsewhere on the canvas with the *Type Tool* (T) to signal the end of text entry.
- In the *Layers panel*, notice that the *layer's thumbnail* has changed to indicate the presence of a warp style.
- Once applied, the *Warp Text dialog box* can be reopened to alter the appearance of the text. To do so, select the affected type layer in the *Layers panel* and then click on the *Create warped text icon* in the *Options bar* to launch the *Warp Text dialog box*.

Rulers, Guides and the Grid

The following resources, rulers, guides and the grid, can be useful when the designer needs to position content precisely, for example, when working to achieve alignment among elements, particularly text. For more about the role of alignment in design, refer to *Chapter 2: The Elements and Principles of Design.*

Rulers can be displayed along the top and left edges of the document window (Figure 7.13). To turn the rulers on or off, access the *View menu* and select the *Rulers menu command* [View menu > Rulers | ⌘R]. The rulers' unit of measure reflects the application's units, a setting available in the *Preferences dialog box*

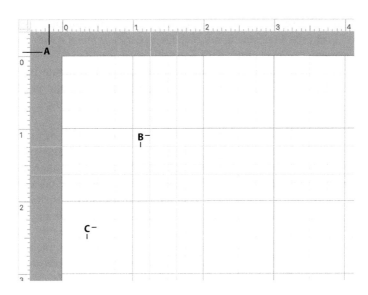

Figure 7.13

Rulers, guides and the grid: (A) rulers, (B) guides (cyan lines) and (C) the grid.

[Photoshop CC menu > Preferences > Units & Rulers…]; options include pixels, inches, centimeters, millimeters, points and picas. *Note: The Preferences dialog box* can be accessed by double-clicking on a ruler. The unit of measure can also be changed by right-clicking (Control + click) on a ruler and selecting an option from the provided list.

Guides appear as nonprinting lines overtop an image in the workspace (see Figure 7.13). Guides can be moved, removed and also locked in position to avoid being accidentally moved. There are multiple methods for bringing a guide on to the canvas; here are two.

- *Option 1:* Drag a guide onto the workspace from one of the rulers.
  - Confirm that the rulers are available along the top and left sides of the document window.
    - If the rulers are not present, turn them on. Go to the *View menu* and select the *Rulers menu command* [View menu > Rulers | ⌘R].
  - Position the cursor over one of the rulers.
    - Notice that the cursor icon changes to a filled arrow.
  - Press and hold the mouse button down and then drag the cursor from the ruler onto the canvas.
    - Accompanying the cursor is the guide (a straight line) and a tooltip indicating the guide's position (e.g., X, Y).
  - When the guide is in the desired location, release the mouse button.
    - In position, the guide is a cyan line (a shade of blue).

- *Option 2:* Use the *New Guide… menu command* to generate a guide.
  - From the *View menu*, select the *New Guide… menu command* [View menu > New Guide…].
  - The *New Guide dialog box* provides options to define the guide's *orientation* (i.e., Horizontal, Vertical) as well as the *position* for the guide.

Guides remain in position and visible until a guide is moved or its visibility is turned off. Use the *Move Tool* (V) to reposition guides on and around the canvas. To delete a guide, position the cursor over the guide, then click and hold down the mouse button and drag the guide to the corresponding ruler and then release the mouse button. To hide or toggle off the visibility of all guides, access the *View menu* and select the *Show menu command* and then *Guides* [View menu > Show > Guides | ⌘;]. Guides can also be locked in position or removed from the image file via the View menu [View menu > Lock Guides | View menu > Clear Guides]. For additional information about other guide options, including *New Guide Layout…* and *New Guides from Shape*, access the *Photoshop Online Help.*

The *grid* is another helpful resource for laying out image elements symmetrically (see Figure 7.13). This feature can be turned on via the *View menu* and the *Show Grid menu command* [View menu > Show Grid | ⌘'].

The *Snap to* feature assists with precise placement of selection edges and cropping borders. The designer can select what they would like to *Snap to* (i.e., Guides, Grid, Layers, Slices, Document, Bounds, All, None) via the *View menu* [View menu > Snap to]. When *Snap to* is active and the designer is moving an object, the object may jerk across the image as though it is being attracted by a magnet. Just as this feature can be turned on via the *View menu*, it can also be disabled there [View menu > Snap].

Tool Tip: To nudge an object, changing its position by a small amount, use the *arrow keys* on the keyboard to reposition an object 1 pixel at a time. Holding down the *Shift key* on the keyboard while pressing the *arrow key* moves an object by 10 pixels.

Looking Ahead

This chapter contains a lot of information about Photoshop. Spend time experimenting with the tools and features until you feel comfortable working with the concepts presented. An end-of-chapter activity awaits when you are ready for a fresh challenge. Read through the provided brief, and then be creative. Utilize the Photoshop skills developed here in combination with the design principles and color theory presented in earlier chapters to create an effective and eye-catching design. Then, when you are ready to proceed, the next chapter introduces the art of digital photography and its role in graphic design.

Discussions

Discussion 7.1: Scaling Proportionally

In *Exercise 7.1*, Step 11, a hot air balloon was scaled proportionally, the width and height of the image changed at the same time. When resizing an image, why is it important to scale proportionally? Is this more or less important when working with images of people? Why or why not?

Discussion 7.2: Types of Layers

Look at the *Layers panel* presented in Figure 7.14 and identify the following elements:

- Type layer
- Layer style
- Warped type layer
- Layer group

- Hidden layer
- Rasterize type layer
- Linked layers

Based on the contents of the Layers panel, we cannot tell what the image looks like. Why not?

Figure 7.14

Discussion 7.2, Layers panel.

Activity

Activity 7.1: Create a Postcard

Activity brief: Create a postcard for a destination (city or country) of your choice. For this activity, you are encouraged to use your own photographs, or the provided photos of London, England, available on the book's companion website.

Activity files: Ch07-Ex03A-photo.jpg, Ch07-Ex03B-photo.jpg, Ch07-Ex03C-photo.jpg, Ch07-Ex03D-photo.jpg, Ch07-Ex03E-photo.jpg, Ch07-Ex03F-photo.jpg, Ch07-Ex03G-photo.jpg, Ch07-Ex03H-photo.jpg, Ch07-Ex03I-photo.jpg, Ch07-Ex03J-photo.jpg, Ch07-Ex03K-photo.jpg

Guidelines

1. Use at least three photographs in the design. Feel free to use more, but target at least three.
2. Include a text element that identifies the location.

File Properties

Image size: 4.25 in. × 6 in. (horizontal postcard) or 6 in. × 4.25 in. (vertical postcard)
Resolution: 150 ppi
Color mode: CMYK
File naming: Use yourlastname-city/country-name.psd as the file name, for example, hughes-london.psd

Exercise File(s) Available on the Companion Website, URL

Ch07-Ex01-photo.jpg | *Exercise 7.1* file, Ascension, Albuquerque International Balloon Fiesta, Albuquerque, New Mexico.
Ch07-Ex02.psd | *Exercise 7.2* file, Ascension, Albuquerque International Balloon Fiesta, Albuquerque, New Mexico.
Ch07-Ex03A-photo.jpg | *Activity 7.1* file. London, England.
Ch07-Ex03B-photo.jpg | *Activity 7.1* file. London, England.
Ch07-Ex03C-photo.jpg | *Activity 7.1* file. London, England.
Ch07-Ex03D-photo.jpg | *Activity 7.1* file. London, England.
Ch07-Ex03E-photo.jpg | *Activity 7.1* file. London, England.
Ch07-Ex03F-photo.jpg | *Activity 7.1* file. London, England.
Ch07-Ex03G-photo.jpg | *Activity 7.1* file. London, England.
Ch07-Ex03H-photo.jpg | *Activity 7.1* file. London, England.
Ch07-Ex03I-photo.jpg | *Activity 7.1* file. London, England.
Ch07-Ex03J-photo.jpg | *Activity 7.1* file. London, England.
Ch07-Ex03K-photo.jpg | *Activity 7.1* file. London, England.

URL: http://www.crcpress.com/9780367075347

External Links Mentioned in the Chapter

Photoshop Online Help | https://helpx.adobe.com/photoshop

8

Digital Photography in Design

First things first, let's answer an obvious question, why include a chapter on photography in a graphic design book? The answer is found in the media and images that we consume. Look around—you are likely to spot multiple designs that are based on or include photographs. These may be photorealistic images (actual photos) or graphics that include altered or stylized photos.

Photography is one of the means that the designer has for acquiring an image; another is to create an image from scratch. Many of us are fortunate to carry a camera with us wherever we go, the camera on our cell phone. This accessibility makes it easy to capture something seen in passing, an unfolding event or a reference for later use. Many photos taken in a day can be described as snapshots. These are photos that we *take* with little thought about the shot's composition or overall quality of the image. In contrast, the photograph that we *make* ideally includes some forethought and planning in order to achieve a compositionally strong image that is effective in attracting and holding the viewer's attention.

Controlling Exposure

At its most basic, photography is the art of capturing light. This was originally done on glass, then on film and these days using image sensors in digital cameras that record data. Cameras utilize three elements, *aperture, shutter speed* and *ISO*, to control the amount of light captured, or the *exposure* of the photo. *Exposure* refers to the lightness or darkness of an image.

The Exposure Triangle

The *Exposure Triangle* is composed of aperture, shutter speed and ISO (Figure 8.1). In the triangle, as in a camera, these three elements work together to generate the exposure of a photo. When one element is adjusted, the other two elements must also be adjusted in order to maintain consistent exposure across photos, which is the desired outcome.

Cameras shooting in an automatic mode (Auto), including cell phone cameras, will determine the appropriate settings for aperture, shutter speed and ISO based on the amount of available light when a photo is taken. However, it is important to understand these elements in order to adjust them as needed to accommodate a subject or location or to achieve a particular look in a photo.

Aperture is an adjustable opening in the camera lens that limits the amount of light passing through the lens and hitting the image sensor. As the aperture is adjusted, the *depth of field* changes, affecting how much of the photo is in *focus* or is completely sharp. When the aperture is small, little light is let into the lens (less

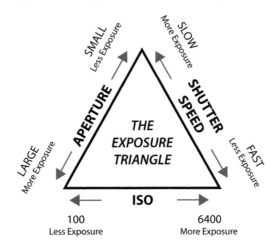

Figure 8.1

The Exposure Triangle. Use the Exposure Triangle to decide how to adjust exposure. When the exposure for one element is increased (a red arrow), the exposure for one or both of the remaining elements must be reduced (the blue arrows) in order to maintain consistent exposure across photos.

exposure), which produces a large depth of field. A large depth of field means that more of the photo is in sharp focus. As the aperture is opened or "stopped up," more light is let into the lens (more exposure), which produces a shallower depth of field. In a photo with a shallow depth of field, the subject may be in focus while the background or foreground is out of focus or blurry. Compare the depths of field (large vs. shallow) in the two photos of sunflowers in Figure 8.2. Notice the relative blurriness of the background in the photo illustrating shallow depth of field.

Unit of measure: f-stop // A *stop* is a doubling or halving of the amount of light let into the camera lens when taking a photo.

Examples: (less exposure) f/64, f/32, f/16, f/11, f/8, f/5.6, f/4, f/2.8, f/1.4 (more exposure)

Shutter speed determines how long the camera shutter stays open to let light in when the shutter release button is pressed. Shutter speed can also affect the clarity of a shot caused by a subject's movement or the camera not being held still. A fast shutter speed provides less exposure and freezes the action within a photo. A slow shutter speed provides more exposure and the potential for blurred motion. Compare the photos of flowing water in Figure 8.3; notice the effect that varying shutter speeds has on the appearance of the water.

Unit of measure: second

Examples: (less exposure) 1/2000, 1/1000, 1/500, 1/250, 1/125, 1/60, 1/30, 1/15, 1/8, 1, 2 (more exposure)

Figure 8.2

Aperture examples: (A) large depth of field (ISO 100, f/22, 1/30th); and (B) shallow depth of field (ISO 100, f/5.6, 1/800th). Sunflowers, Emerald Isle, North Carolina.

Figure 8.3

Shutter speed examples: (A) fast shutter speed (ISO 100, f/11, 1/180th), Jasper National Park, Alberta, Canada; and (B) slow shutter speed (ISO 560, f/22, 1/6th), Fuller Falls, Fundy National Park, New Brunswick, Canada.

How Slow is Too Slow for a Handheld Camera?

When a camera's shutter speed is set to a value slower than 1/60th of a second (e.g., 1/30th, 1/8th, 1 second), a *tripod* (a three-legged support for a camera) or a *monopod* (a one-legged support for a camera) should be used to combat movement created when holding the camera. The movement is natural and to be expected as it is caused by the photographer's breathing. If you do not have access to a tripod or monopod, try placing your camera on a sturdy surface (e.g., a table or a parked car) to provide the necessary support and minimize camera movement and associated blur.

ISO refers to the sensitivity of a digital camera's image sensor; this is the equivalent to ASA film speed* for film cameras. ISO allows the photographer to use the ideal combination of aperture and shutter speed when the amount of available light would normally prevent him or her from doing so. However, increasing the ISO

---

* ASA is a scale created by the American Standards Association that is no longer widely used. Now, most film is labeled by ISO, which was created in 1987 by the International Organization for Standardization.

Figure 8.4

ISO examples: (A) low ISO (ISO 800, f/4.0, 1/60th); and (B) high ISO (ISO 3200, f/3.5, 1/6th). Balloon glow, Albuquerque International Balloon Fiesta, Albuquerque, New Mexico.

reduces the quality of the photo as it introduces noise or graininess into the image. Fortunately, as digital cameras continue to advance, the effect of using a high ISO is less noticeable. Compare the clarity of the photos taken at an evening hot air balloon glow that use different ISO values (ISO 800 vs. ISO 3200) (Figure 8.4). In the close-up of the photo that uses ISO 3200, there is a bit of noise and the areas of color are not as clear as those in the photo that uses ISO 800. *Note:* If you do not notice much difference between the photos, that is okay, just know that ISO *can* be a factor in certain scenarios such as night photography.

Unit of measure: Values that correspond to the ASA scale for film, with a higher ISO number corresponding to a more sensitive sensor

Examples: (less exposure) 100, 200, 400, 800, 1600, 3200, 6400 (more exposure)

Seeing the Shot

The design concepts presented in *Chapter 2: The Elements and Principles of Design* also apply to photography, and consideration of these can help the photographer "see the shot" through the camera's lens. *Seeing the shot* refers to looking at a scene and selectively isolating a subject or area of interest. What is left out of the photo is often as important as what is included, because this can minimize distractions and center attention on the subject.

Figure 8.5

Seeing the shot, low-tech aperture.

A helpful practice for isolating a subject is to use your hands to narrow your field of view. Hold your hands as shown in Figure 8.5, then look through the "aperture" (the space created between your hands) and scan your environment. What around you would make an interesting photo? Just as a camera narrows your area of view to frame a photo, so too does this simple technique.

Types of Camera Shots

To expand this discussion of framing a photo, let's review the basic types of camera shots used in photography. *Note:* These are also some of the same camera shots used in cinematography and videography. This common language is useful when communicating the visual elements of a shot, particularly the size of the subject and its relationship with the background.

A. *Extreme long shot* (ELS) or *extreme wide shot* (EWS): The ELS is used to show the space in which the visual story is taking place and thus is sometimes referred to as an *establishing shot*. The subject may be shown in the distance.

B. *Long shot* (LS) or *wide shot* (WS): The LS shows the entire subject without filling the frame. Instead, the shot may be dominated by the background. This shot often sets the scene and can serve as an establishing shot in place of an ELS/EWS.

C. *Medium shot* (MS): The MS shows part of the subject in detail. When the subject is a person, the MS generally frames him or her from the waist up. The focus of the shot may be the subject, although some background is still showing.

Graphic Design: Learn It, Do It

Figure 8.6

Camera shots: (A) extreme long shot (ELS); (B) long shot (LS); (C) medium shot (MS); (D) medium close-up (MCU); (E) close-up (CU); and (F) extreme close-up (ECU). In flight over the Rio Grande, Albuquerque, New Mexico.

D. *Medium close-up* (MCU): The MCU shows the subject in more detail, falling between the MS and the CU. For a person as a subject, the MCU usually frames him or her from the chest or shoulders up.

E. *Close-up* (CU): The CU fills the frame with the subject. This could be a person's head or face, or the person's hands if he or she is holding something important.

F. *Extreme close-up* (ECU): The ECU features a small area or detail of the subject. For a person, this could be their eyes or mouth.

Each of these shots used for the same subject would create a unique photo with a distinctive focal point or area of attention, as shown in Figure 8.6.

Photographic Composition

When looking through the viewfinder of a camera or at the screen of a cell phone, you are making decisions about composition. *Composition* is how you choose to frame the photo you are about to make. There are four elements that contribute to strong photographic composition: *subject and background*, *sense of balance*, *point of view*, and *simplicity*.

Subject and Background

Photographs that contain layers of content in the foreground, midground and background of the image can achieve a sense of depth in a two-dimensional medium.

Figure 8.7

Subject and background. Alpacas at Eastland Alpacas, Mount Joy, Pennsylvania.

The 2-week-old alpaca in the foreground of the photo in Figure 8.7 is in focus and is the main subject of the photo. However, by including the two other alpacas in the background, the viewer's eye is drawn from the baby alpaca across the rest of the photo. When framing a shot, do not just concentrate on the subject, look at what is happening around it, particularly in the background. Use this opportunity to adjust your position or to zoom in on the subject in order to eliminate distracting background elements or to zoom out to provide needed context for the subject.

Sense of Balance

Balance can refer to the position of the subject in the image frame or the overall balance of the photo. Looking at the overall photo, a straight *horizon line** provides stability to the image. A crooked or angled horizon line can distract from the overall impact of a photo as the viewer tries to reconcile the unexpected horizon line. Take time in the field to look at the horizon line and adjust the

---

* A horizon line is the physical or visual boundary where the sky separates from land or water.

Figure 8.8
Rule of thirds (A) photo, (B) photo with rule of thirds gridlines shown. Sheep at the Hill of Tara, County Meath, Ireland.

camera as needed to achieve an accurate horizon. Similarly, if photographing a building, observe its lines and ensure that they are appropriately perpendicular or parallel to the ground. In *Chapter 9: Photo Editing in Photoshop*, the process for straightening an angled horizon line in Photoshop is presented.

The *rule of thirds* is an important concept when it comes to positioning a subject to create a more engaging and balanced photo. The rule of thirds involves mentally overlaying a tic-tac-toe grid on the image, dividing the image into nine equal parts using two horizontal and two vertical gridlines (Figure 8.8). Position the important elements in the shot along these gridlines or at the intersections where these gridlines meet. *Note:* Some cameras have a menu item that allows you to turn on gridlines in the viewfinder. These gridlines are a guide intended to help you frame the shot and will not show up in the photo.

The rule of thirds is based on the idea that an off-centered composition is more pleasing to the eye and looks more natural than one where the subject is placed right in the middle of the frame. This technique also encourages the photographer to make creative use of the negative space, the empty areas around the subject. *Note:* This *rule* is really just a "suggestion," and when intentionally broken, center positioning of a subject can have a powerful visual impact. But in general, the rule of thirds is a good starting point for any composition.

Positioning the Horizon Line

Use the rule of thirds to guide your placement of the horizon in a shot. A photograph with the horizon in the middle of the frame can cut the photo in half and create a sense of indifference within the viewer. However, putting the horizon line higher will focus attention on the land, while putting the horizon line lower will give prominence to the sky.

The horizon does not have to align exactly with the horizontal gridlines; positioning it off-center closer to the top or bottom of the frame will generally produce a more pleasing composition than a centered horizon. This rule can be applied when in the field shooting the photo, or it can also be used during production when you edit the photo, cropping excess parts of the photo.

Point of View

Photos taken at eye level generally result in a neutral effect on the viewer. Changing the angle of the shot can create new perspectives and engaging photos. Whether that means elevating yourself on a stepladder or lowering yourself to ground level, such changes will introduce variety into your photos. When photographing children or animals, position yourself and your camera at their levels, so the camera lens is eye level with the subject. This simple adjustment will increase the viewer's engagement with the subject and produce a stronger photo.

Varying points of view can also be used to elicit an emotional response from the viewer:

- *High angle*: When a subject is photographed from *above* eye level, the photo can have the effect of making the subject seem vulnerable, weak or frightened.
- *Low angle*: When a subject is photographed from *below* eye level, the photo can have the effect of making the subject look powerful, heroic or dangerous.
- *Tilt*: When the camera is set at an angle so the horizon line is not level, this can express a disoriented or uneasy state.

Simplicity

When you look at a scene with your naked eye, your brain quickly picks out subjects of interest. In contrast, the camera does not discriminate, it captures everything in front of it, which can result in a cluttered, messy photo with no central focal point. So before taking a photo, choose your subject, then select the type of shot that frames the subject well. Be aware of other objects in the shot, and try to keep them in the background or make them part of the visual story. The photo of a bull elk (Figure 8.9) isolates the animal from the rest of the herd that was grazing in the campground. Singling out the bull and shifting positions to place him against a simple background (no cabins or RVs included in the shot) allows the viewer to focus their attention on the bull.

Graphic Design: Learn It, Do It

Figure 8.9

Simplicity, Bull elk, Estes Park, Colorado.

Photo Tips

In addition to these fundamentals, the following composition tips are simple and effective ways to elevate snapshots to photographs. These tips are also useful for general composition, whether applied to a photo or other type of image.

- *Fill the frame*: Zoom in on the subject to fill the frame or get closer to the subject (if possible and *if safe*). Doing so will help the viewer know what is important in the shot and where the attention should be focused.
- *Avoid the middle* (a.k.a. rule of thirds): Many cameras have an autofocus feature set to the center of the lens. This feature makes it natural to position a subject in the center of the frame and take a shot. However, positioning the subject in the center of the image can create static, boring photos. Refer to the earlier discussion of the rule of thirds and the benefits that this technique can provide.

Figure 8.10

Leading lines. Breckenridge Ski Resort, Breckenridge, Colorado.

- *Leading lines*: Use lines to control the way the viewer's eyes move around the photo. Converging lines (think of receding railroad tracks) provide a strong sense of perspective and depth, drawing the viewer into a photo (Figure 8.10). Curved lines can lead the viewer on a journey around the frame, leading them toward the main subject. These lines may take form in fences, roads, buildings or telephone wires, or they may be implied by the subject's *sightline*, the way that a person or animal is looking.
- *Creative with colors*: Bright colors attract the viewer's attention, especially when they are used in contrast with complementary colors. Think back to the color schemes presented in *Chapter 3: Color in Design*. These color combinations can be used to create effective color contrasts, for example, using a splash of bright color against a monochromatic background. Be selective about how the subject is framed, in order to exclude unwanted colors from the photo.
- *Aspect ratio*: A collection of photos taken with a point-and-shoot or DSLR (digital single-lens reflex) camera may include a majority of horizontal images. The physical design of DSLR cameras encourages horizontal photos. However, sometimes a subject would be better served with a vertical photo, or this change of orientation may provide a more interesting perspective. For cell phone photographers, the natural inclination may be to take vertical photos given the device's form. If this sounds familiar, make a point to turn your screen 90° and take a horizontal photo instead.

Although the general shape of some subjects suggests a natural orientation, such as a beach (horizontal) or a skyscraper (vertical), try taking photos of the same

Figure 8.11

Visual orientation, landscape (horizontal) vs. portrait (vertical). Lupine, Prince Edward Island National Park, Prince Edward Island, Canada.

subject in both directions. Notice how the unexpected shot (e.g., the vertical photo of a beach) can narrow the field of view. As you experiment with the orientation of photos, remember to use the camera's zoom feature to take the best type of shot to feature the subject. Compare the two photos of a field lupine (Figure 8.11). The height of the plants supports the use of vertical orientation; however, the number and variety of plants support the use of horizontal orientation. Our take-away from this example should be that there is more than one right answer in design (and in life). The photographer should take both photos; the designer should try both options before deciding which photo best serves the overall design.

Stock Images

For certain projects, the designer may need to look beyond their own photographs or illustrations to complete the task at hand. On such occasions, consider the use of stock images. *Stock images* are existing works that can be licensed, paying a fee to the author of the work or to an agency for use of the work. Using stock images can save time, since the images are ready for use as soon as the licensing fee is paid, and money, since the licensing fee may be less than the costs associated with hiring a photographer to capture a specific photo. Assessing the project's needs *and* budget will guide the decision on the number of images to license and the kind of license that is appropriate for the project (e.g., royalty-free license* or Creative Commons license†).

---

* A royalty-free license refers to being able to use the image freely after the initial license has been purchased, without additional royalties; it *does not* mean that there is no cost for a license.
† A Creative Commons (CC) license is used when an author wants to give people the right to share, use and build on a work that the author has created.

A Web search for "stock images" generates a lengthy list of prospective online sources. Included in this list is *Adobe Stock* (https://stock.adobe.com), Adobe's contribution to the stock image market featuring images, videos, templates and 3D objects. Other potential sources include *Creative Commons* (https://creativecommons.org), *Getty Images* (https://www.gettyimages.com) and *Shutter Stock* (https://www.shutterstock.com).

Note to photographers: Many stock image websites not only license images but also purchase images for use. Consider this as a possible outlet for your work.

Copyright

This is an appropriate time to discuss copyright and your rights as a designer. Copyright protects your rights to display, publish or reproduce copies of your creative work. It also prevents others from copying, publishing or adapting your work without your permission.

Putting a copyright notice (©) on work is not required, but its presence tells others that the work is copyrighted. In Photoshop, a watermark, text or a logo superimposed on an image can be easily added to an image to discourage *copyright infringement*, someone claiming the image as their own. The process for creating and applying a watermark is presented in *Chapter 9: Photo Editing in Photoshop*, "Adding a Watermark."

In the United States, legal protection of a copyrighted work lasts for the life of the author plus 70 years. For designers interested in registering copyright, visit the U.S. Copyright Office website (https://www.copyright.gov) for information and process requirements.

In most cases, you own the copyright to your work the moment you create it, as soon as an idea has been transferred from your mind to a *fixed form of expression*, something drawn or created and saved on a computer. An exception to this is the *"Work Made for Hire" doctrine*. When the designer works for someone else as a full-time employee, the employer is considered the author and automatic copyright owner of any work that the designer creates within the scope of their employment. If the designer is working as an independent contractor, their work can legally be "work made for hire" only if this is specified in their contract. For more information on this subject, refer to the references at the end of this chapter (see *External Links Mentioned in the Chapter*).

Copyright vs. Trademark

A copyright protects any completed graphic element. Copyright gives the original creator certain exclusive rights, such as the right to reproduce the work, publish the work, make adaptations and communicate the work to the public.

A trademark covers a broad range of design elements, including logos and product shape and design. These are brand marks that give a particular product or service a distinct identity or help distinguish between various products or services.

Where copyright ownership arises from authorship or original creation, trademark ownership arises from use in the marketplace. It is the distinct identity of the brand that is protected.

Copyright Infringement

Let's take a moment to state the obvious, *do not* use someone else's work without their permission; doing so is *copyright infringement*. Copyright infringement occurs when someone makes copies or commercially exploits a work without the copyright owner's permission.

If you happen to create a similar work independently, this is not infringement; the second work must actually be copied from the first work to be considered infringement. If you use another designer's work for reference, problems can arise. The standard for infringement is whether the second work is "substantially similar" to the original work.

Fair Use

Fair use will excuse an otherwise infringing use under certain limited circumstances, such as noncommercial or educational uses. *Transformative works* may also be fair use. A work is transformative when the copyright material is "transformed in the creation of new information, new aesthetics, new insights and understanding" (Kattwinkel 2018).

Looking Ahead

This introduction to photography included the Exposure Triangle and the elements that control exposure, the types of camera shots available and composition techniques that can strengthen our photos. In the next chapter, we expand our set of Photoshop tools, review basic photo editing practices, and discuss alternate sources of photos along with the role of copyright in the design process.

Discussions

Discussion 8.1: Camera Shots

When you take a photo, what type of camera shot do you generally use? What is your "go-to" camera shot? Here is a refresher of the types of camera shots: extreme long shot (ELS), long shot (LS), medium shot (MS), medium close-up (MCU), close-up (CU) and extreme close-up (ECU). How do your choice of subject and your location influence the type of camera shot that you use?

Discussion 8.2: The Elements of Composition

Survey your current surroundings, and identify a potential subject to photograph. Without taking any photos, discuss how you could apply each of the four elements of composition to strengthen your shots. As a refresher, the elements of composition include subject and background, sense of balance, point of view and simplicity. Which element of composition would have the greatest impact on the resulting photo? Why?

Activities

Activity 8.1: Scavenger Hunt

Take a series of photographs based on the following list of subjects:

1. Lights
2. Pattern
3. Red
4. Reflection
5. Writing
6. Food
7. Flowers/leaves
8. Architecture
9. Looking up
10. Your choice

Guidelines

- Interpret the list as you wish, but just try to take the photos in a creative way. Think outside of the box.
- Do not edit, crop or apply effects to the photos; use them straight out of the camera (or cell phone).
- If you cannot find a particular subject to photograph, move on and then revisit the skipped subject once the others have been found.
- Take your time and think about each subject.

Activity 8.2: Composition-Based Scavenger Hunt

Take a series of photographs that illustrate the following elements of photographic composition:

1. Subject and background
2. Sense of balance
3. Point of view
4. Simplicity

5. Fill the frame
6. Avoid the middle
7. Leading lines
8. Creative with colors
9. Aspect ratio: Using the same subject, take two photos, one horizontal and one vertical
10. Your choice

Guidelines

- Interpret the list as you wish, but just try to take the photos in a creative way. Think outside of the box.
- Do not edit, crop or apply effects to the photos; use them straight out of the camera (or cell phone).
- If you cannot find an example of a particular element, move on and then revisit the skipped element once the others have been found.
- Take your time and think about each subject.

External Links Mentioned in the Chapter

Stock Images

Adobe Stock | https://stock.adobe.com

Creative Commons | https://creativecommons.org

Getty Images | https://www.gettyimages.com

Shutter Stock | https://www.shutterstock.com

9

Photo Editing in Photoshop

Even after the most successful photo shoots, there are photographs that need edits or adjustments to strengthen the images. Photo editing is easily completed in Photoshop. The intended goal of photo editing is to strengthen a photo's composition (refer to *Chapter 8: Digital Photography in Design*) in preparation for output, whether print or digital. This chapter presents situations that necessitate photo editing and identifies tools and processes that can be used to address these issues. *Tip:* There is often more than one way to complete many of these edits. So, try the suggested tools and processes, then as you explore additional tools, revisit these situations and try alternate methods.

Notes to the Reader

- This chapter provides a series of exercises created to allow you to practice the presented techniques. To avoid becoming overwhelmed by the tools and processes, pace yourself; *do not* complete all of the exercises in one work session.
- The photographs used in the chapter exercises are available via the book's companion website for your use to practice the photo editing techniques.

- This chapter is most effective when you have the Photoshop application open in front of you while reading. This will allow you to learn and then do, navigating the interface and utilizing the tools. If you do not have access to the application, the included screen captures will serve as visual references for much of the content.

A Subset of Image Editing Tools

The following image editing tools are presented in addition to the tools introduced in *Chapter 6: Getting Started in Photoshop*. After reading the tools' descriptions, drawn from the *Photoshop Online Help*, locate the tools in the *Tools panel* (refer to the *Photoshop CC 2019 Tools Panel Overview*, see Figure 6.9); remember that some of these tools may be hidden.

Crop and Slice Tools
- The *Crop Tool* (C) trims images.

Retouching Tools
- The *Spot Healing Brush Tool* (J) removes blemishes and objects.
- The *Clone Stamp Tool* (S) paints with a sample of an image.
- The *Healing Brush Tool* (J) paints with a sample or pattern to repair imperfections in an image.
- The *Red Eye Tool* (J) removes the red reflection caused by a camera flash.

These tools are presented in the context of photography; however, they can also be used to edit other images in Photoshop.

Back Up before Editing

When a photograph is opened in Photoshop for the first time, the *Background layer* in the Layers panel contains the image content. Before photo editing begins, it is a good practice to duplicate the Background layer. This allows edits to be performed on the copy of the layer (*Background copy*), preserving the original Background layer as an easily accessible reference to the original photo.

Exercise 9.1: Duplicate the Background Layer

Exercise file: **Ch09-Ex01-photo.jpg** (Figure 9.1)

Step 1: Create a copy of the Background layer. There are multiple ways to complete this task; here are two options.

- *Option 1:* Duplicate the Background layer via the *Layer menu*.

Figure 9.1

Exercise 9.1 file. Iceberg at the dock, Bridgeport, Newfoundland and Labrador, Canada.

- Begin at the *Layer menu* in the application bar and select the *Duplicate Layer... menu command* [Layer menu > Duplicate Layer...].
- In the *Duplicate Layer dialog box*, shown in Figure 9.2, name the new layer or accept the provided name, *Background copy*.
- Click *OK* to create the new layer.

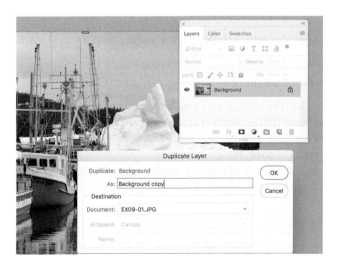

Figure 9.2

Duplicate Layer dialog box, Layer menu > Duplicate Layer....

- *Option 2:* Duplicate the Background layer in the *Layers panel.*
  - Open the *Layers panel* from the *Window menu* [Window menu > Layers].
  - From the *Layers panel menu* available in the upper-right corner of the window, select *Duplicate Layer....*
  - In the *Duplicate Layer dialog box*, name the new layer or accept the provided name, *Background copy.*
  - Click *OK* to create the new layer.
- The new layer will be positioned *above* the original Background layer in the Layers panel, refer to Figure 9.3.

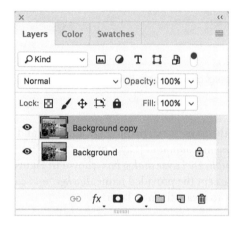

Figure 9.3

Duplicated layer (*Background copy*) in the Layers panel, Window menu > Layers.

Step 2: Save the image file as a *Photoshop document,* Ch09-Ex01.psd.

- Now that the file contains two layers, it should be saved as a *Photoshop Document* (PSD), which is capable of containing more than one layer.
  - From the *File menu,* select the *Save As... menu command* [File menu > Save As...].
  - In the *Save As dialog box,* confirm that *Photoshop* is selected in the *Format dropdown menu.*

Photo Editing Workflow

The following *Photo Editing Workflow* can be useful when assessing the needs of a photo. The workflow serves as a checklist of what *can be done* to strengthen a photo. The suggested order is intentional, first addressing the overall size and orientation of the photo, then focusing on necessary touch-ups and repairs, and concluding with enhancements to bring out the details, textures and colors in the photo. Special processes, such as adding a watermark and combining multiple photos to create a panorama round out the workflow. Apply these steps as needed, recognizing that not all steps will be relevant to a particular photo.

Photo Editing Workflow

1. Compositional Edits
   a. Straighten the photo
   b. Crop for content
   c. Photo orientation (Landscape [Horizontal] vs. Portrait [Vertical], vice versa)

2. Touch-Up Edits
   a. Spot and blemish removal
   b. Patching areas
   c. Red eye removal

3. Enhancements
   a. Color and tone adjustments
   b. Filters

4. Special Processes
   a. Photomerge (a.k.a. Panorama)
   b. Watermark

Photo edits are generally applied on a photo-by-photo basis, with some exceptions. For example, when the same edit needs to be performed to multiple photos (e.g., resizing, tonal change, file naming) Photoshop provides the *Batch command* [File menu > Automate > Batch...]; for instructions on how to use Batch, access the *Photoshop Online Help*.

Destructive vs. Nondestructive Changes

Edits performed in Photoshop can be categorized as either *destructive* or *nondestructive. Destructive edits* save over the original image, preventing the designer from returning to that original image. In contrast, *nondestructive edits* are saved as steps in a process, which can be undone or hidden allowing the designer to return to the original image.

Compositional Edits

Edits made to strengthen the overall composition of a photo can have a dramatic impact on the visual appeal of the image. Changes in this area include straightening a photo to correct a slanted horizon line or a tilted building, cropping a photo to increase attention on the subject and changing a photo's orientation to improve the framing of the subject. Each of these changes can be completed using the *Crop Tool* (C).

Refer to Figure 9.4 for a view of the Options bar when the *Crop Tool* (C) is selected; this view presents the properties associated with the tool. The following property descriptions are drawn from the Photoshop tooltips:

A. *Aspect Ratio menu:* Select a preset aspect ratio or crop size.
B. *Swap Width and Height:* Swaps width and height values.
C. *Clear:* Clear aspect ratio values.
D. *Straighten:* Straighten the image by drawing a line on it.
E. *Overlay Options:* Set overlay options for the Crop Tool. *Note:* The overlay guides can be turned off here; select "Never Show Overlay."
F. *Set additional crop options.*
G. *Delete Cropped Pixels:* Determines if pixel data outside the crop box is retained or deleted.
H. *Content-Aware:* Fill areas outside the original image.
I. *Reset:* Reset the crop box, image rotation and aspect ratio settings.

When the *Crop Tool* (C) is selected in the Tools panel, a *crop box* appears around the photo. The content *inside* the crop box will be preserved when the edit is performed. The size of the crop box can be adjusted using the *crop handles* available on each side and in each corner of the crop box. When one of the crop handles is selected, a visual guide or *overlay* appears on the photo. The default overlay* is the *rule of thirds*. The overlay is intended to assist with compositional adjustments and to provide a preview of the edit. These guides are only visible within Photoshop—they will *not* appear in the final image.

Figure 9.4

Options bar, Crop Tool selected: (A) Aspect Ratio menu, (B) Swap Width and Height, (C) Clear, (D) Straighten, (E) Overlay Options, (F) Set additional crop options, (G) Delete Cropped Pixels, (H) Content-Aware, and (I) Reset.

---

* *Overlay options* include Rule of Thirds, Grid, Diagonal, Triangle, Golden Ratio and Golden Spiral.

Graphic Design: Learn It, Do It

Straightening a Photo

When the *Crop Tool* (C) is used to straighten a photo, the photo is rotated, then the canvas is automatically resized to accommodate the rotated pixels and the excess canvas is trimmed.

Exercise 9.2: Straighten the Horizon Line Using the Crop Tool

Exercise file: **Ch09-Ex02-photo.jpg** (Figure 9.5)

Figure 9.5

Exercise 9.2 file. Icebergs, Twillingate, Newfoundland and Labrador, Canada.

Step 1: Select the Crop Tool (C) in the Tools panel and review the tool's properties in the Options bar.

Step 2: Rotate the photo to straighten the horizon line; here are two options to try.

- *Option 1:* Straighten the photo using the *Straighten feature*,* available as a property for the Crop Tool (C) in the Options bar.
    - Click the *Straighten button* in the Options bar, which changes the cursor's appearance to the *Straighten Tool*.
    - Using the *Straighten Tool*, position the cursor along the horizon line or another line that can be used to straighten the image.
    - Hold down the mouse button and draw a *reference line* along the line that needs to be straightened or made parallel with an edge of the

---

* The *Straighten feature* is available via both the Crop Tool (C) and the Ruler Tool (I). The Ruler Tool (I) can straighten the photo, however excess canvas is left in the image. The most efficient way to straighten *and* trim a photo is using the Crop Tool (C).

photo. *Tip:* The reference line can be short; it does not need to span the width or height of the photo.

- A *tooltip* appears adjacent to the cursor displaying the angle of rotation that will be applied when the mouse button is released.
- Once the line is drawn, release the mouse button. The photo will straighten according to the reference line (Figure 9.6).
- If satisfied with the straightening, commit the change (Step 3). Or, if dissatisfied, cancel the rotation (Step 3).

Figure 9.6

Exercise 9.2, Step 2.

- *Option 2:* Straighten the photo *by hand* using the rotate command.
  - Position the cursor *outside* of the crop box and look for the cursor's appearance to change into a curved double-headed arrow; this is the symbol for rotate.
  - When the cursor appears as a curved double-headed arrow, press and hold down the mouse button, then move the cursor to rotate the photo. The crop box remains fixed, and only the photo rotates behind the box.
  - When satisfied with the rotation, release the mouse button and commit the change (Step 3). Or, if dissatisfied, cancel the rotation (Step 3).

Step 3: Commit or cancel the straighten, and crop the photo.

- When satisfied with the changes, press the *Return/Enter key* on the keyboard *or* click the *Commit button* ✓ in the Options bar to apply the changes.

- If dissatisfied, press the *ESC key* on the keyboard or click the *Cancel button* ⊘ in the Options bar to cancel the changes.
- The Options bar also provides the ability to *Reset* the changes and try again.

Cropping a Photo

Cropping a photo can strengthen its composition by removing unwanted portions of the image. Such an edit can also reframe a subject to improve the overall balance within a photo. The designer can select to preserve or discard the cropped pixels for later use (nondestructive vs. destructive edit) in the Options bar when the Crop Tool (C) is selected (see Figure 9.4).

Exercise 9.3: Apply the Rule of Thirds Using the Crop Tool

Exercise file: **Ch09-Ex03-photo.jpg** (Figure 9.7)

Figure 9.7

Exercise 9.3 file. Making friends at Eastland Alpacas, Mount Joy, Pennsylvania.

Step 1: Select the Crop Tool (C) and review the tool properties in the Options bar. From the Aspect Ratio dropdown menu, select Original Ratio to constrain the dimensions of the crop box.

- Select the *Crop Tool* (C) in the Tools panel.
- In the Options bar, select *Original Ratio* from the *Aspect Ratio dropdown menu* (Ratio).
- Apply any other properties as desired in the *Options bar* (i.e., overlay options, delete cropped pixels) to control the behavior of the tool.

Step 2: Use the provided Rule of Thirds overlay to crop the photo so the subjects fall along or near an intersection of gridlines. There are multiple ways to use the Crop Tool (C); here are three options to try:

- *Option 1:* Draw a *crop box* over the area of the photo to be kept.
- *Option 2:* Drag the *crop handles* from a side or corner of the photo to the desired positions.
  - *Tip:* Adjusting a corner crop handle will change the crop boundaries on two sides of the photo at once.
- *Option 3:* In the *Options bar,* select *Ratio* from the *Aspect Ratio dropdown menu.* Then, enter numerical values in the Width and Height fields.
  - For example, enter "2" in the first field (Width) and "3" in the second field (Height). This creates a vertical crop box that uses a 2:3 ratio (e.g., 4 in. × 6 in.).
  - Click the *Swap Height and Width icon* to generate a horizontal crop box that uses a 3:2 ratio (e.g., 6 in. × 4 in.).

Step 3 (Optional): Reposition the photo within the crop box if needed.

- Position the cursor *within* the crop box.
- Hold down the mouse button and move the cursor to reposition the photo within the crop box.
  - Use this technique to position the subjects of the photo near a rule of thirds gridline or near an intersection of these gridlines (Figure 9.8).
- When satisfied with the repositioned photo, release the mouse button.

Figure 9.8

Exercise 9.3, Step 3; Crop box visible around selection; Crop handles present on sides and in corners of crop box; Rule of Thirds overlay visible within crop box.

Step 4: Commit or cancel the crop.

- When satisfied with the change, press the *Return/Enter key* on the keyboard or click the *Commit button* ✓ in the Options bar to apply the change.
- If dissatisfied, press the *Escape key* on the keyboard or click the *Cancel button* ⊘ in the Options bar to cancel the change.
- The *Options bar* also provides the ability to *Reset* the edit and try again.

Application Tip: Maintaining the Original Ratio

When using the Crop Tool (C), the *Aspect Ratio dropdown menu* located in the Options bar provides an option for *Original Ratio*, which maintains the ratio of the photo's original dimensions; this option links the width and height. When a crop handle is moved to adjust the photo's width, the crop boundary for height moves proportionally. Using *Original Ratio* is particularly important when cropping a photo that will be framed to ensure that the edited photo fits the frame opening.

Changing a Photo's Orientation

The *Crop Tool* (C) can also be used to change a photo's orientation from *Landscape* (horizontal) to *Portrait* (vertical) or vice versa. Use this technique to improve the framing of a subject or to eliminate distracting elements within a photo.

Exercise 9.4: Change Orientation (Landscape/Portrait) Using the Crop Tool

Exercise file: **Ch09-Ex04-photo.jpg** (Figure 9.9)

Step 1: Select the Crop Tool (C) and review the tool properties in the Options bar. Reset the Aspect Ratio dropdown menu if values persist from the previous exercise.

- Select the *Crop Tool* (C) in the Tools panel.
- Reset the *Aspect Ratio dropdown menu* by selecting "Ratio" and then pressing the *Clear button* if values are listed in the width and height fields.
- *Tip:* Before cropping the photo, be sure to review the horizon line and *straighten* the photo as needed using the Crop Tool (C).

Step 2: Rotate the crop box, so it is vertical.

- Press the *Swap Height and Width icon* in the Options bar, which changes the orientation of the crop box.

Figure 9.9

Exercise 9.4 file. Irish country cottage, Inis Mór, County Galway, Ireland.

Step 3: Reposition the photo within the crop box, as needed, to strengthen the compositional position of the subjects (Figure 9.10).

- Position the cursor *within* the crop box.
- Hold down the mouse button and move the cursor to reposition the photo within the crop box.
- When satisfied with the repositioned photo, release the mouse button.

Figure 9.10

Exercise 9.4, Step 3.

Graphic Design: Learn It, Do It

Step 4: Commit or cancel the change.

- When satisfied with the change, press the *Return/Enter key* on the keyboard or click the *Commit button* ✓ in the Options bar to apply the change.
- If dissatisfied, press the *Escape key* on the keyboard or click the *Cancel button* ⊘ in the Options bar to cancel the change.
- The *Options bar* also provides the ability to *Reset* the edit and try again.

Touch-Up Edits

Performing touch-up edits on a photo can enhance the image by eliminating distracting elements whether small or large. From removing dust spots to repairing areas and eliminating red eyes, these edits contribute to the overall impact of the photo.

Tip: When touching up a photo, use the *Zoom Tool* (Z) to increase or decrease the view of the area to be edited [View menu > Zoom In (⌘+) | Zoom Out (⌘−)]. Changing the view can help you achieve a clean and complete edit with no stray edges or gaps in the touch-up.

Spot Removal

The *Spot Healing Brush Tool* (J) is the default image repair tool in Photoshop. The tool can be used to seamlessly blend content cloned from a sample area into a target area. To use the Spot Healing Brush Tool (J), click on the spot or blemish to be eliminated, and Photoshop works out the rest. Repeat as needed. To repair a larger area, click and drag the tool to paint the affected area.

Refer to Figure 9.11 for a view of the Options bar when the *Spot Healing Brush Tool* (J) is selected; this view presents the properties associated with the tool:

- A. *Brush Options:* Set the Size (Brush diameter), Hardness, Spacing, Angle, Roundness.
- B. *Mode:* Normal, Replace, Multiply, Screen, Darken, Lighten, Color, Luminosity.
- C. *Type: Content-Aware:* Compares surrounding areas to seamlessly fill the selection while retaining important details such as shadows; *Create Texture:* Uses pixels in the selection to create a texture; *Proximity Match:*

Figure 9.11

Options bar, Spot Healing Brush Tool selected: (A) Brush Options, (B) Mode, (C) Type, and (D) Sample All Layers.

Uses pixels around the edge of the selection to find an area to use as a patch.

D. *Sample All Layers:* Uses data from all visible layers to resolve the issue. Deselect "Sample All Layers" to sample only from the active layer, the selected layer in the Layers panel.

Exercise 9.5: Remove Dust Spots Using the Spot Healing Brush Tool

Exercise file: **Ch09-Ex05-photo.jpg** (Figure 9.12)

Note: In the provided photo, dust spots are visible in the blue sky.

Figure 9.12

Exercise 9.5 file. Overlooking the Badlands, Badlands National Park, South Dakota.

Step 1: Select the Spot Healing Brush Tool (J) and review the tool properties in the Options bar.

- Choose the *Spot Healing Brush Tool* (J) in the Tools panel.
- In the Options bar, use the following properties to control the behavior of the tool:
  - *Brush Options:* Adjust the *size* of the brush to fit the spot that is being removed. *Tip:* A brush that is slightly larger than the area being fixed works best; this allows the entire area to be covered with one click.
  - *Type:* Set the *source sampling type* to *Content-Aware*; this mode works out how to best fill the area.

Step 2: Remove the dust spots from the sky.

- Click once on the spot that is being removed or for larger areas use the brush to paint (Figure 9.13). The edit should be visible immediately.
  - If there are multiple spots to remove, adjust the brush size as needed between repairs to fit the brush to the targeted spots.
  - *Tip:* Press the *right-bracket key* (]) on the keyboard to increase the size of the brush, or press the *left-bracket key* ([) to decrease the size of the brush.

View 1   **View 2**

Figure 9.13

Exercise 9.5, Step 2, View 1: Dust spots circled; *View 2:* Dust spots corrected.

Removing Large Areas of Content

When there is a large area of the photo that needs to be removed, the Spot Healing Brush Tool (J) may not be able to effectively address the size of the repair. In this situation, try using a *Content-Aware Fill* to complete the edit. When using *Content-Aware*, Photoshop uses the area around the selection to determine the best fix for the selected area.

Exercise 9.6: Remove a Large Area Using a Content-Aware Fill

Exercise file: **Ch09-Ex06-photo.jpg** (Figure 9.14)

Step 1: Use a selection tool (e.g., Lasso Tools [L], Marquee Tools [M]) to select the area of the photo that will be removed. In the provided photo, start by removing

---

Figure 9.14

Exercise 9.6 file. Looking up to St. Colman's Cathedral, Cobh, County Cork, Ireland.

the red boat in the lower-right corner of the photo. Be sure to include the boat's reflection on the water in the selection.

- *Tip:* To *add to an existing selection*, press and hold down the *Shift key* on the keyboard while selecting the additional content. To *remove an area from a selection*, press and hold down the *Option key* on the keyboard while selecting the content.

Step 2: Apply a fill based on the area surrounding the selection.

- Go to the *Edit menu* and select the *Fill… menu command* [Edit menu > Fill…].
- In the *Fill dialog box*, select *Content-Aware* from the *Contents dropdown menu* (Figure 9.15).
- Click *OK* to perform the fill.

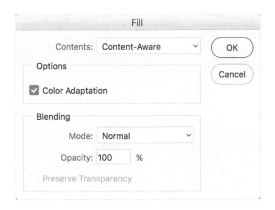

Figure 9.15

Fill dialog box, Edit menu > Fill....

Step 3: Deselect the selection area.

- From the *Select menu,* choose the *Deselect menu command* [Select menu > Deselect | ⌘D].

Step 4 (Optional): Use the same Content-Aware Fill to remove other elements from the photo, for example, the man on the ramp or the lamp pole and its attached wires.

Step 5 (Optional): Crop the photo using the Original Ratio aspect ratio to reduce the amount of negative space created by the removal of the boat (Figure 9.16).

Cloning Areas of a Photo

Photoshop provides the means to replicate content within a photo for use elsewhere in the same image. There are two tools that can perform this action with varied results: the *Clone Stamp Tool* (S) and the *Healing Brush Tool* (J). The *Clone Stamp Tool* (S) produces an exact copy of the sample area in the new location, while the *Healing Brush Tool* (J) blends the copy into the new location. There will be occasions when each tool is needed to perform a specific edit.

Both of these tools necessitate setting a *source point* within the image before the sample area can be copied. The source point serves as a kind of anchor point from which the sample area will be based as it is painted elsewhere in the image. *Tip:* When locating a source point, look for an area with similar coloring, lighting and texture as the destination area to help the sample match seamlessly.

Figure 9.16

Exercise 9.6, Step 5.

Refer to Figure 9.17 for a view of the Options bar when the *Clone Stamp Tool* (S) is selected; this view presents the properties associated with the tool. The following property descriptions are drawn from the Photoshop tooltips:

A. *Brush Preset picker:* Click to open the brush preset picker.
B. *Brush Options:* Set the Size (Brush diameter), Hardness, Spacing, Angle, Roundness.
C. *Brush Settings panel shortcut:* Toggle the Brush Settings panel.
D. *Clone Source panel shortcut:* Toggle the Clone Source panel.
E. *Mode:* Effect Mode.
F. *Opacity:* Set opacity for stroke.

| A | B | C D | E | F | G | H | I | J | K | L | M |

Figure 9.17

Options bar, Clone Stamp Tool selected, (A) Brush Preset picker; (B) Brush Options; (C) Brush Settings panel shortcut; (D) Clone Source panel shortcut; (E) Mode; (F) Opacity; (G) Pressure for Opacity; (H) Flow; (I) Airbrushed-style build-up effects; (J) Stroke offset; (K) Sample; (L) Ignore adjustment layers; and (M) Pressure for Size.

G. *Pressure for Opacity:* Always use Pressure for Opacity. When off, Brush Preset controls pressure.

H. *Flow:* Set flow rate for stroke.

I. *Airbrushed-style buildup effects:* Enable airbrushed-style buildup effects.

J. *Stroke offset:* Use same offset for each stroke.

K. *Sample:* Clone sample mode (Current Level, Current & Below, All Layers).

L. *Ignore adjustment layers:* Turn on to ignore adjustment layers when cloning.

M. *Pressure for Size:* Always use Pressure for Size. When off, Brush Preset controls pressure.

Exercise 9.7: Replicate Part of a Photo Using the Clone Stamp Tool

Exercise file: **Ch09-Ex07-photo.jpg** (Figure 9.18)

Figure 9.18

Exercise 9.7 file. Chipmunk, Zion National Park, Utah.

Step 1: Select the Clone Stamp Tool (S), and review the tool properties in the Options bar.

- Choose the *Clone Stamp Tool* (S) in the Tools panel.
- In the *Options bar*, adjust the size of the brush, as needed, in preparation for replicating the animal.
  - *Tip:* Select a brush size that fits within the head of the chipmunk.

Step 2: Set a source point to sample.

- Position the cursor over the spot that will serve as the *source point.*
  - The source point should be located within the *sample area*, the part of the photo to be copied.
- Press and hold down the *Option key* on the keyboard, which will cause the cursor's appearance to change.
- While continuing to hold down the Option key, click the mouse button once on the source point.
- Release the Option key.

Step 3: Paint in another area of the photo to replicate the content from the sample area.

- Move the cursor to another area of the photo.
  - *Note:* As the cursor moves from the source point to the painting area, the cursor previews a brush tip's worth of content from the *sample area.*
- Begin painting.
  - The brush is painting with content from the sample area.
  - The brush and the source point are linked; as the brush moves, the source point also moves in relation to the original source point (Figure 9.19).

Note: If the *Clone Stamp Tool* (S) is used without first setting a source point, Photoshop provides the following alert: *Could not use the clone stamp because the area to clone has not been defined (option-click to define a source point).* If this occurs, click *OK* to close the message window, then set a source point (see Step 2).

Step 4 (Optional): Repeat this exercise using the *Healing Brush Tool* (J) instead of the *Clone Stamp Tool* (S) and compare the results.

- Select the *Healing Brush Tool* (J) in the Tools panel.
- Set a source point to sample (see Step 2).
- Move the cursor to another area of the photo and begin painting.
- Compare the results of the two tools.
  - The *Clone Stamp Tool* (S) makes an exact, *full color* replica of the chipmunk.
  - The *Healing Brush Tool* (J) blends the exact replica into the target area resulting in a *lighter* copy of the chipmunk.

When you need or want to create a *reversed* clone of the chipmunk, as shown in Figure 9.20, try the following technique.

Figure 9.19

Exercise 9.7, Step 3.

Exercise 9.7 (Alternate): Reverse Cloned Content

Exercise file: **Ch09-Ex07-photo.jpg** (see Figure 9.18)
Overview: A new layer will first be created to contain the cloned content. Then, the content on the new layer will be flipped horizontal.

Step 1: Create a new blank layer (Layer 1) in the Layers panel. This is the layer on which the cloned chipmunk will be created.

- From the *Window menu,* select the *Layers menu command* [Window menu > Layers].
- Click once on the *Create a new layer icon* located along the bottom edge of the Layers panel.
  - This action adds a new layer (Layer 1) to the Layers panel.
  - The new layer is active, which means that this is where the cloned chipmunk will be created.

Step 2: Select the Clone Stamp Tool (S) and choose "All Layers" from the Sample dropdown menu in the Options bar.

Step 3: Set a source point to sample.

- Position the cursor over the chipmunk's eye in the sample area; this will serve as the *source point.*

- Press and hold down the *Option key* on the keyboard, then click the mouse button once on the source point.
- Release the Option key.

Step 4: With the new layer selected, paint in another area of the photo to replicate the content from the sample area.

- Confirm that *Layer 1* is selected in the *Layers panel*.
  - If Layer 1 is not selected, click once on the layer to select it.
- Move the cursor to another area of the photo away from the original chipmunk.
- Begin painting; the brush should paint with content from the sample area.
  - *Note:* Do not worry if the cloned chipmunk overlaps with the original as the clone is on its own layer and can be repositioned as needed.
- If the painting strays beyond the cloned chipmunk to include unwanted portions of the background, use the *Eraser Tool* (E) to clean up any edges along the clone.

Step 5: Flip the cloned subject and reposition it as needed.

- With Layer 1 still selected, from the *Edit menu*, select the *Transform menu command* and then the *Flip Horizontal command* [Edit menu > Transform > Flip Horizontal].
  - This action flips the cloned chipmunk.
- Use the *Move Tool* (V) to reposition the cloned chipmunk as desired.

Figure 9.20

Exercise 9.7, Alternate.

Graphic Design: Learn It, Do It

Removing Red Eye

Red eye is created when light from a camera's flash bounces off the blood vessels in a person's or animal's eyes.* The *Red Eye Tool* (J) removes the red reflection caused by the flash. Red eye is more often encountered when taking photos in a darkened room, because in this space, the subject's iris is wide open. *Tip:* Many cameras offer a red eye reduction feature to prevent red eye. If your camera supports this feature, turn it on and save yourself this step when photo editing.

Refer to Figure 9.21 for a view of the Options bar when the *Red Eye Tool* (J) is selected; this view presents the properties associated with the tool.

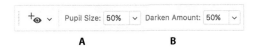

A   B

Figure 9.21

Options bar, Red Eye Tool selected: (A) Pupil Size and (B) Darken Amount.

A. *Pupil Size:* Increase or decrease the area affected by the Red Eye tool.
B. *Darken Amount:* Sets the darkness of the correction.

Tip: When the cursor is positioned over the name of one of these properties, a slider is available, which can be dragged side to side to increase or decrease the property's value.

Exercise 9.8: Remove Red Eye Using the Red Eye Tool

Exercise file: **Ch09-Ex08-photo.jpg** (Figure 9.22)
Use the *Zoom Tool* (Z) to increase or decrease your view of the area to be edited before getting started [View menu > Zoom In (⌘+) | Zoom Out (⌘−)].

Step 1: Select the Red Eye Tool (J) and review the tool properties in the Options bar.

- Select the *Red Eye Tool* (J) in the Tools panel.
- In the *Options bar,* use the following properties to control the behavior of the tool.
  - Set the *Pupil Size* to 50%.
  - Set the *Darken Amount* to 100%.

---

* In animals, red eye or eyeshine may appear as a yellow or green glow (not red) due to a special reflective layer in the retina of many animals' eyes. The Red Eye Tool (J) should be able to correct this eyeshine using the process outlined in *Exercise 9.8.*

Figure 9.22

Exercise 9.8 file. Daisy, Lake Toxaway, North Carolina.

Step 2: Eliminate the instances of red eye. *Tip:* Click in the center of each affected area to produce an even repair.

- Click on the affected red eye area within a pupil; the change is immediate.
  - If the darkened area extends beyond the dog's eye, undo the action [Edit menu > Undo | ⌘Z]. Then try it again, having first positioned the cursor in the *center* of the eye.
- Repeat this action for the second eye.

Color and Tonal Edits and Enhancements

Whether converting a color photo to grayscale or increasing the color saturation in a photo, color enhancements can influence the overall mood and impact of an image. There are multiple ways to achieve the desired results, including both nondestructive and destructive methods.

Adjustment Layers

Adjustment Layers are a set of layers that allow the designer to edit any other layer (or layers) without affecting the pixels in an image. Once applied, the visibility of adjustment layers can be toggled off and on, and the adjustment layers can be deleted with affecting the rest of the image. Adjustment layers can be used to affect an entire image or a specific area. When an adjustment layer is applied, the *Properties panel* provides access to associated properties that can refine the adjustment [Window menu > Properties].

What follows is a list of the adjustment layers corresponding to their symbols shown in Figure 9.23, from left to right:

- *Row 1:* Brightness/Contrast, Levels, Curves, Exposure, Vibrance.
- *Row 2:* Hue/Saturation, Color Balance, Black & White, Photo Filter, Channel Mixer, Color Lookup.
- *Row 3:* Invert, Posterize, Threshold, Selective Color, Gradient Map.

As this list indicates, there are many adjustment layers available, more than most designers use during an average work session. This chapter explores three of the most commonly used adjustment layers, Brightness/Contrast, Hue/Saturation and Black & White:

- *Brightness/Contrast:* Adjusts the exposure in an image.
- *Hue/Saturation:* Adjusts the hue, saturation and lightness values.
- *Black & White:* Converts colors to grayscale while providing control of the tonal range.*

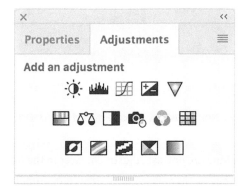

Figure 9.23

Adjustments panel, Window menu > Adjustments.

---

* Tonal range refers to the total number of tones possible in an image. In a black-and-white photo, this equates to the available shades of gray.

Applying a Brightness/Contrast Adjustment Layer

When a photo looks too dark or too light, the Brightness/Contrast adjustment layer can be used to enhance the image. These scenarios are often symptoms of the available light (too little or too much) when the photo was taken.

Exercise 9.9: Use a Brightness/Contrast Adjustment Layer

Exercise file: **Ch09-Ex09-photo.jpg** (Figure 9.24)

Figure 9.24

Exercise 9.9 file. Buoys, North Rustico, Prince Edward Island, Canada.

Step 1: Apply a Brightness/Contrast adjustment layer to the image.

- Select the *Adjustments menu command* from the *Window menu* [Window menu > Adjustments].
- In the *Adjustments panel*, locate and select the *Brightness/Contrast adjustment layer.*
  - Move the cursor over the collection of adjustment layer symbols. When the cursor is positioned over a symbol, the name of the associated adjustment layer is shown.

- Find the *Brightness/Contrast symbol* in the top row and click once on the symbol. This action triggers several events: the *Brightness/Contrast adjustment layer* and its accompanying layer mask are created in the *Layers panel* and the *Properties panel* opens.
- *Note:* The *Adjustments panel* and the *Properties panel* share the same window. Click on the corresponding tab to toggle between panels.

Step 2: Review the contents of the adjustment layer (Brightness/Contrast 1) in the Layers panel (Figure 9.25).

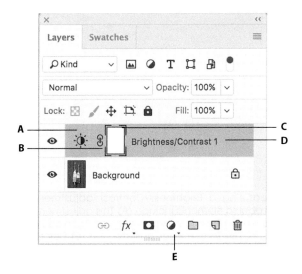

Figure 9.25

Layers panel featuring a Brightness/Contrast adjustment layer, Window menu > Layers. Labeled elements include (A) Layer thumbnail; (B) Link icon: Indicates layer mask is linked to layer; (C) Layer mask thumbnail; (D) Adjustment layer name; and (E) Create new fill or adjustment layer.

- The adjustment layer name (Brightness/Contrast #) features the selected adjustment, Brightness/Contrast, followed by an incremental count (e.g., 1, 2, …).
- Notice the indented position of the adjustment layer and the link icon, which indicates that a *layer mask* is associated with the adjustment layer.
  - The layer mask can be used to isolate the area affected by the adjustment.
  - By default, the adjustment layer is applied to the entire layer to which it has been applied.
  - *Note:* In *Exercise 9.10*, the adjustment layer will be applied to a specific selection instead of to the entire image.

Step 3: Use the elements in the Properties panel to refine the effect of the adjustment layer on the image (Figure 9.26). *Note: The Properties panel*, like the Options bar, is context-sensitive; its content changes depending on which adjustment layer has been applied or is currently selected in the Layers panel.

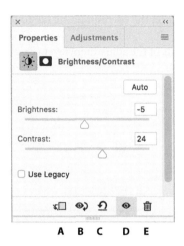

Figure 9.26

Properties panel featuring a Brightness/Contrast adjustment layer, Window menu > Properties. Labeled elements include (A) This adjustment affects all layers below (click to clip layer); (B) Press to view previous state (can also press \); (C) Reset to adjustment defaults; (D) Toggle layer visibility; and (E) Delete this adjustment layer.

- The *Auto button* applies an automatic color correction using the current default setting.
- Click the *Auto button* to see what changes are made to the photo.
- To view the photo in its previous state, before the adjustment was made, press and hold down the *View previous state icon* along the bottom edge of the Properties panel. As long as the mouse button is held down, the previous state is visible. When the mouse button is released, the affected state returns.
- Another way to view the photo in its previous state is by turning off the visibility of the adjustment layer. This can be done by toggling off the *Layer visibility icon* (eye icon) along the bottom edge of the *Properties panel* or in the *Layers panel* located to the left of the layer name.
- To *undo the adjustment state*, here are two options:
  - *Option 1: Delete* the adjustment layer. With the adjustment layer selected in the *Layers panel*, click on the *trashcan icon* along the bottom edge of that panel.

Graphic Design: Learn It, Do It

- *Option 2: Reset* the adjustment layer by returning its values to their defaults (Brightness: 0; Contrast: 0) in the *Properties panel*.
- Adjust the *Brightness* and *Contrast* levels using the properties' sliders or *scrubby sliders*, which appear when the cursor is placed over the name of each property. *Tip:* When experimenting with properties such as Brightness and Contrast, try dragging each slider to its extreme positions to see what kind of effects the related element *can* have on the image. Most image adjustments require subtle corrections, but it is good to recognize what extreme changes look like. On the rare occasion, such extreme changes can produce a unique and successful solution to a design brief.
- *Note:* The *Use Legacy* feature is employed when editing Brightness/Contrast adjustment layers that were created with earlier versions of Photoshop.

Step 4: Save the file (Ch09-Ex09.PSD).

- From the *File menu*, select the *Save menu command* [File menu > Save | ⌘S].
  - Notice that the *Save As dialog box* is presented and that Photoshop suggests saving the file as a *Photoshop Document* since the file now contains multiple layers.
- Save the file as Ch09-Ex09.PSD.

Using a Layer Mask to Isolate an Adjustment Layer

There are occasions when the designer wants to apply an adjustment layer to a particular part of an image and only that part. In this situation, a *layer mask* is created and used to protect the rest of the image from being affected by the adjustment.

Exercise 9.10: Use a Layer Mask to Limit the Effect of a Hue/Saturation Adjustment Layer

Exercise file: **Ch09-Ex10-photo.jpg** (Figure 9.27)
There are multiple ways to create a Quick Mask; two options are presented in this exercise.

- *Option 1:* Use a *selection tool* to isolate a portion of the photo *before* applying the adjustment layer. The selected area will be affected by the adjustment layer.
  - **Step 1:** Use the *selection tool* of your choice to select the red poppies.
    - Consider using one of the following selection tools: *Quick Selection Tool* (W), *Magic Wand Tool* (W) or one of the *Lasso Tools* (L).
  - **Step 2:** Apply a Hue/Saturation adjustment layer to the photo.
    - In the *Adjustments panel*, click on the *Hue/Saturation symbol*, located in the second row.

Figure 9.27

Exercise 9.10 file. Poppies along Emerald Lake, Yoho National Park, British Columbia, Canada.

  - *Or,* locate and hold down the mouse button on the *Create new fill or adjustment layer icon* located along the bottom edge of the *Layer panel.* From the dropdown menu select *Hue/Saturation,* and then release the mouse button.
  - Either technique triggers the creation of the *Hue/Saturation adjustment layer* and its accompanying *layer mask* in the *Layers panel.* The action also opens the *Properties panel.*
- **Step 3:** Change the values (i.e., Hue, Saturation, Lightness) in the *Properties panel* to alter the color of the poppies.
- **Step 4:** Review the contents of the adjustment layer (Hue/Saturation 1) in the *Layers panel,* particularly the *layer mask thumbnail* (Figure 9.28).
  - Look specifically at the *layer mask thumbnail* to see the protected and unprotected areas of the image, based on the selection made in Step 1.
    - The *protected* or unaffected area is shown in black; the adjustment layer does not impact this area.
    - The *unprotected* or affected area, shown in white, is the selection; this area is impacted by the adjustment layer.
  - Once a layer mask has been created, it can be edited to increase or decrease either the protected or unprotected areas (see Step 5).
- **Step 5 (Optional):** Edit the layer mask to increase or decrease the unprotected or affected area.

Graphic Design: Learn It, Do It

Figure 9.28

Exercise 9.10, Step 4.

- Select the *adjustment layer* in the Layers panel, in this example that is Hue/Saturation 1.
- Select the *Brush Tool* (B) in the Tools panel and paint *black* or *white* to alter the layer mask.
  - Painting with black *subtracts* from the selection and reduces the area affected by the adjustment layer.
  - Areas on the adjustment layer painted with white are *added* to the unprotected area.
  - *Note:* Several tools can be used to add or subtract color from a Quick Mask (e.g., Brush Tool [B], Eraser Tool [E], Marquee Tools [M] + Fill).
- *Tip:* To confirm that you are editing the layer mask and not directly on the photo, look to the *document window tab.*
  - In this tab, the current *adjustment layer* (e.g., Hue/Saturation) and "Layer Mask" should be listed.
  - If this information is not shown in the tab, revisit the *Layers panel* and select the *adjustment layer.*
- *Option 2:* Create a Quick Mask *after* the adjustment layer has been applied.
  - **Step 1:** Apply a *Hue/Saturation adjustment layer* to Ch09 Ex10-photo. jpg.
    - In the Adjustments panel, click on the *Hue/Saturation symbol.*

- **Step 2:** Change the values (i.e., Hue, Saturation, Lightness) in the *Properties panel* to alter the appearance of the photo.
  - Note: The entire photo is affected by these changes since no specific selection has been made.
- **Step 3:** Use the Brush Tool (B) to limit the effect of the adjustment layer on the photo using the mask layer. By default, the entire image is unprotected so the mask thumbnail in the Layers panel is all white. Apply black to limit the effect of the adjustment.
  - In the *Layers panel*, click on the *layer mask thumbnail* in the Hue/Saturation adjustment layer.
  - Use the *Brush Tool* (B) to define the protected (unaffected) area, by painting *black* onto the mask layer.
    - In areas where black is applied, the photo returns to its original colors.

Applying Multiple Adjustment Layers

Imagine a scenario in which you want to convert a color photo to black and white while preserving a certain portion of the image in color and then enhancing the color elements; this is the premise for *Exercise 9.11*. The exercise explores applying multiple adjustment layers to a single image. There are multiple solutions to this task, and each image element could be placed on a separate layer or these image elements could be isolated using layer masks. Each solution will be outlined.

When a file contains multiple adjustment layers, the adjustments are stacked in the *Layers panel*. The adjustment layer in the highest position in the Layers panel influences all layers and layer groups below it, including both content layers and other adjustment layers. An adjustment layer can be repositioned within the Layers panel like other layers. Press and hold down the mouse button on the adjustment layer name, then drag the layer to the desired position within the layer stack and release the mouse button.

To limit the effect of an adjustment layer to a single content layer, the adjustment layer can be *clipped* to a layer. Select the adjustment layer, then press the *Adjustment Clips icon* along the bottom edge of the *Properties panel*. The selected adjustment becomes further indented, and the affected layer name is underlined.

Exercise 9.11: Apply Adjustment Layers to Multiple Layers within the Same Image

Exercise file: **Ch09-Ex11.psd** (Figure 9.29)

Exercise brief: Use the adjustment layers listed in the parentheses to alter the appearance of the provided photo. The background of the color photo will be converted to grayscale (Black & White), then the background will be colorized (Hue/Saturation); the umbrella of Figure 1 (left) will change colors (Hue/Saturation), and the overall tone of the photo will be brightened or darkened

Figure 9.29

Exercise 9.11 file. A soft day in Ireland, Glendalough, County Wicklow, Ireland.

(Brightness/Contrast). *Tip:* Before starting this exercise, review the file layers and the content on each layer.

Step 1: Apply a Black & White adjustment layer to the Background copy layer. *Note:* Since a copy of each figure has been placed on separate layers, the Black & White adjustment layer will not affect the coloring of the figures.

- Select the layer (Background copy) that will be affected by the adjustment layer.
- Apply a *Black & White adjustment layer* to the selected layer (Black & White 1).

Step 2: Alter the tones in the background of the photo using the values in the Properties panel. This step allows you to darken or lighten the shades of gray in the background.

- Use the values (i.e., Auto, Tint, color sliders) in the *Properties panel* to alter the tones in the background of the photo
  A. *Auto button:* Applies an automatic color correction using the current default setting.
  B. *Tint:* Provides a shortcut to the *Color Picker (Tint Color)* and applies a selected color to the photo. *Note:* This exercise will achieve the tint effect using a combination of Black & White and Hue/Saturation adjustment layers.

C. *Color Sliders:* Control the image's conversion from color to grayscale: Reds, Yellows, Greens, Cyans, Blues, Magentas. *Note:* When a color image is converted to grayscale, these color sliders continue to influence the appearance of the photo. In the *Exercise 9.11* photo, the connection between the color sliders and the grayscale area can be clearly seen when the Magentas level is changed and the purple umbrella becomes correspondingly lighter or darker in its new grayscale tone.

Step 3: Colorize the background of the photo using a Hue/Saturation adjustment layer. This step adds monochromatic color to the previously grayscale background. *Tip:* It was a cool, rainy day in Ireland when the photo was taken, so consider selecting a color that reflects this tone.

- Select the *Black & White 1 layer* in the Layers panel.
- Apply a *Hue/Saturation adjustment layer* (Hue/Saturation 1).
- In the Properties panel, select the *Colorize checkbox*.
  - *Note:* You may need to *scroll down* to locate the Colorize checkbox.
- Use the *Hue slider* to adjust the color of the background.

Step 4: Change the color of the umbrella for Figure 1 (left) using a Hue/Saturation adjustment layer.

- Select the Figure 1 layer.
- Apply a *Hue/Saturation adjustment layer* (Hue/Saturation 2).
- In the Properties panel, use the *Hue slider* to adjust the color of the umbrella.
  - *Note:* Given its position in the hierarchy of layers, the Hue/Saturation adjustment layer will affect the entire image, until it is *clipped* to the Figure 1 layer.
- While still in the Properties panel, select the *Clip icon*. This action limits the color adjustment to the Figure 1 layer.
  - Notice the additional indentation of the Hue/Saturation adjustment layer and the underline that has been applied to the layer name Figure 1.
- To limit the color change to just the umbrella, create a layer mask to protect the figure (not the umbrella).
  - In the Layers panel, click on the *layer mask thumbnail* in the Hue/Saturation 2 layer to activate the layer mask.
  - In the Tools panel, click once on the *Default Foreground and Background Colors icon* (D), which is located below the foreground and background color chips. This action should set the foreground color to white. Now, click once on the *Switch Foreground and Background Colors icon* (X) to set the foreground color to black; this color will be used limit the effect of the adjustment layer.
  - Use the *Brush Tool* (B) to paint over the figure but not the umbrella using *black*, since the goal is to protect this area from the adjustment

layer. As black is painted, the original color of the figure returns. *Tip:* Since the Hue/Saturation 2 adjustment layer is clipped to the Figure 1 layer, do not worry about painting beyond the edges of the figure. However, be careful not to paint black over the umbrella as this would interfere with the effect of the adjustment layer on the umbrella.

Step 5: Change the tone of the overall photo using a Brightness/Contrast adjustment layer. *Note:* To apply this adjustment to the entire image, the adjustment layer needs to be the topmost layer in the Layers panel (Figure 9.30). The adjustment layer can be reordered once created, or to proactively place the adjustment layer in the correct position, select the current topmost layer and then apply the adjustment layer.

- Select the topmost layer in the Layers panel.
- Apply a *Brightness/Contrast adjustment layer.* Reorder this layer (Brightness/Contrast 1) if needed to move it to the top of the Layers panel.
- In the Properties panel, use the *Brightness and Contrast sliders* to adjust the overall tone of the photo.
  - Brightening the image emphasizes the details including the low-hanging clouds.

Figure 9.30

Exercise 9.11, Step 5, Layers panel, Window menu > Layers.

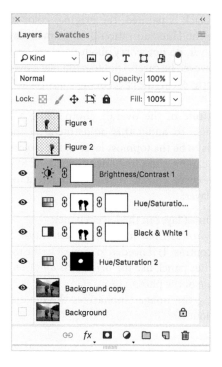

Figure 9.31

Exercise 9.11, Alternate, Layers panel, Window menu > Layers.

- Darkening the image creates a moody photo that captures the atmosphere of the rainy day.

Step 6: Save the image (Ch09-Ex11.PSD).

- From the *File menu*, select the *Save menu command* [File menu > Save | ⌘S].

The same results can be achieved using just the Background copy layer in the provided file. In this scenario, layer masks protect certain image elements from specific adjustment layers (Figure 9.31).

Exercise 9.11 (Alternate): Apply Multiple Adjustment Layers to a Single Layer

Exercise file: **Ch09-Ex11.psd** (see Figure 9.29)

Note: Only the Background copy layer will be used for this alternate solution. So, turn off the visibility of the Figure 1 and Figure 2 layers.

Step 1: Apply a Black & White adjustment layer to the Background copy layer.

Step 2: Colorize the background of the photo using a Hue/Saturation adjustment layer.

Step 3: Create a layer mask on each of the adjustment layers created in Step 1 and 2 to limit the layers' effects.

- Use the *Brush Tool* (B) to paint a *black Quick Mask* over Figure 1 (left) and Figure 2 (right).
  - As black is applied on each layer mask, the adjustment layer's effect disappears from the figures and their umbrellas.

Step 4: Change the color of the umbrella for Figure 1 (left) using a Hue/Saturation adjustment layer.

- To proactively limit the influence of the Hue/Saturation adjustment layer, select the purple umbrella.
  - The selected area is what will be the affected area.

Step 5: Change the tone of the overall photo using a Brightness/Contrast adjustment layer.

Step 6: Save the image.

Alternatives to Adjustment Layers

For designers who prefer not to use adjustment layers, the same color and tonal adjustments can be completed as *destructive* edits. The color adjustment tools are available under the *Image menu* and the *Adjustments menu command*. The list of adjustments includes those used in recent exercises (i.e., Brightness/ Contrast, Hue/Saturation, Desaturate [a.k.a. Black & White]) [Image menu > Adjustments > Brightness/Contrast]. Keep in mind that as destructive edits, there are limited ways to undo these changes, including Undo [Edit menu > Undo | ⌘Z], Step Backward [Edit menu > Step Backward] and the History panel [Window menu > History]. If the file has not been saved since the adjustment was applied, you can also use the Revert menu command [File menu > Revert].

Filters

Just as you might apply a filter to an Instagram photo, Photoshop provides a variety of filter options for designers. The list of available filters is available under the *Filter menu* (Figure 9.32). Some filter changes are subtle (e.g., Blur), while others are dramatic (e.g., Distort > Twirl; Stylize > Oil Paint). Applying any filter is considered a destructive edit.

Considerable time can be spent exploring and experimenting with filters and their associated properties. As time permits, open a photo and try applying

Figure 9.32

Filter menu.

different filters to the image. In the meantime, this chapter explores a few commonly used filters including Sharpen, Blur and Artistic:

- *Sharpen:* Focus a selection and improve its clarity [Filter menu > Sharpen > Sharpen]. There are several sharpen filters, which focus blurred images by increasing the contrast of adjacent pixels.
  - *Tip:* Be careful not to oversharpen an image, which can divert attention from the subject.
- *Blur/Blur Gallery:* Soften a selection or an entire image; these filters can be useful for retouching.
- *Artistic filters:* Filters in the Filter Gallery apply painterly effects (e.g., Dry Brush, Palette Knife, Watercolor), as shown in Figure 9.33 [Filter menu > Filter Gallery...].

Many filters present properties available to adjust the impact of the filter. When changes are made to filter properties, be patient waiting for the effect to be applied. Generally, the larger the file, the longer it takes for the filter to be applied.

The Filter Gallery provides a preview window in which a selected filter can be previewed before it is applied to the image file, as shown in Figure 9.33. Controls located below this preview window allow you to zoom in, zoom out and move the image within the window in order to view the effect of the selected filter on a particular area of the photo. Use these features to your advantage as you experiment with filters.

Figure 9.33

Filter Gallery, Rough Pastels currently selected, Filter menu > Filter Gallery....

Exercise 9.12: Apply an Artistic Filter to Alter the Appearance of a Photo

Exercise file: **Ch09-Ex12-photo.jpg** (Figure 9.34)

Step 1: Create multiple copies of the Background layer (refer to *Exercise 9.1: Duplicate the Background Layer*).

- Open the *Layers panel* from the *Window menu* [Window menu > Layers].
- From the *Layers panel menu* available in the upper-right corner of the window, select *Duplicate Layer....*
- In the *Duplicate Layer dialog box*, accept the provided name *Background copy.*
- Click *OK* to create the new layer.
- Repeat this process several times to create multiple copies of the photo.

Step 2: Apply a unique filter on each layer, renaming the layer name to reflect the name of the applied layer.

- Select a layer in the *Layers panel* and make sure that this layer is *currently visible* and *not hidden by layers above it* in the layer stacking order.
  - *Tip:* Turn off or on visibility of layers to ensure that the selected layer is visible.

Figure 9.34

Exercise 9.12 file. A water view, Peggy's Cove, Nova Scotia, Canada.

- From the *Filter menu*, select a filter to apply to the layer content.
- If satisfied with the filter, click *OK* to accept the effect.
- Then, rename the layer entering the name of the filter as the layer name. If dissatisfied with the filter, click *Cancel* or Undo the action [Edit menu > Undo | ⌘Z].
- Repeat this process to sample additional filters. Each time, be sure to verify which layer is selected and currently visible.

Step 3: Save the image as a PSD file to preserve the layers (Ch09-Ex12.PSD).

- Select the *Save menu command* from the *File menu* [File menu > Save | ⌘S].

Once multiple filters have been applied to different layers within the file, you have the ability to compare and contrast the filters by turning on and off the visibility of layers.

Applying Multiple Filters in the Filter Gallery

It is possible to apply multiple filters within the *Filter Gallery* to an image (Figure 9.35). To do this, it is first necessary to create a new *effect layer* for each additional filter by clicking on the *New effect layer icon* located along the bottom of the Filter Gallery window. The behaviors of effect layers are similar to those of layers within the Layers panel. The stacking order of the effect layers can be rearranged; the visibility of each effect layer can be toggled on and off; and an effect layer can be deleted.

Figure 9.35

Filter Gallery, Filter menu > Filter Gallery...: (A) New effect layer and (B) Delete effect layer.

Special Processes

Adding a Watermark

If you plan to post your photos or other images online, it is a good practice to add a watermark to these images before sharing them. A watermark can be a useful way to promote your name and/or the name of your business. Using a watermark lets viewers know who owns the rights to an image. Although watermarking will not protect your images 100%, it will deter some people from using your images without permission.

To create a *reusable* watermark, a *custom brush* is created. The custom brush is saved in the Photoshop preferences (on the computer). *Note:* The process of resetting Photoshop to the *Default Workspace* discards any custom brushes that have been created. To avoid having to recreate the brush, the designer can either export the brush or save the brush to a new library, which can be reloaded after the workspace has been reset.

Exercise 9.13: Create and Apply a Watermark

Exercise file: **Ch09-Ex13-photo.jpg** (Figure 9.36)

Step 1: Create a new file in Photoshop with file properties that correspond to the intended output of the image (e.g., online or print). For this exercise, we plan to

Figure 9.36

Exercise 9.13 file. The Gateway Arch, Gateway Arch National Park, St. Louis, Missouri.

post the photo online. So, select the Web tab, and select *Web Small* from the Blank Document presets.

- Begin at the *File menu* and select the *New... menu command* [File menu > New... | ⌘N].
- In the *New Document dialog box*, look for the *Web* set, and from the "Blank Document Presets" select *Web Minimum* (1024 × 768 px @ 72 ppi).
- Click *Create* to generate the image file.

Step 2: Use the Type Tool (T) to create a line of black text for the watermark. Or, move a copy of a logo from another source to this new file. *Note:* If the logo is in color, convert it to grayscale before moving it to the new file.

- Select the *Type Tool* (T) in the Tools panel and set the typographic properties in the Options bar to match your personal preferences.

- Set the *Foreground Color* to *black* (or *gray* for a multidimensional feel) in the *Options bar.*
- Position the cursor over the canvas, click once and create a line of text.
  - *Tip:* If the text does not appear on the canvas, double-check the *Text Color* in the Options bar, and if the color chip is white, double-click on the color chip to change the color to black or gray.
- When finished creating the text, click on the *Move Tool* (V) in the Tools panel.

Special Characters, a.k.a. Glyphs

To add special characters to the watermark (e.g., ©, accents), access the *Glyphs panel* from the *Window menu* [Window menu > Glyphs]. This panel contains punctuation, superscript, subscript, symbols, special characters and glyphs from other languages (Figure 9.37).

With a text box created and active, double-click on the glyph that you want to add to your design, and it will appear on the canvas. Recently used glyphs are stored at the top of this panel for easy access.

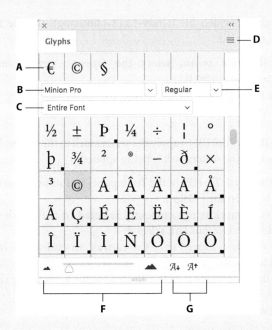

Figure 9.37

Glyphs panel, Window menu > Glyphs, (A) Recent Glyphs; (B) Set the font family; (C) Set Font Category; (D) Glyphs panel menu; (E) Set the font style; (F) Zoom (Out | In); (G) Scale Glyphs (Scale Down | Scale Up).

Step 3: Select the watermark.

- Select the *Rectangular Marquee Tool* (M) in the Tools panel.
- Draw a *bounding box* (selection) around the watermark.

Step 4: Create a brush based on the selected watermark using the *Define Brush Preset...* menu command under the Edit menu. Once created, the new brush will be available in the Brush Catalog.

- From the *Edit menu*, select *Define Brush Preset...* [Edit menu > Define Brush Preset...].
- In the *Brush Name dialog box*, enter a name for the new brush.
- Click *OK* to create the brush.

Step 5: Save your work. *Tip:* Saving this file as a Photoshop Document allows for future edits and adjustments to the design without having to recreate the watermark from scratch.

- From the *File menu*, select the *Save As... menu command* [File menu > Save As... | ⇧⌘S].

Step 6: Open the provided file (Ch09-Ex13-photo.jpg), the file to which the watermark will be added.

- From the *File menu*, select the *Open... menu command* [File menu > Open... | ⌘O].
- Browse to the provided exercise file, Ch09-Ex13-photo.jpg.
- Click *Open*.

Step 7: Use the Brush Tool (B) to apply the watermark to the image. *Tip:* Be aware of the layer to which the watermark is being applied.

- Select the *Brush Tool* (B) in the Tools panel and adjust the properties (e.g., Brush Size, Opacity, Color).
- If the watermark is not currently selected in the *Brush Preset picker* located in the Options bar, select it.
- As the cursor is moved over the canvas, an outline of the watermark should be visible.
- When the watermark is in the desired location, *click once* (Figure 9.38).
  - *Note:* Painting with the *Brush Tool* (B) creates multiple instances of the watermark.

The next time the watermark is to be added to an image, select the *Brush Tool* (B) and click once. *Note:* This process can also be used to create a new brush that is not a watermark, instead a shape, logo or other mark that may be used frequently.

Graphic Design
Learn It, Do It

Figure 9.38

Exercise 9.13, Step 7.

Creating a Panorama (Photomerge)

Multiple photos can be combined into one continuous image, a panorama, via the *Photomerge* command. Three photos taken at Bryce National Park were combined to produce the panorama presented in Figure 9.39. In order for the Photomerge command to be successful, the source photos should overlap by at least a third, but no more than 60%. Too little overlap and the tool may be unable to assemble the panorama; too much overlap and the tool may not be able to blend the images. The photos to be combined can be horizontal or vertical.

Photoshop provides several options for the combining of photos into a panorama in the Photomerge dialog box (Figure 9.40). Let's review these options before proceeding to *Exercise 9.14: Create a Panorama Using Photomerge.*

The *Layout* options (i.e., Auto, Perspective, Cylindrical, Spherical, Collage, Reposition) are used to create a pleasing composition.

Figure 9.39

Panorama. Thor's Hammer as seen from Sunset Trail, Bryce National Park, Utah.

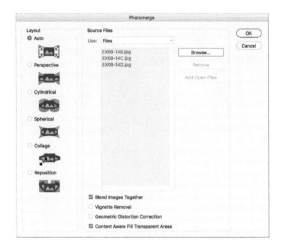

Figure 9.40

Photomerge dialog box, File menu > Automate > Photomerge....

The following descriptions are drawn from the *Photoshop Online Help*:

A. *Auto:* Photoshop analyzes the source images and applies either a Perspective, Cylindrical or Spherical layout, depending on which produces a better photomerge.

B. *Perspective:* Creates a consistent composition by designating one of the source images (by default, the middle image) as the *reference image*. The other images are then transformed (repositioned, stretched or skewed as necessary) so that overlapping content across layers is matched.

C. *Cylindrical:* Reduces the "bow-tie" distortion that can occur with the Perspective layout by displaying individual images as on an unfolded cylinder. Overlapping content across files is still matched. The reference image is placed at the center. This is best suited for creating wide panoramas.

D. *Spherical:* Aligns and transforms the images as if they were for mapping the inside of a sphere, which simulates the experience of viewing a 360° panorama. If you have taken a set of images that cover 360°, use this for 360° panoramas. You might also use Spherical to produce nice panoramic results with other file sets.

E. *Collage:* Aligns the layers and matches overlapping content and transforms (rotate or scale) any of the source layers.

F. *Reposition:* Aligns the layers and matches overlapping content but does not transform (stretch or skew) any of the source layers.

The other available options (i.e., Blend Images Together, Vignette Removal, Geometric Distortion Correction, Content Aware Fill Transparent Areas) affect how the photos are combined and the handling of any gaps or empty spaces generated during the photomerge process. The following descriptions are drawn from the *Photoshop Online Help*:

A. *Blend Images Together:* Finds the optimal borders between the images and creates seams based on those borders, and color matches the images. With Blend Images Together turned off, a simple rectangular blend is performed. This may be preferable if you intend to retouch the blending masks by hand.
B. *Vignette Removal:* Removes and performs exposure compensation in images that have darkened edges caused by lens flaws or improper lens shading.
C. *Geometric Distortion Correction:* Compensates for barrel, pincushion or fisheye distortion.
D. *Content Aware Fill Transparent Areas:* Seamlessly fill the transparent areas with similar image content nearby.

Tips: Taking Photos for a Panorama (Photomerge)

The quality of the source photos plays a large role in the success of the panoramic compositions. Use the following tips to help increase the quality of your source photos.

Tip 1: Create photo markers before and after a series of photos

- Before taking the first photo in the series, place your hand in front of the camera lens being careful not to touch the lens or point the camera to the ground and take a photo.
  - The subject of this photo marker does not matter, just make it something that is easily identifiable as a marker (e.g., your hand, the ground).
- Take another marker shot when you are finished taking the series of photos for the panorama.
- When reviewing your photos, these photo markers will make it easier to locate the series of photos earmarked for Photomerge among other photos taken of the scene.
- If you take multiple series of photos (a good tip), this technique also lets you know where one series of panorama photos ends and another begins.

Tip 2: Body position

- Before you begin taking a series of photos, assess the scene and plant your feet shoulder-width apart in the direction of your expected last shot. Then, wind yourself around to the starting shot.

- As you take photos (overlapping each photo by at least 30%), unwind yourself so you are looking forward (with your body positioned in line with your feet) for the final photo.
- This technique can provide stability and prevent you from overextending your reach and taking uneven photos.

Tip 3: Keep the camera level

- Avoid tilting the camera or changing the camera's height while taking the photos. If available, use a tripod or monopod to provide camera stability.

Tip 4: Avoid the zoom

- Maintain an equal distance between the camera and the scene while taking the photos; do not zoom in or out between photos.

Tip 5: Consistent exposure

- When possible, take the photos when the scene is evenly lit.
- The blending features in Photomerge can help smooth out some differences in exposure; however, extreme differences (e.g., photographing a scene that is in both shadow and sunlight) make alignment with the photos difficult.

Exercise 9.14: Create a Panorama Using Photomerge

Exercise files: **Ch09-Ex14A-photo.jpg**, **Ch09-Ex14B-photo.jpg**, **Ch09-Ex14C-photo.jpg**, **Ch09-Ex14D-photo.jpg**, **Ch09-Ex14E-photo.jpg** (Figure 9.41)

Step 1: Select the photos that will be combined.

- Begin at the *File menu* and select the *Automate menu command,* then the *Photomerge…* command [File menu > Automate > Photomerge…].
- In the *Photomerge dialog box,* look for the "Source Files" header and below that select either *Files* or *Folder* from the *source dropdown menu* (see Figure 9.40).
- Click *Browse…* and navigate to the series of photos.

Figure 9.41

Exercise 9.14 files. Bryce National Park, Utah.

Graphic Design: Learn It, Do It

- Select the three photos that will be used for the panorama (Ch09-Ex14B-photo.jpg, Ch09-Ex14C-photo.jpg, Ch09-Ex14D-photo.jpg).
  - Do not select the photo markers, the photos taken before and after the series of photos.

Step 2: Use the available options in the Photomerge dialog box to adjust the layout of the photos and the appearance of the final panorama.

- Under the "Layout" header, select the *Auto* option.
- Below the list of files to be used, select the checkboxes for both *Blend Images Together* and *Content Aware Fill Transparent Areas*.

Step 3: Initiate the photomerge and create a panorama.

- Click the *OK* button.
- Photoshop creates a multilayer image from the source images, blending where the images overlap (Figure 9.42).

Step 4 (Optional): As needed, use the Crop Tool (C) to eliminate any unwanted content within the panorama.

Step 5: Save the file (Ch09-Ex14.psd).

- Select the *Save As menu command* from the *File menu* [File menu > Save As...].
- Use the following file name for the panorama, Ch09-Ex14.psd.
- Confirm that the *Format dropdown menu* lists "*Photoshop.*"

Figure 9.42

Photomerge complete. Layers panel, Window menu > Layers.

After creating a panorama using this combination of options, repeat the process selecting a different *Layout* option. Once created, compare and contrast the resulting panoramas. Depending on the subject matter and the series of photos, the ideal combination of options will vary. So, it is important to try different combinations and select the final panorama image based on the results.

Looking Ahead

Use the *Photo Editing Workflow* and the associated steps presented in this chapter to strengthen your photos. Revisit the presented tools and processes to increase your ease and comfort applying the necessary edits.

This chapter has presented you with a lot of information regarding photo editing practices. Additional photographs are available via the book's companion website for your use to practice working with the tools and the processes. Utilize the Photoshop skills developed here to create visually appealing and dynamic images.

Discussion

Discussion 9.1: Can You Believe What You See?

In this digital age, can you believe what you see? Looking at magazine covers at a newsstand or images online, are you skeptical about the authenticity and the accuracy of what you see? Why is it important to question these images?

What incentive does a magazine or website have for featuring modified photos? What impact can photos that have been modified, particularly photos of celebrities and athletes, have on the viewer?

Should the media be required to inform consumers that images have been digitally altered? What would this look like? Should a label or a symbol be added as a kind of watermark to denote alterations? Would this apply to any photo edits, including straightening the horizon or removing red eye from a photo?

Activities

Activity 9.1: Photo Editing Your Photos

Review the photos that were taken as part of the *Chapter 8: Digital Photography in Design* activities. Apply the necessary photo editing techniques to these photos to strengthen their composition and overall impact. Use the *Photo Editing Workflow* as a checklist of possible edits as you assess the needs of each photo.

When the edits on a particular photo are complete, change the file name (e.g., appending "-v2" to the end of the file name) when saving the file [File menu > Save As…]. This allows for a side-by-side comparison of the photo pre- and post-edits.

Activity 9.2: Stylize a Photo

Select one of the photos taken as part of the *Chapter 8: Digital Photography in Design* activities and apply a combination of adjustment layers and filters to create a stylized image.

What impact do these edits have on the subject of the photo and the overall presentation of the image?

Exercise File(s) Available on the Companion Website, URL

Ch09-Ex01-photo.jpg | *Exercise 9.1* file. Iceberg at the dock, Bridgeport, Newfoundland and Labrador, Canada.

Ch09-Ex02-photo.jpg | *Exercise 9.2* file. Icebergs, Twillingate, Newfoundland and Labrador, Canada.

Ch09-Ex03-photo.jpg | *Exercise 9.3* file. Making friends at Eastland Alpacas, Mount Joy, Pennsylvania.

Ch09-Ex04-photo.jpg | *Exercise 9.4* file. Irish country cottage, Inis Mór, County Galway, Ireland.

Ch09-Ex05-photo.jpg | *Exercise 9.5* file. Overlooking the Badlands, Badlands National Park, South Dakota.

Ch09-Ex06-photo.jpg | *Exercise 9.6* file. Looking up to St. Colman's Cathedral, Cobh, County Cork, Ireland.

Ch09-Ex07-photo.jpg | *Exercise 9.7* file. Chipmunk, Zion National Park, Utah.

Ch09-Ex08-photo.jpg | *Exercise 9.8* file. Daisy, Lake Toxaway, North Carolina.

Ch09-Ex09-photo.jpg | *Exercise 9.9* file. Buoys, North Rustico, Prince Edward Island, Canada.

Ch09-Ex10-photo.jpg | *Exercise 9.10* file. Poppies along Emerald Lake, Yoho National Park, British Columbia, Canada.

Ch09-Ex11.psd | *Exercise 9.11* file. A soft day in Ireland, Glendalough, County Wicklow, Ireland.

Ch09-Ex12-photo.jpg | *Exercise 9.12* file. A water view, Peggy's Cove, Nova Scotia, Canada.

Ch09-Ex13-photo.jpg | *Exercise 9.13* file. The Gateway Arch, Gateway Arch National Park, St. Louis, Missouri.

Ch09-Ex14A-photo.jpg, Ch09-EX14B-photo.jpg, Ch09-EX14C-photo.jpg, Ch09-EX14D-photo.jpg, Ch09-EX14E-photo.jpg | *Exercise 9.14* files. Bryce National Park, Utah.

URL: http://www.crcpress.com/9780367075347

External Links Mentioned in the Chapter

Photoshop Online Help | https://helpx.adobe.com/photoshop

Typography in Design

Type is a key element of design; it is equal in importance to graphics. A contributing factor to the tone and mood of an image, type is integral to the overall success or failure of a design. However, type is often one of the final elements incorporated. This chapter outlines the goals of type in design and encourages the designer to utilize typography in a meaningful way. *Typography* refers to the style and appearance of the printed word.

The chapter begins with an overview of type and related terminology. This includes distinguishing characteristics used to identify type. Familiarity with this terminology will facilitate discussions of typefaces and their classifications into one of four type categories. Type assessment in the forms of legibility and readability are presented along with techniques for improving these attributes. Finally, the methods for adjusting the appearance of type in the Adobe Creative Cloud are discussed.

Typography Terminology

First, here is some basic terminology. It is important to recognize and understand the fundamental elements of type and how they relate to one another.

- *Character* or *glyph:* The basic typographic element. This refers to any individual letter, number or punctuation mark.
- *Letterform:* A term used to refer to a letter's shape.
- *Typeface:* The specific letterform design of an alphabet including its characters and symbols. Each typeface is known by a name, such as Arial, Cambria and Times New Roman.
  The term *typeface* originated during times of movable type.* Blocks of wood or metal contained a relief image of a character on one surface, called the *face.*
- *Font:* A complete character set within a typeface in one particular size and style. This includes upper- and lowercase, numerals, punctuation marks, and any special characters contained in the typeface. Fonts are *also* specific computer files that contain all the characters within a typeface.
  During times of movable type, a *font* referred to a collection of pieces of wood or metal type. They were a specific size and, therefore, could only print one size character. Contemporary print processes can reproduce almost any size character from one digital font. Therefore, the terms *font* and *typeface*, while distinct, are often used interchangeably.
- *Type family:* The collection of all the sizes and styles of a typeface, under the name of the typeface. For example, all the styles and sizes of Helvetica form the Helvetica family. A type family may contain variations, but a strong visual continuity exists because the variations are all based on common design characteristics.

The Anatomy of Type

As we dissect the basic anatomy of type, refer to Figure 10.1. First, look to the guide lines used to measure different aspects of type. The *baseline* is the invisible horizontal line on which all type sits. In a typeface, the height of lowercase letters that have no ascenders or descenders is referred to as the *x-height.* The *meanline*

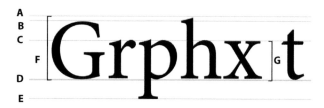

Figure 10.1

Typography guide lines: (A) cap line, (B) ascender line, (C) meanline, (D) baseline, (E) descender line, (F) cap height, and (G) x-height. *Typeface:* Minion Pro.

---

* Movable type was used to print newspapers and other publications until the late nineteenth century when it was replaced by linotype.

　　　　　　　　　　　　　　　　　Graphic Design: Learn It, Do It

is based on the height of the letter "x." The height of this line varies depending on the font being used. The height of most lowercase letters that extend above the x-height reach the *ascender line* (e.g., b, d, h, k, l). The exception is the letter "t," which generally does not reach the ascender line. In the opposite direction, lowercase letters that continue below the baseline extend to the *descender line* (e.g., g, j, q). In certain typefaces, some capital letters (e.g., J, Q) reach this line. Just as x-height is used to measure lowercase letters, the *cap line* is used to measure the *cap height*, the height of a capital letter above the baseline.

Figure 10.2 highlights some of the components and characteristics used to describe type. *Tip:* Do not get overwhelmed with terminology in this chapter; use the provided figures for reference as you get started.

- *Stroke:* A line that forms letters.
- *Bowl:* The curved stroke that encloses parts of letters (e.g., B, P, R, b, p) creating a counter.
- *Apex:* The point at the top of a character where two strokes meet (e.g., A, N, M).
- *Descender:* The part of a lowercase or capital letter that extends below the baseline (e.g., j, p, q, y, Q and sometimes J). The exception to this label is the lower part of the letter "g," which is referred to as a *loop* whether it is fully or partially closed.
- *Ascender:* The part of a lowercase letter that extends above the x-height, usually continuous with a main stroke (e.g., h, l, t).
- *Serif:* A flare or wedge-shaped form at the end of a letterform's strokes.
- *Finial:* A tapered or curved end of letters (e.g., c, e).
- *Counter:* The enclosed or partially enclosed negative space of a letterform (e.g., M, O, c, d). The exception to this label is the enclosed part of the letter "e," which is referred to as the *eye*.
- *Arm:* A horizontal stroke that does not connect to a stroke at one or both ends, such as the top of the capital letters "E" or "T."
- *Tittle:* Name for the dot above the letters "i" and "j."
- *Crossbar:* Connects two strokes, as in the capital letters "A" or "H."

Figure 10.2

Typography components: (A) bowl, (B) apex, (C) crossbar, (D) descender, (E) ascender, (F) serif, (G) finial, (H) counter, (I) arm, (J) tittle, (K) loop, and (L) stroke. *Typeface:* Minion Pro.

Typography's Units of Measure

The basic units of measurement used when working with type are points and picas. Type size is measured in *points* from the top of the ascender to the bottom of the descender (Figure 10.3). A *pica [pronounced: pahy*-kuh] is used to measure width, such as the width of a column or a *gutter*, the space between columns. Picas are more convenient than inches because smaller spaces can be measured in whole units instead of fractions.

Point, pica and inch conversations:

- One point = 1/72 of an inch
- One pica = 12 points
- One inch = 6 picas or 72 points

Designed | 72 pt.

Figure 10.3

Type size. *Typeface:* Big Caslon Medium.

Categories of Type

Typefaces can be classified in one of four primary categories of type: *serif, sans serif, script or decorative.* Within certain categories, there are subgroups of typefaces. For more information about these subgroups, access the reference at the end of this chapter (see *External Links Mentioned in the Chapter*).

1. *Serif:* Serif typefaces possess a flare or wedge-shaped form at the ends of the main strokes of characters, which is called a serif (Figure 10.4). Serif

Baskerville **Rockwell**
Bodoni 72 Garamond
Onyx Playfair Display
Times New Roman
American Typewriter

Figure 10.4

Examples of Serif typefaces.

typefaces are regularly used for lengthy blocks of text in print documents (e.g., newspapers, magazines). Online, serif typefaces are often used for headlines and body text providing contrast to sans serif typefaces.

- *Subgroups include:* Old Style, Transitional, Modern, Slab
- *Examples:* Garamond, Onyx, Times New Roman

2. *Sans Serif:* In French, the word "sans" means *without*, so sans serif typefaces are those without serifs on the ends of strokes (Figure 10.5). Sans serif letterforms are typically the same thickness all the way around; they are considered *monoweight*. Sans serif typefaces are widely used for online and mobile content as their wide, open lettering is easy to read on screens.

- *Subgroups include:* Grotesque, Square, Geometric
- *Examples:* Arial, Futura, Helvetica

Arial   Verdana
Britannic Bold Corbel
Futura   Tahoma
Geneva   Skia
Helvetica **Impact**

Figure 10.5

Examples of Sans Serif typefaces.

3. *Script:* This category includes typefaces that appear to have been hand-lettered (Figure 10.6). Script typefaces include scripts that connect, scripts that do not connect, scripts that look like handwriting, and scripts that look like traditional calligraphy. Scripts should not be used for long

Apple Chancery
Brush Script *Blacksword*
Edwardian Script *Mistral*
Lucida Blackletter
Snell Roundhouse *SignPainter*

Figure 10.6

Examples of Script typefaces.

blocks of text or instances of all caps as they are challenging to read and can distract from the message that is being communicated.

- *Subgroups include:* Formal, Casual
- *Examples:* Brush Script, Edwardian Script, Mistral

4. *Decorative:* These typefaces are distinctive and often ornamental (Figure 10.7). They provide an easy way to add personality to a design. However, since decorative typefaces are so distinctive, it is best to use them sparingly. Decorative fonts are often used on posters and in advertisements to attract attention.
   - *Subgroups include:* Grunge, Graffiti
   - *Examples:* Curlz, Stencil, Playbill

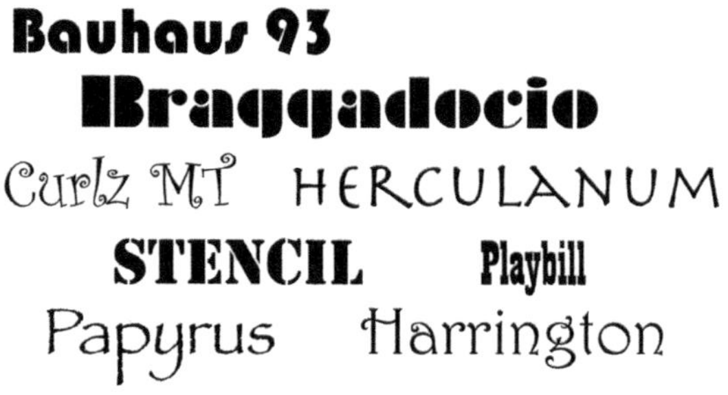

Bauhaus 93
Braggadocio
Curlz MT HERCULANUM
STENCIL   Playbill
Papyrus   Harrington

Figure 10.7

Examples of Decorative typefaces.

Adobe Fonts and Additional Sources

The Adobe applications come loaded with access to a lengthy list of fonts. These fonts are OpenType, a cross-platform font file format developed by Adobe and Microsoft. The OpenType format offers cross-platform compatibility, the same font file works on macOS and Windows computers. For more information about OpenType, access the reference provided at the end of this chapter (see *External Links Mentioned in the Chapter*).

Adobe's list of fonts is available as a *font dropdown menu* in both the *Options/ Control bar** and the *Character panel* in the Adobe Creative Cloud applications. This menu provides a list of fonts along with a "Sample" of each font (Figure 10.8). Fonts can be filtered based on type categories (*default:* All Classes), user-designated "favorite fonts" (star icon), and fonts similar to the currently selected font (double-wave icon). Access to the Adobe Typekit (Tk), a subscription service for fonts, is also available from this menu.

---

* The name of the bar that contains tool properties and is located below the application bar varies across applications; in Photoshop this bar is referred to as the *Options bar*, and in both Illustrator and InDesign the bar is known as the *Control bar*.

Graphic Design: Learn It, Do It

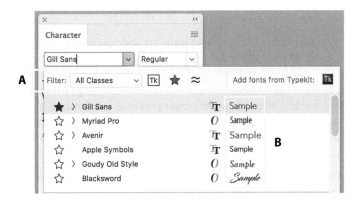

Figure 10.8

Photoshop Character panel: (A) sample typefaces; (B) *Row 1* (left to right): Show only fonts with classifications; Show fonts from Typekit (Tk); Show favorite fonts (star icon); Show similar fonts (double-wave icon); Add fonts from Typekit.

Should the occasion arise when the designer wants to expand their font options, font websites are resources similar to stock image websites. On these sites, some fonts are free for personal use, while others are available for purchase or license. Similar to acquiring a stock image, the designer should review the licensing options carefully. In addition to Adobe's *Typekit* (http://www.typekit.com), other potential sources include *DaFont.com* (http://www.dafont.com) and *Font Squirrel* (http://www.fontsquirrel.com).

Monospaced vs. Proportional Fonts

The same word can take up varying amounts of horizontal space depending on the nature of the selected typeface. The lines of text in Figure 10.9 illustrate the difference between *monospaced* and *proportional* fonts. In the monospaced font every letterform occupies the same horizontal space. In contrast, the space occupied by the proportional font varies based on the width of individual characters.

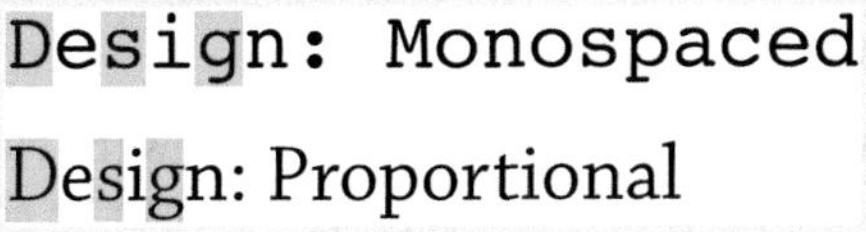

Design: Monospaced

Design: Proportional

Figure 10.9

Monospaced vs. proportional fonts. *Typeface:* Monospaced: Courier (40 pt.)/ Proportional: Chaparral Pro (40 pt.).

Legibility and Readability

Typography is assessed in terms of both legibility and readability. As designers, we need to be aware of both attributes when creating and formatting text. *Legibility* addresses the clarity of individual characters and words. Building on this, *readability* refers to the clarity of extended amounts of text (e.g., paragraph or page of text). Readable text affects how the viewer processes information in a design.

So, what makes a typeface readable? The short answer is a combination of factors. For a more thorough and useful response, let's review some of these factors that contribute to readable type.

Contrast: Contrast is achieved when two or more elements are markedly different from one another, for example, using serif typeface for a headline and sans serif typeface for body copy. Contrast is among the six principles of design introduced in *Chapter 2: The Elements and Principles of Design*. In typography, contrast can be created using typeface, size, style, color or weight.

Contrasts in type are used to reinforce *visual hierarchy*, a sense of order and organization within a design. The visual hierarchy helps to direct the viewer to the most important information first, and then guides the viewer's attention through the rest of the design.

Measure: The length of a line of text is known as its *measure*. An even measure is easy to read across multiple lines or a block of text. The use of columns can contribute to an even measure.

Here are a few tips related to line length:

- *Tip 1: Be mindful of where lines of text end*
  - Short lines or single words left hanging at the end of a paragraph are known as *widows*; those found at the top of a column are known as *orphans*.
  - In typography, it is a good practice to avoid widows and orphans to encourage visual balance and an ease of reading.
- *Tip 2: Limit centered text*
  - Limit the use of center alignment to headlines or single lines of text.
  - Avoid using center alignment for blocks of text.
  - Centered text requires that the viewer visually redefine the starting point for each line when reading. This is wasted energy and a potentially disrupting action.

Spacing: Use negative space in and around text to allow the viewer's eyes to easily scan the page. The following formatting properties can be adjusted to alter the amount of space between letters, words and lines.

- *Kerning [pronounced: kur-ning]:* The distance between two characters; how close or far apart characters are horizontally. This property is particularly useful for angled letters (e.g., A, V, W), when more negative space exists around the letterforms.

- *Tracking:* The horizontal distance between characters in a large block of text (or a word or a sentence).
- *Leading* [*pronounced: led*-ing]: The vertical space between rows of type, measured from baseline to baseline. Adjusting leading is similar to changing the line spacing in a word processing application (e.g., single spacing vs. double spacing). For easy-to-read blocks of text, the leading value should be *greater* than the font size, up to 1.5 times as great. For example, a 12 pt. font could successfully use leading between 12 and 18 pts.

Figure 10.10 illustrates these properties at work. In View 1, "Visit Your/NATIONAL/PARKS" presents the application's default spacing between the letters and the lines of text. In View 2, *tracking* has increased the spacing between the letters in "Visit Your." This change justifies the text on the first two lines, "Visit Your/NATIONAL," now vertically begin and end together. Next, *kerning* has decreased the space between the letters "P" and "A" in "PARKS," bringing the letters closer

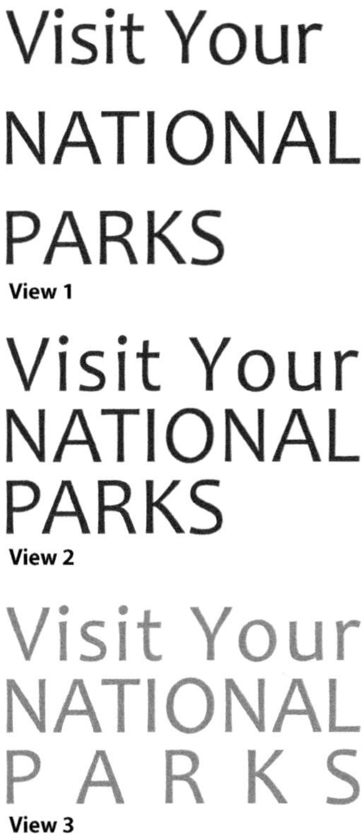

Visit Your
NATIONAL
PARKS
View 1

Visit Your
NATIONAL
PARKS
View 2

Visit Your
NATIONAL
P A R K S
View 3

Figure 10.10

Spacing example: tracking, kerning, leading. *View 1:* default spacing; *View 2:* spacing adjustments applied; and *View 3:* final design. *Typeface:* Candara.

together for a more natural look. Finally, *leading* has decreased the space between the three lines of text, bringing them closer together for a more polished look. In View 3, the tracking of "PARKS" has been increased to match the justification of the other two lines and the text color has been changed to create the final design.

Emphasis: When a term or phrase warrants special attention, use italics (most popular) or bold for emphasis. *Tip:* Avoid using underline for emphasis as this formatting suggests that the item is linked, as in hyperlinked, even when presented on a printed page. Across a project, choose one form of emphasis and be consistent. Too much emphasis can be distracting and can disrupt readability.

Contrast, measure, spacing and emphasis influence the layout of a single word, line or block of text and therefore the viewer's processing of the message. Working in unison, these factors contribute to increased readability of text.

Tips for Working with Multiple Typefaces

Tip 1: Limit of 3.

* Use no more than *three typefaces* in a single project.
* If this sounds too limiting, remember that within each typeface, there are multiple font sizes and styles (e.g., italics, bold, strong).

Tip 2: Similar x-height.

* When incorporating multiple typefaces into a design, select fonts that have a *similar x-height*. This detail will help with the alignment of characters and words.

Adobe's Type Properties

Applications in the Adobe Creative Cloud (Photoshop, Illustrator and InDesign) provide the means to create and alter text. Across applications, text created using the *Type Tool* (T) can be adjusted via the formatting properties available in the *Options/Control bar*. Additional formatting properties can be accessed through the *Character* and *Paragraph panels*. The paths to access these panels vary by application; however, once opened, the panels' formatting properties are similar across applications.

Accessing the Character and Paragraph Panels

* *Photoshop:* Window menu, select Character or Paragraph [Window menu > Character|Paragraph]
* *Illustrator:* Window menu, select Type, then Character or Paragraph [Window menu > Type > Character|Paragraph]
* *InDesign:* Window menu, select Type & Tables, then Character or Paragraph [Window menu > Type & Tables > Character|Paragraph]

Graphic Design: Learn It, Do It

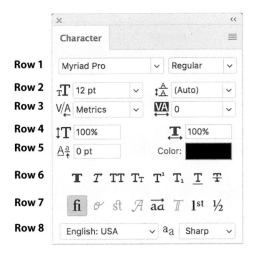

Figure 10.11

Character panel (Photoshop), properties listed beginning with *Row 1 (left to right):* Search for and select fonts (*default:* Myriad Pro), Set the font style (*default:* Regular); *Row 2:* Set the font size, Set the leading; *Row 3:* Set kerning between two characters, Set the tracking for the selected characters; *Row 4:* Vertically scale, Horizontally scale; *Row 5:* Set the baseline shift, Set the text color; *Row 6:* Faux Bold, Faux Italic, All Caps, Small Caps, Superscript, Subscript, Underline, Strikethrough; *Row 7:* Standard Ligatures, Contextual Alternates, Discretionary Ligatures, Swash, Stylistic Alternates, Tilting Alternates, Ordinals, Fractions; and *Row 8:* Set the language on selected characters for hyphenation and spelling, Set the anti-aliasing method (i.e., None, Sharp, Crisp, Strong, Smooth).

The *Character panel* provides options for formatting characters and letterforms (Figure 10.11). A tooltip containing the name of the property appears when the cursor is positioned over a symbol in this panel. These tooltips can be helpful while you are becoming familiar with the formatting properties.

The *Paragraph panel* provides formatting options for text, including alignment, justification, indentation, space before or after a paragraph and hyphenation (Figure 10.12). You may be familiar with some of these formatting properties as they are frequently used in word processing.

- *Alignment:* This property arranges content in a straight line and uses even spacing between words. Alignment options include Left, Center, Right (Figure 10.13). *Note:* These examples use *Lorem Ipsum placeholder text* for content; placeholder text is discussed in *Chapter 13: Page Layout.*
  - *Left-aligned text:* The left side of the paragraph is straight (or *flush*) and the right side is *ragged.*
  - *Center-aligned text:* Text is aligned down the vertical center of a block of text, so ragged edges are present on both the left and right sides. Centered text should only be used for short amounts of text, as it is demanding to read due to the variations in line length.

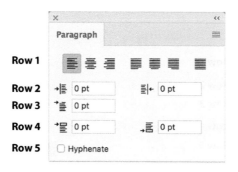

Row 1

Row 2   0 pt   0 pt

Row 3   0 pt

Row 4   0 pt   0 pt

Row 5   Hyphenate

Figure 10.12

Paragraph panel (Photoshop), properties listed beginning with *Row 1 (left to right)*: Align (Left align text, Center text, Right align text), Justify (Justify last left, Justify last centered, Justify last right), Justify All; *Row 2*: Indent left margin, Indent right margin; *Row 3*: Indent first line; *Row 4*: Add space before paragraph, Add space after paragraph; and *Row 5*: Automatic hyphenation.

- *Right-aligned text:* A ragged edge is produced on the left side of the paragraph and the straight edge on the right. The viewer is continually searching for the beginning of each line as this varies through a block of text due to the ragged edge. Text that uses this alignment is challenging to read.

Lorem ipsum dolor sit amet, consectetuer adipiscing elit, sed diam nonummy nibh euismod tincidunt ut laoreet dolore magna aliquam erat volutpat. Ut wisi enim ad minim veniam, quis nostrud exerci tation ullamcorper suscipit lobortis nisl ut aliquip ex ea commodo consequat. Duis autem vel eum iriure dolor in hendrerit in vulputate velit esse molestie consequat, vel illum dolore eu feugiat nulla

View 1

Lorem ipsum dolor sit amet, consectetuer adipiscing elit, sed diam nonummy nibh euismod tincidunt ut laoreet dolore magna aliquam erat volutpat. Ut wisi enim ad minim veniam, quis nostrud exerci tation ullamcorper suscipit lobortis nisl ut aliquip ex ea commodo consequat. Duis autem vel eum iriure dolor in hendrerit in vulputate velit esse molestie consequat, vel illum dolore eu feugiat nulla

View 2

Lorem ipsum dolor sit amet, consectetuer adipiscing elit, sed diam nonummy nibh euismod tincidunt ut laoreet dolore magna aliquam erat volutpat. Ut wisi enim ad minim veniam, quis nostrud exerci tation ullamcorper suscipit lobortis nisl ut aliquip ex ea commodo consequat. Duis autem vel eum iriure dolor in hendrerit in vulputate velit esse molestie consequat, vel illum dolore eu feugiat nulla

View 3

Figure 10.13

Alignment options: Left-aligned text, Center-aligned text, Right-aligned text. *Typeface:* Myriad Pro.

Lorem ipsum dolor sit amet,
consectetuer adipiscing elit,
sed diam nonummy nibh
euismod tincidunt ut laoreet
dolore magna aliquam erat
volutpat.
Ut wisi enim ad minim
veniam, quis nostrud exerci
tation ullamcorper suscipit
lobortis nisl ut aliquip ex ea
commodo.
Duis autem vel eum iriure
dolor in hendrerit in vulputate velit.

View 1

Lorem ipsum dolor sit amet,
consectetuer adipiscing elit,
sed diam nonummy nibh
euismod tincidunt ut laoreet
dolore magna aliquam erat
volutpat.
Ut wisi enim ad minim
veniam, quis nostrud exerci
tation ullamcorper suscipit
lobortis nisl ut aliquip ex ea
commodo.
Duis autem vel eum iriure
dolor in hendrerit in vulputate velit.

View 2

Lorem ipsum dolor sit amet,
consectetuer adipiscing elit,
sed diam nonummy nibh
euismod tincidunt ut laoreet
dolore magna aliquam erat
volutpat.
Ut wisi enim ad minim
veniam, quis nostrud exerci
tation ullamcorper suscipit
lobortis nisl ut aliquip ex ea
commodo.
Duis autem vel eum iriure
dolor in hendrerit in vulputate velit.

View 3

Lorem ipsum dolor sit amet,
consectetuer adipiscing elit,
sed diam nonummy nibh
euismod tincidunt ut laoreet
dolore magna aliquam erat
v o l u t p a t .
Ut wisi enim ad minim
veniam, quis nostrud exerci
tation ullamcorper suscipit
lobortis nisl ut aliquip ex ea
c o m m o d o .
Duis autem vel eum iriure
dolor in hendrerit in vulputate   velit.

View 4

Figure 10.14

Justification examples: (A) justify last left; (B) justify last centered; (C) justify last right; and (D) justify all. *Typeface:* Myriad Pro.

- *Justification:* This option produces neat, straight edges on both sides of a block of text (Figure 10.14). Justified text presents a formal appearance, and the text tends to take up less room than other alignments. However, to create the straight edges on each side of the block of text requires the words to be unevenly spaced. Gaps of white space (a.k.a. *rivers*) can appear awkwardly throughout the text. Justification options include Justify last line left, Justify last line centered, Justify last line right and Justify All.

Selecting Type for a Project

When it comes right down to it, selecting typefaces for a project is a subjective activity, and there is generally more than one right option. Your experiences and your environment will often influence your decision as much as any other factor. So, experiment with your design and try different solutions. As suggested in *Chapter 4: Defining the Project*, generating multiple options provides a good basis of comparison and conversation. Plan to solicit feedback from your peers and your client, as applicable. Think about how the typographic element(s) can enhance an overall design. Here are three goals for type within a design:

- *Readability:* The type should be easy to see and understand.
- *Functionality:* The type should communicate the intended message.
- *Engagement:* The type should attract and hold the viewer's attention.

With these goals in mind, revisit the project's stated purpose. What best suits the needs of the project and its audience? Does the subject matter naturally lend itself to one of the four type categories? Are there thematic or historical references that inspire the selection of a particular typeface? How might contrast be created among the type elements?

With the answers to these questions in hand, think about the hierarchy of information and its logical presentation. What information is most important? What is secondary? Think about how this organization of information can influence the viewer's comprehension of the message. Now, utilize the available typefaces and your ability to alter their appearance as necessary to incorporate meaningful text into your designs.

Looking Ahead

This chapter presented a great deal of information about type and its properties. Take some time to apply this knowledge to your work in Photoshop or look forward to applying these ideas in Illustrator and InDesign. Up next is an introduction to Adobe Illustrator, its workspace, tools and working with vector images.

Discussion

Discussion 10.1: Typeface Goals

When selecting typefaces for a project, the goals of readability, functionality and engagement should be priorities. In this context, *engagement* is described as attracting and holding the viewer's attention. Identify at least three ways that you could increase the engagement of the text presented in Figure 10.15, View 1. Which type properties would you adjust first?

If the position of the words is changed (see Figure 10.15, View 2), how does this affect the readability and functionality of the text?

Graphic Design: Learn It, Do It

View 1

Graphic Design | Learn It
Do It

View 2

Figure 10.15

Discussion 10.1. Typeface: American Typewriter.

Activity

Activity 10.1: Type Properties

Create a new document in the application of your choice. Use the *Type Tool* (T) to create a multiline block of text: HAVE A//GOOD DAY. Use the properties available via the *Character* and *Paragraph panels* to complete the following text edits:

- Change the font, its size and its color.
- Change the kerning to bring the letters "A V" closer together.
- Increase the tracking on Line 2, so the words "GOOD DAY" fit below Line 1.

External Links Mentioned in the Chapter

Font Resources

Adobe's Typekit | http://www.typekit.com

DaFont.com | http://www.dafont.com

Font Squirrel | http://www.fontsquirrel.com

Getting Started with Illustrator

Adobe Illustrator is the industry standard for creating vector images and artwork. Vectors are objects created using mathematical equations. No pixels are used in vector images, so the images can be resized without concern for pixelation or degradation of image quality. Vector images can be created from scratch or based on a photo or other image.

Illustrator Overview

This chapter begins with a high-level overview of Illustrator, introducing its workspace and tools. Some of these elements will be familiar from Photoshop, and others may seem foreign. Significant differences between the applications are noted throughout this chapter.

Illustrator provides an extensive collection of tools. This chapter features a subset of these, tools selected to get you quickly creating in Illustrator. When you are ready to expand your personal toolset, access the *Illustrator Online Help* resource, which is available at all times via the *Help menu* [Help menu > Illustrator Help...].

Notes to the Reader

This chapter is most effective when the Illustrator application is open in front of you while reading. This will allow you to learn and then do, navigating the interface and utilizing the tools. If you do not have access to the application, the included screen captures will serve as visual references for much of the content.

Creating an Illustrator File

When Illustrator opens, a *Home Screen** appears welcoming the designer to the application (Figure 11.1). In this dialog box, select either the *Create New...* or the *Open... button* located along the left side of the window to get started. Let's choose the *Create New... button*, which launches the *New Document dialog box*.

In the *New Document dialog box*, Illustrator provides a series of preset values based on the project type and expected output (Figure 11.2); these sets include Mobile, Web, Print, Film & Video and Art & Illustration. To proceed, select a set; let's choose the *Print set* and from the *Blank Document Presets* select *Letter* (612 × 792 pt.). Take a moment to review the *Preset Details*, the file properties

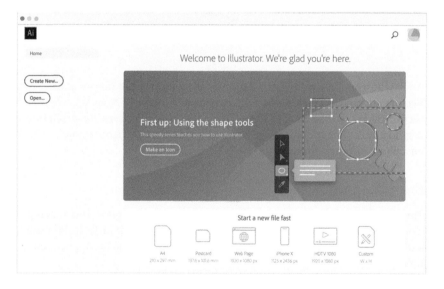

Figure 11.1

Home Screen dialog box.

---

* To disable the *Home Screen,* go to the Illustrator CC menu and access Preferences > General... and deselect *Show The Home Screen When No Documents Are Open.*

Graphic Design: Learn It, Do It

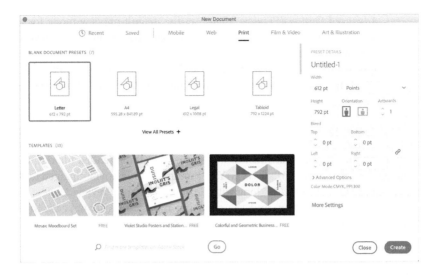

Figure 11.2

New Document dialog box, Print set > Letter preset selected.

associated with this selection. Once a blank document preset has been selected, the following preset properties can be reviewed and modified as needed to accommodate a project.

Preset Details (descriptions drawn from *Illustrator Online Help*)

- *Name:* Specify the name for this new document (*Default:* Untitled-1).
- *Size:* Specify the size of the artboard. [The working area in the file is referred to as the *artboard.*]
  - Width/Height, Unit of Measure.
- *Orientation:* Specify a page orientation for the document: Portrait (vertical) or Landscape (horizontal).
- *Artboards:* Specify the number of artboards in the document.
- *Bleed* (Top, Bottom, Left, Right):* Specify the position of the bleed along each side of the artboard. To use different values for different sides, delink the dimensions by clicking the chain icon.
- *Advanced Options/Color Mode:* Specify a color mode for the document (*Default:* CMYK Color).
- *Advanced Options/Raster Effects:* Specify the resolution for raster effects[†] in the document (*Default:* High [300 ppi]).

---

* A document *bleed* is the small area around the edge of a document that extends beyond the finished content on the page. When the document is printed, the bleed can be trimmed off in order to create a finished design that extends to the edge of the page.

† *Raster effects* are effects that produce pixels instead of vectors data.

- *Advanced Options/Preview Mode:* Set the default preview mode for the document (i.e., *Default* displays artwork created in the document in vector view with full color; *Pixel* displays artwork with a rasterized (pixelated) appearance; *Overprint* provides an "ink preview" that approximates how blending, transparency and overprinting will appear in color-separated output).

Unlike creating a new document in Photoshop, no *Resolution* field is provided since Illustrator's vector images are *resolution independent.* Another distinction between applications is that Illustrator assumes that the intended file output is print, so the default *Color Mode* is CMYK. The *Color Mode* can be changed under the *Advanced Options header,* along with *Raster Effects* and *Preview Mode.*

Click the *Create button,* and the resulting illustration file appears in the Illustrator workspace.

Artboards in Illustrator

A single Illustrator file can contain multiple artboards (1–1,000 artboards per document depending on the size of the artboards). Think of an artboard as a page (or a workspace) within a multipage document. When a finished design is exported, each artboard can be saved in a separate file or combined into a single file.

Saving an Illustration File

It is a good habit to save a new illustration file *before* creating content in the illustration. This practice can help the designer avoid losing work should the application or computer freeze and need to be restarted while they areworking. Throughout this book, you will be encouraged to save your work, early and often.

To save a new file, access the *File menu* and select the *Save As… menu command* [File menu > Save As… | ⇧⌘S]. This action launches the *Save As dialog box,* shown in Figure 11.3; here the file can be named, if this was not done when

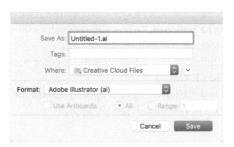

Figure 11.3

File menu > Save As….

Graphic Design: Learn It, Do It

creating the illustration file (in the *New Document dialog box*). *Tip:* When naming the file, remember to avoid using special characters and spaces in the file name. Also, be careful to not overwrite the provided file extension, which is included in the *Save As field*. This file extension matches the current file format (shown in the *Format dropdown menu*). Native Illustrator files are *Adobe Illustrator*, which use the (AI) file extension. If the file format needs to be changed, do so via the *Format dropdown menu*, selecting the desired file type. *Do not* type the desired file extension into the *Save As field* and assume the file type will be changed; this technique *will not* work and can prevent the file from opening in the future due to a disconnect between the listed file extension and the actual file type.

Finally, before saving the file, know *where* the illustration file will be saved. Select an appropriate location,* and then click the *OK button*. This action launches the *Illustrator Options dialog box*, which provides additional file options including compatibility with earlier versions of the application, compression and transparency. Click the *OK button* to accept the default values and to open the newly created illustration file in the workspace.

Illustrator Workspace Introduction

The Illustrator workspace is presented in Figure 11.4; the workspace is composed of the following labeled elements (descriptions drawn from *Illustrator Online Help*):

A. The *Illustrator menu bar*, also referred to as the *application bar*, provides access to the application's menus and menu commands.
B. The *Control panel* displays options for the currently selected *object*.
C. The *Tools panel* contains tools for creating and editing images, artwork and page elements.
D. The *document window* displays the file. [As previously stated, the working area is referred to as the *artboard*, this is where the image will be created.] If more than one file is open at a time, document windows can be tabbed and, in certain cases, grouped and docked.
E. The *status bar* is part of the document window; information about the image file is displayed here, including the image's current zoom level, current artboard in use, navigation control for multiple artboards and current tool in use.
F. *Panels* help the designer monitor and modify their work. By default, the Properties, Layers and Libraries panels are open. Additional panels can be accessed via the *Window menu*.

Adobe provides the ability to reset the Illustrator workspace to the *default workspace* when opening the application. Resetting the workspace returns the

---

* *Tip:* For designers using the macOS, pressing the down arrow located to the right of the *Where field* provides additional options for navigating to a specific location on the computer.

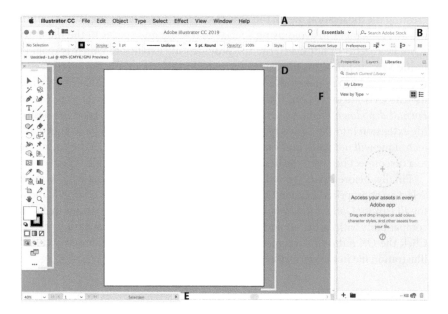

Figure 11.4

Illustrator workspace. (A) Illustrator menu / application bar, (B) Control panel, (C) Tools panel, (D) Document window, (E) Status bar, and (F) Panels.

tools and panels to their default settings. This option is useful while getting to know the workspace as you experiment with tools and their settings. To reset the workspace, hold down the following keyboard keys when starting Illustrator: *Option + Command + Shift* (macOS) or *Alt + Control + Shift* (Windows).

The Illustrator Menu Bar

Located at the top of the application's window, the *Illustrator menu bar* consists of a series of menus, including Illustrator CC, File, Edit, Object, Type, Select, Effect, View, Window and Help. Clicking on a menu name presents a list of related menu commands.

The Control Panel

Below the Illustrator menu bar in its default location, is the *Control panel*, which is *context-sensitive*; the contents change based on the *object* that is selected on the artboard. *Note:* In Photoshop, this area is referred to as the *Options bar*, and it is content-sensitive based on the *tool* that is selected in the Tools panel.

The top row of the Control panel includes the following shortcuts and options: a shortcut to the Home Screen (house icon); Arrange Documents dropdown menu;

Graphic Design: Learn It, Do It

Figure 11.5

Instances of the Control panel when different objects are selected on the artboard: (A) No Selection, (B) Path selection and (C) Type selection.

a shortcut to the Learn panel* (lightbulb icon); Workspace dropdown menu[†]; and a Search field (Adobe Stock, Adobe Help).

Figure 11.5 presents multiple instances of the Control panel, illustrating its contents when different objects are selected on the artboard (i.e., No Selection, Path selected and Type selected). Some tool properties available in the Control panel (e.g., stroke weight and brush definition) are common across objects, while others are specific to a particular object.

Tip: If the Control panel is not visible in the workspace, access: Window menu > Control.

The Tools Panel

Generally located on the left side of the application's workspace, the *Tools panel* provides designers with an extensive collection of tools with which to create. The *Illustrator CC 2019 Tools Panel Overview* presented in Figure 11.6 and continued in Figure 11.7 lists all of the Illustrator tools organized by broad function-based categories: Select, Draw, Paint, Type, Modify and Navigate. This guide is also available as a printable PDF file on the book's companion website. *Tip:* This is a useful reference to have available when learning the tools, their names and locations. A brief description of each tool's functionality is available via the *Illustrator Online Help*.

Tip: If the Tools panel is not visible in the workspace, access: Window menu > Toolbars > Advanced.

When interacting with the Tools panel, if the cursor hovers over a tool icon, the name of that tool appears as a *tool tip*[‡] adjacent to the cursor pointer (Figure 11.8). A *keyboard shortcut* is listed to the right of the tool name, when available. The designer can use keyboard shortcuts to select tools in the Tools panel and avoid shifting their attention between the artboard and the Tools panel while working on an illustration.

---

* The *Learn panel* provides a list of tutorials, project ideas and application updates; this panel can also be accessed via the Window menu [Window menu > Learn].

† *Workspace layouts* include the following options: Automation, Essentials (*default*), Essentials Classic, Layout, Painting, Printing and Proofing, Tracing, Typography and Web. These options can also be accessed via the Window menu [Window menu > Workspace].

‡ *Tool tips* are labels or short descriptions displayed when the cursor hovers over a tool or property. This feature is available across all Adobe applications and can be controlled via the application's preferences [Illustrator CC menu > Preferences > General > Show Tool Tips].

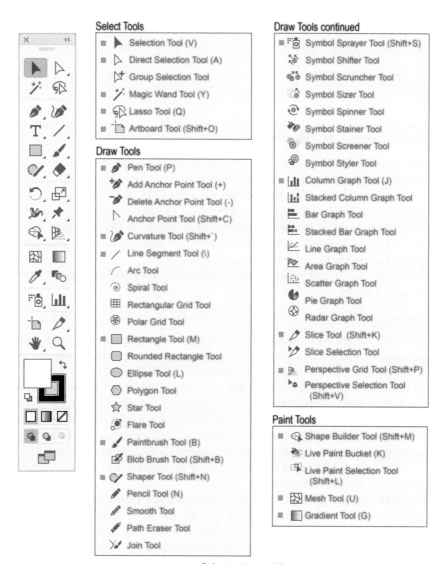

Select Tools

- ▶ Selection Tool (V)
- ▷ Direct Selection Tool (A)
- ▷⁺ Group Selection Tool
- ⚡ Magic Wand Tool (Y)
- ⟋ Lasso Tool (Q)
- ⧈ Artboard Tool (Shift+O)

Draw Tools

- ✒ Pen Tool (P)
- ✒⁺ Add Anchor Point Tool (+)
- ✒⁻ Delete Anchor Point Tool (-)
- ⌐ Anchor Point Tool (Shift+C)
- ✒ Curvature Tool (Shift+`)
- ⁄ Line Segment Tool (\)
- ⌒ Arc Tool
- ◎ Spiral Tool
- ⊞ Rectangular Grid Tool
- ⊛ Polar Grid Tool
- ▢ Rectangle Tool (M)
- ▢ Rounded Rectangle Tool
- ◯ Ellipse Tool (L)
- ⬡ Polygon Tool
- ☆ Star Tool
- ◎ Flare Tool
- ✎ Paintbrush Tool (B)
- ✎ Blob Brush Tool (Shift+B)
- ◔ Shaper Tool (Shift+N)
- ✏ Pencil Tool (N)
- 〰 Smooth Tool
- ✎ Path Eraser Tool
- ⟆ Join Tool

Draw Tools continued

- ⬚ Symbol Sprayer Tool (Shift+S)
- ⬚ Symbol Shifter Tool
- ⬚ Symbol Scruncher Tool
- ⬚ Symbol Sizer Tool
- ⬚ Symbol Spinner Tool
- ⬚ Symbol Stainer Tool
- ⬚ Symbol Screener Tool
- ⬚ Symbol Styler Tool
- ⫿ Column Graph Tool (J)
- ⫿ Stacked Column Graph Tool
- ☰ Bar Graph Tool
- ☰ Stacked Bar Graph Tool
- ⬳ Line Graph Tool
- ⬳ Area Graph Tool
- ⬚ Scatter Graph Tool
- ◕ Pie Graph Tool
- ⊛ Radar Graph Tool
- ⟋ Slice Tool (Shift+K)
- ⟋ Slice Selection Tool
- ⬚ Perspective Grid Tool (Shift+P)
- ⬚ Perspective Selection Tool (Shift+V)

Paint Tools

- ⬚ Shape Builder Tool (Shift+M)
- ⬚ Live Paint Bucket (K)
- ⬚ Live Paint Selection Tool (Shift+L)
- ⬚ Mesh Tool (U)
- ▢ Gradient Tool (G)

■ Default tool in group | Keyboard shortcuts included in parentheses

Figure 11.6

Illustrator CC 2019 Tools Panel Overview.

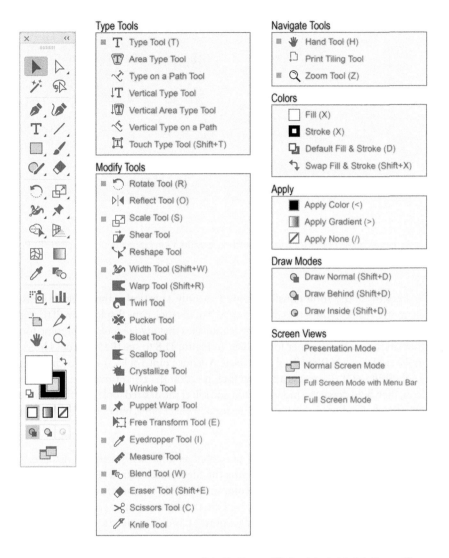

Type Tools

■ T Type Tool (T)
   ⬚T̲ Area Type Tool
   ⤢ Type on a Path Tool
   ↓T Vertical Type Tool
   ↓⬚T̲ Vertical Area Type Tool
   ⤢ Vertical Type on a Path
   ⬚T̲ Touch Type Tool (Shift+T)

Modify Tools

■ ↻ Rotate Tool (R)
   ▷|◀ Reflect Tool (O)
■ ⬚ Scale Tool (S)
   ⬚ Shear Tool
   ⤴ Reshape Tool
■ ⬭ Width Tool (Shift+W)
   ◀ Warp Tool (Shift+R)
   ⟳ Twirl Tool
   ✖ Pucker Tool
   ◀●▶ Bloat Tool
   ⬔ Scallop Tool
   ⬤ Crystallize Tool
   ⬤ Wrinkle Tool
■ ⤢ Puppet Warp Tool
   ⬚ Free Transform Tool (E)
■ ⤢ Eyedropper Tool (I)
   ⤢ Measure Tool
■ ⬚ Blend Tool (W)
■ ◆ Eraser Tool (Shift+E)
   ✂ Scissors Tool (C)
   ✐ Knife Tool

Navigate Tools

■ ✋ Hand Tool (H)
   ⬚ Print Tiling Tool
■ ◌ Zoom Tool (Z)

Colors

   ☐ Fill (X)
   ■ Stroke (X)
   ⬚ Default Fill & Stroke (D)
   ↰ Swap Fill & Stroke (Shift+X)

Apply

   ■ Apply Color (<)
   ▦ Apply Gradient (>)
   ⬚ Apply None (/)

Draw Modes

   ◉ Draw Normal (Shift+D)
   ◑ Draw Behind (Shift+D)
   ◉ Draw Inside (Shift+D)

Screen Views

   Presentation Mode
   ⬚ Normal Screen Mode
   ⬚ Full Screen Mode with Menu Bar
   Full Screen Mode

■ Default tool in group | Keyboard shortcuts included in parentheses

Figure 11.7

Illustrator CC 2019 Tools Panel Overview continued.

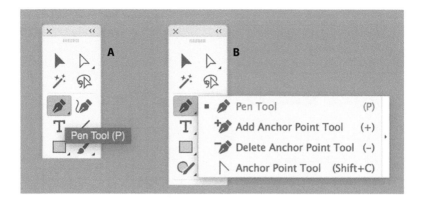

Figure 11.8

Tools panels: (A) Pen Tool *tool tip* and associated *keyboard shortcut;* and (B) Pen Tool selected, *hidden tools* visible.

Looking at the Tools panel in Figure 11.6, only a portion of the available tools is currently visible. Notice that more than half of the tool icons display a small triangle in their lower-right corner; this triangle indicates that *hidden tools* are present, tools that share space with other tools. Refer to Figure 11.8 to see the Pen Tool's hidden tools: Add Anchor Point Tool (+), Delete Anchor Point Tool (−) and Anchor Point Tool (Shift + C). To access a hidden tool, position the cursor over the visible tool icon, then hold down the mouse button and select the desired tool from the provided list of tools. Keyboard shortcuts can be used to select *some*, but not all, hidden tools.

The Document Window

By default, a *document window* is presented as a *tab* within the workspace. As shown in Figure 11.9, the tab contains the file name, zoom level (e.g., 100%, the current degree of magnification), color mode (CMYK) and preview mode (GPU Preview). When more than one file is open, the document windows are presented in a group of tabs docked below the Control panel. To select a specific file, click on its tab and the corresponding document window appears in front of the other open files. A tab can be rearranged by clicking on and dragging the window tab to

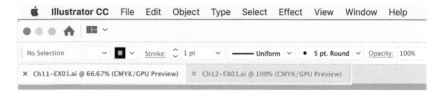

Figure 11.9

Document window tabs.

Graphic Design: Learn It, Do It

a new location within the group of tabs. To undock or *float* a document window from a group of windows, drag the window tab out of the group. *Tip:* If an open file is ever "misplaced" or not visible in the workspace, click on the *Window menu* and scroll to the bottom of this menu for a list of open files. Select the name of the desired file, and it will be brought to the forefront of all open files.

The Status Bar

The *status bar* is available for each illustration file. Located in the lower-left corner of the document window, the status bar displays the active image's current magnification (e.g., 40%), artboard navigation and current tool (*default*) (see Figure 11.4). To display other types of information in this bar, click the right arrow in the status bar, and from the *Show menu* select one of the available options (i.e., Artboard Name, Current Tool, Date and Time, Number of Undos or Document Color Profile).

Panels

In addition to being accessed from the Control panel, object properties can be accessed from individual *panels*. Panels help the designer monitor and modify images and their elements. The list of available panels is accessible from the *Window menu*. When a panel name is selected in the list, the associated panel is displayed in the workspace. A checkmark located to the left of the panel name indicates that the respective panel is open in the workspace.

A Subset of Tools

The following subset of tools is selected from the Tools panel. Accompanying the selected tools are each tool's keyboard shortcut command, if available, and the tool's respective description drawn from the *Illustrator Online Help*. As you read these descriptions, locate the tools in the Tools panel, refer to the *Illustrator CC 2019 Tools Panel Overview* (see Figure 11.6). Remember that some of these tools may be hidden.

Selection Tools

- The *Selection Tool* (V) selects entire objects.
- The *Direct Selection Tool* (A) selects points or path segments within objects.
- The *Lasso Tool* (Q) selects points or path segments within objects.

Draw Tools

- The *Pen Tool* (P) draws straight and curved lines to create objects.
  - The *Add Anchor Point Tool* (+) adds anchor points to paths.
  - The *Delete Anchor Point Tool* (−) deletes anchor points from paths.
  - The *Anchor Point Tool* (Shift + C) changes smooth points to corner points and vice versa.

- The *Line Segment Tool* (\) draws individual straight-line segments; related line tools include *Arc*, *Spiral*.
- The *Rectangle Tool* (M) draws squares and rectangles. Other shapes include *Rounded Rectangle, Ellipse* (L), *Polygon, Star.*
- The *Paintbrush Tool* (B) draws freehand and calligraphic lines, as well as art, patterns and bristle brush strokes on paths.

Navigate Tools

- The *Hand Tool* (H) moves the Illustrator artboard within the illustration window.
- The *Zoom Tool* (Z) increases and decreases the view magnification in the illustration window.

The lower portion of the Tools panel contains several useful features shown in Figure 11.10.

Colors

- The *Fill* (X) and *Stroke* (X) *Colors* set fill color and set stroke color.
- *Default* Fill and Stroke Colors (D).
- *Swap* Fill and Stroke Colors (Shift + X).
- Color options: *Color* (<), *Gradient* (>), *None* (/).

Drawing Modes

- Draw Normal (Shift + D to switch modes)
- Draw Behind (Shift + D to switch modes)
- Draw Inside (Shift + D to switch modes)

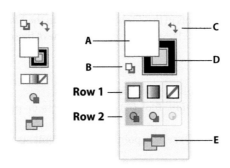

Figure 11.10

Tools panel: Single-column display (*left*); Two-column display (*right*). Colors: (A) Fill Color (X), (B) Default Fill and Stroke Colors (D), (C) Switch Fill and Stroke Colors (Shift + X), (D) Stroke Color (click to activate) (X). *Row 1:* Color (<), Gradient (>), None (/). *Row 2:* Draw Normal, Draw Behind, Draw Inside (Shift + D to shift modes) and (E) Change Screen Mode.

Change Screen Mode

- Presentation (Shift + F)
- Normal Screen Mode (F)
- Full Screen Mode with Menu Bar (F)
- Full Screen Mode (F)

Note: Additional tools are introduced in *Chapter 12: Illustrator Continued.*

In Illustrator (and InDesign), color is presented as either a *Fill* or a *Stroke*,* which is different than the Foreground and Background Colors used in Photoshop. A vector shape can contain color (Fill) and/or be outlined by color (Stroke).

Illustrator provides three options for the Fill and Stroke Colors of a path or object: Color, Gradient† and None. These options can be used in a variety of combinations, as shown in Figure 11.11. The color options can be selected *before* creating an object or applied *after* an object has been created. Panels accessed from the *Window menu* provide additional options for Color (i.e., Color, Color Guide, Color Themes and Swatches) and Gradient (i.e., Gradient).

Once a stroke has been applied, its properties can be adjusted in the *Control panel* or the *Stroke panel* (Figure 11.12) [Window menu > Stroke].

It is time to put this information to use. *Exercise 11.1* is designed to help you explore the Illustrator workspace and become familiar with the processes of creating and saving an illustration file. Review the exercise brief and get started.

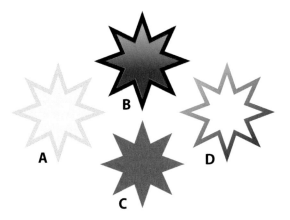

Figure 11.11

Color options: (A) *Fill:* Color, *Stroke:* Color; (B) *Fill:* Gradient, *Stroke:* Color; (C) *Fill:* Color, *Stroke:* None; and (D) *Fill:* None, *Stroke:* Gradient.

---

* The term *stroke* was first introduced in *Chapter 1: Breaking Down Design*, as a line used to outline a shape or an object.

† A *gradient* is a graduated blend of colors.

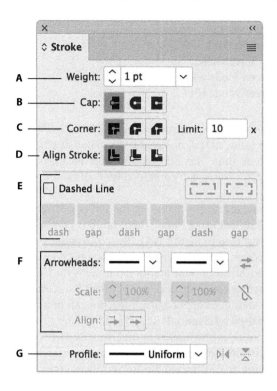

Figure 11.12

Stroke panel, Window menu > Stroke: (A) Weight; (B) Cap (Butt Cap, Round Cap, Projecting Cap); (C) Corner (Miter Join, Round Join, Bevel Join); (D) Align Stroke (Align Stroke to Center, Align Stroke to Inside, Align Stroke to Outside); (E) Dashed Line; (F) Arrowheads; and (G) Profile (variable width strokes are available to create a more hand-drawn look).

Exercise 11.1: Create, Save and Add Content to an Illustration File

Exercise brief: Create and save an illustration file, then use the following tools to add content to the file: Rectangle Tool (M), Paintbrush Tool (B) and Pen Tool (P).

Step 1: Create a new illustration file using the Print set and the Letter size (612 × 792 pt.).

- Begin at the *File menu* and select the *New... menu command* [File menu > New... | ⌘N].
- In the New Document dialog box, click on the Print set and from the Blank Document Presets select Letter (612 × 792 pt.).
- Click *Create* to generate the illustration file.

Step 2: Save the new illustration file as an Adobe Illustrator file. Use *Ch11-Ex01* for the file name, *Adobe Illustrator* for the file format and select an appropriate location for the file (Ch11-Ex01.ai).

- With the new file open in the workspace, access the *File menu* and select the *Save As... menu command* [File menu > Save As... | ⇧⌘S].
- In the *Save As dialog box*, enter the file name, *Ch11-Ex01*, verify the *Format* (Adobe Illustrator (ai)) and navigate to an appropriate location.
- Click *Save*.
- This action launches the *Illustrator Options dialog box*, click *OK* to accept the default settings and save the illustration file.
  - The additional file options include compatibility with earlier versions of Illustrator, compression and transparency.

Step 3: Add content to the illustration file using the Rectangle Tool (M).

- Select the *Rectangle Tool* (M) in the Tools panel, and then move the cursor over the artboard.
- Click and hold down the mouse button while moving the cursor diagonally away from its starting point.
  - A tool tip appears during this step adjacent to the cursor listing the dimensions of the shape being created (i.e., W: Width; H: Height).
- When the shape reaches its desired size, release the mouse button.
  - The colors of the shape reflect the current *Fill* and *Stroke Colors*, which are visible in the lower portion of the Tools panel (see Figure 11.10).

Until another tool is selected, in the Tools panel or using a keyboard shortcut, the active tool will remain the Rectangle Tool (M). *Tip:* The *Selection Tool* (V) is a good "neutral" tool to select between tasks; this choice can prevent additional content from being accidentally added to the illustration file.

Step 4: Change the Fill and Stroke Colors of the rectangle. To complete this change, first select the shape using the Selection Tool (V).

- Choose the *Selection Tool* (V) in the Tools panel and click once on the shape created in Step 3.
  - If the *Fill Color* of the shape is *None*, the *stroke of the shape* must be clicked in order to select the shape.
  - *Note:* When the *Fill Color* of the shape is *None*, there is no content to click on within the shape. Symbolically, *None* is represented by a white square with a red diagonal line through it in the Tools panel and in other instances of color chips.
- Use the *Fill* and *Stroke color chips* in the lower portion of the Tools panel *or* in the Control panel to change the *Fill Color*.

- In the Tools panel, if the *Fill Color* is in the foreground of the color chips (in front of the Stroke Color), double-click on the Fill Color.
  - However, if the *Stroke Color* is in the foreground, click once on the Fill Color to activate it (bringing it to the foreground of the color chips or the active position), then double-click on the Fill Color.
- Double-clicking on the Fill Color opens the familiar *Color Picker dialog box* (Figure 11.13), which presents multiple methods for representing a color (i.e., HSB, RGB, #: Hexadecimal, CMYK). Refer to *Chapter 3: Color in Design* for a review of the different color modes.
- Click anywhere within the gradient located on the left side of the *Color Picker dialog box* to select a new Fill Color.
  - To change the range of available colors within the gradient, click on the desired hue in the spectrum of colors located to the right of the gradient.
  - The new color will be shown *above* the current color chip located near the center of the dialog box.
- Click *OK* to change the Fill Color.

To change the Stroke Color, use the same process. First, confirm that the *Stroke Color* in the Tools panel is in the active position (in front of the Fill Color); then, double-click on the Stroke Color to open the *Color Picker dialog box*.

Step 5: Save the file.

- Return to the *File menu* and select *Save* [File menu > Save] or try the following keyboard shortcut command, ⌘S (Command + S).

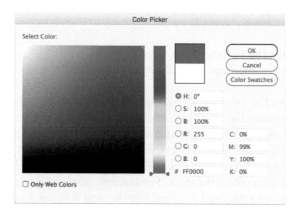

Figure 11.13

Color Picker dialog box.

Graphic Design: Learn It, Do It

Congratulations, you have created your first vector. Let's pause here and discuss vectors and their components.

Introduction to Vectors

Vector images are made up of a collection of paths. A *path* is composed of one or more straight or curved *segments*. The path featured in Figure 11.14 is made up of two curved-line segments. At the beginning and end of each segment is an *anchor point*. An anchor point located at the end of a path is referred to as an *endpoint*.* A path can be *closed*, such as the rectangle created in *Exercise 11.1*; or, a path can be *open*, such as the wavy line in Figure 11.14. A closed path begins and ends at the same endpoint, while an open path has two distinct endpoints. The shape of a path can be changed by adjusting its anchor points, direction lines or the path segment itself.

Direction lines are used to achieve curved-line segments. At the end of each direction line is a *direction point*, which can be moved using the *Direct Selection Tool* (A). The *angle* of a direction line determines the *slope* of a curve, while the *length* of a direction line determines the *height* or *depth* of a curve.

The *Selection Tool* (V) is used to select an entire path (or object). With the path selected, it can be resized, rotated or repositioned. Notice the *handles* positioned on the sides and in the corners of the shape; these handles can be used to alter the shape. In contrast, the *Direct Selection Tool* (A) is used to select a specific anchor

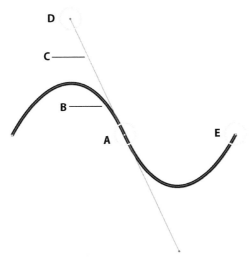

Figure 11.14

A path and its components: (A) anchor point, (B) path segment, (C) direction line, (D) direction point, and (E) endpoint.

---

* All endpoints are anchor points; however, not all anchor points are endpoints.

---

11. Getting Started with Illustrator   221

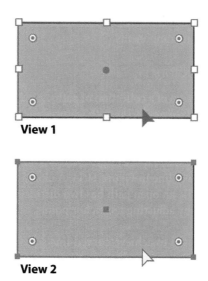

View 1

View 2

Figure 11.15

Selected paths: *View 1*: selected with Selection Tool (V), and *View 2*: selected with Direct Selection Tool (A).

point, a group of anchor points or a direction point. A selected anchor point or direction point can be repositioned to affect a path segment. The rectangles in Figure 11.15 illustrate the differences between paths selected by the *Selection Tool* (V) and the *Direct Selection Tool* (A).

Let's apply this information to the *Exercise 11.1* illustration file.

Step 6: Use the Paintbrush Tool (B) to create an open and a closed path.

- Select the *Paintbrush Tool* (B) in the Tools panel and paint an open path (e.g., the letters "C" or "S") and a closed path (e.g., the letter "O").
- Make sure that each path has a *Fill Color* and a *Stroke Color* applied to it. If needed, select the path using the *Selection Tool* (V) and apply the necessary color(s). Notice how the open path creates a straight line of the Fill Color between the two endpoints.

Step 7: Use the Direct Selection Tool (A) to adjust the shape of the closed path.

- First, deselect all objects on the artboard. This is easily accomplished via the *Select menu* and the *Deselect menu command* [Select menu > Deselect | ⇧⌘A].
- Choose the *Direct Selection Tool* (A) in the Tools panel and click once on the stroke of the closed path.

- This action makes visible all of the anchor points used to create the path.
- When the cursor rolls over the path (*path*) or an anchor point (*anchor*), corresponding labels are displayed.
- Position the cursor over an anchor point and then click once on the anchor point to select it.
  - When selected, the anchor point is filled in (blue square) and any associated direction lines (and direction points) are also selected.
- Click and hold down the mouse button on the same anchor point and move the mouse.
  - As the position of the mouse changes, the shape of the path changes.
- When satisfied with the altered shape, release the mouse button.
- Use the *Direct Selection Tool* (A) to fine-tune the shape by changing the position and length of a direction handle.
  - Click on and drag a *direction point*, which controls the direction line (*handle*).
  - *Tip:* Remember, the *angle* of a direction line determines the *slope* of a curve, while the *length* of a direction line determines the *height* or *depth* of a curve.

There are times when a path has too many or too few anchor points to achieve the desired shape. Illustrator provides tools to facilitate each of these scenarios.

- The *Delete Anchor Point Tool* (−) deletes anchor points from a path.
- The *Add Anchor Point Tool* (+) adds anchor points to paths.

Note: These tools are hidden tools sharing space with the *Pen Tool* (P). Let's use each of these tools to alter the appearance of the closed path.

Step 8: Remove or add anchor points from the closed path to alter its appearance.

- First, deselect all objects on the artboard [Select menu > Deselect | ⇧⌘A].
- Use the *Direct Selection Tool* (A) to click once on the closed path to make visible all of its anchor points.
- Select the *Delete Anchor Point Tool* (−) and click once on one of the anchor points.
  - This action eliminates the selected anchor point, which affects the overall shape of the path.
  - *Note:* If the *Delete Anchor Point Tool* (−) is clicked anywhere else on the artboard, the following Illustrator alert is presented, *Please use the delete anchor point tool on an anchor point of a path.* Click *OK* or press the *ESC key* on the keyboard to close this window and try again.
- Select the *Add Anchor Point Tool* (+) and click on the path to add an anchor point.

- *Note:* If the *Add Anchor Point Tool* (+) is clicked anywhere else on the artboard, the following Illustrator alert appears, *Please use the add anchor point tool on a segment of a path.* Click *OK* or press the *ESC* key on the keyboard to close this window and try again.
- Use the *Direct Selection Tool* (A) to adjust the position of the new anchor point and/or its direction lines (and direction points).

Step 9: Save the file.

- Select *Save* from the *File menu* [File menu > Save | ⌘S].

Corner Points and Smooth Points

Paths use two kinds of *anchor points*, corner points and smooth points, to connect line segments, as shown in Figure 11.16. A *corner point* indicates that a path changes direction abruptly. A *smooth point* joins path segments that are

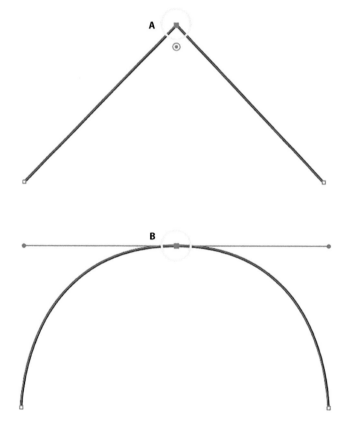

Figure 11.16

Points: (A) corner point and (B) smooth point.

Graphic Design: Learn It, Do It

connected as a continuous curve. A smooth point includes one or two direction lines, which can be repositioned to impact the curvature of the path segment. A path can be created using a combination of corner and smooth points or one type exclusively. *Note:* A corner point can be converted into a smooth point, and vice versa.

Introducing the Pen Tool

The *Pen Tool* (P) is one of the most popular tools in Illustrator for drawing paths. Depending on how it is used, the Pen Tool (P) can create *either* corner points or smooth points.

- *Corner Point:* Click and release the mouse button to create a corner point.
- *Smooth Point:* Click and hold down the mouse button *and* move the mouse away from the anchor point to create a direction line (and direction point), *then* release the mouse button. This action creates a smooth point. *Tip:* If you forget to hold down the mouse button while moving the mouse, use the *Undo menu command* to step backward and try again [Edit menu > Undo | ⌘Z].

Let's use the Pen Tool (P) to create a series of paths that utilize the different point types. Before starting each path, read through the provided steps in their entirety and review the corresponding figure, which provides a sort of blueprint or guide for the steps involved.

Step 10: Turn on the Document Grid [View menu > Show Grid | ⌘'].

- The *Document Grid* is a useful resource when creating evenly spaced or aligned path segments. This will be helpful in the upcoming tasks.

Step 11: Use the Pen Tool (P) to re-create the path in Figure 11.18; this path is made of corner points exclusively.

In preparation for creating this path, select the *Pen Tool* (P) and then set the *Fill Color* to *None** and the *Stroke Color* to *Black*. When the cursor is positioned over the artboard, notice its appearance; the tool state indicates that it is prepared to begin a path (see Figure 11.17A).

The path will be created working from left to right, beginning at the endpoint represented by the green dot in Figure 11.18.

- *Endpoint 1:* Click once and release the mouse button to create the first anchor point (*Endpoint 1*).

---

* A *Fill Color* other than *None* can prevent the designer from seeing parts of the path as it is being created. *Tip:* Apply a Fill Color after the path has been created.

Pen Tool States

The appearance of the cursor changes depending on how the Pen Tool (P) is being used; each state represents an action in progress or an action that is about to be performed. A guide to these *Pen Tool states* is presented in Figure 11.17 as a reference. Two views of each tool state are provided: the first view features the Pen Tool (P) as it appears naturally; the second instance presents the crosshair option, which is visible when the *Caps Lock key* on the keyboard is turned on while using the Pen Tool (P). *Tip:* Do not get overwhelmed by the different tool states, they are simply included for reference. The more that you work with the Pen Tool (P), the more familiar the tool states will become.

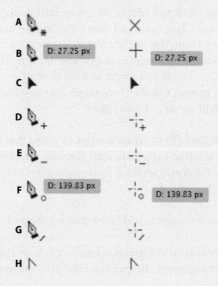

Figure 11.17

Pen tool states, default appearance *(left)*, crosshair appearance *(right)*: (A) prepared to begin path; (B) in progress creating or editing path (with grid coordinates); (C) mouse button is pressed; (D) ready to add an anchor point to path; (E) ready to remove an anchor point from path; (F) hovered over beginning point of path or to close path; (G) hovered over endpoint of existing path to continue path; and (H) ready to convert path or anchor point.

- Move the cursor to the right, into position for *Anchor Point 2*.
  - While the cursor is moving across the artboard, its appearance includes a tool tip displaying grid coordinates (see Figure 11.17B).
- *Anchor Point 2:* Click once and release the mouse button to create the second anchor point.

Graphic Design: Learn It, Do It

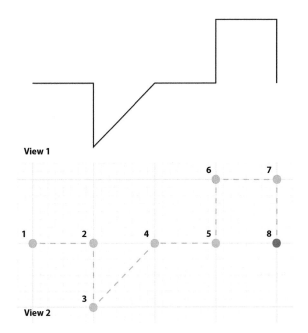

Figure 11.18

Path created using corner points. *View 1:* finished path; *View 2:* guide for creating the path; *Endpoints:* green and red dots; *Anchor points:* blue dots; *Path segment:* dashed line.

- Move the cursor down, into position for *Anchor Point 3.*
  - *Tip:* Holding down the *Shift key* on the keyboard while moving the cursor constrains the angle of the path to 45°, 90°, 135° or 180°. Release the Shift key *after* the anchor point has been created to preserve the angle.
- *Anchor Point 3:* Click once and release the mouse button to create the third anchor point.
- Continue working from left to right following the guide provided in Figure 11.18. Create an anchor point at each of the blue dots.
  - As the cursor moves from position to position, a preview of the path accompanies the cursor along with a tool tip containing grid coordinates.
- *Endpoint 8:* Click once and release the mouse button to create the final anchor point at the red dot (*Endpoint 8*).
- Press the *Return/Enter key* on the keyboard to end the path.
  - Move the cursor and notice that the cursor has returned to its original appearance, confirming that the path has ended (see Figure 11.17A).

Step 12: Save the file.

- From the *File menu*, select *Save* [File menu > Save | ⌘S].

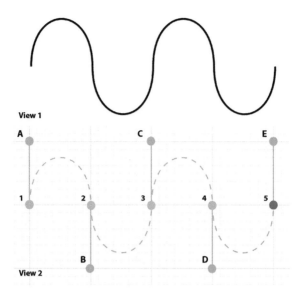

Figure 11.19

Path created using smooth points. *View 1:* finished path; *View 2:* guide for creating the path; *Endpoints:* green and red dots; *Anchor points:* blue dots; *Direction lines:* orange lines; *Direction points:* orange dots; *Path segment:* dashed line.

Step 13: Use the Pen Tool (P) to re-create the path in Figure 11.19; this path is made up of only smooth points.

In preparation for creating this path, select the *Pen Tool* (P) and then set the *Fill Color* to *None* and the *Stroke Color* to *Black*. When the cursor is positioned over the artboard, notice its appearance, the tool state indicates that it is prepared to begin a path (see Figure 11.17A).

The path will be created working from left to right, beginning at the endpoint represented by the green dot in Figure 11.19. *Do not* click on the orange dots; these represent *direction points* (not anchor points), which are created naturally when a direction line (orange line) is generated.

- *Endpoint 1:* Click and hold down the mouse button to create the first anchor point (*Endpoint 1*) *and* move the cursor to *Direction Point A, then* release the mouse button.
  - Onscreen, you should see the anchor point and a direction line (and direction point) above *and* below the anchor point (*Endpoint 1*).
  - *Note:* The direction lines (and points) do not contain content and will not be seen in the final illustration. These elements are used to control the appearance of the path.
- Move the cursor to the right, into position for *Anchor Point 2.*

Graphic Design: Learn It, Do It

- *Anchor Point 2:* Click and hold down the mouse button to create the second anchor point (*Anchor Point 2*) *and* move the cursor to *Direction Point B, then* release the mouse button.
- Move the cursor to the right, into position for *Anchor Point 3.*
- *Anchor Point 3:* Click and hold down the mouse button to create the third anchor point (*Anchor Point 3*) *and* move the cursor to *Direction Point C, then* release the mouse button.
- Continue working from left to right following the guide provided in Figure 11.19. Create an anchor point at the next blue dot along with a corresponding direction line (and direction point).
- *Anchor Point/Endpoint 5:* Click and hold down the mouse button to create the final anchor point (*Endpoint 5*) *and* move the cursor to *Direction Point E, then* release the mouse button.
- Press the *Return/Enter key* on the keyboard to end the path.
  - Move the cursor and notice that the cursor has returned to its original appearance, confirming that the path has ended (see Figure 11.17A).

Step 14: Save the file.

- From the *File menu,* select *Save* [File menu > Save | ⌘S].

It is good to practice creating corner and smooth points. Most illustrations created with the Pen Tool (P) use a combination of corner points *and* smooth points, so let's review the steps involved with that process next.

Step 15: Use the Pen Tool (P) to reproduce a path created using a combination of corner and smooth points (Figure 11.20). There are multiple ways to create this path; two options are presented.

- *Option 1:* Use *both* corner and smooth points while the path is being created. This process involves converting anchor points as they are created to accommodate the transitions between the straight- and curved-line segments.
  Working from left to right, follow the guide provided in Figure 11.20 to create the path.
  - *Endpoint 1:* Create a corner point by clicking once and releasing the mouse button (*Endpoint 1*).
  - Move the cursor to the right, into position for *Anchor Point 2.*
  - *Anchor Point 2:* Create a corner point by clicking once and releasing the mouse button (*Anchor Point 2*).
  - *Convert Anchor Point 2:* Now, convert the corner point into a smooth point.

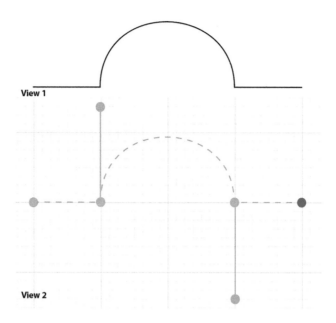

View 1

View 2

Figure 11.20

Path created using corner points and smooth points. *View 1:* finished path; *View 2:* guide for creating the path; *Endpoints:* green and red dots; *Anchor points:* blue dots; *Direction lines:* orange lines; *Direction points:* orange dots; *Path segment:* dashed line.

- *Why?* The smooth point (and its direction line and direction point) will produce the first half of the curved path between *Anchor Points 2* and *3.*
- With the cursor positioned over *Anchor Point 2,* click and hold down the mouse button *and* move the cursor to *Direction Point A,* then release the mouse button.
  - The only visible difference onscreen will be the addition of a *direction line* (and a *direction point*) attached to *Anchor Point 2.*
  - This action *converts* the corner point into a smooth point.
- Move the cursor to the right, into position for *Anchor Point 3.*
- *Anchor Point 3:* Create a smooth point by clicking and holding down the mouse button (*Anchor Point 3*) *and* moving the cursor to *Direction Point B,* then release the mouse button.
  - This smooth point controls the second half of the curved path between *Anchor Points 2* and *3.*
- *Convert Anchor Point 3:* Now, convert the smooth point into a corner point.

Graphic Design: Learn It, Do It

- *Why?* If the smooth point was left as is, and then *Anchor Point 4* was created, the line segment between *Anchor Points 3* and *4* would be curved and not straight.
- Position the cursor over *Anchor Point 3*, then click and release the mouse button.
- This action *converts* the smooth point into a corner point.
- Move the cursor to the right, into position for *Anchor Point 4.*
- *Endpoint 4:* Click once and release the mouse button to create the final anchor point at the red dot (*Endpoint 4*).
- Press the *Return/Enter key* on the keyboard to end the path.
- *Option 2:* Create all of the anchor points as corner points, then use the *Anchor Point Tool* (Shift + C) to convert *Anchor Points 2* and *3* into smooth points. Then, use the *Direct Selection Tool* (A) to alter direction lines in order to flatten the appropriate line segments.

Working from left to right, follow the guide provided in Figure 11.20 to create this path.

- Create a corner point at each of the four anchor points, represented by the green, blue and red dots in Figure 11.20.
  - Click once and release the mouse button to create a corner point.
  - Move the cursor into position for the next anchor point.
  - Repeat these steps.
  - After the final anchor point is created (*Endpoint 4*), press the *Return/Enter key* on the keyboard to end the path.
- Select the *Anchor Point Tool* (Shift + C) from the Tools panel.
  - This tool will be used to convert the second and third corner points into smooth points.
  - *Note:* The *Anchor Point Tool* (Shift + C) is a hidden tool sharing space with the *Pen Tool* (P).
- Convert *Anchor Point 2* from a corner point into a smooth point.
  - Position the cursor over *Anchor Point 2,* then click and hold down the mouse button. While still holding down the mouse button, move the cursor to *Direction Point A, then* release the mouse button.
  - During this conversion process, the first line segment will become curved as direction lines are created (Figure 11.21); that is okay.
- Flatten the first line segment, located between Anchor Points 1 and 2, by returning *Direction Point C* to *Anchor Point 2.*
  - Choose the *Direction Selection Tool* (A) in the Tools panel.
  - Position the cursor over the *Direction Point C.* Press and hold down the mouse button and move the direction point toward *Anchor Point 2.*
    - As the direction line is shortened, the first line segment flattens.
  - When the first line segment is flat, release the mouse button.

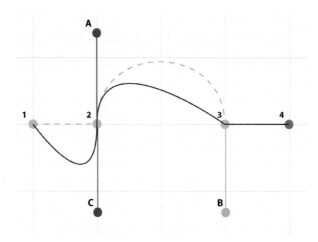

Figure 11.21

Path created using corner points and smooth points.

- Convert *Anchor Point 3* from a corner point into a smooth point.
  - Select the *Anchor Point Tool* (Shift + C) from the Tools panel.
  - Position the cursor over *Anchor Point 3*, then click and hold down the mouse button *and* move the cursor to *Direction Point B, then* release the mouse button.
- Flatten the last line segment by returning *Direction Line B* to *Anchor Point 3.*
  - Choose the *Direction Selection Tool* (A) in the Tools panel.
  - Position the cursor over the *Direction Point B.* Press and hold down the mouse button *and* move the direction point toward *Anchor Point 3.*
  - When the last line segment is flat, release the mouse button.
- The path should now resemble Figure 11.20.

Nice work re-creating the paths represented in Figures 11.18 through 11.20.

Step 16: Save the file.

- Select *Save* from the *File menu* [File menu > Save | ⌘S].

Well done, you have completed your first Illustrator exercise. Hopefully, you are becoming familiar with the Illustrator workspace. Before continuing, let's discuss some *Need to Know Fundamentals,* important nuggets of information that will facilitate your work in Illustrator.

Need to Know Fundamentals

Undoing Your Work

When performing a task, it is helpful to know how to undo that task. Under the *Edit menu*, the *Undo... menu command* allows the most recent operation to be undone [Edit menu > Undo | ⌘Z]. Illustrator supports multiple levels of Undo. In case too many tasks are undone, Illustrator also provides a *Redo menu command* [Edit menu > Redo | ⇧⌘Z].

To undo all of the changes made to a file since it was last saved, select the *Revert menu command* available from the *File menu* [File menu > Revert]. This menu command returns an image file to its last saved state.

Shape Tools

By default, the *shape tools* create rectangles, rounded rectangles and ellipses. These tools can also create squares, rounded squares and circles, respectively. To do so, hold down the *Shift key* on the keyboard while drawing the shape. *Tip:* Release the mouse button *before* the Shift key to preserve the shape.

Objects created using the shape tools can be created from the center point of the shape outward. *Tip:* Turn on the *Document Grid* before attempting this technique [View menu > Show Grid | ⌘']. Use an intersection of guidelines as the center point for a shape, growing the shape out from that point. Place the cursor at one of these intersection points, then hold down the *Option key* while drawing the shape outward from the center point. *Tip:* Release the mouse button *before* the Option key to preserve the shape.

To create a circle using this method, hold down *both* the *Shift* and *Option keys* before or while using the *Elliptical Marquee Tool* (M) to draw the circle. Release the mouse button *first*, then the Shift and Option keys to preserve the shape.

Closing an Open Path

There will be times when the designer needs to close an open path, such as the letter "C." One way to close this shape is by using the *Pen Tool* (P).

Start by first deselecting all objects on the artboard [Select menu > Deselect | ⇧⌘A]. Then, choose the *Pen Tool* (P) in the Tools panel and position the cursor over one of the endpoints of the open path. When positioned over an endpoint, the cursor appearance changes (see Figure 11.17E). Click once on the *endpoint*; this action continues the path where it previously ended.

Now use the *Pen Tool* (P) to continue the path to the other endpoint. When the cursor is close to the endpoint, its appearance changes (see Figure 11.17F). Click on the *endpoint* to close the path. The cursor should return to its original state (see Figure 11.17A).

Creating and Applying a Gradient

A *gradient* is a graduated blend between two or more colors or between shades of the same color. *Gradient* is one of the *Fill* and *Stroke Color* options for an object in both Illustrator and InDesign. Gradients can be *linear, radial* or *freeform*, as shown in Figure 11.22. A *Linear gradient* presents shades from the *starting color stop* to the *ending color stop* in a straight line. A *Radial gradient* presents shades from the starting color stop to the ending color stop in a circular pattern. A *Freeform gradient** presents a combination of colors within a shape in such a way that the blending appears natural.

In the Adobe Creative Cloud applications, gradients are defined by a series of color stops in a gradient bar. A *stop* is the point where a gradient changes from one color to another. In the *Gradient panel* (Figure 11.23), each stop is identified by a circle located beneath the *gradient slider* [Window menu > Gradient]. By default, the *midpoint* of a gradient is 50% between the colors. The position of the midpoint, represented by a diamond icon above the gradient slider, can be adjusted to affect the distribution of colors.

There are multiple ways to apply a gradient to an object; here is one method.

- First, select an object using the *Selection Tool* (V).
- Next, choose the *Gradient Tool* (G) from the Tools panel.
- Using the Gradient Tool (G), click once on the object.
  - This action fills the object with the *Gradient* value shown in the *Tools panel* (below the Fill and Stroke Colors) (Figure 11.24, View 1).

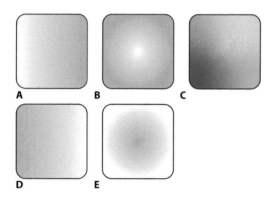

Figure 11.22

Gradient examples: (A) linear, (B) radial, (C) freeform, (D) linear reversed, and (E) radial reversed.

---

* The *Freeform gradient* was added to Illustrator in the Illustrator CC 2019 release; it can only be applied on the fill of an object. In contrast, Linear and Radial gradients can be applied to *both* the fill and the stroke of an object.

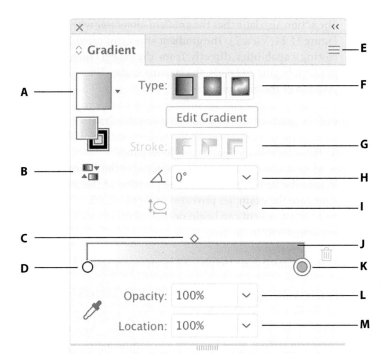

Figure 11.23

Gradient dialog box, Window menu > Gradient: (A) Gradient (Gradient Swatches available from dropdown menu); (B) Reverse; (C) Midpoint (diamond icon); (D) Starting color stop; (E) Gradient panel menu; (F) Type (Linear, Radial, Freeform); (G) Stroke (Apply gradient within stroke, Apply gradient along stroke, Apply gradient across stroke); (H) Angle; (I) Aspect Ratio; (J) Gradient slider; (K) Ending color stop; (L) Opacity; and (M) Location.

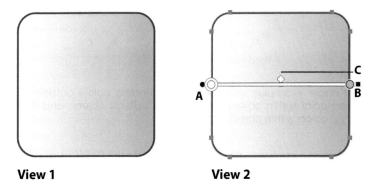

View 1   **View 2**

Figure 11.24

Gradient Annotator, *View 1:* Gradient, *View 2:* Gradient annotator: (A) starting color stop, (B) ending color stop, and (C) midpoint.

- The action also launches the *gradient annotator* within the object (see Figure 11.24, View 2). The gradient annotator provides basic gradient editing capabilities directly from the object, including where the gradient begins and ends, the starting and ending color stops and the position of the midpoint.

The angle of the gradient can be changed using the Gradient Tool (G).

- Select the *Gradient Tool* (G) in the Tools panel.
- Draw a line across the object corresponding to the desired gradient angle.
  - Where the line begins marks the position of the *starting color stop*. Compare the examples provided in Figure 11.25.
  - *Note:* The gradient can begin outside of the object limiting the colors presented within the shape.

The gradient annotator can also be used to change a color in the gradient.

- To initiate a change, double-click on the *color stop* to be changed.
- This action launches either the *Color* or *Swatches panel* providing multiple ways to adjust the color [Window menu > Color | Swatches].
- The gradient reflects any change in color immediately.

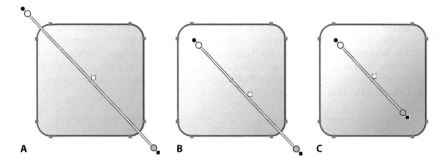

Figure 11.25

Gradient angle examples: (A) starting and ending colors outside of object; (B) starting color within object, ending color outside object; and (C) starting and ending colors within object.

The colors in a gradient can also be adjusted via the *Gradient panel* [Window menu > Gradient]. Here additional colors can be added to a gradient creating a multicolor gradient, as shown in Figure 11.26. In the following example, colors from the *Swatches panel* will be added to the gradient slider [Window menu > Swatches].

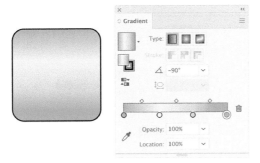

Figure 11.26

Multicolor gradient and corresponding Gradient panel with dropdown arrow highlighted, Window menu > Gradient.

- Position the cursor over a color in the Swatches panel.
- Then, click and hold down the mouse button while dragging the color from the Swatches panel to the Gradient panel. Position the cursor over the gradient slider where the new color will be added and then release the mouse button.
  - The gradient should reflect the additional color.
- Continue adding colors as desired.
  - As colors are added, additional midpoints are created between the color stops, allowing for further gradient adjustments.

Colors can also be removed from a gradient.

- In the Gradient panel, position the cursor over the color stop that will be removed.
- Then, click and hold down the mouse button while dragging the color stop down, away from the gradient slider.
- Once the color box has been removed, release the mouse button; the change will be seen immediately.

If a gradient will be used repeatedly, it can be saved as a *Gradient Swatch* for future use. In the *Gradient panel*, look for the circled dropdown arrow located to the right of the thumbnail of the gradient in Figure 11.26.

- Click once on this arrow to open the associated options.
- In the lower-left corner, click on the *Add to Swatches icon.*
  - The new gradient (*Default:* New Gradient Swatch 1) is now available in the *Swatches panel* (Figure 11.27).

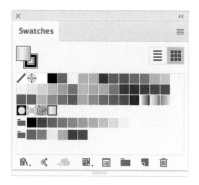

Figure 11.27

Swatches panel including new multicolor gradient, Window menu > Swatches.

- The new gradient can be renamed by double-clicking on the associated thumbnail in the *Swatches panel* and entering a name in the *Swatch Options dialog box*.

Creating Complex Shapes

The Shape Builder Tool

An easy way to combine individual shapes is using the *Shape Builder Tool* (Shift + M). The following description is drawn from the *Illustrator Online Help (Tools Gallery)*.

- The *Shape Builder Tool* (Shift + M) merges simple shapes to create custom, complex shapes.

In Figure 11.28, View 1, a series of shapes drawn with the Pen Tool (P) create a simple house. Drawn as separate closed paths, each of the five shapes is on its

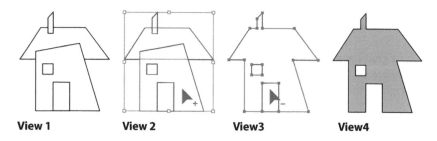

View 1   **View 2**   **View3**   **View4**

Figure 11.28

Shape Builder example: *View 1:* individual paths, *View 2:* paths selected, *View 3:* paths combined, and *View 4:* finished path.

own sublayer in the Layers panel. The *Shape Builder Tool* (Shift + M) can be used to combine the house, roof and chimney shapes into a single shape. Then the door and window will be subtracted from the new shape creating negative space within the shape.

In Figure 11.28, View 2, all of the shapes have been selected using the *Selection Tool* (V) in preparation for the Shape Builder Tool (Shift + M). Select the *Shape Builder Tool* (Shift + M) and position the cursor over the house. Click and hold down the mouse button while drawing a line from the house to the roof and the chimney; avoid intersecting the line with the door and window. As the line is drawn, the soon to be combined shapes are filled with a pattern of small dots. When the pattern is present in the desired areas, release the mouse button. This action triggers the merging of the shapes into a single shape, as shown in Figure 11.28, View 3.

The *Shape Builder Tool* (Shift + M) will now be used to remove the door and window from the shape, creating negative spaces in the shape. Hold down the *Option key* on the keyboard and notice the subtle change to the appearance of the cursor, a negative sign (−) is now present indicating that content will be subtracted from the shape. Continue to hold down the Option key while clicking once on the door and once on the window. To confirm that these areas were removed from the house shape, fill the house with a new fill color. The door and window are in fact negative areas, holes in the larger shape.

Compound Shapes and Compound Paths

Another way to combine shapes is via the *Pathfinder panel* [Window menu > Pathfinder]. Figure 11.29 features the available *Shape Modes* effects. Notice how each affects a pair of overlapping circles and the color of the resulting compound shape. A *compound shape* is editable art composed of two or more objects, each assigned a shape mode. When a compound shape is created, the resulting shape assumes the appearance of the topmost object, as seen in Figure 11.29B and E. The *Direction Selection Tool* (A) can be used to edit components of the compound shape.

The *Pathfinder* effects provide additional ways to create new shapes out of overlapping objects. Apply Pathfinder effects via the Pathfinder panel or from the Effects menu [Effects menu > Pathfinder]. These effects are illustrated in

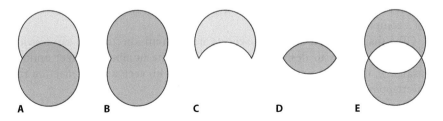

A   B   C   D   E

Figure 11.29

Shape Modes effect examples: (A) Original objects, (B) Unite, (C) Minus Front, (D) Intersect, and (E) Exclude.

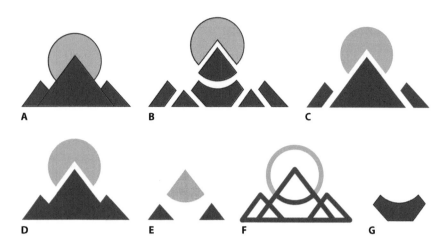

Figure 11.30

Pathfinder effect examples: (A) Original objects, (B) Divide, (C) Trim, (D) Merge, (E) Crop, (F) Outline, and (G) Minus Back.

Figure 11.30. When the resulting shape is composed of multiple shapes, these shapes have been spaced out to highlight their shapes and appearances (e.g., Examples B, C, D). Notice the mix of attributes among the examples: most possess fill colors, and some possess stroke colors.

A compound shape can be returned to its original separate objects by *releasing* the compound shape. *Expanding* a compound shape maintains the shape of the compound object, but the individual components can no longer be selected.

Any object that has a hole in it, such as the compound shape shown in Figure 11.29E or the completed house with the door and window in Figure 11.28, View 4, is referred to as a *compound path*. A compound path contains two or more paths that are painted so that holes appear where paths overlap. When created, all objects in the compound path take on the paint and style attributes of the backmost object in the stacking order.

Compound paths act as *grouped objects* and appear as <Compound Path> items in the Layers panel. The *Direct Selection Tool* (A) can be used to select part of a compound path.

The shapes created using these effects are often unexpected and can provide creative solutions to design challenges. Given the number of effect options available, it is worth spending getting familiar with each and its effect on the overlapping shapes.

Looking Ahead

Many new concepts and approaches to creating content have been presented in this chapter. Spend time experimenting with the tools and repeating the processes until you feel comfortable navigating the workspace, creating and saving a file. The more time spent experimenting with paths, vectors and compound shapes, the more familiar they will become. *Chapter 12: Illustrator Continued* builds on the Illustrator basics, expanding your use of the application. The fundamentals of type and tracing a photograph are presented.

Discussion

Discussion 11.1: The Scalability Factor

A major incentive behind creating a logo as a vector image is the scalability of the image, the ability to increase or decrease the size of the logo without degrading its quality. This is a useful property for branding purposes. What logo(s) have you seen used in different sizes? How and where were the logos used?

Activities

Activity 11.1: Brush Options

Create a new illustration file and write out your name using the *Paintbrush Tool* (B). Then, use the *Direct Selection Tool* (A) to adjust the anchor points that create the paths in your name. Similarly, add or delete anchor points to the paths until you are satisfied with the lettering. Now, adjust the appearance of the lettering (the selected paths) via the *Brushes panel* [Window menu > Brushes]. From the *Brushes panel menu*, select the *Open Brush Library command* to access additional options. Try some of the artistic brushes, such as Artistic > Artistic_ Calligraphic | Artistic_ChalkCharcoalPencil | Artistic_Paintbrush. How do these brushes affect the presentation of your name? Remember the stated goals of selecting a typeface: Readability, Functionality and Engagement; the same goals apply here (Figure 11.31).

Activity 11.2: Share a Little Love

Create a valentine (Figure 11.32). However, to make this activity more challenging, draw only *half* of the heart using the *Pen Tool* (P) or the *Paintbrush Tool* (B). Then, generate a reflected second half of the heart using the *Reflect command* [Object menu > Transform > Reflect…]. Reposition the halves and join them using the *Join command* [Object menu > Path > Join | ⌘J]. Finally, use the *Line Segment Tool* (\) to create paths that appear to pierce the heart, the addition of *Stroke Arrowheads* finishes the illustration. When finished, export a copy of the valentine and email it to a friend or family member. Share your work, and in the process brighten someone's day.

Reflect and Copy

There are several ways that the drawn half of the heart could be replicated and reflected in order to create the second half of the heart. Using the *Reflect*

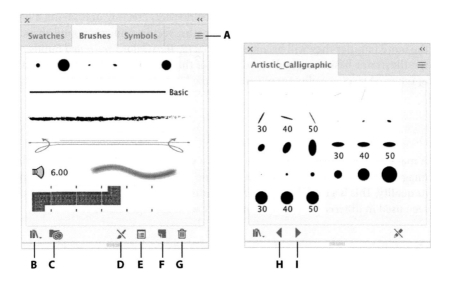

Figure 11.31

Brushes panel: (A) Brushes panel menu, (B) Brush Libraries Menu, (C) Libraries Panel, (D) Remove Brush Stroke, (E) Options of Selected Object, (F) New Brush, (G) Delete Brush, (H) Load Previous Brush Library, and (I) Load Next Brush Library.

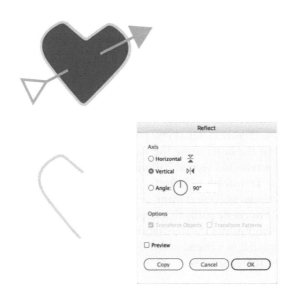

Figure 11.32

Activity 2, Reflect dialog box [Object menu > Transform > Reflect...].

command is a straightforward way to achieve the desired results [Object menu > Transform > Reflect...]. In the *Reflect dialog box*, Illustrator provides the means to copy the path that is being reflected. To duplicate the path, press the *Copy button* instead of the *OK button* to complete the transformation.

Joining Paths

To join the paths, *Zoom In* on one pair of endpoints [View menu > Zoom In | ⌘+]. Using the *Direct Selection Tool* (A), select the two endpoints; try drawing a box around the ends of the two paths to select the endpoints. Once the endpoints are selected, access the *Object menu* and select the *Path menu command* and then *Join* [Object menu > Path > Join | ⌘J]. This action joins one end of the heart. Repeat the process to join the other end and produce a *closed path*. Once the path is closed, fill it with color or a gradient.

Exporting the File

When the illustration is complete, go to the *File menu* and select the *Export menu command* and then *Export As...* [File menu > Export > Export As...]. From the *Format dropdown menu*, select *JPEG (jpg)*, a universally accessible file format. Give the file a name, and know where it will be exported when the *Export button* is pressed. The JPEG file should easily attach to an email message.

Exercise File(s) Available on the Companion Website, URL

Ch11-Illustrator-CC-2019-Tools-Overview.pdf | *Illustrator CC 2019 Tools Panel Overview*

URL: http://www.crcpress.com/9780367075347

External Links Mentioned in the Chapter

Illustrator Online Help | https://helpx.adobe.com/illustrator

12

Illustrator Continued

Building on the Illustrator fundamentals presented in the previous chapter, this chapter introduces Illustrator's unique approach to layers and sublayers. Then, additional tools are presented expanding the designer's toolkit. *Exercise 12.1* features a variety of ways to eliminate content and divide shapes. Attention then shifts to creating type in Illustrator and some of the techniques and properties available for creative text use in design. *Exercise 12.2* provides an outlet to practice these tools and processes. Finally, in *Exercise 12.3* an illustration is created based on a photograph; the vector-based trace image highlights the designer's ability to easily craft a stylized image.

Understanding Layers in Illustrator

Layers are a key component to a designer's ability to create and edit an image in Illustrator, just as they were in Photoshop. They allow for a sense of depth to be created in a two-dimensional image. Layers can also be used to incorporate text into an image. Every illustration file contains at least one layer. However, unlike Photoshop, Illustrator utilizes *sublayers*. A single layer can contain multiple sublayers, as seen in Figure 12.1. Clicking on the *disclosure triangle* located to the left of the *document layer name* expands the layer, revealing sublayers and their stacking order. A new layer can be created within an illustration file, but it must be a deliberate action, otherwise, new paths, objects and type are added to the file on sublayers. The number of layers and sublayers in a file is only limited by the computer's memory.

The Layers Panel

The *Layers panel*, featured in Figure 12.1, is accessible from the *Window menu* [Window menu > Layers]. In this panel, all of the layers and sublayers in an illustration are listed. The Layers panel provides the designer with the ability to control the visibility of layers (and sublayers), lock layers (and sublayers), create

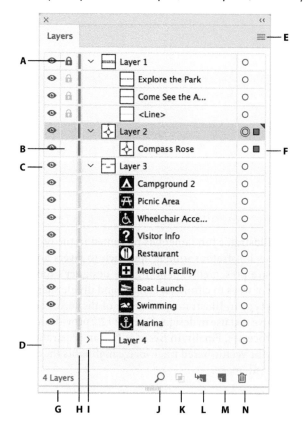

Figure 12.1

Layers panel, Window menu > Layers: (A) Locked layer toggle (lock icon), (B) Unlocked sublayer (no lock icon), (C) Visibility toggle (eye icon), (D) Hidden layer (no eye icon), (E) Layers panel menu, (F) Selected object indicator (filled square), (G) Number of layers in the file, (H) Layer color identifier, (I) Disclosure triangle, (J) Locate Object, (K) Make/Release Clipping Mask, (L) Create New Sublayer, (M) Create New Layer, and (N) Delete Selection.

Figure 12.2

Layer color identifier. *Typefaces:* Impact/News Gothic MT.

new layers, and delete selected layers (and sublayers). Additional commands and options can be accessed via the *Layers panel menu*, available in the upper-right corner of the panel. The currently selected sublayer is identified by the filled square located to the right of the sublayer name. A related indicator is also present next to the corresponding layer name.

Application Tip: In order to edit an object in Illustrator, the object's layer or sublayer must be selected in the Layers panel. Each layer has a unique color associated with it and its sublayers, this is the layer color identifier. In Figure 12.2,* the red bounding box corresponds to the red color label of Layer 2 and its sublayers, shown in Figure 12.1.

Managing, Renaming and Deleting Layers

Layers and sublayers can be *reordered* and *deleted* in the Layers panel. To change the *stacking order* of a sublayer, click on a sublayer name and hold down the mouse button while dragging the sublayer up or down within the Layers panel. A *highlight line* will appear where the sublayer will be placed when the mouse button is released. The same technique can be used to reorder layers. When the stacking order of a sublayer is changed within the Layers panel, the visibility of that sublayer's content within the artboard may be impacted. If content is "missing" on the artboard, it is likely hidden behind another layer's content.

---

* Figure 12.2 displays a series of symbols available in Illustrator [Window menu > Symbols, Symbol Library: Maps]. In this context, a *symbol* is an art object that can be reused in a file.

The topmost layer in the Layers panel is closest to the viewer. Within a layer, the topmost sublayer is closest to the viewer among the other sublayers. The stacking order of sublayers can also be adjusted under the *Object menu* using the *Arrange menu command* (i.e., Bring to Front ⇧⌘] | Bring Forward ⌘] | Send Backward ⌘[| Send to Back ⇧⌘[) [Object menu > Arrange].

Layers and sublayers can be *renamed* by double-clicking on the default name (e.g., Layer 1, <Line>) and typing in a new name.

Deleting a layer or *sublayer* is a straightforward process; select the layer or sublayer to be deleted, then click on the *Trashcan icon* located along the bottom edge of the *Layers panel*. This task can also be performed via the *Layers panel menu*. Deleting a sublayer removes its content from the illustration. Deleting a layer eliminates all of its sublayers and their contents from the illustration.

Layer-Friendly File Types

Certain file types support layers, meaning these file types preserve layer information and make the layers available across work sessions. The Adobe Illustrator (AI) is one such file type. An Adobe Illustrator file does not flatten an illustration's layers and sublayers; the saving process does not discard layer information.

Another file type that supports layers is the *Tagged-Image File Format* (TIFF; TIF). Illustrator files can be *exported* to a TIFF file (or to a Photoshop Document [PSD]). However, if a file containing layers is opened in another application, such as Preview, the illustration will be presented as a flattened image without layers.

When the time comes to save an illustration file, if the file contains layers, be sure to select a file type that supports layers in case the image needs to be edited later. This sounds obvious, but when this is forgotten it creates unnecessary work for the designer. Without editable layers, making changes to an illustration can be time consuming and can sometimes mean re-creating the image.

Once an illustration file has been saved with its layers preserved, it is typical to save or export another instance of the image to share with others who do not have access to Illustrator. This second file differs from the Adobe Illustrator file because it is *flat*, meaning it does not contain layer information. *Exercise 12.3* includes a step to save a copy of the illustration as a PDF file, which can be shared with and opened by others.

Let's first add to our collection of Illustrator tools, expanding our ability to create an engaging and effective illustration.

The Eraser Tool and Tools for Dividing Content

Once a path is created, it is important to know how to alter that path. *Chapter 11: Getting Started with Illustrator*, introduced the *Delete Anchor Point Tool (−)* and its ability to reshape a path by deleting single or multiple anchor points.

Graphic Design: Learn It, Do It

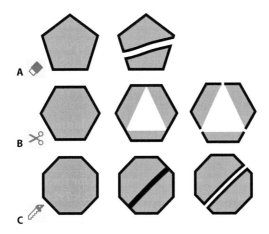

Figure 12.3

Tools: (A) Eraser Tool (Shift + E), (B) Scissors Tool (C), and (C) Knife Tool.

Figure 12.3 features three other tools that can be used to eliminate content or to divide a shape: Eraser Tool (Shift + E), Scissors Tool (C) and Knife Tool. Though their results are similar, each tool behaves slightly differently. The following descriptions are drawn from the *Illustrator Online Help*:

A. The *Eraser Tool* (Shift + E) erases any area of the object over which you drag [the tool].
B. The *Scissors Tool* (C) cuts paths at specified points.
C. The *Knife Tool* cuts objects and paths.

The *Eraser Tool* (Shift + E) is an efficient way to eliminate content from an illustration. When working with vector images, the Eraser Tool (Shift + E) erases content and closes the remaining paths.

The *Scissors Tool* (C) cuts a path allowing part of an object to be deleted or separated from the rest of the object. This tool *does not* close the remaining paths. *Note:* In order to function as expected, the Scissors Tool (C) must be used on a path or an anchor point. If the *Scissors Tool* (C) is clicked anywhere else on the artboard, the following Illustrator alert appears, *Please use the scissors tool on a segment or an anchor point (but not an endpoint) of a path*. If this message appears, click *OK* or press the *ESC key* on the keyboard to close the window and try again.

The *Knife Tool* cuts an object and closes the paths along the cutline. This tool does not eliminate content, it simply divides an object or path.

Let's try using these tools in order to compare and contrast their behaviors firsthand. *Exercise 12.1* is designed to put these tools to use and also to practice creating *polygons*, shapes with at least three straight sides and angles.

Exercise 12.1: Using the Eraser, Scissors and Knife Tools

Exercise brief: Create a new illustration file and populate it with polygons. Then, experiment with the following tools: Eraser Tool (Shift + E), Scissors Tool (C) and Knife Tool. Pay particular attention to the state of the remaining shapes after each tool is used.

Step 1: Create and save a new illustration file in Illustrator (Ch12-Ex01.ai).

- Begin at the *File menu* and select the *New... menu command* [File menu > New... | ⌘N].
- In the *New Document dialog box*, look for the *Print set*, and from the *Blank Document Presets* select *Letter* (612 × 792 pt.).
- Click *Create* to generate the illustration file.
- Return to the *File menu* and select the *Save As... menu command* [File menu > Save As... | ⇧⌘S].
- In the *Save As dialog box*, enter the file name, *Ch12-Ex01*, verify the *Format* (Adobe Illustrator [ai]) and navigate to an appropriate location.
- Click *Save*, which launches the Illustrator Options dialog box.
- In the Illustrator Options dialog box, accept the default values, and click *OK* to save the illustration file.

Step 2: Create three polygons using a different number of sides for each shape. Each shape should possess a Fill Color and Stroke Color.

- Select the *Polygon Tool* in the Tools panel, then position the cursor over the artboard.
  - *Note:* The Polygon Tool is a hidden tool sharing space with the Rectangle Tool (M).
- Click the mouse button once on the artboard where the center of the shape will be placed, and the *Polygon dialog box* appears (Figure 12.4).
  - Here values for *Radius* (distance from the center of the shape to the edge) and *Sides* (the number of sides for the shape, e.g., three sides for a triangle) can be entered.

Figure 12.4

Polygon dialog box.

- Accept the default values or enter custom values and click *OK* to create the shape.
- Repeat this process entering unique values in the *Polygon dialog box* to create two more polygons.
- Confirm that each shape possesses a visible *Fill Color* and a *Stroke Color*.
  - If needed, select the shapes using the Selection Tool (V) and apply the necessary color via the Tools panel or the Control panel.

Step 3: Use the Eraser Tool (Shift + E) to eliminate part of a polygon.

- Choose the *Eraser Tool* (Shift + E) in the Tools panel and move the cursor toward one of the polygons.
- Click and hold down the mouse button and then paint over part of the polygon. When the mouse button is released, the area that was painted over is eliminated.
  - Notice that the remaining shape has a stroke around its entirety, including along the recently erased area(s). Similarly, if additional shapes were created during the process, they also possess a stroke.

Step 4: Use the Scissors Tool (C) to remove or cut out part of a polygon.

- Select the *Scissors Tool* (C) in the Tools panel and move the cursor over the second polygon. *Tip:* For this tool to work, it has to begin *on* the path of the shape.
- Click and release the mouse button as though creating a corner point.
- Move the cursor to another path in the shape, click and release the mouse button.
- Continue this process as desired, to "cut out" part of the polygon.
- Now, choose the *Selection Tool* (V) and click on one of the newly created shapes. Move the new shape away from its original position to highlight the new shape.
  - Notice that the edges created during this process *do not* possess strokes.

Step 5: Use the Knife Tool to cut a polygon into multiple pieces.

- Choose the *Knife Tool* in the Tools panel and move the cursor toward the third polygon.
- Beginning *outside* of the polygon, click and hold down the mouse button, then draw a line that enters and exits the polygon. Release the mouse button.
  - The path of the Knife appears within the shape. Closed paths were created, each possessing strokes along the cutline.
- Deselect all objects on the artboard [Select menu > Deselect | ⇧⌘A].
- Use the *Selection Tool* (V) to select and move one of the pieces of the polygon away from its original position to highlight the new shape.

Step 6: Save the file.

- Select *Save* from the *File menu* [File menu > Save | ⌘S].

Nice work, you have just sliced and diced a series of shapes. Familiarity and comfort using these tools comes with practice. If you need some additional shapes to dissect, try using the *Star Tool*, another hidden tool that shares space with the *Rectangle Tool* (M).

The process for using the *Star Tool* is similar to the *Polygon Tool*. Position the cursor over the artboard where the center of the star is to be positioned. Then, click once to open the *Star dialog box* (Figure 12.5). Here values for *Radius 1* (distance from the center to the innermost points), *Radius 2* (distance from the center to the outermost points) and *Sides* (the number of sides for the star) can be entered. Accept the default values or enter custom values and click *OK* to create the star.

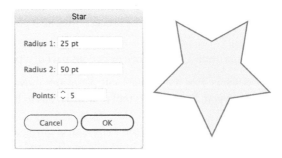

Figure 12.5

Star dialog box and resulting star.

Before proceeding to the Type Tool (T), let's review some *Need to Know Fundamentals* that pertain to *Exercise 12.1.*

Need to Know Fundamentals

Transforming Paths

The appearance of a path can also be altered through the use of transform commands. A collection of these commands can be found within the *Effect menu*, specifically under the *Illustrator Effects header* and the *Distort & Transform menu command*. Figure 12.6 illustrates the available options: Free Distort; Pucker & Bloat; Roughen; Transform (i.e., Scale, Move, Rotate, Reflect); Tweak; Twist; and Zig Zag. When selected, each of these options launches a corresponding dialog box presenting related properties that can be adjusted to affect the selected object.

Tip: Be sure the *Preview checkbox* in the dialog box is checked in order to view the adjustments as they are made.

Graphic Design: Learn It, Do It

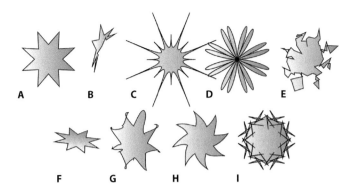

Figure 12.6

Transforming Paths examples, Effect menu > Distort & Transform: (A) Original path, (B) Free Distort, (C) Pucker, (D) Bloat, (E) Roughen, (F) Transform, (G) Tweak, (H) Twist, and (I) Zig Zag.

Selecting Paths and Objects

Multiple tools can be used to select objects in Illustrator. While the *Selection Tool* (V) and the *Direction Selection Tool* (A) are go-to tools for many designers, here are a few alternatives. The following descriptions are drawn from the *Illustrator Online Help*:

- The *Magic Wand Tool* (Y) selects objects with similar attributes.
- The *Lasso Tool* (Q) selects points or path segments within objects.

These tools could be used to select any of the shapes created in *Exercise 12.1*.

Using the Type Tools

Now, on to the *Type Tool* (T) and a sample of the many ways that text can be created in Illustrator. When type is created, a new *sublayer* is added to the Layers panel. Once created, type can be edited for content and appearance. Illustrator provides multiple ways to add text to an illustration, similar to Photoshop. These methods are represented in Figure 12.7.

A. *Point type* is a horizontal or vertical line of text that begins where the cursor is positioned when the mouse button is clicked in the illustration. Entering text at a point is a useful way to add a few words to an illustration. When point type is created, each line of type is independent, the length of the line expands or collapses as the content is edited, but it does not automatically wrap to the next line.

B. *Area type* (a.k.a. *Paragraph type*) uses boundaries to control the flow of characters, either horizontally or vertically. Entering text this way is useful when you want to create multiple lines or paragraphs.

C. *Type on a path* flows along the edge of an open or a closed path.

Save Your Work, Early and Often.

A

This practice will help you avoid losing work should the application or computer freeze and need to be restarted while you are working. Throughout the book, you will be encouraged to save your work, early and often.

B

C

Figure 12.7

Examples of the three methods used for creating type in Photoshop: (A) point type, (B) area type, and (C) type on a path. *Typeface:* Myriad Pro.

Converting between Point Type and Area Type

Type can be converted from *point type* to *area type* in order to adjust the flow of characters within a bounding box. Similarly, *area type* can be converted to *point type* to make each text line flow independently from the others. To convert the type, first select the type on the artboard using the Selection Tool (V). Then, from the *Type menu*, select the appropriate menu command, *Convert To Area Type* or *Convert To Point Type* [Type menu > Convert To Area Type | Convert To Point Type].

When *area type* is converted to *point type*, a carriage return is added at the end of each line of type (except the last line). Be aware that when area type is converted to point type, all characters that overflow the bounding box are deleted. To avoid losing text, adjust the bounding box so that all type is visible *before* the conversion.

When a text element is selected on the artboard, the *Control panel* displays the properties available for adjustment (Figure 12.8). These options include the following labeled properties (from left to right):

A. Fill
B. Stroke
C. Shortcut to Stroke panel
D. Stroke Weight
E. Variable Width Profile
F. Shortcut to Transparency panel
G. Opacity

Graphic Design: Learn It, Do It

| A | B | C | D | E | F | G | H | I | J | K | L | M |

Control panel, Type Tool options: (A) Fill; (B) Stroke; (C) Shortcut to Stroke panel; (D) Stroke Weight; (E) Variable Width Profile; (F) Shortcut to Transparency panel; (G) Opacity; (H) Recolor Artwork; (I) Shortcut to Character panel | Shortcut to Paragraph panel; (J) Align (Left, Center, Right); (K) Make Envelope; (L) Align to Selection; and (M) Shortcut to Transform panel.

H. Recolor Artwork
I. Shortcut to Character panel | Shortcut to Paragraph panel
J. Align (Left, Center, Right)
K. Make Envelope
L. Align to Selection
M. Shortcut to Transform panel

The *Character* and *Paragraph panels* (Figure 12.9) provide additional properties and greater options for formatting and adjusting type. The *Character panel* provides options for formatting characters. Use the *Paragraph panel* to change the formatting of columns and paragraphs. Many of the typography elements presented in *Chapter 10: Typography in Design* can be found in these panels, both of which are accessible via shortcuts in the *Control panel* or from the *Window menu* [Window menu > Type > Character | Paragraph].

Let's take time to explore the Type Tools, beginning with the *Area Type Tool* and the *Type on a Path Tool. Note:* Both of these tools are hidden tools sharing space with the *Type Tool* (T). Next, the process of creating outlines, converting editable type into unique paths for each letterform, is presented. *Exercise 12.2* encompasses multiple ways to work with and alter text. After each new technique,

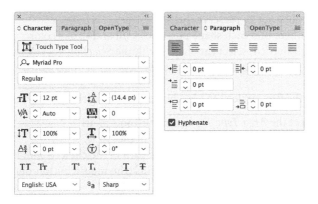

Character panel, Window menu > Type > Character; Paragraph panel, Window menu > Type > Paragraph.

---

12. Illustrator Continued

you will be prompted to save the illustration file, a step that is included as a reminder to save your work as you go.

Exercise 12.2: Working with the Type Tools

Exercise brief: Create an illustration file and experiment with type, including type *in* and *on* a path.

Step 1: Create and save an illustration file in Illustrator (Ch12-Ex02.ai).

- Go to the *File menu* and select the *New... menu command* [File menu > New... | ⌘N].
- In the *New Document dialog box*, look for the *Print set* and from the *Blank Document Presets* select *Letter* (612 × 792 pt.).
- Click *Create* to generate the illustration file.
- Return to the *File menu* and select *Save As...* [File menu > Save As... | ⇧⌘S].
- In the *Save As dialog box*, enter the file name, *Ch12-Ex02*, verify the *Format* (Adobe Illustrator [ai]) and navigate to an appropriate location.
- Click *Save*, which launches the Illustrator Options dialog box.
- In the Illustrator Options dialog box, accept the default values and click *OK* to save the illustration file.

Step 2: Create two circles on the artboard, each possessing a Fill Color and Stroke Color.

- Select the *Ellipse Tool* (L) from the Tools panel.
- Draw two circles on the artboard.
  - *Tip:* Remember that holding down the *Shift key* on the keyboard constrains the shape to a *circle*. Release the mouse button *before* the Shift key to preserve the shape.
- Confirm that each shape possesses a fill and stroke color.
  - If needed, select the shapes with the *Selection Tool* (V) and apply the necessary color(s) via the *Control panel* or *Tools panel*.

Step 3: Fill the first circle with placeholder text using the Area Type Tool.

- Select the *Area Type Tool* from the Tools panel.
- Position the cursor over the edge of the circle.
  - When the cursor overlaps the path of the circle, a *path* label appears.
- When the *path* label is visible, click the mouse button once. The shape fills with placeholder text.
  - *Note:* If the *Area Type Tool* is clicked anywhere else on the artboard, the following Illustrator alert appears: *You must click on a non-compound, non-masking path to create text inside a path.* Click *OK* or press the *ESC key* on the keyboard to close this window and try again.

Graphic Design: Learn It, Do It

- Notice that the fill and stroke of the circle have been replaced by the text. The previously filled shape is now being used for its shape as a *type area*.

Step 4: Justify the placeholder text within the circle, and turn off hyphenation.

- When the text is created, the text is automatically selected.
  - Use this opportunity to *justify* the text.
- Select the *Justify with last line aligned left* option in the *Paragraph panel* [Window menu > Type > Paragraph].
  - *Note:* Justifying the text emphasizes the shape of the type area.
- Still in the Paragraph panel, deselect the *Hyphenate checkbox*, which turns off hyphenation in the selected text.

Placeholder Text

Illustrator provides *placeholder* or *dummy text* when the Type Tool (T) is used. This dummy text, referred to as *Lorem Ipsum*, has been a standard in the printing industry since the 1500s. Lorem Ipsum is popular with designers because it uses a regular distribution of words, punctuation and variable sentence length (Figure 12.10). The Latin dummy text is also less distracting than the results of using random keystrokes to fill a text field. For more information about Lorem Ipsum, refer to the references at the end of this chapter (see *External Links Mentioned in the Chapter*).

Lorem ipsum dolor sit amet, consectetuer adipiscing elit, sed diam nonummy nibh euismod tincidunt ut laoreet dolore magna aliquam erat volutpat. Ut wisi enim ad minim veniam, quis nostrud exerci tation ullamcorper suscipit lobortis nisl ut aliquip ex ea commodo consequat. Duis

Figure 12.10

Example of Lorem Ipsum placeholder text. *Typeface:* Myriad Pro.

There will be times when a duplicate path is needed either as part of a design or to compare paths (Figure 12.11). There are several ways to replicate a path,

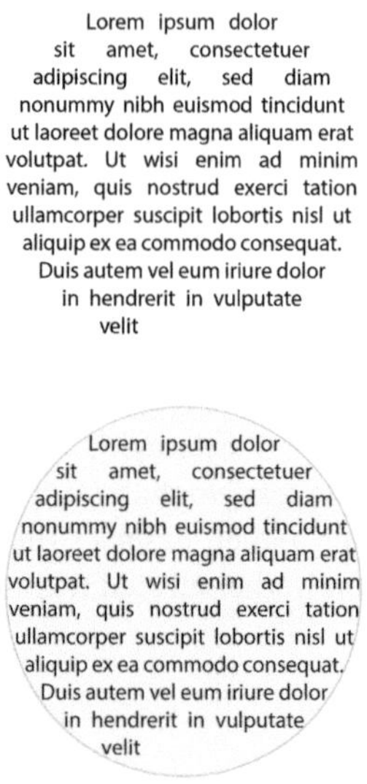

Lorem ipsum dolor
sit amet, consectetuer
adipiscing elit, sed diam
nonummy nibh euismod tincidunt
ut laoreet dolore magna aliquam erat
volutpat. Ut wisi enim ad minim
veniam, quis nostrud exerci tation
ullamcorper suscipit lobortis nisl ut
aliquip ex ea commodo consequat.
Duis autem vel eum iriure dolor
in hendrerit in vulputate
velit

Lorem ipsum dolor
sit amet, consectetuer
adipiscing elit, sed diam
nonummy nibh euismod tincidunt
ut laoreet dolore magna aliquam erat
volutpat. Ut wisi enim ad minim
veniam, quis nostrud exerci tation
ullamcorper suscipit lobortis nisl ut
aliquip ex ea commodo consequat.
Duis autem vel eum iriure dolor
in hendrerit in vulputate
velit

Figure 12.11

Exercise 12.2, Creating Area Type. *Typeface:* Myriad Pro.

including using the *Copy* and *Paste menu commands* [Edit menu > Copy (⌘C) | Paste (⌘V)]; here is an alternative that can be performed from the artboard. First, select the path with the *Selection Tool* (V), then hold down the *Option/Alt key* on the keyboard while dragging the selected path to a new location. The original path remains in its location while a copy is made and moved to the new location. *Tip:* When preparing to drag the selected path to a new location, *do not* position the cursor over the path's center point. Otherwise, the center point will be relocated and a copy of the path will not be created.

Step 5: Make a copy of the path from Step 4 (circle containing justified text) before proceeding. Use this copy for Step 6.

Step 6: Apply Fill and Stroke Colors to the copy of the path created in Step 5.

- First, deselect all objects on the artboard [Select menu > Deselect | ⇧⌘A].
- Choose the *Direct Selection Tool* (A) from the Tools panel.
- Using the *Direct Selection Tool* (A), position the cursor *on the path* of the circle and click once.
  - Look to the Tools panel and specifically the *Fill* and *Stroke color chips*, which currently reflect *None* as their content.
- Apply both a *Fill* and a *Stroke Color* to the shape (see Figure 12.11).

Notice how the text spans the width of the circle and is very close to the edge of the stroke. If the weight (a.k.a. thickness) of the stroke was increased,

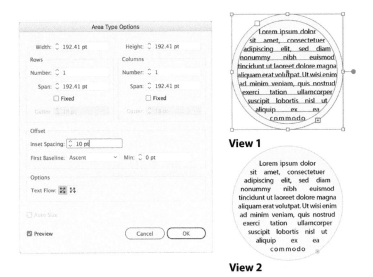

View 1

View 2

Figure 12.12

Area Type Options dialog box, Type menu > Area Type Options…, *View 1:* type with inset spacing (10 pt.); and *View 2:* deselected path.

the stroke would overlap the text interfering with the readability of the text. The solution to this formatting challenge is found under the *Type menu* in the *Area Type Options dialog box* (Figure 12.12) [Type menu > Area Type Options…]. *Tip:* Select the circle before navigating to the Type menu. Look for the *Offset header* and specifically, the *Inset Spacing field*. Increase this value and watch as a *margin* is created between the edge of the circle and the text. *Tip:* Be sure the *Preview* feature is turned on in order to view the change. As the inset spacing increases, the available space for the text decreases. A square outlined in red containing a red plus sign is now present at the end of the visible text. This is the symbol for *overset* or *overmatter text*, which appears when there is too much text for the text area and some of the text is currently not visible.

To view the overset text, select the path with the *Selection Tool* (V), then double-click on the *overset symbol*. *Tip:* It can be challenging to click on the correct location, so consider first zooming in on the path to increase visibility of the work area [View menu > Zoom In | ⌘+]. Illustrator creates a duplicate circle with the remaining text shown (Figure 12.13). The blue line connecting the two shapes, and more specifically the connected text fields, indicates that the text is *threaded*. Threaded text is a topic covered in *Chapter 14: Getting Started with InDesign*. For now, we can use the *Type Tool* (T) to either select all of the text and resize it to fit in one circle, *or* highlight and delete the overset text in the second circle, then delete the empty path that held the overset text.

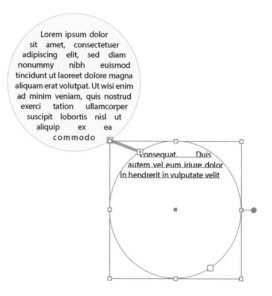

Figure 12.13

Area Type with overset text shown.

Step 7: Adjust the inset spacing of the path to increase readability of the text.

- Use the properties available in the *Area Type Options dialog box* to increase the inset spacing [Type menu > Area Type Options...].
  - *Tip:* Be sure the *Preview* feature is turned on in order to view the change.

Step 8: Save the file.

- Select *Save* from the *File menu* [File menu > Save | ⌘S].

Step 9: Create placeholder text along the stroke of the remaining circle (created in Step 2) using the Type on a Path Tool (Figure 12.14).

- Select the *Type on a Path Tool* from the Tools panel.
- Position the cursor *on the edge* of the circle. The position of the cursor is where the text will begin.
  - When the cursor overlaps the path of the circle, a *path* label appears.
- When the *path* label is visible, click the mouse button once.
  - *Note:* If the *Type on a Path Tool* is clicked anywhere else on the artboard, the following Illustrator alert appears, *You must click on a non-compound, non-masking path to create text along a path.* Click *OK* or press the *ESC key* on the keyboard to close this window and try again.
- Placeholder text fills the circumference of the circle.
- Notice that the fill and stroke of the circle have been replaced by the text on a path.

Graphic Design: Learn It, Do It

Figure 12.14

Exercise 12.2, Creating Type on a Path. *Typeface:* Myriad Pro.

The size of the placeholder text is based on the current font size, which is listed in the *Character panel* [Window menu > Type > Character]. If the font size is too small or too large, try the following. *Undo* the previous action [Edit menu > Undo | ⌘Z], then change the font size in the *Character panel*, and repeat the *Type on a Path action.*

When the type on a path is selected using the *Selection Tool* (V), brackets are visible at the beginning and end of the type and at the midpoint (Figure 12.15). The *beginning bracket* controls where the text begins along the path. The *ending bracket* controls where the text ends along the path. The *midpoint bracket* can be used to rotate the text along the path, changing the overall position of the text. The midpoint bracket can also be used to flip the text to the other side of the path. For the Type on a Path example shown in Figure 12.14, flipping the text would move the text *into* the circle.

In Figure 12.16, the *midpoint bracket* has been rotated counterclockwise, which rotated the text in the same direction along the path.

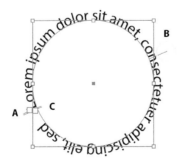

Figure 12.15

Type on a Path: (A) beginning bracket at the start of the text, (B) midpoint bracket located between the beginning and ending brackets, and (C) ending bracket at the end of type.

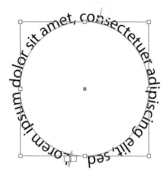

Figure 12.16

Type on a Path: midpoint bracket (circled) rotated.

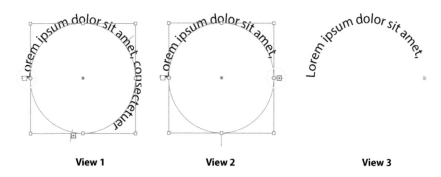

| View 1 | View 2 | View 3 |

Figure 12.17

Type on a Path: *View 1:* beginning bracket repositioned, *View 2:* ending bracket repositioned, and *View 3:* limited text along a path.

The beginning and ending brackets limit where text appears along a path (Figure 12.17). In Figure 12.17, View 1, the *beginning bracket* has been repositioned clockwise, which *decreases* the amount of visible text. Notice that the ending bracket now includes the *overset symbol*, a square outlined in red containing a red plus sign, which indicates that there is too much text for the text field. In Figure 12.17, View 2, the *ending bracket* has been repositioned counterclockwise to further limit the amount of text visible along the path. The resulting limited presentation area is displayed in Figure 12.17, View 3, including the overset symbol.

Step 10: Adjust the placeholder text along the stroke so all of the text is visible. There is more than one way to accomplish this task, including resizing or editing the text.

Graphic Design: Learn It, Do It

Step 11: Save the file.

- From the *File menu* select *Save* [File menu > Save | ⌘S].

Step 12: Add an artboard to the illustration file to have some more room to work.

- Open the *Artboards panel* from the *Window menu* [Window menu > Artboards].
- In the Artboards panel, click on the *New Artboard symbol* (Figure 12.18).

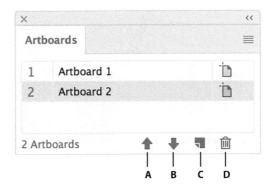

Figure 12.18

Artboards panel, Window menu > Artboards: (A) Move Up, (B) Move Down, (C) New Artboard, and (D) Delete Artboard.

Step 13: On the new artboard, create an open path using the tool of your choice (e.g., Pen Tool [P], Paintbrush Tool [B]) and fill the path with placeholder text using the Type on a Path Tool. *Tip*: Remember from *Chapter 11: Getting Started with Illustrator*, an open path has two distinct endpoints (e.g., the letters "C" or "S").

- Select the *Paintbrush Tool* (B) from the Tools panel and create an open path.
- Once the path is created, select the *Type on a Path Tool* and click once on the path where the text should begin.
  - Placeholder text fills the path along the stroke of the path.
  - Notice that the *Fill* and *Stroke Colors* of the path have been changed to *None*.
- *Optional:* Use the *midpoint bracket* to flip the text to the other side of the path. Notice that this changes the direction of the text (Figure 12.19).

Step 14: Save the file.

- Select *Save* from the *File menu* [File menu > Save | ⌘S].

Just as there are properties that affect Area Type, properties exist for Type on a Path; these are available via the Type menu [Type menu > Type on a Path > Type

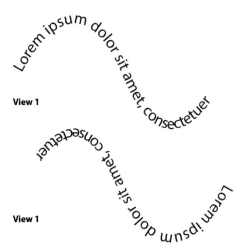

View 1

View 1

Figure 12.19

Type on a Path, open path: *View 1:* default type presentation; and *View 2:* flipped type presentation.

on a Path Options…]. In the *Type on a Path dialog box,* options include *Effect* (Rainbow, Skew, 3D Ribbon, Stair Step, Gravity); *Flip; Align to Path* (Ascender, Descender, Center, Baseline) and *Spacing* (Figure 12.20). For information about how to use these options, access the *Illustrator Online Help.*

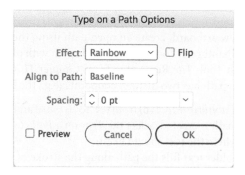

Figure 12.20

Type on a Path dialog box, Type menu > Type on a Path > Type on a Path Options….

Let's try one more type technique. In preparation for this, first add one more artboard to the illustration file (see Step 12).

Step 15: On the new artboard, use point type to create a word or line of text. The font size of this text should be at least 60 pt.

- Select the *Type Tool* (T) from the Tools panel.

Graphic Design: Learn It, Do It

- Click once and type in a word or line of text.
- Resize the text as needed via the *Character panel* so the font size is at least 60 pt. [Window menu > Type > Character].

Step 16: Convert the text into a series of anchor points.

- Using the *Selection Tool* (V) click on the text.
- From the *Type menu*, select the *Create Outlines menu command* [Type menu > Create Outlines | ⇧⌘O].
  - *Note*: Until the text is selected with the *Direct Selection Tool* (A), the change will not be apparent.

The appearance of each letter or word can be altered selecting specific anchor points with the *Direct Selection Tool* (A) and moving these anchor points (Figure 12.21).

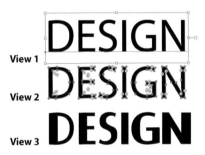

View 1

View 2

View 3

Figure 12.21

Type examples: *View 1:* type selected with Selection Tool; *View 2:* Type menu > Create Outlines, selected with Direction Selection Tool; and *View 3:* customized text. *Typeface:* Myriad Pro.

Step 17: Customize the appearance of the text using the Direct Selection Tool (A).

- Choose the *Direct Selection Tool* (A) from the Tools panel.
- Use the *Direct Selection Tool* (A) to select the text.
  - To select a single letter, click once on the letter.
  - To select multiple letters or an entire word, press and hold down the mouse button, then draw a box around the letters. When the box surrounds the desired letters, release the mouse button.
- Notice the anchor points that form the path of each letterform.
  - These anchor points can be modified individually or in groups.
- First, *deselect* all of the anchor points [Select menu > Deselect | ⇧⌘A].
- Position the cursor over an anchor point, then click on the anchor point to select it.
  - When the cursor hovers over an anchor point, an *anchor* label appears.

- With an anchor point selected, click and hold down the mouse button, and move the cursor. When satisfied with the altered shape, release the mouse button.
  - *Tip:* Multiple anchor points can be selected by drawing a box around the anchor point to select them.
- Repeat this step to continue customizing the text.

Step 18: Save the file.

- Select *Save* from the *File menu* [File menu > Save | ⌘S].

Good job, you have created and edited text using several of the available tools. Let's wrap up this exercise with some related *Need to Know Fundamentals*.

Need to Know Fundamentals

Stylize Effects

Photoshop provides Layer Styles as an easy way to apply effects (e.g., drop shadow) to type and content. In Illustrator, many of these same effects are available under the *Effect menu*, specifically under the *Illustrator Effects header* and the *Stylize menu command* (Figure 12.22). When selected, each option opens a related dialog box. *Tip:* Be sure to select the object using the *Selection Tool* (V) *before* the effect is applied.

Figure 12.22

Effect menu > (Illustrator Effects) Stylize.

Graphic Design: Learn It, Do It

Drop Shadow

Feather

Inner Glow

Outer Glow

Round Corners

Scribble

Figure 12.23

Examples of Stylize effects: Effect menu > (Illustrator Effects) Stylize, Drop Shadow, Feather, Inner Glow, Outer Glow, Round Corners and Scribble. *Typeface:* Myriad Pro.

Examples of the *Stylize effects* are presented in Figure 12.23; each line of text reflects the applied effect.

Once an effect has been applied to an object, it can be edited via the *Appearance panel* [Window menu > Appearance]. Figure 12.24 features the "Drop Shadow" example from the previous figure selected on the artboard. Clicking on the underlined *Drop Shadow shortcut* in the *Appearance panel* launches the associated *Drop Shadow dialog box* where the current effect can be adjusted.

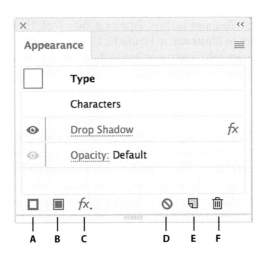

Figure 12.24

Appearance panel, Window menu > Appearance: (A) Add New Stroke, (B) Add New Fill, (C) Add New Effect, (D) Clear Appearance, (E) Duplicate Selected Item, and (F) Delete Selected Item.

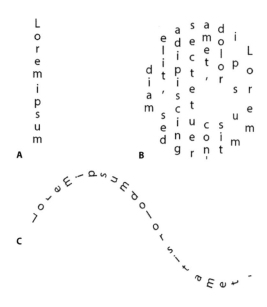

Figure 12.25

Vertical type examples: (A) Vertical Type Tool, (B) Vertical Area Type Tool, and (C) Vertical Type on a Path Tool.

Vertical Type

Illustrator provides vertical alternatives to the type tools: *Vertical Type Tool, Vertical Area Type Tool* and *Vertical Type on a Path Tool.* These options afford a designer flexibility, as illustrated in Figure 12.25. The formatting properties in the Character and Paragraph panels as well as in the Control panel adjust accordingly to support the change in text direction.

Image Tracing a Photograph

Illustrator provides the designer with the ability to trace a photograph. This process converts a resolution-dependent, bitmap image into a resolution-independent, vector image. This effect is frequently used for posters and stylized designs. There are multiple options to choose from when it comes to how the photograph is translated based on the desired amount of colors and level of detail. Figure 12.26 illustrates five color options applied to the same segment of a photograph of the Old Faithful Geyser in Yellowstone National Park. Compare the amount of colors used in each example along with the clarity and detail of the subject matter. Looking from left to right, the examples contain increasingly more paths and thus greater detail.

Let's use this process to create a poster promoting Yellowstone National Park in *Exercise 12.3.* Review the exercise brief, and then get started.

Graphic Design: Learn It, Do It

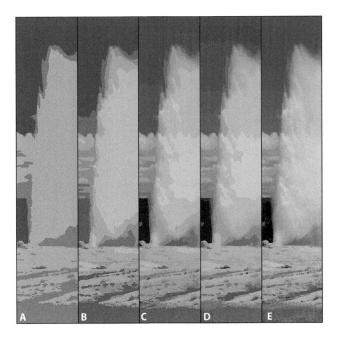

Figure 12.26

Image Trace, Tracing Presets: (A) 3 Colors, (B) 6 Colors, (C) 16 Colors, (D) Low Fidelity Photo, and (E) High Fidelity Photo.

Exercise 12.3: Creating a Poster

Exercise brief: Create a vector-based poster that incorporates a photograph and creative use of text in the illustration.

    Exercise file: **Ch12-Ex03-photo.jpg** (Figure 12.27)

Step 1: Create and save an illustration file in Illustrator (Ch12-Ex03.ai).

- Go to the *File menu* and select *New...* [File menu > New... | ⌘N].
- In the *New Document dialog box,* look for the *Art & Illustration set* and from the *Blank Document Presets* select *Poster* (1296 × 1728 pt.) [18 × 24 in.].
- Customize the file by making the following changes to the default properties.
  - Change the *Color Mode* to CMYK.
  - Click on the *More Settings button* and under the *Advanced header,* set the *Raster Effects* to High (300 ppi). Click the *Create Document button* to return to the *New Document dialog box.*
- Click *Create* to generate the illustration file.
- Return to the *File menu* and select *Save As...* [File menu > Save As... | ⇧⌘S].

Figure 12.27

Exercise 12.3 file. Old Faithful Geyser, Yellowstone National Park, Wyoming.

- In the *Save As dialog box*, enter the file name, *Ch12-Ex03*, verify the *Format* (Adobe Illustrator [ai]) and navigate to an appropriate location.
- Click *Save*, which launches the Illustrator Options dialog box.
- In the Illustrator Options dialog box, accept the default values and click *OK* to save the illustration file.

Step 2: Place the provided photograph on the artboard. *Tip:* Resist the urge to drag and drop the file onto the artboard. Instead, use the following method:

- Go to the *File menu* and select the *Place... menu command* [File menu > Place... | ⌘P].
- Navigate to the provided photograph file (available on the book's companion website). Then click *Place*. This action creates a "loaded cursor" that has the photograph file associated with it.
- Position the cursor in the upper-left corner of the illustration file and click once to place the photograph. *Note:* Do not be alarmed when the photo spans well beyond the artboard.

Once placed, the photograph should be selected on the artboard. Look to the *Control panel* (Figure 12.28) and review the available options.

Graphic Design: Learn It, Do It

A		B	C	D	E	F	G	H	I	J

Figure 12.28

Control panel while photograph is selected: (A) Status of photograph (Embedded/ Unembedded) including Color Mode and Resolution, (B) Edit Original image, (C) Converts Image into Tracing Image, (D) Mask, (E) Crop Image, (F) Shortcut to Transparency panel, (G) Opacity, (H) Align to Selection, (I) Shortcut to Transform Panel, and (J) Isolate Selected Object.

Step 3: Resize the photograph as needed to fit the artboard.

- *Zoom out* to see the photograph in its entirety [View menu > Zoom Out | ⌘-] (Figure 12.29).
- Choose the *Selection Tool* (V) from the Tools panel, and position the cursor over the handle in the lower-right corner of the photograph (see Figure 12.29A).
- Hold down the *Shift key* on the keyboard to preserve the proportions of the image frame, *then* hold down the mouse button and drag the handle to the lower-right corner of the artboard.
  - *Note:* When the photograph is resized to fit the entire image on the artboard, the photograph does not fill the artboard, there is a white gap to the right of the photograph (see Figure 12.29B).

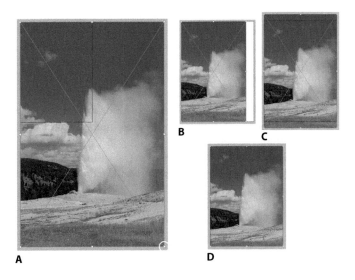

Figure 12.29

Photograph placed [File menu > Place…]: (A) initial placement of photograph (too large), (B) resized photograph (too small), (C) resized and repositioned photograph (too large), and (D) cropped image (Crop Image button pressed).

- Using the same combination of the *Shift key* and dragging the cursor, resize the photograph (larger) so it covers the entire artboard.
- Reposition the photo so there is a balance between the sky and the ground included on the artboard (see Figure 12.29C).
- To remove the excess areas of the photograph, click the *Crop button* in the *Control panel*. Use the *handles* on each side and in the corners of the photograph to trim the excess areas of the photo (see Figure 12.29D). When the handles are positioned at the edge of the artboard, press the *Return/Enter key* on the keyboard.
  - The following Illustrator alert may appear: *Cropping a linked file embeds a copy of the original. The original file at the linked location is not affected.* If this message appears, click *OK* or press the *ESC key* on the keyboard to close the window and try again.
- *Deselect* the photograph [Select menu > Deselect | ⇧⌘A].

Now that the photograph has been successfully placed on the artboard, save the file and continue working.

Step 4: Save the file.

- From the *File menu* select *Save* [File menu > Save | ⌘S].

Step 5: Use Image Trace to create paths based on the photograph.

- In the *Control panel* click on the dropdown arrow positioned to the right of the *Image Trace button*. This dropdown list of *Tracing Presets* offers multiple options (i.e., High Fidelity Photo, Low Fidelity Photo, 3 Colors, 6 Colors, 16 Colors, Shades of Gray, Black and White Logo, Sketched Art, Silhouettes, Line Art, Technical Drawing).
- Let's begin with the *Low Fidelity Photo option*.
  - Why select Low Fidelity Photo? Low Fidelity Photo will emphasize the color shape nature of the vector image. It will contain more colors than the self-described 3, 6 or 16 Colors options, but fewer than High Fidelity Photo. Fewer paths will be created than if High Fidelity Photo was selected, which will make selecting and editing specific paths easier.
- Select the *Low Fidelity Photo option*.
  - When this option is selected, the following Illustrator alert may appear, *Tracing may proceed slowly with this large image. Would you like to continue? Note*: To reduce the image size, rasterize to a lower resolution using Object menu > Rasterize. If this message appears, click *OK* or press the *ESC key* on the keyboard to close the window.

The photo is traced; content previously presented as pixels is now a collection of color shapes corresponding to the original photograph. Once the *Image Trace* is

Graphic Design: Learn It, Do It

complete, zoom in on the image [View menu > Zoom In | ⌘+]. The color shapes will not become pixelated no matter the degree of magnification. *Tip:* To return the image to a workable view, use the *Fit Artboard in Window* option from the *View menu* [View menu > Fit Artboard in Window | ⌘0].

Step 6: Save the file.

* From the *File menu* select *Save* [File menu > Save | ⌘S].

To edit the traced image, the color groups first need to be separated and then ungrouped. Begin by selecting the traced image with the *Selection Tool* (V), then clicking on the *Expand button* in the *Control panel*. This action allows the designer to view the shapes that comprise the image, a series of *blue outlines* (Figure 12.30). These paths are currently *grouped*. When objects or paths are *grouped*, multiple objects are treated as a single unit. Grouped objects can be moved or transformed without affecting their attributes and relative positions.

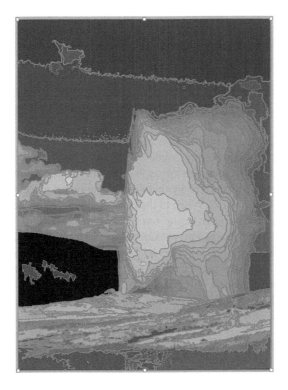

Figure 12.30

Image Trace, Expand.

In order to select and modify a single path, the paths must be *ungrouped*. To ungroup the paths, first make sure that they are selected using the *Selection Tool* (V) and then from the *Object menu*, select the *Ungroup menu command* [Object menu > Ungroup | ⇧⌘G]. Once this action is complete, individual paths can be selected and edited.

Step 7: Separate the color groups to allow for individual paths to be edited.

- With the traced image selected, click the *Expand button* in the *Control panel*.
  - When this action is complete, the image should appear as a series of blue outlines.
- From the *Object menu*, select the *Ungroup menu command* [Object menu > Ungroup].
  - Once this action is complete, the color shapes can be selected as individual paths.
- Deselect all [Select menu > Deselect | ⇧⌘A].
- Using the *Direct Selection Tool* (A), move the cursor over the sky of the image and look for the outline of a color shape to appear. When one of these areas is visible, click the mouse button once to select the specific path. If too much of the image is selected, simply deselect all and try again.

Just like with any other path, color shapes can be altered, changing their colors (fill and stroke), adjusting the anchor points, affecting their shape and deleting the path.

Illustrator provides an *Isolation Mode*, which can be used to edit a path, sublayer, compound shape or symbol, without affecting other content. Content not associated with the selected item appears grayed out and cannot be edited. The Isolation Mode can be entered by double-clicking on an object on the artboard using the *Selection Tool* (V). When in the Isolation Mode, a gray bar appears above the workspace containing an *arrow icon* that can be used to exit the current level. Next to the arrow icon, the current *Containing Layer* and the *Current Isolation Object* are listed (Figure 12.31). *Note:* It is possible to go several layers deep within the Isolation Mode, so it may be necessary to click the arrow icon multiple times to exit Isolation Mode and return to the artboard.

Try using the Isolation Mode to edit a specific path, for example, the topmost layer of blue sky. Consider eliminating the hook shown in Figure 12.32.

Step 8 (Optional): Simplify the sky in the upper-left corner of the image.

- *Zoom in* on the area of interest [View menu > Zoom In | ⌘+].
- In order to simplify the sky, eliminate the two color shapes identified as "1" and "2" in Figure 12.32A.

Graphic Design: Learn It, Do It

Figure 12.31

Isolation Mode: (A) Back one level/Exit Isolation Mode, (B) Containing Layer, and (C) Current Isolated Object.

- Use the *Selection Tool* (V) to select each of the color shapes.
- Once selected, press the *Delete key* on the keyboard to eliminate each shape.
- When Shape 2 is deleted, a hole in the blue sky is created. This empty area will be filled when Shape 4 is edited.
- *Tip:* Select Shape 1, then hold down the *Shift key* on the keyboard and click on Shape 2. Used in this capacity, the Shift key adds to a current selection.
- Double-click on Shape 3 (the second band of blue in the image) using the *Selection Tool* (V) to enter the *Isolation Mode*.
  - The goal is to eliminate the two projections identified in Figure 12.32B. There are several ways to accomplish this goal; here is one method.
- First, *deselect* all anchor points [Select menu > Deselect | ⇧⌘A].
- Select the *Lasso Tool* (Q) and draw a selection area around one of the projections.
  - This action selects the anchor points used to create the projection (see Figure 12.32C).
- Now press the *Delete key* on the keyboard to eliminate these anchor points.
- Repeat the same process with the second projection.

---

12. Illustrator Continued

Figure 12.32

Exercise 12.3, Step 8: (A) shape identification, (B) projections identified, (C) Lasso Tool selection, (D) endpoints, and (E) anchor points added and adjusted.

- When completed, Shape 3 appears to have a straight line between the remaining sections of the path (see Figure 12.32D). This straight line is actually Illustrator closing the gap between the two newly created endpoints.
- Use the *Pen Tool* (P) to *join* these two endpoints.
  - *Tip:* To close an open path, with the Pen Tool (P) selected, position the cursor over one of the two endpoints, then click once. Now, move the cursor over the second endpoint, and click once. This simple process creates a path between the anchor points, which can now be modified.
- To camouflage the straight path, use the *Add Anchor Point Tool* (+) to add several anchor points, then use the *Anchor Point Tool* (Shift + C) to convert the corner points to smooth points, which blend more naturally with the contours of the path (see Figure 12.32E).
  - *Tip:* Remember that adjusting the *direction handle* affects the created curve.
- When satisfied with the changes made, press the *arrow icon* to exit the *Isolation Mode*.

Graphic Design: Learn It, Do It

Figure 12.33

Exercise 12.3, Step 8 completed.

- It is time patch the hole in the image using Shape 4. Double-click on Shape 4, the top band of blue, to enter the *Isolation Mode.*
- Use the tools and techniques available to cover the white hole. Consider simplifying the path along the top of the white area, then repositioning the remaining anchor points to cover the negative space. *Note:* Text will be added to the image in this area, which will cover the patch job, so do not get too carried away trying to replicate the uneven edge of Shape 4 that was created during the tracing process (Figure 12.33).

Step 9: Save the file.

- From the *File menu* select *Save* [File menu > Save | ⌘S].

The bands of color in the sky reflect the gradation of colors in the original photograph. The subtle shades of blue were converted into bands of related colors during the image tracing process. For the designer who prefers a solid color for the sky, this is a simple edit to complete. Select the sky paths and change the fill color, which limits the sky color from three shades of blue to one (Figure 12.34). *Note:* Simplifying the sky to a single color may highlight some stray color shapes along the previous path edges. These stray paths can be left as is, selected and deleted or changed so their color matches the sky.

Let's add some text to the design. First, add a headline and subhead that use a stylized typeface to stand out from the image. Then, for something unexpected, we create a path in the shape of the blowing mist from the geyser's spray, and this path will be filled with text. However, before we begin creating text, let's first lock the traced sublayers in the Layers panel to avoid unintentionally selecting and adjusting the image. When we want to make changes to any of these layers, we need to unlock the layers. A new layer will be created to hold the text and text-related elements.

Figure 12.34

Exercise 12.3, Sky simplified.

Step 10: In the Layers panel, lock the *Layer 1. Note:* By locking Layer 1 all of its sublayers are automatically locked.

- If the *Layers panel* is not open, open it from the *Window menu* [Window menu > Layers].
- In the Layers panel, click once in the empty column positioned to the left of the layer name (Layer 1). A *lock icon* should appear indicating that the layer and its sublayers are now locked.

Step 11: In the Layers panel, create a new layer, which will contain the text elements.

- In the *Layers panel,* create a new layer using either the *Create New Layer icon* along the bottom of the panel, or select *New Layer...* from the Layers panel menu (Figure 12.35).

Step 12: Use the Type Tool (T) to create a headline for the poster celebrating Yellowstone National Park's status as the "World's First National Park."

- Confirm that Layer 2 is currently selected in the *Layers panel.*
- Select the *Type Tool* (T) from the Tools panel.
- Create a text headline for the poster.

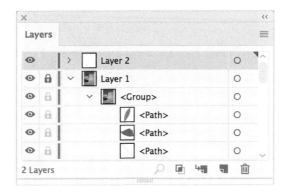

Figure 12.35

Layers panel, Layer 2 created, Layer 1 locked.

If your text includes multiple lines or a headline and a subhead, consider using contrasting typefaces and sizes to establish a sense of hierarchy within the text. With the headline in position, let's create a mist-shaped path for the text.

Step 13: Create a closed path that follows the natural shape of the geyser's mist. Then use the *Area Type Tool* to place text within the path.

- Use the *Pen Tool* (P) or the *Paintbrush Tool* (B) to draw a path around the mist located to the right of the geyser's plume of water (Figure 12.36).
  - Be sure the path begins and ends at the same anchor point.
  - Use the *Direct Selection Tool* (A) as needed to adjust the path.
  - *Tip:* For ease of use, set the *Fill Color* to None and the *Stroke Color* to a color that contrasts with the traced image in the background.
- Once the path is created, select the *Area Type Tool* and position the cursor along the edge of the path. Click once to fill the area with placeholder text.
- Replace the placeholder text with copy that describes the attributes or landmarks of Yellowstone National Park.
  - The link to the Yellowstone National Park website is included at the end of this chapter for reference and inspiration.
  - However, be mindful of copyright infringement as you look to outside sources; be sure to provide the appropriate attributes for the source(s) of any outside text included in the design.
- Adjust the *font size* and the *shape of the area path* as needed to accommodate the text.
  - Turn off *hyphenation* to increase the readability of the text.
  - Add a subtle *drop shadow* to the text to help it stand out from the background image [Effect menu > (Illustrator Effects) Stylize > Drop Shadow...].

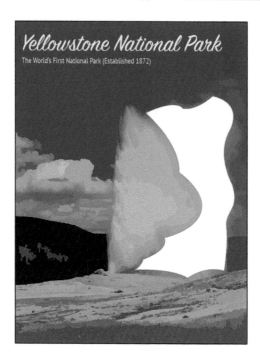

Figure 12.36

Area path.

Step 14: Save the file and take a moment to appreciate your work (Figure 12.37).

- Select *Save* from the *File menu* [File menu > Save | ⌘S].

Nice work, you have demonstrated your ability to create in Illustrator using a selection of its tools and processes. There is one final step to perform before closing the illustration file and the application. The step is to save a copy of the poster as a PDF file, a file format that can be easily accessed by others.

Step 15: Save a PDF version of the illustration.

- From the *File menu*, select *Save As...* [File menu > Save As... | ⇧⌘S].
- In the *Save As dialog box*, choose *Adobe PDF (pdf)* from the *Format dropdown menu*.
- Click *Save*, an action that launches the *Save Adobe PDF dialog box* (Figure 12.38).
- Review the available options, then accept the default values and click the *Save PDF* button.
- Locate and open the PDF file to verify its content and to view your work.

Now, you have finished *Exercise 12.3*, well done.

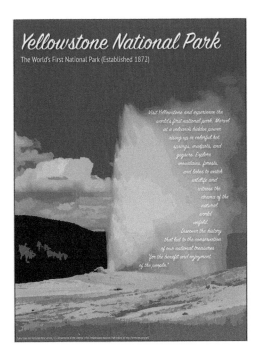

Figure 12.37

Exercise 12.3 completed.

Looking Ahead

This chapter presented a lot of information about Illustrator. Spend time revisiting the exercises and experimenting with the tools and features until you feel comfortable working with the concepts presented. Then, when you are ready to proceed, the next chapter focuses on page layout and the elements that go into the overall page design of a document.

Discussion

Discussion 12.1: Creative Text Presentation

Type on a Path allows for the creative presentation of text in an illustration. How do you envision using this feature? What shaped path would you create for the type? What benefits are provided with the use of *Type on a Path*? Now, think about the audience's experience, what readability challenges accompany the use of *Type on a Path* and *Area Type*? How can you proactively plan to avoid these challenges?

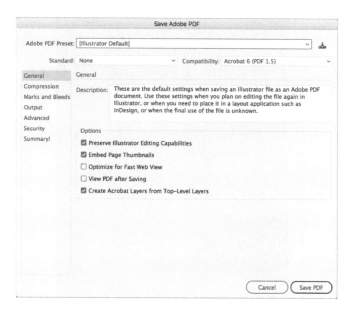

Figure 12.38

Save As PDF dialog box.

Activity

Activity 12.1: Create a Personal Logo

Use Illustrator to create a logo for yourself that includes your name. Design the logo for personal branding, specifically for use on a business card, letterhead, jacket or ball cap.

Use the brainstorming techniques presented in *Chapter 4: Defining the Project* to get started. When capturing your initial ideas, consider the following:

- *Your Name:* Identify which name you will incorporate, your full name, a single name (first, middle or last name), a nickname or your initials.
- *Inspiration:* Focus on what you do (skills, hobbies) and how these ideas could be visually represented.
- *Sense of Self:* List five words that you use to describe yourself. If appropriate, ask others to do the same. Review the terms for ideas and concepts that could be incorporated into the logo.
- *Colors:* Think about the role of color in the logo, consider color significance and symbolism (refer to *Chapter 3: Color in Design*).

Graphic Design: Learn It, Do It

Once production has begun, pay attention to the following concepts:

- *Keep It Simple:* Focus on one or two ideas. Do not try to incorporate all of your brainstorming ideas into a single design.
- *Use Negative Space:* Think about ways to include visible breaks for the eye into the logo. Use the principles of design to achieve balance between the figure and the ground, refer to *Chapter 2: The Elements and Principles of Design.*
- *Typography Matters:* Incorporate your name into the design from the start; it should not be an afterthought. Select a type category that supports the ideas that you wish to communicate in the logo (refer to *Chapter 10: Typography in Design*).

Exercise File(s) Available on the Companion Website, URL

Ch12-Ex03-photo.jpg | *Exercise 12.3* file. Old Faithful Geyser, Yellowstone National Park, Wyoming.

Ch12-Ex03.pdf | *Exercise 12.3* file, Poster.

URL: http://www.crcpress.com/9780367075347

External Links Mentioned in the Chapter

Illustrator Online Help | https://helpx.adobe.com/illustrator

Lorem Ipsum | https://www.lipsum.com

Yellowstone National Park | https://www.nps.gov/yell/

13

Page Layout

When discussing page layout, we are referring to a design that brings together images and text into a single document. The size of the document may vary in terms of dimensions or volume (e.g., single page vs. multipage), but the underlying goal is the same, to create an arrangement of content that presents a clear and cohesive message, in other words, visual hierarchy. As described in *Chapter 2: The Elements and Principles of Design*, visual hierarchy refers to a sense of order within a design that aids in identifying what is most important. The principles of design can be used to achieve visual hierarchy; they include Balance, Alignment, Repetition, Contrast, Proximity and Space. For a refresher of these design principles, refer to *Chapter 2: The Elements and Principles of Design*. Successful page layout supports visual hierarchy and does not distract from the content.

The Grid System

One of the most popular techniques used to achieve these results is the *grid system*. At its core, the grid system is a method used to divide a page or screen into defined areas, which are used to present content. The grid system can be traced back to early handwritten manuscripts, yet it remains a widely used layout technique in contemporary design. One explanation for this longevity is that grids work across platforms from print layouts to Web-based designs that support multiple devices and various screen sizes.

A *grid* is a structure that divides a page into columns or modules. These defined areas provide an underlying structure on which the designer can arrange page content. This system affords flexibility in where content is placed. At the same time, the structure encourages consistency and the ability to reproduce the layout across a project. The consistency that is created benefits both the designer as well as the viewer who understands where content will be presented.

Each grid is made up of a combination of the following parts (Figure 13.1):

- *Format:* The format is the area where the design is placed. In print design, the format is the page; in Web design, the format is the browser window.
- *Margins:* Margins are the negative spaces between the edge of the format and the content.
- *Columns, rows and gutters:* Columns are vertically defined areas within a grid. The horizontal equivalent to a column is the row. The space between columns or rows is known as the gutter or alley.
- *Modules:* Modules are individual areas of space created from the intersections of columns and rows. Vertical groups of modules together create columns; horizontal groups create rows.

Types of Grids

The designer has multiple types of grids from which to choose in order to accommodate the content and needs of a project. When deciding on which grid to use, it is helpful to first sketch the general layout and see which of the following grids is best suited to the arrangement.

- *Manuscript grid* or *single-column grid:* The manuscript grid is the simplest grid structure. It is essentially a rectangular area that occupies most of the space inside the format (Figure 13.2). The manuscript grid works well for continuous blocks of text or the presentation of images.
- *Multicolumn grid:* As its name suggests, the multicolumn grid is composed of multiple columns (Figure 13.3). The number of columns depends on the content and the dimensions of the output. The columns can be used to create zones for different kinds of content.
- *Modular grid:* The modular grid divides a page into modules (Figure 13.4). The intersections of columns, rows and gutters create a matrix of modules or cells. A modular grid provides more control than a multicolumn grid, which can be beneficial for complex layouts. Each module in the grid can contain a small chunk of information, or adjacent modules can be combined to form blocks.

Graphic Design: Learn It, Do It

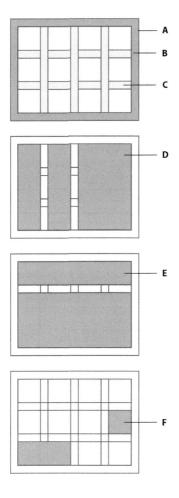

Figure 13.1

Grid components: (A) format, (B) margins, (C) gutters, (D) columns, (E) rows, and (F) modules.

- *Baseline grid:* The baseline grid is an underlying structure that guides the vertical spacing in a design. Using this type of grid is like writing on a lined piece of paper (Figure 13.5). The grid ensures that the bottom of each line of text (a.k.a. its baseline) aligns with the vertical spacing. It is primarily used for horizontal alignment and for hierarchy.

Keep in mind that when it comes to page layout, there is generally more than one viable solution for a project. In fact, it is a good practice to develop more than one solution and assess the strengths of each before finalizing the arrangement of content.

Lorem ipsum dolor sit amet, consectetuer adipiscing elit, sed diam nonummy nibh euismod tincidunt ut laoreet dolore magna aliquam erat volutpat. Ut wisi enim ad minim veniam, quis nostrud exerci tation ullamcorper suscipit lobortis nisl ut aliquip ex ea commodo consequat. Duis autem vel eum iriure dolor in hendrerit in vulputate velit esse molestie consequat, vel illum dolore eu feugiat nulla facilisis at vero eros et accumsan et iusto odio dignissim qui blandit praesent luptatum zzril delenit augue duis dolore te

Figure 13.2

Manuscript grid.

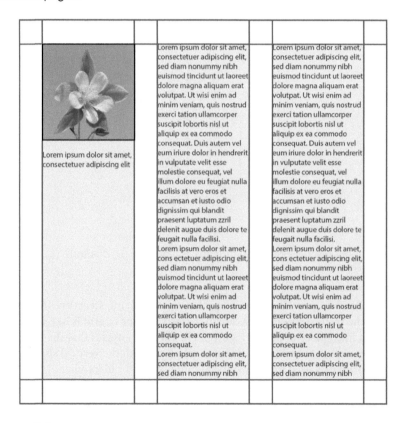

Figure 13.3

Multicolumn grid.

Graphic Design: Learn It, Do It

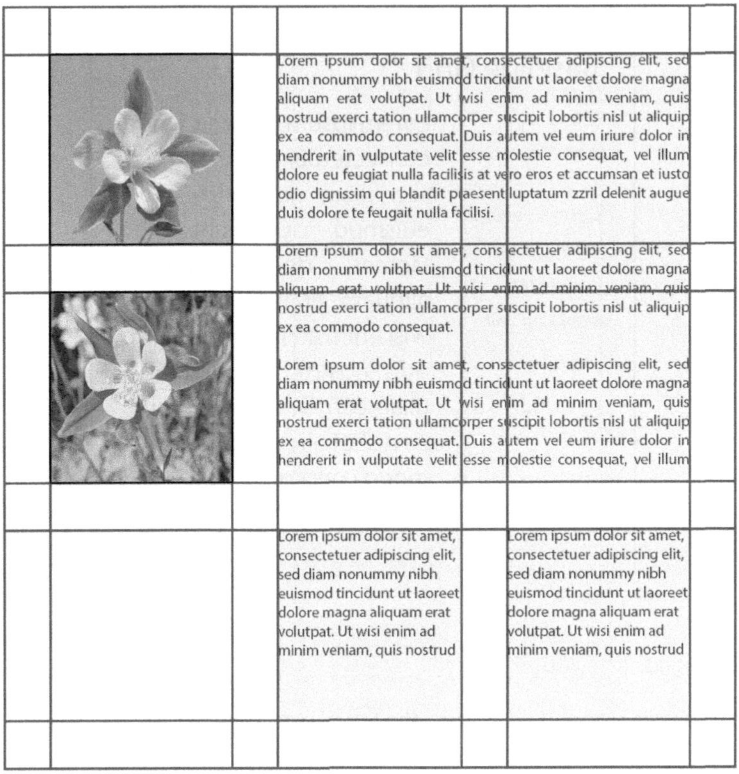

Figure 13.4

Modular grid.

As a designer, you may be tasked with creating page layouts for a variety of outputs. However, whether designing a business card, brochure or magazine page, the grid system provides a structure on which to develop visual hierarchy. The degree of complexity may vary among projects, but the underlying goal is the same, to create a design that utilizes the design principles to effectively communicate its message.

Designing a Business Card

Now let's apply these ideas to a series of tasks. We begin with a business card, a document that is limited in its finished size, but impactful when making a first impression with potential clients. Among the goals of a business card is to create a personal connection between you and a potential client. When you distribute a business card, you are inviting the recipient to connect with you.

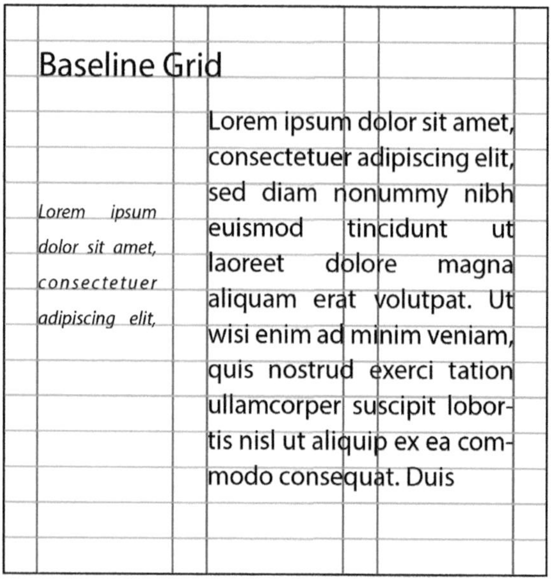

Baseline Grid

Lorem ipsum
dolor sit amet,
consectetuer
adipiscing elit,

Lorem ipsum dolor sit amet,
consectetuer adipiscing elit,
sed diam nonummy nibh
euismod tincidunt ut
laoreet dolore magna
aliquam erat volutpat. Ut
wisi enim ad minim veniam,
quis nostrud exerci tation
ullamcorper suscipit lobortis nisl ut aliquip ex ea commodo consequat. Duis

Figure 13.5

Baseline grid.

A business card should include the following components:

- *Logo and tagline:* The company logo and tagline (or slogan) are used to convey the company's identity visually through use of color, fonts and text.
- *Name and functional job title:* Use these elements as an opportunity to introduce yourself and what you do.
- *Contact information:* Provide relevant contact details while keeping personal information private. If most of your business and communications are done online, do not include your physical street address on the business card. If location is relevant to your business (e.g., wedding photography), consider listing your city or town on the business card but leave off your street address. You can always provide the physical street address on future communications or invoices once a relationship has been established. Think about your safety.
- *Website:* If you have an online platform to share examples of your work, include that link on the business card. Online portfolios are discussed in detail in *Chapter 16: Bringing It All Together.*
- *Social media profiles:* If you are professionally active on social media, provide channels that are relevant to your field. Be strategic about where potential clients can view a sample of your work. However, do not overwhelm your audience with a lengthy list of social media channels. Save that for your website.

- *White space a.k.a. negative space:* Use negative space to provide balance to the content presented on the business card. Again, avoid overwhelming your audience.

The dimensions of a finished business card in the United States and Canada are 3.5 in. × 2 in. (89 mm × 51 mm). In much of Europe, the standard business card is 3.346 in. × 2.165 in. (85 mm × 55 mm). These varying sizes are mentioned as a reminder that it is important to understand your client, the client's needs and the context of the project before you begin laying out a document.

For the purposes of this discussion, we use the U.S. standard size (3.5 in. × 2 in.). When setting up the document, an additional one-quarter inch (0.25 in.) is added to the dimensions to accommodate the bleed area (3.75 in. × 2.25 in.). The bleed area is an additional one-eighth inch (0.125 in.) of space on each side of the business card for design elements that extend beyond the finished size of the card (Figure 13.6). The bleed area will be trimmed off of the document, so its contents will not be seen in the finished business card.

In addition to designing the front of a business card, the layout of the document provides an opportunity for content on the back of the business card as well. The back of the card can be used to present a company logo or tagline or to present a translated version of the front of the card if business is regularly done in a second language. The back of the card can also be left blank, as space to write a message.

In addition to deciding whether a business card will be single or double sided, the choice of orientation (horizontal vs. vertical) must be made. Although horizontal business cards are the norm for most U.S. companies, vertical business cards are also used. A vertical orientation may be used to stand out from other cards and companies. A vertical orientation may also be used by companies and individuals who do business in foreign markets, where characters are read from top to bottom.

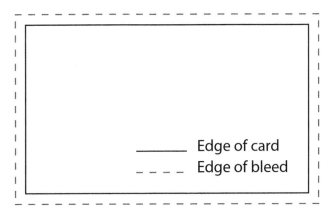

Figure 13.6

Standard business card including bleed.

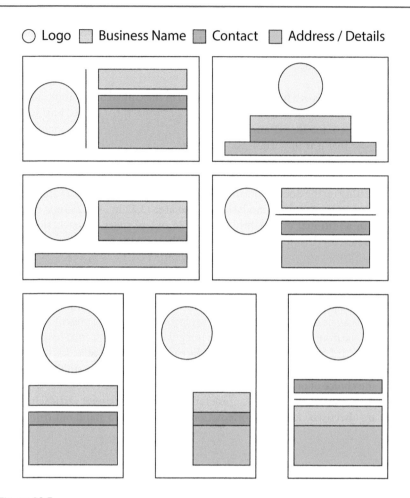

○ Logo ▢ Business Name ▢ Contact ▢ Address / Details

Figure 13.7

Sample business card layouts.

As shown in Figure 13.7, there are multiple ways to present the standard information included on a business card using either orientation.

For those designers seeking an unexpected layout, alternate shapes can be used for business cards (e.g., squares and mini-cards). Just be aware of potential costs when utilizing nontraditional options. *Tip:* Contact a printing service to price out the costs associated with different layout options (e.g., dimensions, single vs. double sided and full color) before committing to a specific design.

Let's see how much space is available for content on a standard business card and which orientation you prefer. *Exercise 13.1* initiates the design process using sketches on paper to capture your initial ideas and preferences.

Exercise 13.1: Draft a Business Card

Exercise brief: Create a business card for yourself or your business (current or hypothetical). Design the business card to include the contact information that you would expect to find on such a card.

Exercise file: **Ch13-Ex01.pdf** Business card templates (horizontal and vertical)

Download and print a copy of the *Business Card Template*, which is available as a PDF file on the book's companion website. Or, create your own template in Illustrator based on the provided dimensions of a standard business card. Use the template to capture your ideas *on paper*. Create at least three variations of your business card. Repeating the task encourages you to consider different options when it comes to the arrangement of card elements. With your sketches in hand, answer the following questions:

- What information is most important on the business card?
- How do the principles of design contribute to the visual hierarchy of information on the business card?
- How are the individual design principles being used?
  - *Balance:* How has the visual weight of the elements (e.g., company logo and contact information) been balanced?
  - *Alignment:* How has alignment been used to create order and organization within the design? Do visual connections exist among the elements on the business card?
  - *Repetition:* How is repetition being used in the elements of the business card (e.g., font, color and line)? How does the repetition create rhythm or a feeling of organized movement across the business card?
  - *Contrast:* How is contrast being used to emphasize specific elements within the design? What elements represent opposing elements (e.g., fonts, colors and lines)?
  - *Proximity:* What is the main focal point on the business card? What kinds of visual connections exist among the content?
  - *Space:* How is space being used to avoid clutter and confusion? How are the positive and negative spaces being used to effectively present information in the layout of the business card?
- How could a grid help organize the arrangement of elements on the business card?

Based on your responses to these questions, revise the sketches or begin again. Remember that the design process is cyclical: design, review, revise and repeat. The goal in these revisions is to strengthen the business card design before you begin creating the document in an Adobe Creative Cloud application. *Tip:* It is often easier to print another copy of the *Business Card Template* and start the sketching fresh, rather than revising an existing design.

Designing a Brochure

Our next task is to create a brochure to promote a company or an event. As shown in Figure 13.8, there are multiple options to choose from when designing a folded brochure. For our purposes, we will focus on the tri-fold brochure using a landscape orientation for the paper.

In a tri-fold brochure, three equal sections are created by folding the side panels over the middle. Most tri-folds bend the right side first and then the left side. Based on this order, when opened, the brochure reads from left to right. When laying out any brochure, it is important to ask, "What will the viewer see first?" Keep in mind the order in which content is presented and consumed. For the tri-fold brochure (Figure 13.9), the numbered panels correspond to the order in which content is generally presented and ideally consumed.

Each one of the six sections of a tri-fold brochure serves a purpose in the overall presentation of information. Locate each section in Figure 13.9 after reading its description.

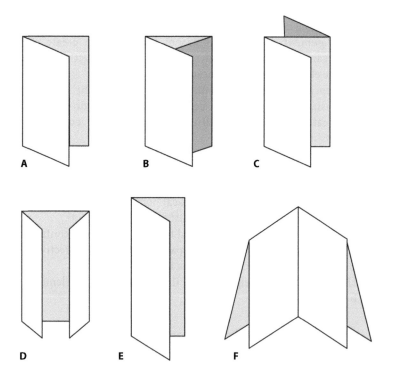

Figure 13.8

Brochure layouts: (A) half-fold, (B) tri-fold, (C) Z-fold, (D) three-panel gate fold, (E) vertical half fold and (F) French fold (quarter fold).

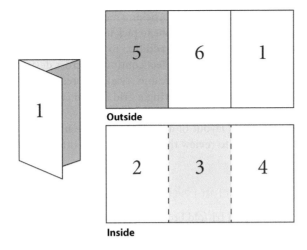

Figure 13.9

Tri-fold brochure layout, sections labeled.

- *Section 1 (Front Cover):* As the front cover of the folded brochure, this panel generally contains an image and the name of the company or event. This information should be eye-catching and placed in the top third of the design in order to be visible in a brochure rack. The cover design should entice the viewer to pick up and open the brochure and continue reading.
- *Section 2 (Inside Front Cover):* The brochure is unfolded to show the inside front cover, Section 2. This panel often contains both questions and answers that introduce the company or the event.
- *Sections 3 (Inside Back Cover) and 4 (Inside Panel):* When the inside panel (Section 5) is opened, Sections 3 and 4 are visible. The middle and right panels generally contain additional information about the subject. Consider using headers and bulleted lists to organize the content, to avoid overwhelming the viewer with too much text.
- *Section 5 (Inside Panel):* This inside panel is visible when the brochure is first opened. The space sometimes contains extra information or it may be used as an order form or survey.
- *Section 6 (Back Cover):* The back cover is generally reserved for contact information or a map. If the brochure will be mailed to audiences, the back panel serves as a place for the mailing address and postage. *Note:* If Section 5 contains a form that will be completed and returned to event organizers, this back panel should be reserved for the mailing address and a designated postage area.

Beyond the arrangement of content, there are several design challenges associated with creating a brochure. First, how will the brochure stand out visually among other brochures in a crowded brochure rack? The goal of the cover panel is to generate enough interest for someone to pick up the brochure in order to learn more about the company or event. In addition to attracting attention, the overall design of the brochure should also reflect continuity across design. This includes consistency in fonts (e.g., typeface, size and style), the presentation of images and overall alignment of content. Employing a grid system can help you achieve an organized arrangement of content.

Let's review the basic layout of a tri-fold brochure using a paper mock-up. *Exercise 13.2* is designed to review the presentation of information in the folded brochure.

Exercise 13.2: Draft a Tri-Fold Brochure

Exercise brief: Mock up a tri-fold brochure on paper. Use the provided template and fold it to become familiar with the available areas for content and the order in which each section is seen.

Exercise files: **Ch13-Ex02.pdf** Tri-fold brochure template

Download and print a copy of the *Tri-Fold Brochure Template*,* which is available as a PDF file on the book's companion website. Fold the template along the dashed lines. First, fold the right panel into the center, then the left panel. With the folded template in hand, review how the brochure opens and the order of the sections seen.

Now select a subject, either an organization that you support or an event that you attend, and sketch content related to that subject on each panel of the folded template.

Note: Included at the end of *Chapter 15: InDesign Continued* is an activity that reviews the process for setting up a document to create a tri-fold brochure.

With your sketch in hand, answer the following questions:

- What information is most important on the brochure? Where is this information located?
- How do the principles of design contribute to the visual hierarchy of information presented on the brochure?
- How are the design principles being used?
  - *Balance:* How has the visual weight of the elements been balanced?
  - *Alignment:* How has alignment been used to create order and organization within the brochure? Do visual connections exist among the elements on different panels?
  - *Repetition:* How is repetition being used in the elements of the brochure (e.g., font, color and line)? How does the repetition create rhythm or a feeling of organized movement across the brochure?

---

* If you have the ability to print double-sided, do so for the *Tri-Fold Brochure Template*. If not, print both pages and then place the backs of these pages together to create a homemade version of the double-sided template.

Graphic Design: Learn It, Do It

- *Contrast:* How is contrast being used to emphasize specific elements within the design? What elements represent opposing elements (e.g., fonts, colors and lines)?
- *Proximity:* What is the main focal point on the brochure? What kinds of visual connections exist among the content on the inside and outside of the brochure?
- *Space:* How is space being used to avoid clutter and confusion? How are the positive and negative spaces being used to effectively present information in the layout of the brochure?
- How could a grid help organize the arrangement of elements on the brochure?

Designing a Magazine Page

The next subject of page layout that we address is a magazine page. There is quite a bit of terminology involved in this section. An understanding of these terms will further discussions of layout techniques that promote readability and the impact of the overall design. *Note:* Many of the page elements presented here in the context of a magazine can be applied to other documents as well.

Let's begin with a few familiar terms, *margins* and *columns*. These universal properties are applicable across various document types. Set during the document creation process, values for margins and columns can later be adjusted as needed. During production, these areas are represented by document guides (Figure 13.10). The guides will not be visible in the final document output.

Margins are the areas along the outer edges of a printed page. These areas are often left empty due to a printer's inability to print to the edge of a page. For many consumer printers, this margin is at least one-quarter inch (0.25 in.) on

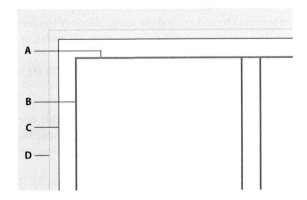

Figure 13.10

Document guides: (A) margin guide, (B) column guide, (C) document edge, and (D) bleed guide.

Figure 13.11

Bound document, larger margins along inside edges to accommodate binding.

all sides of a document. While the width of a document's margins is generally consistent on each of the four sides of a page, the values can vary depending on the needs of the project. For bound projects, such as a magazine or book, the inside margins may be larger than the others to accommodate the binding process (Figure 13.11).

Columns are another page element used to present and contain content. As discussed during the introduction of the grid systems, the use of columns can encourage a sense of consistency across a document. Columns can also be used to increase the ease of readability for large blocks of text. A column limits the length of a line of text making it easier for a reader to scan a line and move on to the next. On pages that include both text and images, columns provide flexibility for the presentation of text next to and around the image. *Note:* All pages use at least one column in their document setup; one column spans the width of the page from left margin to right margin.

The following questions are generally raised once columns are introduced into page layout:

- *How many is too many columns?* The answer to this question depends in part on the dimensions of the document page, specifically the width. When a column can only fit two to three words per line, consider reducing the number of columns on the page.
- *Should text in columns be justified?* Not necessarily. Text presented in columns can be justified to highlight the evenness of the columns. Similarly, justification is often used when wrapping text around an object, a technique presented in *Chapter 15: InDesign Continued*. In this scenario, justified text emphasizes the shape of the object and any offset

Graphic Design: Learn It, Do It

space or margin between the text and the object. However, remember the challenges of justified text discussed in *Chapter 10: Typography in Design*, including but not limited to widows, orphans and rivers.

The space between columns, the *gutter*, is what separates columns of content. As such, the gutter is generally treated aesthetically as negative space, a visual break for the eye. The width of the gutter can be set when a document is created and then adjusted as needed.

Additional page elements defined during the document creation process include bleed and slug. These areas fall *outside* of the document page, and while not seen by the reader, they serve as useful references for the designer. Both the bleed and slug areas are specified when the document is created and then discarded when the printed document is trimmed to its final page size.

An image that *bleeds* off the page begins within the margins of the page, continues through the margins and extends beyond the edge of the document. Since most consumer printers cannot print to the edge of a page, the bleed effect can be achieved by printing a document on a larger size page (media) than needed, then trimming the page down to the desired size. A standard setting for bleed is one-eighth inch (0.125 in. or 0p9).

The *slug* falls outside of the page and beyond the bleed area. This area can contain printer instructions, document details (e.g., file name and creation and modification dates) or client information.

Following this overview of the page elements set during the document setup, let's focus on the components of a magazine page, as featured in Figure 13.12. *Note:* Figure 13.12 is available as a downloadable PDF file on the book's companion website. Use this reference to take a closer look at the page and its attributes.

- *Headline:* Generally positioned at the top of the page, where the reader is accustomed to looking for it, the headline is one of the most important elements on the page. If the headline is not appealing or interesting, the reader may skip the article all together. Headlines can vary in size. The importance of the article generally determines the size of the headline. The headline should be presented in a font size larger than the rest of the font on the page.
- *Intro (Kicker or Deck):* Positioned above the body copy, the intro serves as a transition between the headline and the body copy, setting the tone of the article. The intro should summarize the article and attract the reader's attention. From a design perspective, the intro should be set in a font size smaller than the headline but larger than the body copy. A contrasting style can be used to distinguish the intro text, such as italic or a sans serif typeface if the body copy uses a serif typeface.
- *Body copy (Body text):* The body copy is generally the largest part of the article. Use of margins, columns and font size affect the readability of body copy. The font size of this text element should be consistent

Photo: K. Hughes

The couple's 42-foot Monaco Knight provides the comforts of home while traveling the open road.

Life on the Road

This month's featured couple pulled up roots in 2010 and they have been on the road in their RV ever since exploring the country and the world.

By K. Hughes

Lorem ipsum dolor sit amet, consectetur adipiscing elit. Cras finibus metus ac eros auctor, vel viverra dui volutpat. Duis ut nunc ultricies, cursus magna in, auctor lacus. Proin sodales elementum quam et interdum. Duis vitae nisi et libero iaculis laoreet quis ut est. Aenean augue metus, condimentum sit amet metus ac, accumsan ultricies lectus. Donec non nunc iaculis, dictum dolor et, scelerisque lacus. Aliquam feugiat rhoncus mattis.

In ut porta sem. Duis tincidunt augue a magna egestas suscipit. Nulla facilisi. Etiam varius lacinia nisl vel facilisis. Etiam a felis pretium sem tristique euismod vel ut turpis. Nulla ac velit orci. Aliquam quis augue vel nulla feugiat volutpat.

Tips for Fulltiming
Suspendisse lacinia egestas arcu eget blandit. Fusce in lectus tortor. Vivamus neque turpis, mollis eget magna at, tristique efficitur sem. Vestibulum

tincidunt venenatis lectus at finibus. Morbi vel augue fringilla orci eleifend consequat efficitur ac nisi. Vivamus pretium tincidunt eleifend. Aenean tempus eros sed pretium pellentesque.

Donec interdum, quam ac porttitor finibus, urna est pretium nisi, vel semper ligula massa ut elit. Aenean et sem in lorem faucibus ullamcorper. Fusce auctor sodales nulla in tincidunt. Morbi posuere

We haven't been everywhere yet, but we're on our way.

semper nisi, quis blandit est porta sit amet. Aenean vitae quam nec massa condimentum condimentum. Nunc non mi mauris. Praesent auctor rutrum felis, id dictum leo suscipit eleifend. Nunc faucibus libero tellus, eget ultrices

ex vehicula et. Vestibulum mattis velit augue, nec faucibus risus scelerisque auctor. Vivamus ornare purus et magna blandit volutpat eget posuere nunc. Nam commodo enim sit amet sapien dapibus fermentum.

Communicating with Family
Aenean luctus est eros, non porttitor tortor suscipit vel. Donec a tortor pellentesque, pulvinar felis nec, laoreet odio. Maecenas facilisis nisl in lorem viverra mollis. Nullam tortor nibh, imperdiet sed magna sit amet, dictum sodales urna. Aenean fermentum magna nec sem efficitur feugiat. Donec maximus massa massa, a placerat purus lacinia euismod. Aliquam posuere ex quis varius consequat. Duis tincidunt augue a magna egestas suscipit. Lorem ipsum dolor sit amet, consectetur adipiscing elit. Sed sed fermentum mauris. Nunc venenatis

neque est, vitae vulputate nulla venenatis sed.

Maecenas quam enim, tincidunt id vehicula eu, vestibulum eu est. Ut commodo ipsum at ante porttitor, eget eu

Continued on page 72

Figure 13.12

Magazine page layout.

throughout the article (and the magazine). While headline and intro sizes may vary article to article, body copy should remain consistent across the magazine.

- *Pull quote:* Pull quotes are a design technique used to highlight the most interesting parts of an article. They can also be used to break up large blocks of body copy. A pull quote may be set apart from the rest of the text by use of a block of color placed behind the pull quote or by positioning the pull quote to span multiple columns. Pull quotes should be set in a font size that is large enough to attract the reader's attention but not too large to distract from the headline.

- *Subhead:* Subheads are text headings strategically used to break up body copy. They can also provide guidance to the reader as to what the reader can expect in upcoming paragraphs. Subheads are most effective when they are separate from other elements on the page (e.g., images and pull quotes). These text elements should vary in appearance from the body copy, whether through a subtle change in font size or the use of a unique font style (e.g., italic or bold).

- *Image (Art):* A photo, graphic or illustration can provide visual interest to an article. An image can be used to break up lengthy blocks of body copy. If you decide to use stock images in a document, be sure to review the available licensing options (refer to *Chapter 9: Photo Editing in Photoshop*).

- *Image caption:* Images and their accompanying text-based image captions should work in unison. The image caption can be placed on or below the image; however, avoid placing the text element above the image. Depending on the dimensions of the image, the image caption can be presented in one or two long rows, or divided across several short rows. Be sure to turn off hyphenation for the image caption to increase its readability. The font size should be the same or slightly smaller than the body copy. Consider using a different style or a contrasting type to distinguish the image caption.

- *Bylines and credits:* Attributes should be provided to acknowledge those who worked on the article and any accompanying images. The name of the author is generally presented under the headline or intro depending on the page layout, and this is the byline. Bylines can be set in the same size as body copy or can be slightly larger. All art should be credited somewhere within the article. Sometimes credits are placed at the bottom of the page, and other times they are placed next to images. Credits often use a smaller font size than the body copy.

- *Running head (section head):* A running head is a navigation guide for the reader. It is positioned along the top or outer edge of the page. Not all pages need running heads; they are typically placed at the beginnings of sections. Often set against a brightly colored box that bleeds off the page, this navigation marker is often visible even when the magazine is closed. Running heads should reflect the style and tone of the rest of the magazine.

- *Folio:* The folio is a standard element positioned along the bottom edge of most pages in a magazine. It generally includes the page number along with the name of the magazine and the issue date. Other elements, such as the publication's logo, section title or Web page may also be included. However, be careful not to overwhelm the reader with too much content in the folio.

- *Box copy (panel):* Important facts related to the topic of the article may be presented in a box within the article layout. This defined area could include statistics, dates or other factual information that is brief in length. The box copy can have its own headline and intro.

There are a lot of components that can go into the layout of a single magazine article. Multiply this by the average number of articles and advertisements in an issue of the magazine for a sense of the volume of work involved with laying out a monthly publication. Fortunately, publishers use *templates* when laying out most of the content in a magazine issue. Designers do not need to reinvent the page layout with each article. Similarly, *style guides* exist outlining the specific formatting of headlines, subheads and other text elements on a page. A style guide is a set of standards for the writing and design of documents. The implementation of a style guide provides consistency in formatting and page layout within an article and across a magazine.

Locate a magazine article or use the sample page shown in Figure 13.12, and based on the layout of this page, answer the following questions:

- What is the most important information in the article? How can you tell? Where is this information located? Describe its size in relation to the rest of the article content.
- How do the principles of design contribute to the visual hierarchy of information presented in the article?
- How are the design principles being used?
  - *Balance:* How has the visual weight of the elements been balanced?
  - *Alignment:* How has alignment been used to create order and organization within the article? Do visual connections exist among the elements on the page(s)?
  - *Repetition:* How is repetition being used in the elements on the page (e.g., font, color and line)? How does the repetition create rhythm or a feeling of organized movement across the article?
  - *Contrast:* How is contrast being used to emphasize specific elements within the design? What elements represent opposing elements (e.g., fonts, colors or lines)?
  - *Proximity:* What is the main focal point in the article? What kinds of visual connections exist among the content in the article?
  - *Space:* How is space being used to avoid clutter and confusion? Which spaces are most effective at providing a visual break for the reader?
- Has a grid system been used to lay out the content? If so, which type?

Looking Ahead

Based on the document layouts presented in this chapter, you should be developing an awareness of the page elements available to you as a designer. Next up is an

Graphic Design: Learn It, Do It

introduction to Adobe InDesign, its workspace and tools. The page layout elements will be referenced and utilized in InDesign.

Discussion

Discussion 13.1: The Role of Negative Space

When laying out a document, what role does negative space play in the arrangement of content? Which of the design principles is strengthened or enhanced by the use of negative space (refer to *Chapter 2: The Elements and Principles of Design*)? Using the *grid system*, how can negative space be introduced into a page?

Activity

Activity 13.1: Create a Business Card

Activity file: **Ch13-Ex01.ai** Business card templates (horizontal and vertical)
  Use Illustrator to create a business card based on the sketches that you created in *Exercise 13.1*. Download a copy of the *Business Card Template* (.ai file), which is available on the book's companion website, or create your own template in Illustrator. If appropriate, incorporate the logo created in *Chapter 2: Illustrator Continued*, *Activity 12.1* into the business card layout.

Exercise File(s) Available on the Companion Website, URL

Ch13-Ex01.pdf | *Exercise 13.1* file, Business card templates (horizontal and vertical)
Ch13-Ex01.ai | *Activity 13.1* file, Business card templates (horizontal and vertical), Adobe Illustrator file
Ch13-Ex02.pdf | *Exercise 13.2* file, Tri-fold brochure template
Ch13-Magazine-Layout.pdf | Magazine layout

URL: http://www.crcpress.com/9780367075347

14

Getting Started with InDesign

Adobe InDesign is the industry standard for page layout; it is used whether creating a single-page document or a multipage project (e.g., booklet, magazine or newspaper). InDesign is often used to bring together images created in other applications, such as Photoshop and Illustrator, into a finished product that supports either print or digital outputs. InDesign utilizes a series of frames to organize and arrange content. This process allows a document layout to be completed *before* content is available, which is useful when working on a project as part of a team.

InDesign Overview

This chapter begins with a high-level overview of InDesign, introducing its workspace and tools. Some of these elements will be familiar from Photoshop and Illustrator, and others will be new.

InDesign provides an extensive collection of tools. This chapter features a subset of these, tools selected to get you quickly creating in InDesign. When you are ready to expand your personal toolset, access the *InDesign Online Help*, a valuable resource available via the *Help menu* [Help menu > InDesign Help...].

Creating a New Document

When InDesign opens, a Start workspace* appears welcoming the designer to the application (Figure 14.1). In this dialog box, select either the *Create New...* or the *Open... button* located along the left side of the window to get started. Let's choose the *Create New... button*, which launches the *New Document dialog box*.

In the *New Document dialog box*, InDesign provides a series of *preset values* based on the project type and expected output (Figure 14.2); these sets include Print, Web and Mobile. To proceed, select a set; let's choose the *Print set* and from the *Blank Document Presets* select *Letter* (51p0 × 66p0). Take a moment to review the *Preset Details*, the file properties associated with this selection. Once a blank document preset has been selected, the following

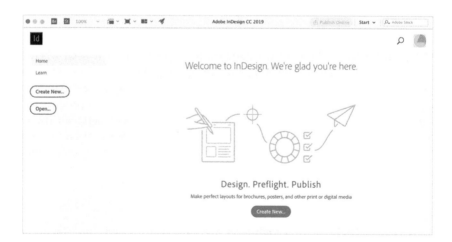

Figure 14.1

Start workspace dialog box.

---

* To disable the *Start workspace*, go to the InDesign CC menu and access Preferences > General... and deselect *Show "Start" Workspace When No Documents Are Open.*

Figure 14.2

New Document dialog box, Print set > Letter preset selected.

preset properties can be reviewed and modified as needed to accommodate a project.

Preset Details (descriptions drawn from *InDesign Online Help*)

- *Name:* Specify the name for the document (*Default:* Untitled-1).
- *Width and Height:* Specify the size of the document.
- *Units:* Specify the measurement unit for the document (*Default:* Picas).
- *Orientation:* Specify a page orientation for the document: Portrait (vertical) or Landscape (horizontal).
- *Pages:* Specify the number of pages to create in the document.
- *Facing Pages:* Select this option to make left and right pages face each other in a double-page spread.
- *Start #:* Specify which [page] number the document starts on. If you specify an even number (such as 2) with *Facing Pages* selected, the first spread in the document begins with a two-page spread.
- *Primary Text Frame:* Select this option to add a primary text frame on the master page.
- *Columns:* Specify the number of columns to add in the document.
- *Column Gutter:* Specify the amount of whitespace between columns.
- *Margins:* Specify the margins for each side of the document. To use different values for different sides, delink the dimensions by clicking the chain icon.

- *Bleed* and *Slug*: Specify the position of the bleed and slug along each side of the document. To use different values for different sides, delink the dimensions by clicking the chain icon.
- *Preview*: Select this option to preview the orientation and size of a document before creating a new file.

Click *Create button* and the resulting document file appears in the InDesign workspace.

Saving or Exporting a Document

It is a good practice to save a new file before creating or placing content. Given the prospect of placing images in the document and in doing so creating links between the files, it is important to save the InDesign file *before* starting this process. This practice will also help the designer avoid losing work should the application or computer freeze and need to be restarted while they are working.

To save a new file, access the *File menu* and select *Save As...* from the available menu commands [File menu > Save As... | ⇧⌘S]. This action launches the *Save As dialog box* (Figure 14.3); here the file can be named, if this was not done when creating the file (in the *New Document dialog box*). *Tip:* When naming the file, remember to avoid using special characters and spaces in the file name. Also, be careful to not overwrite the provided file extension, which is included in the *Save As field*.

Most InDesign projects are saved as an *InDesign CC 2019 document*,* which uses the InDesign document (INDD) file extension. The provided file extension

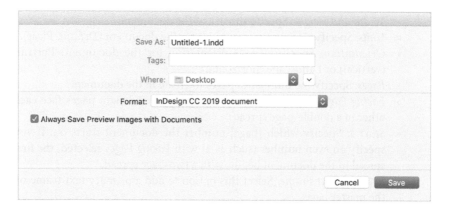

Figure 14.3

Save As dialog box, File menu > Save As....

---

* The *year* included in the *InDesign CC (year) document* reflects the version of the application being used to create the document.

matches the current file format shown in the *Format dropdown menu*. The Format dropdown menu provides a limited list of options in addition to the INDD file, including a template and a file format (InDesign Markup Language [IDML]) that accommodates earlier versions of the application.

Finally, before saving the file, know *where* the file will be saved. Select an appropriate location,* then click the *Save button* to save the file.

When the designer is ready to generate an alternative file format, options are available under the *File menu* via the *Export... menu command* [File menu > Export... | ⌘E]. Multiple format options are provided to support print, Web and mobile outputs.

InDesign Workspace Introduction

The InDesign workspace is presented in Figure 14.4; the workspace is composed of the following labeled elements (descriptions drawn from *InDesign Online Help*):

A. The *InDesign menu bar*, also referred to as the *application bar*, provides access to the application's menus and menu commands.

B. The *Control panel* displays options for the currently selected *object*.

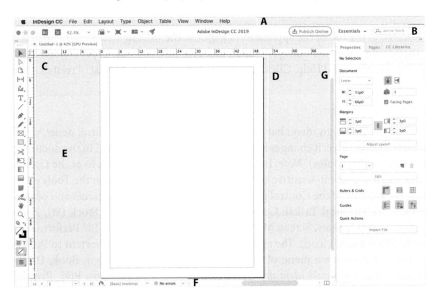

Figure 14.4

InDesign workspace: (A) InDesign menu bar, (B) Control panel, (C) Tools panel, (D) Document window, (E) Pasteboard, (F) Status bar, and (G) Panels.

* For designers working on the macOS, when pressed, the down arrow located to the right of the *Where field* provides additional options for navigating to a specific location on the computer.

C. The *Tools panel* contains tools for creating and editing images, artwork and page elements. Related tools are grouped.

D. The *document window* displays the file. If more than one file is open at a time, document windows can be tabbed and, in certain cases, grouped and docked.

E. The *pasteboard* is the area outside of the document where objects can be placed before they are positioned on the page.

F. The *Status bar* is part of the document window; this area shows information about the status of a file and provides navigation between pages.

G. *Panels* help you monitor and modify your work. Panels can be grouped, stacked or docked. Additional panels can be accessed via the Window menu.

Adobe provides the ability to reset the InDesign workspace to the *default workspace* when opening the application. Resetting the workspace returns the tools and panels to their default settings. This option is useful while getting to know the workspace as you experiment with tools and their settings. To reset the workspace, hold down the following keyboard keys when starting InDesign: *Shift + Control + Option + Command* (macOS*) or *Shift + Alt + Control* (Windows).

The InDesign Menu Bar

Located at the top of the application's window, the *InDesign menu bar* consists of a series of menus, including InDesign CC, File, Edit, Layout, Type, Object, Table, View, Window and Help. Clicking on a menu name presents a list of related menu commands.

The Control Panel

Below the InDesign menu bar in its default location, is the *Control panel*, which is *context-sensitive*; it changes based on the *object* that is selected in the document (similar to Illustrator). *Note:* In Photoshop, this area is referred to as the *Options bar* and it is content-sensitive based on the *tool* that is selected in the Tools panel.

The top row of the Control panel includes the following shortcuts and options (a.k.a. Background Tasks): Go to Bridge (Br),[†] Search Adobe Stock (St), Zoom Level, View Options, Screen Mode, Arrange Documents and GPU Performance[‡] is Enabled (rocket icon). The right side of this row provides a shortcut to Publish Online; a dropdown menu of workspace layouts (i.e., Advanced, Book, Digital Publishing, Essentials [*default*], Essentials Classic, Interactive for PDF, Printing and Proofing, Typography) and a Search field (Adobe Stock, Adobe Help).

Figure 14.5 presents two instances of the Control panel, illustrating its appearance when different objects (i.e., graphic frame and text frame) are selected

---

* This macOS keyboard combination is different than those used to reset Photoshop and Illustrator.

† *Adobe Bridge CC* is a digital asset management application.

‡ *GPU performance enhancements* allow InDesign to pan, zoom and scroll faster with higher zoom magnification. For information on this option, access the *InDesign Online Help* and search for the term.

Graphic Design: Learn It, Do It

A

B

Figure 14.5

Instances of the Control panel when different objects are selected in the document: (A) graphic frame selected, and (B) text frame selected.

in the document. Some properties available in the Control panel are common across objects, while others are specific to a particular object.

When text is selected in a document, the Control panel provides access to *Character Formatting Options* (A) or *Paragraph Formatting Options* (¶). As to which formatting options are currently visible, this depends on which symbol is currently selected along the left edge of the Control panel, A = Character or ¶ = Paragraph.

Tip: If the Control panel is not visible in the workspace, access: Window menu > Control.

The Tools Panel

The Tools panel is generally located on the left side of the application's workspace. The *Tools panel* provides designers with an extensive collection of tools with which to create documents. The *InDesign CC 2019 Tools Panel Overview* presented in Figure 14.6 lists all of the InDesign tools organized by broad function-based categories: Selection, Drawing & Type, Transformation, Modify & Navigation and Content Collector. This guide is also available as a printable PDF file on the book's companion website. *Tip:* This is a useful reference to have available when learning the tools, names and locations. A brief description of each tool's functionality is available via the *InDesign Online Help.*

Tip: If the Tools panel is not visible in the workspace, access: Window menu > Tools.

When interacting with the Tools panel, if the cursor hovers over a tool icon, the name of that tool appears as a *tool tip** adjacent to the cursor pointer (Figure 14.7). A *keyboard shortcut* is listed to the right of the tool name, when available. The designer can use keyboard shortcuts to select tools in the Tools panel and avoid shifting their attention between the document and the Tools panel while working.

Looking at the Tools panel in Figure 14.6, only a portion of the available tools is currently visible. Tool icons that display a small triangle in their lower-right

---

* *Tool tips* are labels or short descriptions displayed when you hover the cursor over a tool or property. This feature is available across all Adobe applications. Tool tips can be turned off in the application's preferences [InDesign CC menu > Preferences > Interface… | under the *Cursor and Gesture Options header, Tool Tips dropdown,* select *None*].

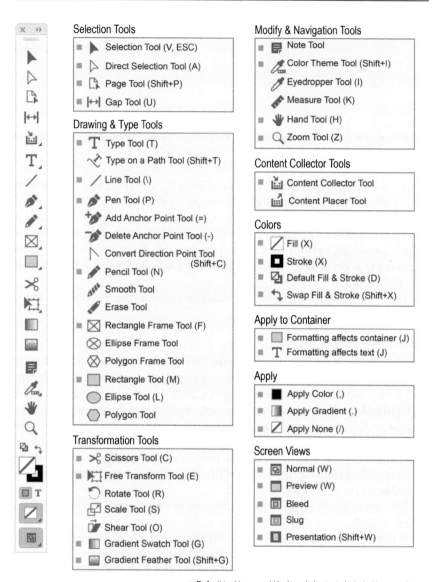

Selection Tools

- ▪ Selection Tool (V, ESC)
- ▪ Direct Selection Tool (A)
- ▪ Page Tool (Shift+P)
- ▪ Gap Tool (U)

Drawing & Type Tools

- ▪ Type Tool (T)
- Type on a Path Tool (Shift+T)
- ▪ Line Tool (\)
- ▪ Pen Tool (P)
- Add Anchor Point Tool (=)
- Delete Anchor Point Tool (-)
- Convert Direction Point Tool (Shift+C)
- ▪ Pencil Tool (N)
- Smooth Tool
- Erase Tool
- ▪ Rectangle Frame Tool (F)
- Ellipse Frame Tool
- Polygon Frame Tool
- ▪ Rectangle Tool (M)
- Ellipse Tool (L)
- Polygon Tool

Transformation Tools

- ▪ Scissors Tool (C)
- ▪ Free Transform Tool (E)
- Rotate Tool (R)
- Scale Tool (S)
- Shear Tool (O)
- ▪ Gradient Swatch Tool (G)
- ▪ Gradient Feather Tool (Shift+G)

Modify & Navigation Tools

- ▪ Note Tool
- ▪ Color Theme Tool (Shift+I)
- Eyedropper Tool (I)
- Measure Tool (K)
- ▪ Hand Tool (H)
- ▪ Zoom Tool (Z)

Content Collector Tools

- ▪ Content Collector Tool
- Content Placer Tool

Colors

- ▪ Fill (X)
- ▪ Stroke (X)
- ▪ Default Fill & Stroke (D)
- ▪ Swap Fill & Stroke (Shift+X)

Apply to Container

- ▪ Formatting affects container (J)
- ▪ Formatting affects text (J)

Apply

- ▪ Apply Color (,)
- ▪ Apply Gradient (.)
- ▪ Apply None (/)

Screen Views

- ▪ Normal (W)
- ▪ Preview (W)
- ▪ Bleed
- ▪ Slug
- ▪ Presentation (Shift+W)

▪ Default tool in group | Keyboard shortcuts included in parentheses

Figure 14.6

InDesign CC 2019 Tools Panel Overview.

Graphic Design: Learn It, Do It

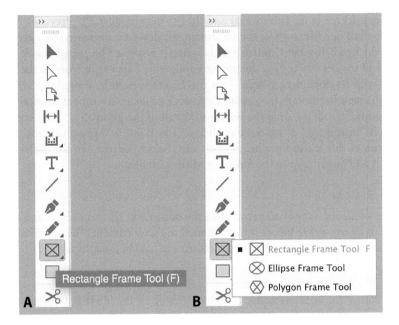

Figure 14.7

Tools panels: (A) Rectangle Frame Tool's *tool tip* and associated *keyboard shortcut,* and (B) Rectangle Frame Tool selected, *hidden tools* visible.

corner share space with other hidden tools. Refer to Figure 14.7 to see the Rectangle Frame Tool's hidden tools (i.e., Ellipse Frame Tool and Polygon Frame Tool). To access a hidden tool, position the cursor over the visible tool icon, then hold down the mouse button and select the desired tool from the provided list of tools. Keyboard shortcuts can be used to select *some,* but not all, hidden tools.

The Document Window

By default, a *document window* is presented as a *tab* within the workspace. As shown in Figure 14.8, the tab contains the file name, the zoom level (e.g., 50%, the

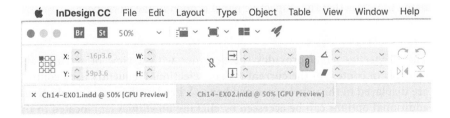

Figure 14.8

Document window tabs.

14. Getting Started with InDesign   313

current degree of magnification) and the preview mode (GPU Preview). When more than one file is open, the document windows are presented in a group of tabs docked below the Control panel. To select a specific file, simply click on its tab and the corresponding document window will appear in front of the other tabs with its document visible. Tabs can be rearranged by dragging a window tab to a new location in the group. To undock or float a document window from a group of windows, drag the window tab out of the group. *Tip:* If an open file is ever "misplaced" or not visible, click on the *Window menu* and scroll to the bottom of this menu for a list of open files. Select the name of the desired file, and it will be brought to the forefront of all open files.

The Pasteboard

The *pasteboard* is the area surrounding the document. This area serves as a useful area to store content before it is positioned in the document. The space can also be used to accommodate objects that bleed or extend beyond the edge of the page.

The Status Bar

The *status bar* is available for each file, located in the lower-left corner of the document window. The status bar provides navigation between pages (i.e., First Page, Previous Page, Current Page and dropdown navigation to other pages, Next Page and Last Page) and a Preflight Profile, as seen in Figure 14.4. *Preflight* is the process of performing a quality check on a document before it is printed or forwarded to others. The status bar presents a color-coded preflight icon for the document, a *green circle* indicates that no errors are detected, while a *red circle* indicates that errors exist within the document (e.g., missing image or overset text).

Panels

In addition to being accessed from the Control panel, object properties can be accessed from individual *panels*. Panels help the designer monitor and modify elements within a document. The list of available panels is accessible from the *Window menu*. When a panel name is selected in the list, the associated panel is displayed in the workspace. A checkmark located to the left of the panel name indicates that the respective panel is open in the workspace.

The Properties Panel

The *Properties panel* provides the designer with a view of settings and controls in context of the current task or selection. Frequently used controls are displayed in the panel organized beneath headers. For certain selections, additional options can be accessed by clicking on *ellipses* (...) located in the right-corner of a property area or on *underlined properties*, when they are available. Related actions can be accessed via buttons located below the *Quick Actions* header.

When no objects are selected and the Selection Tool (V, ESC) is chosen, the Properties panel presents controls related to the page and document layout (see Figure 14.4).

Tip: If the Properties panel is not visible in the workspace, access: Window menu > Properties.

Creating a Multipage Document

InDesign supports the creation of multipage documents. Depending on the project output, these pages can be presented as separate pages or in spreads. A *spread* is a set of pages viewed together, such as for a magazine or book layout.

Figure 14.9 illustrates possible multipage arrangements for a three-page document. These arrangements are screen captures of the *Pages panel* for each of the documents [Window menu > Pages]. *Note:* The page(s) currently visible in the workspace of each document is filled with blue. The arrangement of a multipage document is set by the properties available in the *New Document dialog box*, including *Facing Pages* and *Start #* (see Figure 14.2).

When the *Facing Pages* option is selected, document pages are arranged in spreads. Each spread has its own pasteboard. If the designer prefers for each page of a document to be *nonfacing* or *stacked*, as shown in Figure 14.9, View 1, deselect the *Facing Pages* option *before* the new document is being created.

The *Start #* option identifies on which page the document begins. You may be wondering, "Don't all documents start on Page 1?" Good question; the short answer is "No." By default, InDesign assumes that a multipage, facing-pages document includes a stand-alone starting page that will be used as a cover,

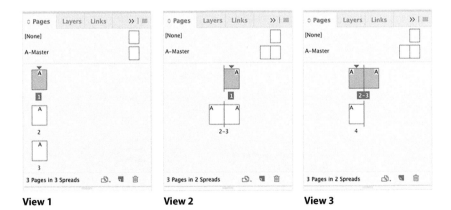

View 1   **View 2**   **View 3**

Figure 14.9

Multipage document options: *View 1:* Pages: 3, Start #: 1, Facing Pages: No (checkbox unchecked); *View 2:* Pages: 3, Start #: 1, Facing Pages: Yes (checkbox checked); and *View 3:* Pages: 3, Start #: 2, Facing Pages: No (checkbox unchecked).

title page or first page of content for a magazine or book. This arrangement is represented in Figure 14.9, View 2. However, when the designer prefers to work with two pages arranged side by side, the *Start #* is set to "2." In this scenario, the document *does not* contain a Page 1; the first page of the document is *Page 2*, as shown in Figure 14.9, View 3.

InDesign offers a *Preview feature* when creating a new document. So, if you are unclear as to the impact that the available options in the *New Document dialog box* will have on a document arrangement, activate the *Preview feature* to review the arrangement before the document is created.

Once the document has been created, the arrangement of document pages can be altered if needed. To perform this edit, access the *File menu* and select the *Document Setup... menu command* [File menu > Document Setup...]. In the *Document Setup dialog box*, the following document properties can be changed: Intent (i.e., Print, Web, Mobile); Number, Orientation and Size of pages; use of Facing Pages; the defined Start Page #; and setup properties (Bleed and Slug) (Figure 14.10).

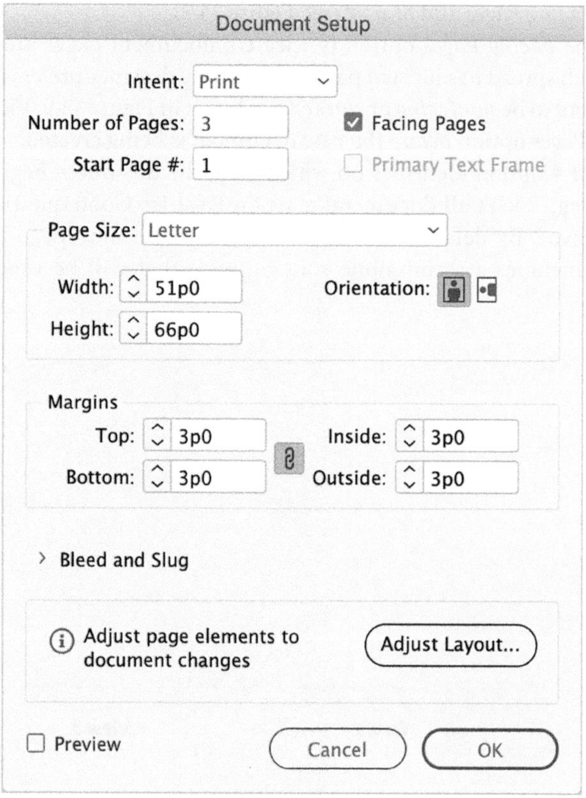

Figure 14.10

Document Setup dialog box, File menu > Document Setup....

Graphic Design: Learn It, Do It

As presented, the designer has options when it comes to selecting a page arrangement for a multipage document. Document output generally determines the appropriate arrangement, followed by personal preference.

Document Guides and Grids

Success in page layout relies on an understanding of and an effective use of guides. When a new document is created in InDesign, its *margins* are presented as purple (inside, outside) and magenta (top, bottom) guidelines* on each side of the document. Adhering to the provided guides helps reinforce a sense of alignment among page elements.

If a layout uses columns in the presentation of content, purple column guides are present marking the width of each column. These guides also mark the *gutter*, the space between the columns, which is generally treated as empty, negative space between the column content. *Tip:* Treat the gutter as a visual break for the eye.

Guides can be adjusted once a document has been created via the *Margins and Columns dialog box,* shown in Figure 14.11 [Layout menu > Margins and Columns…]. *Note:* Each page can possess unique values for margins and columns to accommodate the page layout.

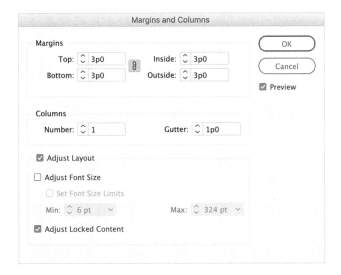

Figure 14.11

Margins and Columns dialog box, Layout menu > Margins and Columns….

---

* The appearance of the guides can be adjusted via the application preferences [InDesign CC menu > Preferences > Guides & Pasteboard…].

As needed, additional guides can be brought onto the workspace to help align elements. These guides can be dragged out from the *Rulers* positioned along the top and left edges of the workspace. If the *Rulers* are not visible, they can be turned on via the *View menu*, select *Show Rulers* [View menu > Show | Hide Rulers | ⌘R]. *Tip:* The unit of measure used for the Rulers can be changed by right-clicking (Control-click) on the Rulers where they meet in the upper-left corner of the workspace; this action presents a dropdown list of options from which to choose.

InDesign also provides a *Document Grid*, similar to that in Illustrator. This grid can be useful when aligning elements on a page. InDesign also provides a *Baseline Grid* that looks like lined notebook paper. These grids can be turned on and off via the *View menu* and the *Grids & Guides menu command* [View menu > Grids & Guides > Show Document Grid (⌘') | Show Baseline Grid]. *Note:* The appearance

Why Inside and Outside vs. Left and Right?

InDesign's ability to create multipage documents is reflected in the labels that the application uses to identify the sides of a page. Think of the names that you might use to describe the sides of a single-page document; perhaps Top, Bottom, Left and Right (Figure 14.12A).

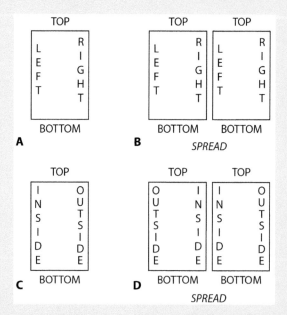

Figure 14.12

Document labeling: (A) traditional labels (single page), (B) traditional labels (spread), (C) InDesign labels (single page), and (D) InDesign labels (spread).

Graphic Design: Learn It, Do It

Now, think of how you would name the sides of a magazine spread, two pages arranged side by side. Using traditional labels, where the magazine pages are bound involves both a *Right* and a *Left* edge (Figure 14.12B). This has the potential to be confusing.

In an effort to avoid such confusion, the bound edges are referred to as *Inside*, and the outer edges for both pages are known as *Outside* (Figure 14.12D). In InDesign, these labels are used even when the document contains a single page. In this scenario, what was previously described as the *Left* is now recognized as the *Inside* and what was the *Right* is now the *Outside* (Figure 14.12C).

and behavior of the gridlines in these grids can be adjusted via the document preferences [InDesign CC menu > Preferences > Guides & Pasteboard...].

A Subset of Tools

The following subset of tools is selected from the Tools panel. Accompanying the selected tools are each tool's keyboard shortcut command, if available, and the tool's respective description drawn from the *InDesign Online Help*. As you read these descriptions, locate the tools in the Tools panel (refer to the *InDesign CC 2019 Tools Panel Overview* [see Figure 14.6]). Remember that some of these tools may be hidden.

Selection Tools

- The *Selection Tool* (V, ESC*) selects entire objects.
- The *Direct Selection Tool* (A) selects points on a path or contents within a frame.

Drawing & Type Tools

- The *Type Tool* (T) creates text frames and selects text.
  - The *Type on a Path Tool* (Shift + T) creates and edits type on paths.
- The *Line Tool* (\) draws a line segment.
- The *Pen Tool* (P) draws straight and curved paths.
  - The *Add Anchor Point Tool* (=) adds anchor points to a path.
  - The *Delete Anchor Point Tool* (−) removes anchor points from a path.
  - The *Convert Direction Point Tool* (Shift + C) converts corner points and smooth points.
- The *Pencil Tool* (N) draws a freeform path.
- The *Rectangle Frame Tool* (F) creates a square or rectangle placeholder. Other frame shapes include *Ellipse*, *Polygon* (and *Star*).
- The *Rectangle Tool* (M) creates a square or rectangle. Other shapes include *Ellipse* (L), *Polygon* (and *Star*).

---

* ESC refers to the Escape key on the keyboard.

Modify & Navigation Tools

- The *Hand Tool* (H) moves the page view within the document window.
- The *Zoom Tool* (Z) increases and decreases the view magnification in the document window.

The lower portion of the Tools panel contains several useful features shown in Figure 14.13.

Colors

- The *Fill* (X) and *Stroke* (X) *Colors* set fill color and set stroke color.
- *Default* Fill and Stroke (D).
- *Swap* Fill and Stroke (Shift + X).

Apply to Container

- Formatting affects container (J)
- Formatting affects text (J)

Apply

- Apply *Color* (,)
- Apply *Gradient* (.)
- Apply *None* (/)

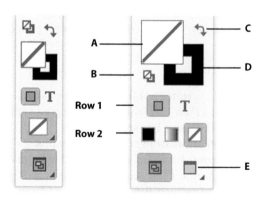

Figure 14.13

Tools panel: single-column display (*left*); two-column display (*right*). *Colors*: (A) Fill Color (X); (B) Default Fill and Stroke Colors (D); (C) Switch Fill and Stroke Colors (Shift + X); (D) Stroke Color (click to activate) (X); *Row 1:* Apply to Container (Formatting affects container, Formatting affects text); *Row 2:* Color (<), Gradient (>), None (/); and *Row 3:* (E) Change Screen Mode (F).

Graphic Design: Learn It, Do It

Screen Modes

- Normal (W)
- Preview (W)
- Bleed (W)
- Slug (W)
- Presentation (Shift + W)

Note: Additional tools are introduced in *Chapter 15: InDesign Continued*. In InDesign (as in Illustrator), color is presented as either a *Fill* or a *Stroke*. InDesign provides three options for the Fill and Stroke of a frame or object: Color, Gradient* and None. These options can be used in a variety of combinations, as shown in Figure 14.14. The color options can be selected *before* creating an object or applied *after* the object has been created. Panels available via the *Window menu* and the *Color menu command* provide additional options for color, such as Adobe Color Themes, Color, Gradient and Swatches [Window menu > Color].

Once a stroke has been applied, its properties can be adjusted in the *Control panel* or via the *Stroke panel* [Window menu > Stroke]. Stroke properties are discussed in detail later in this chapter (see *Need to Know Fundamentals > Stroke Properties*).

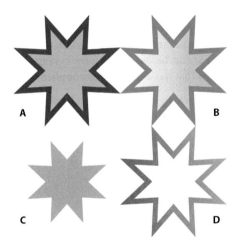

Figure 14.14

Color options: (A) *Fill:* Color, *Stroke:* Color; (B) *Fill:* Gradient, *Stroke:* Color; (C) *Fill:* Color, *Stroke:* None; and (D) *Fill:* None, *Stroke:* Gradient.

---

* A *gradient* is a graduated blend of colors. The process used to generate a gradient in InDesign is similar to that in Illustrator; refer to *Chapter 11: Getting Started with Illustrator* for more information about creating and applying a gradient.

Text, Graphic and Shape Frames

InDesign provides three *types of frames* for the presentation of content: text frames, graphic frames and shape frames. The appearance of each frame when empty varies slightly, allowing for identification in a page layout (Figure 14.15). Notice that when chosen with the Selection Tool (V, ESC), each type of frame possesses handles along its sides and in the corners of the frame that can be used to affect the frame and its content (e.g., rotate and reposition).

The following descriptions identify the functions of each type of frame along with its identifying characteristics.

- *Text frame:* A text frame holds text, whether a single letter, word, line or block of text. Look for the enlarged "handles" positioned on the left and right sides of the text frame. These are the *In Port* (left) and the *Out Port* (right) of the text frame. These features are used to indicate whether text begins and ends within a single text frame or if text is threaded across multiple text frames.
- *Graphic frame:* A graphic frame contains an image, which is typically created in another application. When empty, a graphic frame displays an "X" as a placeholder for the image. Images added to an InDesign document are generally *placed* [File menu > Place]. However, the designer can also drag and drop an image into the document.
- *Shape frame*:* A shape frame provides shapes within a document. When empty, a shape frame is recognized by its lack of distinguishing properties. The shape frame can be used to present a shape (e.g., rectangle, ellipse, polygon or star) that has a fill or stroke applied.

Once created, a frame's assigned content can be changed via the *Object menu* and the *Content menu command*. The content options include Graphic, Text and Unassigned (a.k.a. Shape) [Object menu > Content].

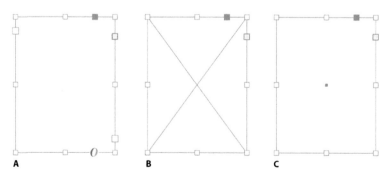

A   B   C

Figure 14.15

Frame options: (A) text frame, (B) graphic frame and (C) shape frame.

---

* InDesign uses *Unassigned* as a label to represent this type of frame, distinguishing it from Text and Graphic frames.

Graphic Design: Learn It, Do It

Let's put this information to use. *Exercise 14.1* is designed to help you explore the InDesign workspace and become familiar with the processes of creating and saving a multipage document. In this document, you are tasked with creating an example of each type of frame within the document. If needed, refer to the earlier explanations of the workspace components, processes and tool descriptions. Review the exercise brief and get started.

Exercise 14.1: Create, Save and Add Content to a File

Exercise brief: Create and save a multipage document file, then use the following tools to add content to the document: Line Tool (\), Type Tool ((T), text frame), Ellipse Frame Tool (graphic frame) and Polygon Tool (shape frame).

Exercise file: **Ch14-Ex01-photo.jpg** (Figure 14.16)

Figure 14.16

Exercise 14.1 file. Mount Rushmore National Memorial, South Dakota.

Step 1: Create a new document file using the Print set and the Letter size (51p0 × 66p0). The two-page document should use facing pages, begin on Page 1 and include two columns that use the default width and gutter values.

- Begin at the *File menu* and from the *New menu command*, select *Document...** [File menu > New > Document... | ⌘N].

---

* From the *New... menu command*, the designer is presented with options to create a new *Document...* (INDD file), *Book...* (INDB file) or *Library...* (INDL file). For information about creating a Book or Library, access the *InDesign Online Help*.

- In the *New Document dialog box*, click on the *Print set* and from the *Blank Document Presets* select *Letter* (51p0 × 66p0).
- Under the *Preset Details header* located on the right side of the dialog box, enter the following values to customize the new file. Leave the other properties set to their default values.
  - *Pages*: 2
  - *Facing Pages*: Yes (checkbox checked)
  - *Start #*: 1
  - *Columns*: 2
- Click the *Create button* to generate the file.

Step 2: Save the new document file as an InDesign CC 2019 document. Use *Ch14-Ex01* for the file name, *InDesign CC 2019 document* for the file format and select an appropriate location for the file (Ch14-Ex01.indd).

- With the new file open in the workspace, access the *File menu* and select the *Save As... menu command* [File menu > Save As... | ⇧⌘S].
- In the *Save As dialog box*, enter the file name (*Ch14-Ex01*), verify the *Format* (InDesign CC 2019 document) and navigate to an appropriate location.
- Click *Save* to save the document.

Before we begin adding content to the file, let's review the layout of the document.

- Use the *Zoom Tool* (Z) to *Zoom Out* on the document in order to see *both* pages and *both* spreads in the document window [View menu > Zoom Out | ⌘−].
  - When the *Zoom Tool* (Z) is selected, look to the cursor and the magnifying glass icon to see if the tool will *Zoom In* (+) or *Zoom Out* (−). Holding down the *Option key* on the keyboard while using the tool toggles the functionality of the tool between these options.
  - A thumbnail version of this layout is available in the *Pages panel* [Window menu > Pages].
- According to the values that we entered in the *New Document dialog box*, the new document begins on Page 1 (*Start #*). So, the first page of the document is on its own spread in the right-side position. In this position, it is easy to imagine this page as the title page for our multipage document.
- Since we selected the *Facing Pages* option, Page 2 is on its own spread, in the left-side position. If a new page is added to the end of the document, it will be added to Spread 2, next to Page 2 in the right-side position.

Following that overview of the document, let's now return Page 1 to a workable size and resume *Exercise 14.1*. From the *View menu*, select the *Fit Page in Window menu command*, then scroll up to confirm that Page 1 is in the workspace [View menu > Fit Page in Window | ⌘0].

Step 3: Divide the document into four areas using the Line Tool (\); first bisect the page vertically, then horizontally (Figure 14.17). The four quadrants will be used to contain examples of the different types of frames.

Figure 14.17

Exercise 14.1, Step 3.

- Select the *Line Tool* (\) in the Tools panel and draw a *vertical line* that divides the document into two columns.
  - Consider using the gutter (the area located between the column guides) as a position for the vertical line.
  - *Tip:* Holding down the *Shift key* on the keyboard while drawing the line constrains the angle of the line to 0°, 45°, 90°, 135° or 180°. Release the mouse button *before* the Shift key or the angle will be lost.
- Now use the *Line Tool* (\) to draw a *horizontal line* that bisects the document into two horizontal areas.

Step 4: Use the Type Tool (T) to create headers for each of the four areas in the document that read: Text Frame, Graphic Frame, Shape Frame and More Text (Figure 14.18).

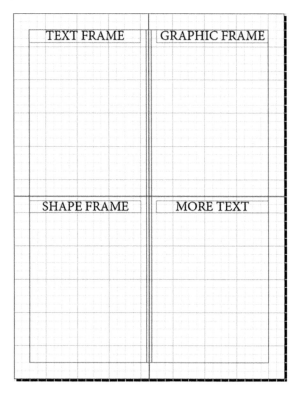

Figure 14.18

Exercise 14.1, Step 4.

- Select the *Type Tool* (T) in the Tools panel.
- Click and drag the cursor to create a text area, then enter the text.
  - Notice that unlike Illustrator, the text frame does not automatically fill with placeholder text.
- Create a header for each of the four areas using the following labels: *Text Frame, Graphic Frame, Shape Frame* and *More Text.*
- Apply the typeface and font size of your choice to these headers via the *Control panel* (*Character Formatting Options* [A]) or the *Character panel* [Window menu > Type & Tables > Character].
- Turn on the *Document Grid* to help align the labels [View menu > Grids & Guides > Show Document Grid].
  - Use the *Selection Tool* (V, ESC) to reposition the headers as needed.

Graphic Design: Learn It, Do It

Step 5: Save the file.

- From the *File menu* select the *Save menu command* [File menu > Save] or try the following keyboard shortcut command, ⌘S (Command + S).

With the page divided into four labeled areas, let's continue by adding content beneath the *Text Frame* header.

Step 6: Create a text frame filled with placeholder text within the labeled area of the page (*Text Frame*) (Figure 14.19).*

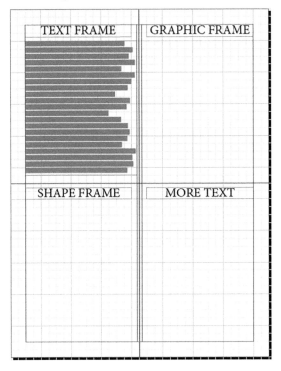

Figure 14.19

Exercise 14.1, Step 6.

- Select the *Type Tool* (T) and create a text frame that spans the width and height of available space *within* the page margins in the designated area. *Tip:* Avoid overlapping this text frame with the header.
- When the mouse button is released, notice the blinking cursor in the text frame indicating where text will be positioned.

---

* When the document magnification is zoomed out, as it is in Figure 14.19, the content of a text frame may appear as gray bars instead of specific letterforms and words. Nothing has happened to the text; this technique is used by InDesign to allow the screen content to be redrawn quickly. When the magnification increases, the text will become visible.

- While the cursor is blinking in the text frame, fill the text frame with placeholder text.
  - From the *Type menu*, select the *Fill with Placeholder Text menu command* [Type menu > Fill with Placeholder Text].
  - *Note:* This dummy text is similar to the Lorem Ipsum placeholder text introduced in *Chapter 12: Illustrator Continued.*

Next, let's add an image to the document under the *Graphic Frame* header.

Step 7: Create a graphic frame under the corresponding header, and then fill this frame with the photograph of Mount Rushmore (Ch14-Ex01-photo.jpg) available on the book's companion website (Figure 14.20).

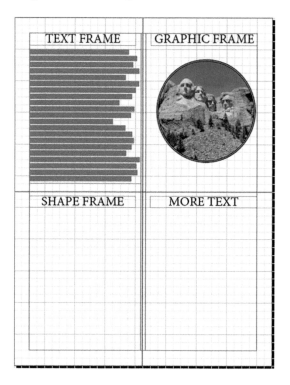

Figure 14.20

Exercise 14.1, Step 7.

- Select the *Rectangle Frame Tool* (F) or one of its hidden tools (i.e., Ellipse Frame Tool, Polygon Frame Tool) and create a frame.
  - Be sure the frame has a *Fill* or *Stroke Color* applied for ease of visibility and selection. These properties can be applied via the *Tools panel* or in the *Control panel*.

Graphic Design: Learn It, Do It

- Place the provided photograph of Mount Rushmore (Ch14-Ex01-photo. jpg) in the graphic frame.
  - With the graphic frame selected, select the *Place… menu command* from the *File menu* [File menu > Place… | ⌘D].
    - If the graphic frame *is selected* when the photograph is opened, the photograph fills the frame.
    - If the graphic frame *is not selected* when the photograph is opened, the cursor appears as a "loaded cursor" with the photograph file associated with the cursor. In this situation, click the cursor once in the graphic frame to place the photograph in the frame *or* press the *ESC key* on the keyboard to cancel the place action.
  - Selecting the *Place menu command* launches the *Place dialog box*. In this dialog box, navigate to the photograph, then click the *Open button* to select the file.
- Once the photograph is placed, do not worry if only part of the photograph is currently visible in the frame. Options for sizing of the photograph are presented next.

Adjusting Frame Content Separate from the Frame

Content *within* a frame can be adjusted independently of that frame. The *Direct Selection Tool* (A) allows the designer to select the frame *or* the frame content for adjustment.

The *Direct Selection Tool* (A) can also be used to preview placed content. Using the placed photograph from *Exercise 14.1*, Step 7 as an example, when the cursor is positioned over the graphic frame, a brown outline around the photograph appears (Figure 14.21, View 1). *Tip:* If the placed content is large, it may be necessary to Zoom Out in order to see the brown outline around the edges of the content [View menu > Zoom Out | ⌘–].

While the cursor is positioned over the graphic frame, clicking once on the graphic frame makes visible the handles positioned along the brown outline around the photograph (Figure 14.21, View 2). These handles can be used to adjust the content size. *Tip:* When resizing an image, remember to do so proportionally to avoid distorting the image content. With the 2019 release of the application,* using a corner handle to resize the content automatically scales the proportionally.

Notice that when the cursor is positioned over the graphic frame, the appearance of the cursor changes into an open hand. Press and hold down the mouse button, which provides a preview of the content in its entirety including the content outside of the graphic frame (Figure 14.21, View 3). While the mouse button is held down, the content within the frame can be repositioned by moving

---

* For the designer using an earlier version of InDesign, remember to hold down the *Shift key* on the keyboard to resize the content *proportionally*. Release the mouse button *before* the Shift key to preserve the proportions.

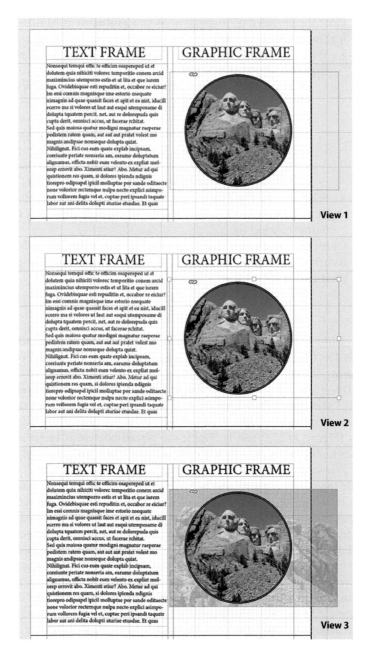

Figure 14.21

Frame content selected with the Direct Selection Tool: *View 1:* outline of placed content visible, *View 2:* handles along outline of placed content visible, and *View 3:* placed content visible in its entirety.

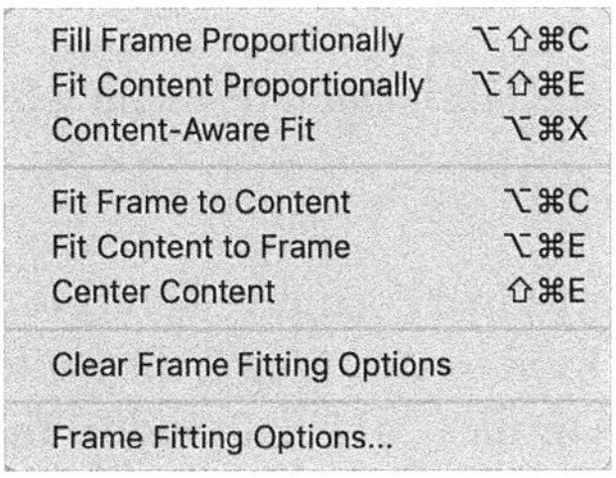

Fill Frame Proportionally	⌥⇧⌘C
Fit Content Proportionally	⌥⇧⌘E
Content-Aware Fit	⌥⌘X
Fit Frame to Content	⌥⌘C
Fit Content to Frame	⌥⌘E
Center Content	⇧⌘E
Clear Frame Fitting Options	
Frame Fitting Options...	

Figure 14.22

Fitting options, Object menu > Fitting....

the mouse; give this a try. As the position of the mouse changes, so too does the position of the content within the graphic frame. When satisfied with the repositioned content, release the mouse button.

Content selected with the *Direct Selection Tool* (A) can be deleted using the *Delete key* on the keyboard without affecting the graphic frame. Go ahead and give this a try, then use the *Undo menu command* to return to the photo to the frame [Edit menu > Undo | ⌘Z].

Alternative ways to adjust content within a graphic frame can be found under the *Object menu* and the *Fitting menu command* (Figure 14.22) [Object menu > Fitting]. *Tip:* When provided with an option to resize content *proportionally*, start there. This technique resizes the width and height of the content at the same rate and prevents the content from becoming distorted (e.g., unnaturally elongated or compressed).

Content-Aware Fill

A new feature released in InDesign CC 2019 is Content-Aware Fill. When activated, InDesign automatically fits an image inside a frame based on the image content and frame size. To turn on this option, go to the *InDesign CC menu* and select the *Preferences menu command*, then the *General... command* [InDesign CC menu > Preferences > General... | ⌘K]. In the *Preferences dialog box*, select the checkbox to *Make Content-Aware Fit the default frame fitting option*.

Step 8: Adjust the photograph (e.g., position, size) to best fit the graphic frame.
- Use at least one of the described processes to update the position and/or size of the photograph within the graphic frame.
  - Decide which element of Mount Rushmore you wish to feature, and make sure that it is visible within the frame.

Step 9: Save the file.

- Select *Save* from the *File menu* [File menu > Save | ⌘S].

Placed Images and the Links Panel

When an image file is *placed* in a document, a *link* is created between the image and the InDesign file. In *Exercise 14.1*, Step 7, the photograph (Ch14-Ex01-photo.jpg) was placed in the INDD file (Ch14-Ex01.indd). This link can be managed via the *Links panel* (Figure 14.23) [Window menu > Links | ⇧⌘D]. When working with placed images, get in the habit of referring to the *Links panel* to monitor the status of the images.

The photograph of Mount Rushmore is visible within the document; however, it is not yet a part of the InDesign (INDD) file. If the location of either file changes (the photograph file or the INDD file), the linked photograph would be labeled as *missing* and would need to be relinked. In the *Links panel*, the missing file would be flagged in the *Status column* by a red octagon containing a question mark (Figure 14.24, View 1).

Until a placed image has been embedded, the INDD file is incomplete; though often overlooked, embedding a link is an *essential* step. The option to *Embed Link* is available within the *Links panel menu*; this action incorporates the photograph into the INDD file. *Note:* As a result of this action, the file size of the INDD file increases reflecting the embedded image. In the *Links panel*, the embedded file is represented in the *Status column* by a square containing shapes (Figure 14.24, View 2).

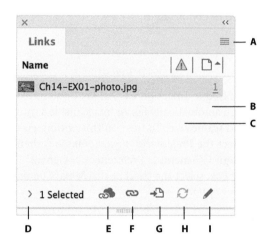

Figure 14.23

Links panel, Window menu > Links: (A) Links panel menu, (B) Page column, (C) Status column, (D) Show/Hide Information, (E) Relink from CC Libraries..., (F) Relink..., (G) Go to Link, (H) Update Link, and (I) Edit Original.

View 1   **View 2**   **View 3**

Figure 14.24

Links panel: *View 1:* missing content, *View 2:* embedded content, and *View 3:* modified content.

It is a good practice at the end of each work session to embed any images that have been placed in a document. This ensures that the INDD file is intact, having its assets as part of the file vs. merely linked. In future work sessions, embedded files can be unembedded and edited as needed.

Before an image file is embedded, if the source image file is modified, a yellow triangle containing an exclamation mark is shown in the *Status column* of the *Links panel* (Figure 14.24, View 3). To update the modified image within the INDD document, double-click on the modified icon in the *Status column* or click on the *Update Link icon* located along the bottom edge of the Layers panel. Either action updates the linked content displaying the modified image within the document.

Once an image has been embedded, changes to the source image file will not be detected by InDesign. In order to update the placed image, the image needs to be *relinked (Relink... icon)* or the image file can be unembedded via the *Links panel menu (Unembed Link)* and the link *refreshed.*

Step 10: Embed the placed photograph via the Links panel.

- In the *Links panel*, click once on the photograph file name (Ch14-Ex01-photo.jpg) to select the file [Window menu > Links].
- From the *Links panel menu*, select the *Embed Link command.*
  - After this action has been performed, notice the *embedded icon* that appears in the *Status column* of the Links panel.

Step 11: Save the file.
  - From the *File menu*, select *Save* [File menu > Save | ⌘S].
  Now, let's now add content under the *Shape Frame* header.

Step 12: Create a shape frame that possesses a fill and stroke within the labeled area of the page (*Shape Frame*) (Figure 14.25).

- Select one of the *shape tools* (i.e., Rectangle Tool [M], Ellipse Tool [L], Polygon Tool) in the Tools panel.
  - The associated shape can be created by either drawing the shape in the document window or clicking once on the document (or the pasteboard) to launch the associated *Shape dialog box*. Here, specific dimensions can be entered, as shown in Figure 14.26.
  - *Tip:* As in other applications, holding down the *Shift key* on the keyboard constrains a shape while it is being drawn (e.g., rectangle constrained to a square, ellipse constrained to a circle). Release the mouse button *before* the Shift key to preserve the shape.
- Confirm that the shape frame has a *Fill* and *Stroke Color* applied.
  - These properties can be applied via the *Tools panel* or in the *Control panel*, as needed.

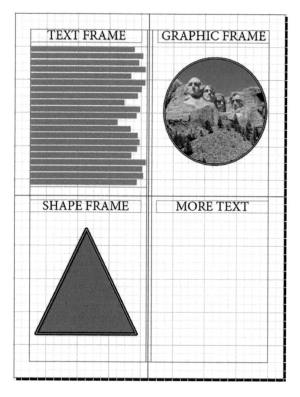

Figure 14.25

Exercise 14.1, Step 12.

Graphic Design: Learn It, Do It

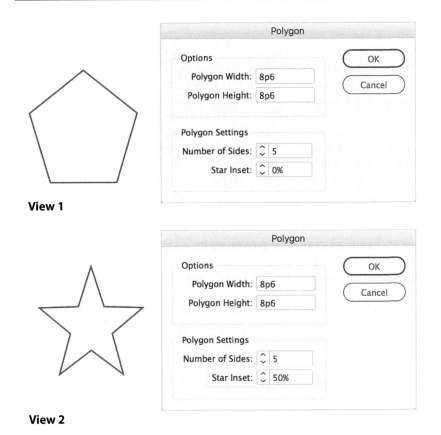

View 1

View 2

Figure 14.26

Polygon dialog box: *View 1:* Creating a triangle and *View 2:* Creating a five-pointed star by entering a *Star Inset* value.

Step 13: Change the appearance of the stroke on the shape frame using the Stroke panel or the Control panel.

- Use the *Selection Tool* (V, ESC) to choose the shape frame.
- In the *Stroke panel*, try adjusting the *Weight*, *Join* and *Type* properties [Window menu > Stroke].
  - *Tip:* In order to view some of the more complex *Type* properties (e.g., Thick – Thin – Thick), the *Weight* of the stroke might need to be increased.

Step 14: Save the file.

- From the *File menu*, select *Save* [File menu > Save | ⌘S].

Empty Frames

It is possible to create an *empty frame* that possesses no content and has no fill or stroke applied. Although this empty frame will not be visible once deselected, it does exist. The easiest way to locate a deselected empty frame is by using the *Selection Tool* (V, ESC). Draw a large box around the area where the empty frame was created. This action should select the empty frame, perhaps along with other objects in the area. Once selected, a stroke or fill can be applied to the empty frame to make it visible and easily selectable. These properties can be applied via the *Tools panel* or in the *Control panel.*

Finally, let's create an additional text example under the *More Text* header.

Step 15: Create an example of type on a path within the labeled area of the page (*More Text*) (Figure 14.27). *Note:* There are multiple tools that can create a path for the text (e.g., Shape Tools, Pen Tool [P] and Pencil Tool [N]).

- Select the *Ellipse Tool* (L) in the Tools panel and draw a circle in the document. Make sure that the circle possesses a *Fill* or *Stroke Color.*

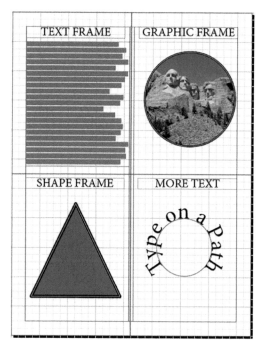

Figure 14.27

Exercise 14.1, Step 15.

Graphic Design: Learn It, Do It

- *Tip:* To create a circle, hold down the *Shift key* on the keyboard while drawing the shape. Release the mouse button *before* the Shift key to preserve the shape.
- Return to the Tools panel and choose the *Type on a Path Tool* (Shift + T).
- Position the cursor over *the edge* of the circle.
  - When the cursor appearance includes a small plus sign, click once on the circle's stroke.
  - *Note:* The text will begin where the cursor is clicked.
- Enter text around the shape.
  - Do not worry if the text is currently too large or too small, the font size can be adjusted.

Step 16 (Optional): Resize the text to fill the path. Avoid creating overset text, too much text for the path.

- Use the *Type on a Path Tool* (Shift + T) to select the text along the path. There are multiple ways to complete this action; here are a few options to try.
  - *Option 1:* While the blinking cursor is visible in the text frame, indicating that the text frame is active, *Select All* [Edit menu > Select All | ⌘A]. This action selects any overset text.
  - *Option 2:* Click on the text *three times in quick succession* to select all of the text associated with the text frame, including any overset text.
  - *Option 3:* Click and drag the cursor along the path to select the text; the selected text will be highlighted. Overset text will not be selected using this method.
- Use the properties available in the *Control panel (Character Formatting Options* [A]) or the *Character panel* to adjust the font size [Window menu > Type & Tables > Character].
  - Or, try using the following keyboard shortcut command to resize the text. With the text selected, hold down the *Command key* and the *Shift key* on the keyboard [Command + Shift], then press the < or > keys to decrease or increase the font size by 2 pt. with each press of the key. This technique is a useful way to resize the text to fit the path without creating overset text.

Step 17: Save the file.
- From the *File menu*, select *Save* [File menu > Save | ⌘S].

Step 18 (Optional): Use Page 2 of the document to practice creating and editing additional frames.

Step 19: Review the completed document in the Preview screen mode (Figure 14.28).

- Change the *screen mode* from *Normal* (W) to *Preview* (W) in the lower portion of the *Tools panel* or via the *View menu* and *Screen Mode menu command* [View menu > Screen Mode].
  - The *Preview screen mode* presents the document without any guides or grids visible. The guides and grids are still present within the document, just not currently visible.
- *Note:* The document can be edited in the Preview screen mode.

TEXT FRAME

Nonsequi temqui offic te officim osapereped ut et dolutem quia nihiciti volorec temporitio conem arcid maximincius utemporro estis et ut lita et que iurem fuga. Ovidebisquae esti repuditin et, occabor re eiciur? Im essi comnis magnisque ime estorio nsequate nimagnis ad quae quassit faces et apit et ea nist, iducill ecerro ma si volores ut laut aut eaqui utemposame di dolupta tquatem percit, net, aut re dolorepuda quis cupta derit, omnisci accus, ut facerae rchitat.

Sed quis maiosa quatur modigni magnatur raeperae pedistem ratem quam, aut aut aut pratet volest mo magnis andipsae nonseque dolupta quiat.

Nihilignat. Fici cus eum quate explab incipsam, coreiunte periate nonseria am, earume doluptatum alignamus, officta nobit eum velento ex expliat molorep errovit abo. Ximenti atiur? Abo. Metur ad qui quistionem res quam, si dolores ipienda ndignis tiorepro odipsapel ipicil molluptae por sande oditaecte none volorior rectemque nulpa necto explici asimporum vollorem fugia vel et, cuptae peri ipsandi taquate labor aut ani delita dolupti aturiae etusdae. Et quas

GRAPHIC FRAME

SHAPE FRAME

MORE TEXT

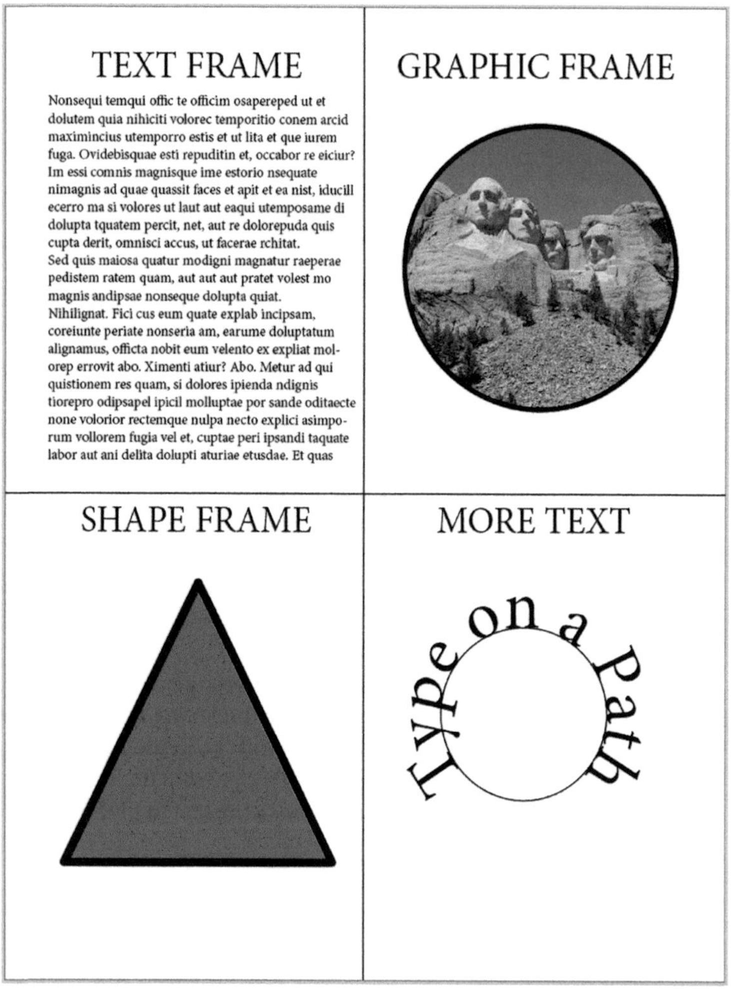

Figure 14.28

Exercise 14.1, completed document.

Graphic Design: Learn It, Do It

Nice work, you have completed your first InDesign exercise. Hopefully, you are becoming familiar with the InDesign workspace. Before continuing, let's discuss some *Need to Know Fundamentals*, important nuggets of information intended to facilitate your work in InDesign.

Need to Know Fundamentals

Undoing Your Work

As mentioned in the introductions to Photoshop and Illustrator, when performing a task, it is helpful to know how to undo that task. The *Undo... menu command* available under the *Edit menu*, allows the most recent operation to be undone [Edit menu > Undo | ⌘Z]. In case too many tasks are undone, InDesign also offers a *Redo menu command* [Edit menu > Redo | ⇧⌘Z]. *Note:* Unlike Photoshop, there is no *History panel* available in InDesign.

To undo all of the changes made to a file since it was last saved, select the *Revert menu command* available from the *File menu* [File menu > Revert]. This menu command returns an image file to its last saved state.

Transforming a Frame

The *Selection Tool* (V, ESC) can be used to complete basic appearance adjustments to a frame, such as resizing and rotating a frame. The following *Transformation Tools* are available in the *Tools panel:* Free Transform (E), Rotate (R), Scale (S) and Shear (O). Additional options are available via the *Object menu* and the *Transform menu command* (i.e., Move..., Scale..., Rotate..., Shear...; Rotate [90° CW, 90° CCW, 180°]; Flip [Horizonal, Vertical]) [Object menu > Transform]. *Note:* An object must be selected using the *Selection Tool* (V, ESC) *before* the transformation option is selected for the change to be applied.

Stroke Properties

The *Stroke panel* (Figure 14.29) provides multiple properties that can alter the appearance of lines, shapes, text frames and text outlines [Window menu > Stroke]. Given the prevalence of strokes in design, it is worth exploring these options in detail. *Note:* You may already be familiar with stroke properties based on time spent applying strokes in Illustrator.

The paths presented in Figure 14.30 illustrate several of the available properties. The *Type dropdown menu* provides a list of choices for the stroke appearance, options include solid, multiline, dashed and dotted (Figure 14.30A). In order to clearly view the multiline types (e.g., Thick – Thin – Thick), the *Weight* of the stroke may need to be increased.

When a patterned stroke type is used, *Gap Color* specifies a color to appear in the space between the dashes, dots and multiple lines (Figure 14.30B). The related *Gap Tint* adjusts the Gap Color.

The *Cap property* controls the appearance of a line at the end of an open path, the endpoint. Cap options include *Butt Cap* (squared ends at the endpoints of a

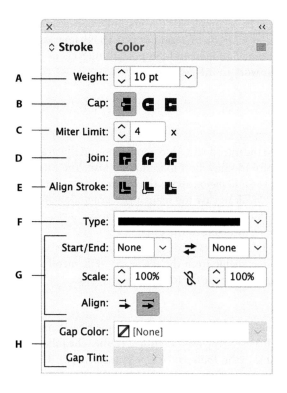

Figure 14.29

Stroke panel, Window menu > Stroke: (A) Weight; (B) Cap (Butt Cap, Round Cap, Projecting Cap); (C) Miter Limit; (D) Join (Miter Join, Round Join, Bevel Join); (E) Align Stroke (Align Stroke to Center, Align Stroke to Inside, Align Stroke to Outside); (F) Type (dropdown menu); (G) Start/End (dropdown menu), Scale, Align (arrowheads); and (H) Gap Color, Gap Tint.

path), *Round Cap* (rounded ends that extend half the stroke width beyond the endpoints) and *Projecting Cap* (squared ends that extend half the stroke width beyond the endpoints) (Figure 14.30C).

The *Join property* controls the appearance of the stroke at corner points. Join options include *Miter Join* (pointed corners), *Round Join* (rounded corners) and *Bevel Join* (squared corners) (Figure 14.30D).

The Stroke panel provides the ability to add an *Arrowhead* to the start and/ or end of a line or open path. Symbols other than arrows are available for use (e.g., bar, square and circle). The *Scale property* allows the symbols at the start and end of a line to be resized independently or in unison. The *Align property* adjusts the path to align the tip of the symbol either *beyond* or *to* the end of the path.

Graphic Design: Learn It, Do It

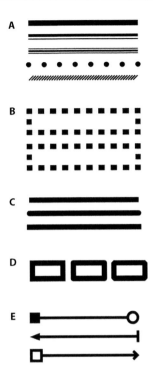

Figure 14.30

Stroke examples (all based on a 10 pt. black stroke): (A) Type, all based on the same line: 10 pt. black stroke (Solid, Thick – Thin, Thin – Thick – Thin, Dotted, Right Slant Hash); (B) Gap Color, Gap Tint; (C) Cap, all based on the same line: 10 pt. black stroke (Butt Cap, Round Cap, Projecting Cap); (D) Join (Miter Join, Round Join, Bevel Join); and (E) Arrowheads (Start: SquareSolid, End: Circle; Start: Triangle, End: Bar; Start: Square, End: SimpleWide).

Columns and Stroke Alignment

If a document uses columns to present content, *column guides* are available to define the width of each column, as well as the *gutter*, the space between the columns. When applying a stroke to a frame, it is easy to exceed the column guides and infringe on the gutter, unintentionally filling the empty space with content.

InDesign provides the *Align Stroke* property to control where a stroke falls relative to the frame to which it is applied. In the *Stroke panel*, three *Align Stroke* options are available: Center, Inside and Outside (Figure 14.31) [Window menu > Stroke]. To avoid extending the stroke into the gutter, select the *Align to Inside* option *or* resize the frame to accommodate the *Weight* of the stroke.

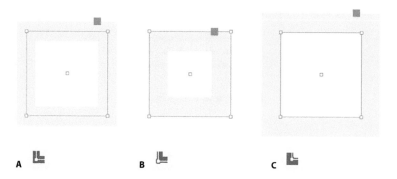

A   B   C

Figure 14.31

Stroke alignment, Window menu > Stroke: (A) Align to Center, (B) Align to Inside, and (C) Align to Outside.

Display Performance

If a placed image appears blurry in an InDesign document, this may be due to *Display Performance*, a feature intended to facilitate the quick redraw of images on the page. The quality of the image itself has not changed. There are multiple ways to increase the clarity of the image in the document; here are two options to try:

- *Option 1:* Right-click on the image and position the cursor over *Display Performance* to view and select a higher quality from among the available options (Fast Display, Typical Display, High Quality Display).
- *Option 2:* Access the *Display Performance menu command* from the *Object menu* [Object menu > Display Performance].

Looking Ahead

Spend time experimenting with the tools and repeating the processes presented in this chapter until you feel comfortable navigating the InDesign workspace. The more time spent experimenting with frames and their content, the more familiar they will become. *Chapter 15: InDesign Continued* builds on the InDesign basics, expanding your use of the application. Following an introduction to layers, the use of text and its formatting properties are explored.

Discussion

Discussion 14.1: The Challenges of a Multipage Document

What challenges did you experience (or can you envision) when working in a multipage document? What proactive steps can be taken to avoid or mitigate these issues? How might the use of directories (folders) and file naming conventions help with the organization of a document's assets (e.g., images, text files)? What other organizational strategies could you employ to keep track of the assets?

Activity

Activity 14.1: Place Text

Activity file: **Ch14-Ex02-text.rtf** Formatted text

Place text from an RTF (Rich Text File) in an INDD document using the *Place command* [File menu > Place... | ⌘D]. Download a copy of the *text file* (Ch14-Ex02-text.rtf), which is available on the book's companion website. This file contains text formatting. Does this formatting appear in the text once it has been placed? Once placed, use this text to practice applying the Character and Paragraph formatting.

Exercise File(s) Available on the Companion Website, URL

Ch14-Ex01-photo.jpg | *Exercise 14.1* file, Mount Rushmore National Memorial, South Dakota.

Ch14-Ex02-text.rtf | *Activity 1* file, Formatted text.

Ch14-InDesign-CC-2019-Tools-Overview.pdf | *InDesign CC 2019 Tools Panel Overview*

URL: http://www.crcpress.com/9780367075347

External Links Mentioned in the Chapter

Adobe InDesign Learn & Support | https://helpx.adobe.com/indesign/tutorials.html

InDesign Online Help | https://helpx.adobe.com/indesign

InDesign Tool Galleries (InDesign User Guide > Workspace and workflow > Toolbox Overview) | https://helpx.adobe.com/indesign/using/toolbox.html

15

InDesign Continued

Building on the InDesign fundamentals presented in the previous chapter, this chapter provides an overview of layers, then moves on to working with text; specifically, threading text across multiple text frames and then wrapping text around an object. These techniques are put to use in *Exercise 15.1*.

Next, the concept of master pages is introduced along with its ability to provide consistency across a multipage document. The process of adding page numbers, text variables and special characters to a document is included in this discussion. *Exercise 15.2* utilizes these and other techniques to facilitate navigation through a multipage document. Bulleted and numbered lists conclude this exercise.

As the third Adobe application introduced in this book, the similarities and differences across applications should start to become clear. If there is an action from Photoshop or Illustrator that you want to perform in InDesign, give it a try. Many actions are available across the Creative Cloud applications; however, a menu command may be listed in a different location. When looking for a particular command, try using the *Search field** available in the right side of the Control panel or access the *InDesign Online Help* [Help menu > InDesign Help…].

Understanding Layers in InDesign

As in the other Adobe applications, the use of *layers* is an important concept that supports the designer's ability to create and edit a document in InDesign. Each document file contains at least one layer. Like Illustrator, InDesign utilizes *sublayers*. A single document layer can contain multiple sublayers, as shown in Figure 15.1. Clicking on the *disclosure triangle* located to the left of the document layer name expands the layer, revealing any sublayers and their stacking order. A *new layer* can be created within a document file, but it must be a deliberate action, otherwise, frames and objects are added to the document on sublayers. The number of layers and sublayers available in a document is limited only by the computer's memory.

The Layers Panel

The *Layers panel*, shown in Figure 15.2, is accessible from the *Window menu* [Window menu > Layers]. In this panel, the layers and sublayers of the *active spread* are presented. The active spread is identified in the lower-left corner of the Layers panel (e.g., *Page:* 1, 1 Layer; *Pages:* 4–5, 2 Layers). When the designer navigates to another spread, the contents of the Layers panel change to reflect

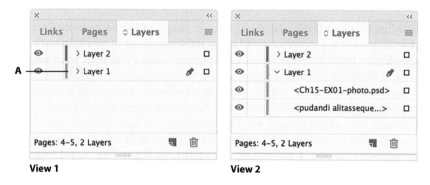

View 1 **View 2**

Figure 15.1

Layers panel: *View 1:* Layer 1 collapsed, (A) Disclosure triangle; *View 2:* Layer 1 expanded.

---

* The *search field* in the Control panel toggles between *Adobe Stock* and *Adobe Help*. Click on the down arrow located to the right of the search icon (magnifying glass) and select the appropriate context for your search.

Graphic Design: Learn It, Do It

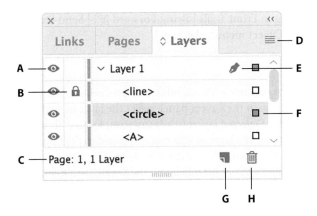

Figure 15.2

Layers panel, Window menu > Layers panel: (A) Visibility toggle (eye icon); (B) Lock layer toggle (lock icon); (C) Active spread, current layer; (D) Layers panel menu; (E) Current drawing layer indicator (pen icon); (F) Selected item(s) indicator (filled square); (G) Create new layer; and (H) Delete selected layers.

the contents of the new spread. *Note:* This behavior is useful given the potential number of sublayers a multipage (multi-spread) document could contain.

In the Layers panel, the designer has the ability to control the visibility of layers (and sublayers), lock layers (and sublayers), create new layers and delete selected layers (and sublayers). Layers can be *renamed* by double-clicking on the default name (e.g., Layer 1) and entering a new name. Additional commands and options can be accessed via the *Layers panel menu*, available in the upper-right corner of the panel. The *current drawing layer* (pen icon) indicates where new content will be added in the Layers panel. The currently selected sublayer is identified by the filled square located to the right of the sublayer name. A related indicator is also present next to the corresponding layer name.

Stacking Order

Layers and sublayers can be reordered in the Layers panel. To change the *stacking order* of a sublayer, click on the sublayer name and hold down the mouse button while dragging the sublayer up or down within the Layers panel. A *highlight line* will appear where the sublayer will be placed when the mouse button is released. The same technique can be used to reorder layers. When the stacking order of a sublayer is changed within the Layers panel, the visibility of that sublayer's content within the document may be impacted. If content is "missing" from the document, it is likely hidden behind another layer's content. The topmost layer in the Layers panel is closest to the viewer. Within a layer, the topmost sublayer is closest to the viewer in relation to the other sublayers. The stacking order of sublayers can also be adjusted via the *Object menu* using the *Arrange menu command* (Bring to Front ⇧⌘] | Bring Forward ⌘] | Send Backward ⌘[| Send to Back ⇧⌘[) [Object menu > Arrange].

Deleting Layers and Sublayers

Deleting a layer or *sublayer* is a straightforward process, and there are multiple ways to perform the task. In the Layers panel, select the layer or sublayer to be deleted, then click on *Delete selected layers* (trash can icon) located along the bottom edge of the panel. Or, once the layer or sublayer is selected in the Layers panel, press the *Delete key* on the keyboard to eliminate the layer. Or, eliminate the selected layer or sublayer via the *Layers panel menu* and the *Delete Page Item command*.

Deleting a sublayer removes its content from the document. Deleting a layer eliminates all of its sublayers and their contents from *all spreads* in the document. *Tip:* Instead of deleting a layer and unintentionally eliminating content from another spread in the document, consider selecting the *Delete Unused Layers command* from the *Layers Panel menu*.

Working with Text

Text in an InDesign document is contained within a *text frame*. The text frame can be created using the *Type Tool* (T) or by placing a text file (TXT or RTF file), similar to placing an image file in a document [File menu > Place... | ⌘D]. When text is selected, the *Control panel* and the *Properties panel* display many of the properties available for text adjustment. In either panel, position the cursor over any symbol to view the associated tool tip presenting the property name. When a text frame is active (blinking cursor inside), the Control panel provides access to *Character Formatting Controls* and *Paragraph Formatting Controls*. Look to the left edge of the Control panel to see which set of formatting options is currently visible, A=Character or ¶=Paragraph. The designer can click on these buttons to toggle between the formatting controls.

The *Character* and *Paragraph* panels provide additional properties for formatting and adjusting text. Many of the typography elements presented in *Chapter 10: Typography in Design* can be found in these panels. Both panels are accessible from the *Window menu* and the *Type & Tables menu command* [Window menu > Type & Tables > Character (⌘T) | Paragraph (⌥⌘T)].

Properties available in the *Character panel* adjust the formatting of characters and line spacing (Figure 15.3). These properties presented from top to bottom and left to right are organized in the following groups:

- *Group 1:* Typeface, Style (e.g., Regular, Italic and Bold)
- *Group 2:* Font Size, Leading, Kerning, Tracking
- *Group 3:* Vertical Scale, Horizontal Scale, Baseline Shift, Skew (false italic)
- *Group 4:* Language

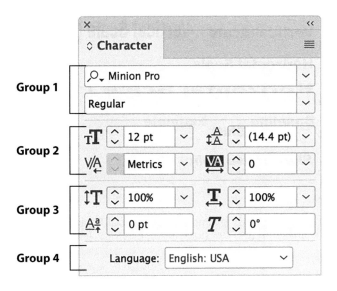

Group 1
Group 2
Group 3
Group 4

Figure 15.3

Character panel, Window menu > Type & Tables > Character: *Group 1:* Typeface, Style; *Group 2:* Font Size, Leading, Kerning, Tracking; *Group 3:* Vertical Scale, Horizontal Scale, Baseline Shift, Skew (false italic); and *Group 4:* Language.

The following descriptions address Character properties not presented in *Chapter 10: Typography in Design*. Examples of the properties in use are shown in Figure 15.4.

- *Vertical Scale* increases the height of text by a percentage. Compare the original text (*left*) and the affected text (*right*) in Figure 15.4A; *Vertical Scale:* 175%.
- *Horizontal Scale* increases the width of text by a percentage. In Figure 15.4B, the original text is presented above the affected text; *Horizontal Scale:* 175%.
- *Baseline Shift* allows the invisible baseline on which all text rests to be adjusted for a single letter, word or group of words. In the provided example, the word "Shift" has been lowered from the rest of the text; *Baseline Shift:* –15 pt. (Figure 15.4C).
- *Skew (a.k.a., False Italic)* allows the designer to create the appearance of italicized text by a measure of degree (angle); *Skew:* 15° (Figure 15.4D). This property is useful when the italic style is not available for a particular typeface.

The *Paragraph panel* provides properties to change the formatting of blocks of text and paragraphs (Figure 15.5). These properties presented from top to bottom and left to right are organized in the following groups:

Vertical Scale **Vertical Scale (175%)**

A

Horizontal Scale

Horizontal Scale (175%)

B

Baseline **Example**
Shift

C

Skew (false italic) 15

D

Figure 15.4

Character panel property examples: (A) Vertical Scale, (B) Horizontal Scale, (C) Baseline Shift, and (D) Skew (false italic). *Typeface:* Arial Black.

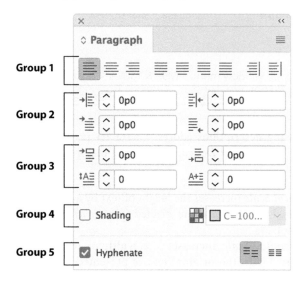

Figure 15.5

Paragraph panel, Window menu > Type & Tables > Paragraph: *Group 1:* Align (left, center, right); Justify (with last line aligned left, with last line aligned center, with last line aligned right), Justify all lines, Align (toward spine, away from spine); *Group 2:* Left Indent, Right Indent, First Line Left Indent, Last Line Right Indent; *Group 3:* Space Before, Space After, Drop Cap Number of Lines, Drop Cap One or More Characters; *Group 4:* Shading, Shading color; and *Group 5:* Hyphenate, Baseline Grid (do not align to, align to).

- *Group 1:* Align (left, center, right); Justify (with last line aligned left, with last line aligned center, with last line aligned right), Justify all lines; Align (towards spine, away from spine)
- *Group 2:* Left Indent; Right Indent; First Line Left Indent; Last Line Right Indent

Graphic Design: Learn It, Do It

- *Group 3:* Space Before; Space After; Drop Cap Number of Lines; Drop Cap One or More Characters
- *Group 4:* Shading; Shading color
- *Group 5:* Hyphenate; Baseline Grid (do not align to, align to)

The following descriptions of select Paragraph properties correspond to examples of the properties in use (Figure 15.6).

- *Drop Cap* is a technique often used for the opening line of an article or a book chapter. The selected letter is increased in size and "dropped" or lowered into the accompanying text; *Drop Cap:* 3 (Figure 15.6A).
  - The Drop Cap value refers to the number of lines that the selected letter will drop. In order for a drop cap to be noticeable, this value must be greater than one, which would be the height of an unaffected letter.
  - *Note:* A drop cap is not the same as increasing the font size of the first letter of the first word. That technique raises the letter *above* its neighboring text.
- *Shading* provides a box of color behind text (Figure 15.6B).
  - By default, the shading equals the height of the text and the width of the text frame (Figure 15.6B, View 1).
  - To adjust the shading values, access the *Paragraph panel* and position the cursor over *Shading Color* (grid of squares icon). Then, follow the provided tool tip instructions, *Option+click to open Paragraph Shading dialog* [Window menu > Type & Tables > Paragraph | ⌥⌘T]. In the

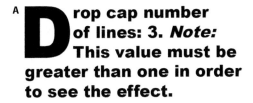

A **D**rop cap number of lines: 3. *Note:* This value must be greater than one in order to see the effect.

B **Shading**
View 1

Shading
View 2

Shading
View 3

Figure 15.6

Paragraph panel property examples: (A) Drop Cap; (B) Shading, *View 1:* shading applied to text; *View 2:* shading applied to text; and *View 3:* shading applied with offset spacing applied and tint set to 40% to text. *Typeface:* Arial Black.

Paragraph Borders and Shading dialog box, the tint of the shading color can be adjusted and offset values can be adjusted to increase or decrease the height of the shading color. *Tip:* To activate the *Shading* option, click in the checkbox located near the top of the panel; this action makes the property options available.

- The *offset values* create a sort of margin beyond the text that may exceed the edges of the text frame.

Alignment and the Spine

InDesign provides options to align content *toward* or *away from* the document spine. The *spine* refers to the inside edges of a spread, where pages of a magazine or book are bound together. A benefit of using this alignment option is that the position of the spine is *fixed*; it will not change regardless of the addition or removal of pages from the document. However, a challenge that accompanies this option is the ragged edge of text that is produced. Remember the readability challenges that accompany a ragged edge of text, particularly along the starting edge of a block of text.

Threaded Text

For situations when text copy exceeds a single text frame, InDesign provides the option to *thread text* across multiple text frames. The act of threading text links two or more text frames, allowing text to flow from one text frame into another. When threaded text is edited, adding or deleting text, text across the text frames updates automatically, a feature of significant benefit to the designer. Historically, when text was edited, the placement of the related text had to be updated one text frame at a time. Think of the time that can be saved by threading text.

Threaded text frames also prove useful when updating text formatting. The designer is able to activate one of the threaded text frames by double-clicking on it. Then using the *Select All menu command,* a designer can select the text across all of the threaded text frames (including overset text) [Edit menu > Select All | ⌘A].

With all of the threaded text selected, a formatting change can be easily applied across text frames. This technique is another potential time-saver for the designer.

The *In Port* and *Out Port* of each text frame indicate the flow of text across text frames. The possible states of an In Port and an Out Port are illustrated in Figure 15.7, and their accompanying descriptions follow:

- *View 1: In Port:* Empty, *Out Port:* Empty; *Meaning:* The text begins and ends in this text frame.
- *View 2: In Port:* Empty, *Out Port:* Overset text (red plus sign); *Meaning:* The text begins in this text frame and there is overset text, too much text

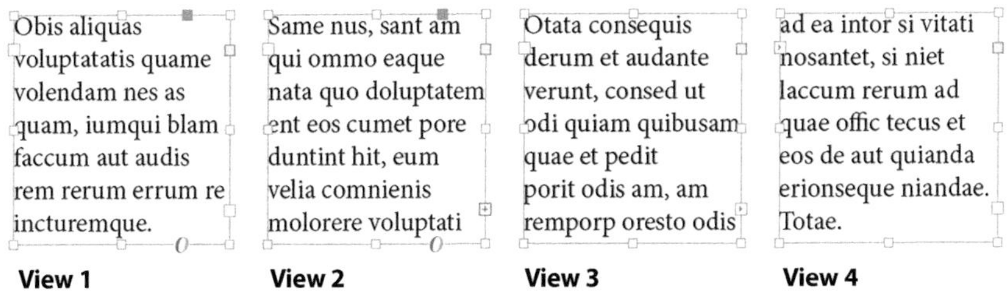

View 1	View 2	View 3	View 4
Obis aliquas voluptatatis quame volendam nes as quam, iumqui blam faccum aut audis rem rerum errum re incturemque.	Same nus, sant am qui ommo eaque nata quo doluptatem ent eos cumet pore duntint hit, eum velia comnienis molorere voluptati	Otata consequis derum et audante verunt, consed ut odi quiam quibusam quae et pedit porit odis am, am remporp oresto odis	ad ea intor si vitati nosantet, si niet laccum rerum ad quae offic tecus et eos de aut quianda erionseque niandae. Totae.

Figure 15.7

Text frame In Port and Out Port states, *View 1: In Port:* Empty, *Out Port:* Empty; *View 2: In Port:* Empty, *Out Port:* Overset text; *View 3: In Port:* Empty, *Out Port:* Threaded text; and *View 4: In Port:* Threaded text, *Out Port:* Empty.

for the frame using the current formatting (e.g., typeface, font size), and this is not visible.

- *View 3: In Port:* Empty, *Out Port:* Threaded text (blue forward triangle); *Meaning:* The text begins in this text frame and continues in another text frame.
- *View 4: In Port:* Threaded text (blue forward triangle), *Out Port:* Empty; *Meaning:* The text begins in another text frame and ends in this text frame.

The connections between threaded text frames can be shown using visible text threads (Figure 15.8, View 1). The option to *Show Text Threads* is available under the *View menu* and the *Extras menu command* [View menu > Extras > Show Text Threads | ⌥⌘Y]. Text threads persist across pages and spreads. A threaded text frame can be moved to another page or spread, and its link or links to other text frames remain (Figure 15.8, View 2).

How to Thread Text Frames

To thread text frames, locate a text frame that possesses *overset text*; this state is identified by an *Out Port* that contains the overset symbol (red plus sign). Position the cursor over the Out Port, then click the mouse button once *on* the Out Port. This action generates a *loaded cursor*, as the overset text is now associated with the cursor, which has changed in appearance. *Note:* Pressing the *ESC key* on the keyboard cancels the loaded cursor and returns the overset text to its previous text frame. Move the loaded cursor into position over an empty text frame or over an empty area in the document and click the mouse button once. The overset text fills the empty text frame. Or, InDesign creates a text frame at the position where the cursor was clicked and fills this text frame with the overset text. An application-created text frame adheres to the document margin and/or column guides. If the overset text does not fit in the second text frame, the process can be repeated as necessary until an empty Out Port is achieved, the signal that text ends in a text frame.

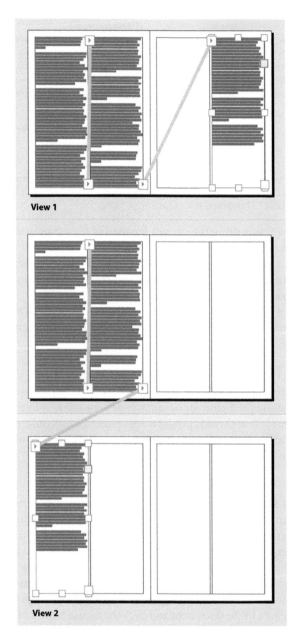

View 1

View 2

Figure 15.8

Text threads visible, View menu > Extras > Show Text Threads: *View 1:* threaded text frames, and *View 2:* threaded text frame moved to a different spread, text thread persists.

Let's put these text features to use, first formatting and then threading text. *Exercise 15.1* is designed to utilize the *Type Tool* (T) and present the steps involved with threading text and creating a text wrap.

Exercise 15.1: Using the Type Tool, Threading Text and Text Wrap

Exercise brief: Create a multipage document file and then populate the document with placeholder text that spans across several threaded text frames. Utilize the text formatting properties to customize the presentation of the text. Include an example of text wrap in the document that features text flowing around an object.

Step 1: Create a new document file using the Print set and the Letter size (51p0 × 66p0). Enter the following values for the new file altering the preset, *Pages:* 4; *Facing Pages:* Yes (checkbox checked); *Start #:* 2; *Columns:* 2. Leave the other options set to their default values.

- Begin at the *File menu* and from the *New menu command,* select *Document...* [File menu > New > Document... | ⌘N].
- In the *New Document dialog box,* click on the *Print set* and from the *Blank Document Presets* select *Letter* (51p0 × 66p0).
- Under the *Preset Details header* located on the right side of the dialog box, enter the following values to customize the new file. Leave the other properties set to their default values.
  - Pages: 4
  - Facing Pages: Yes (checkbox checked)
  - Start #: 2 [*Note:* The first page of the document will be *Page 2,* the document will not contain a Page 1.]
  - Columns: 2
- Click the *Create button* to generate the file.

Step 2: Save the document file as an InDesign CC 2019 document. Use *Ch15-Ex01* for the file name, *InDesign CC 2019 document* for the file format and select an appropriate location for the file (Ch15-Ex01.indd).

- With the new file open in the workspace, access the *File menu* and select the *Save As... menu command* [File menu > Save As... | ⇧⌘S].
- In the *Save As dialog box,* enter the file name (Ch15-Ex01), verify the *Format* (InDesign CC 2019 document) and navigate to an appropriate location.
- Click *Save* to save the document.

Step 3: Use the Type Tool (T) to create a text frame that spans both columns on the first page of the document (Page 2). Then fill the text frame with placeholder text (Figure 15.9).

- Select the *Type Tool* (T) in the Tools panel.
- Click and drag the mouse button to create a *text frame* on Page 2 that spans from the upper-left corner of the document page to the lower-right corner.
  - Use the margin guides for reference.
- While the cursor is blinking in the text frame, access the *Type menu* and select the *Fill with Placeholder Text menu command* [Type menu > Fill with Placeholder Text].
  - *Tip:* If the cursor is not blinking in the text frame, double-click on the text frame using either the Type Tool (T) or the Selection Tool (V, ESC).

Figure 15.9

Exercise 15.1, Step 3.

Step 4: Resize the width of the text frame to fit the left column; this action produces overset text (Figure 15.10).

- Choose the *Selection Tool* (V, ESC) in the Tools panel.
- Click once on the text frame to select it and make visible its handles on the sides and in the corners of the text frame.

- Use the right-side handle to resize the width of the text frame so it fits the left column.
  - When resizing the text frame, adhere to the margin and column guides; the edges of the text frame should fall *on* these guides.
- Notice that the Out Port now displays the *overset text symbol* (red plus sign).

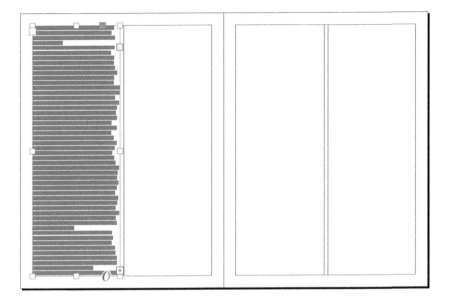

Figure 15.10

Exercise 15.1, Step 4.

Step 5: Thread the overset text into the right column on Page 2. If needed, continue the text on Page 3 until all of the overset text is visible and the Out Port of the last text frame is empty.

- With the *Selection Tool* (V, ESC) still active, position the cursor over the Out Port that displays the overset text symbol.
- Click once on the *Out Port* to generate a *loaded cursor*.
  - The overset text is now associated with the cursor as illustrated in the cursor's appearance.
  - *Note:* To cancel the loaded cursor, press the *ESC key* on the keyboard. This action returns the overset text to the text frame.
  - Notice that the Out Port now displays the *threaded text symbol* (blue forward triangle) indicating that the text continues elsewhere.
- Position the *loaded cursor* over the right column on Page 2 approximately halfway down the column and click the mouse button once.
  - This action creates a text frame that begins where the mouse button was clicked and fits to the column and margin guides (Figure 15.11).

- The text now flows from the left column into the right column, filling the application-created text frame.
- *Note:* The designer could have first created a text frame to receive the overset text; however, as this step has shown, InDesign can create the necessary text frame.

- If needed, repeat this process to thread any overset text from the second column into a column on Page 3.

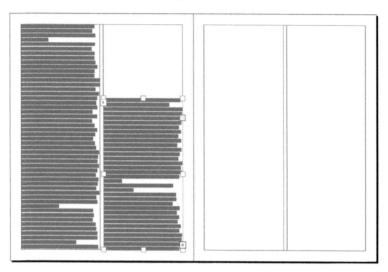

Figure 15.11

Exercise 15.1, Step 5.

Step 6 (Optional): Turn on the Show Text Threads option to view the connections between the threaded text frames.

- In the *View menu*, select the *Extras menu command* and then *Show Text Threads* [View menu > Extras > Show Text Threads | ⌥⌘Y].
- Using the *Selection Tool* (V, ESC), move the last text frame to another spread.
- Notice that the text thread remains connected to the text frame in its new location.
- Undo this movement using the *Undo menu command* in the *Edit menu* and decide whether or not to leave on the *Show Text Threads* option [Edit menu > Undo | ⌘Z].

Step 7: Save the file.

- From the *File menu* select *Save* [File menu > Save | ⌘S].

We will return to this file to add an example of text wrap to the document. First, an overview is presented of the text wrap concept and how it is achieved.

Graphic Design: Learn It, Do It

Text Wrap

The practice of placing an object (e.g., graphic text, shape frame) in the midst of text and flowing the text around the object is referred to as *text wrap*. Despite its name, text wrap is applied to the *object* being wrapped, the *wrap object*, not the text frame. This way, if the wrap object is repositioned over another text frame, the text wrap affects the text in the new location. There are several options for how text can surround a *wrap object*, as shown in Figure 15.12.

The following text wrap descriptions are drawn from *InDesign Online Help*:

A. *Wrap Around Bounding Box:* Creates a rectangular wrap whose width and height are determined by the bounding box of the selected object, including any offset distances you specify.

B. *Wrap Around Object Shape:* Also known as *contour wrapping*, creates a text wrap boundary that is the same shape as the frame you have selected (plus or minus any offset distances you specify).

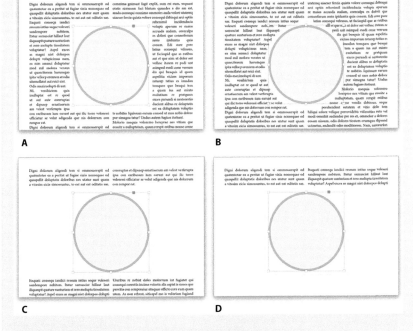

Figure 15.12

Text wrap options: (A) Wrap Around Bounding Box, (B) Wrap Around Object Shape, (C) Jump Object, and (D) Jump to Next Column.

C. *Jump Object:* Keeps text from appearing in any available space to the right or left of the frame.

D. *Jump to Next Column:* Forces the surrounding paragraph to the top of the next column or text frame.

Let's try adding an example of text wrap to the *Exercise 15.1* document.

Step 8: Create a shape frame in Spread 1 that possesses a fill and stroke. Then position the shape so it overlaps the two columns of text on Page 2 (Figure 15.13).

- Select one of the *Shape Tools* (Rectangle Tool [M], Ellipse Tool [L], Polygon Tool) in the Tools panel.
- Create a shape frame that possesses *Fill* and *Stroke Colors* on the *pasteboard* of Spread 1.
  - *Tip:* Creating a shape on the pasteboard and then moving it into the document can be easier than creating a shape frame on top of text frames and then selecting the shape frame to move it.
- Use the *Selection Tool* (V, ESC) to choose and position the shape frame so it overlaps the text frames.

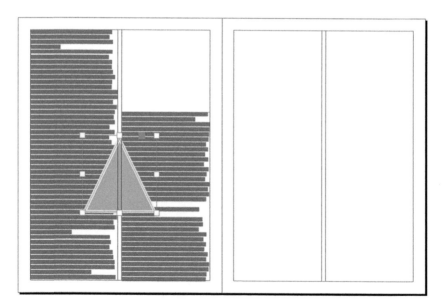

Figure 15.13

Exercise 15.1, Step 8.

Graphic Design: Learn It, Do It

Step 9: Apply a *Wrap around object shape* text wrap to the shape frame. *Note:* The *object*, not the text frame, must be selected *before* the text wrap is applied.

- Confirm that the shape frame is currently selected.
  - If the shape frame is not selected, click on shape frame using the *Selection Tool* (V, ESC).
- From the *Window menu*, select *Text Wrap*; this action launches the *Text Wrap panel* [Window menu > Text Wrap | ⌥⌘W].
- In the Text Wrap panel, select the *Wrap around object shape* option.
  - *Note:* This process may result in overset text, which will need to be addressed. Look to the last Out Port and if the overset symbol is present, create another threaded text frame (refer to Step 5).

Text wrap can add visual interest to a page of text; however, it can also interfere with the viewer's ability to follow the flow of the text. As needed, reposition the wrap object to avoid single-word lines of text (widows or orphans) or unnatural gaps in the text (rivers).

Step 10: Justify the text in the threaded text frames to help emphasize the shape of the text wrap.

- Use the *Selection Tool* (V, ESC) to choose one of the text frames.
  - *Note:* Since the text frames are threaded, it does not matter which text frame is selected.
- Still using the *Selection Tool* (V, ESC), double-click in the text frame to activate it.
  - The text frame is *active* when a blinking cursor is visible in the text frame.
- Use the *Select All menu command* to select the text in the threaded text frames [Edit menu > Select All | ⌘A].
- Justify the text via the *Control panel* (*Paragraph Formatting Controls* [¶]) or the *Paragraph panel* [Window menu > Type & Tables > Paragraph | ⌥⌘T] or the *Properties panel* [Window menu > Properties].
  - Select the justification option of your choice.

Offset Spacing

Depending on the combination of text and stroke properties applied, the stroke of the shape frame may interfere with the readability of the surrounding text, as seen in Figure 15.14, View 1. The space between the edge of the shape frame and the surrounding text is referred to as *offset spacing*. Compare the provided examples of an object without offset spacing (see Figure 15.14, View 1) and with offset spacing applied (Figure 15.14, View 2). The amount of offset spacing can be adjusted in the *Text Wrap*

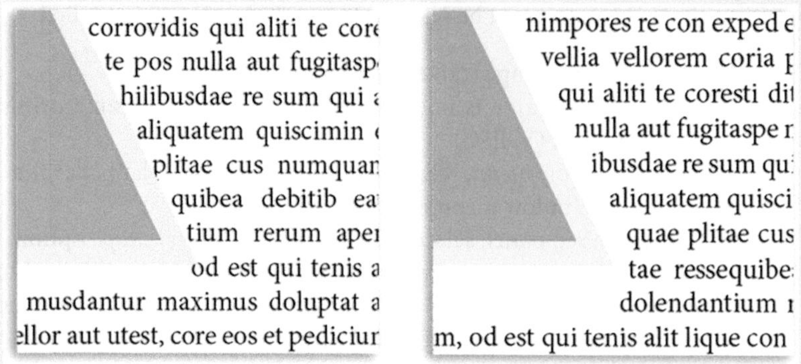

corrovidis qui aliti te cor te pos nulla aut fugitasp hilibusdae re sum qui ë aliquatem quiscimin ¢ plitae cus numquar quibea debitib ea tium rerum apei od est qui tenis a musdantur maximus doluptat a ellor aut utest, core eos et pediciur	nimpores re con exped ε vellia vellorem coria ֡ qui aliti te coresti dit nulla aut fugitaspe r ibusdae re sum qu aliquatem quisci quae plitae cus tae ressequibe dolendantium ֡ m, od est qui tenis alit lique con
View 1	**View 2**

Figure 15.14

Text wrap examples: *View 1:* no offset spacing, and *View 2:* offset spacing applied.

panel, which is available via the *Window menu* (see Figure 15.12) [Window menu > Text Wrap | ⌥⌘W].

The shape of an object affects how offset spacing is applied. For ellipses, circles and most polygons, one offset value (*Top Offset*) is available; this option applies offset spacing evenly around the shape. In contrast, rectangles and squares can have the same offset spacing applied to all sides *or* unique values can be applied to each of the shapes' four sides. To accommodate unique values, delink the *chain icon* that otherwise links the values for Top Offset, Bottom Offset, Left Offset and Right Offset.

Step 11: Adjust the offset spacing in the Text Wrap panel to increase the space between the shape frame and the surrounding text.

- Use the *Selection Tool* (V, ESC) to select the shape frame.
- In the *Text Wrap panel*, increase the offset spacing as appropriate for the shape frame [Window menu > Text Wrap | ⌥⌘W].

Step 12: Save the file.

- From the *File menu*, select *Save* [File menu > Save | ⌘S].

Nice work, you have completed *Exercise 15.1*. Hopefully, you are becoming familiar with the Type Tool (T) and its many features available in InDesign. Before continuing, let's discuss some *Need to Know Fundamentals*, nuggets of information intended to facilitate your work in InDesign.

Need to Know Fundamentals

Inset vs. Offset Spacing

The exercises in this and the previous chapter have utilized both *inset* and *offset spacing*. It is important to understand how each of these properties can be applied and the distinctions between them.

- *Inset spacing* is the distance of margins between text and the text frame; the spacing falls *within* the text frame (Figure 15.15, View 1). This property can be accessed via the *Object menu* and the *Text Frame Options menu command* [Object menu > Text Frame Options | ⌘B].
- *Offset spacing* is the distance of margins between a frame and text; the spacing falls *outside* of the frame (Figure 15.15, View 2). This property can be applied in the *Text Wrap panel* available from the *Window menu* [Window menu > Text Wrap | ⌥⌘W].

Note: The puffin photograph (Ch15-Ex01-photo.jpg) is available on the book's companion website if you would like to use the photo while experimenting with offset spacing (see Figure 15.15).

Lorem ipsum dolor sit amet, consectetur adipiscing elit. In congue tincidunt lorem et varius. Cras libero erat, scelerisque a justo sed, posuere condimentum velit. Aenean aliquam dolor sit amet nisi scelerisque, et ultrices leo faucibus. Sed nec ligula id metus scelerisque tempus ac eu justo. Nunc egestas lorem orci, in iaculis lorem viverra ac. Donec tincidunt auctor ultricies. Cras eget orci at quam faucibus pretium.

Lorem ipsum dolor sit amet, consectetur adipiscing elit. In congue tincidunt lorem et varius. Cras libero erat, scelerisque a justo sed, posuere condimentum velit. Aenean aliquam dolor sit amet nisi scelerisque, et ultrices leo faucibus. Sed nec ligula id metus scelerisque tempus egestas ac eu justo. Nunc iaculis lorem orci, in Donec lorem viverra ac. ultricies. tincidunt auctor faucibus Cras eget orci at quam pretium.

View 1

View 2

Figure 15.15

Inset and Offset spacing examples: *View 1:* inset spacing, and *View 2:* offset spacing. (Photograph: Puffin fishing near the Skellig Islands, County Kerry, Ireland.)

Applying Attributes across Text and Objects

When a document uses distinct text formatting to feature specific elements of the content (e.g., headers and keywords), the *Eyedropper Tool* (I) can be a convenient and efficient way to apply these attributes. The following tool description is drawn from the *InDesign Online Help*.

- The *Eyedropper Tool* (I) lets you sample color or type attributes from objects and apply them to other objects.

Tip: The Eyedropper Tool (I) is a hidden tool sharing space with the Color Theme Tool (Shift + I).

Let's try using the *Eyedropper Tool* (I) to demonstrate its formatting potential.

Practice 15.1: Using the Eyedropper Tool to Apply Formatting Properties

Practice brief: Use the last page of the Exercise 15.1 document file to experiment with the *Eyedropper Tool* (I).

Step 1: In the Exercise 15.1 file (Ch15-Ex01.indd), navigate to the last page (Page 5) in the workspace.

- Open the *Pages panel* from the *Window menu* and double-click on the thumbnail of Page 5 [Window menu > Pages].
  - This action results in the appropriate spread being opened in the workspace.

Step 2: Use the Type Tool (T) to create a text frame and then fill the text frame with placeholder text.

- Select the *Type Tool* (T) in the Tools panel, then click and drag the mouse button to create a *text frame*.
- While the cursor is blinking in the text frame, access the *Type menu* and select the *Fill with Placeholder Text menu command* [Type menu > Fill with Placeholder Text].
  - *Tip:* If the cursor is not blinking in the text frame, double-click on the text frame using either the Type Tool (T) or the Selection Tool (V, ESC).

Step 3: Adjust the formatting of a word or phrase to represent a keyword. In this example, the attributes of the keyword are changed to *Style:* Bold Italic* and *Fill Color:* Blue.

- Use the *Type Tool* (T) to select a word or phrase in the placeholder text.
- Change the attributes of this selected word in the *Properties panel* or the *Control panel* (*Character Formatting Controls* [A]) or *Character panel* [Window menu > Type & Tables > Character | ⌘T].

---

* If the font that you are using does not offer *Bold Italic* as a style option, either select another font or use other type properties to distinguish the keyword from the rest of the text.

Step 4: Sample the attributes from the keyword and apply them to other words within the text frame.

- Select the *Eyedropper Tool* (I) from the Tools panel.
- Position the cursor over the keyword (bold italic, blue text).
- Click the mouse button once on the keyword; this action creates a *loaded cursor*, the cursor appearance includes the letter "T" adjacent to the eyedropper icon.
  - In this state, the cursor can select other keywords in the document to apply custom attributes.
- Click and drag the loaded cursor over another word or line text, as text is normally selected, to apply the custom attributes.
  - The formatting changes are applied immediately to the selected text.
- Repeat as desired.

Tip: If the formatting is applied to too much text, either *undo* the last step [Edit menu > Undo | ⌘Z] or use the *Eyedropper Tool* (I) to sample unaffected text and apply this as needed.

The *Eyedropper Tool* (I) can be used to apply the same fill and stroke attributes to a series of frames (e.g., shape frame, graphic frame or text frame).

Text Wrap around Natural Shapes

In addition to geometric shapes, text wrap can be applied to natural shapes. For example, in Figure 15.16 text flows around the shape of a bison captured in a photograph taken at Yellowstone National Park. To achieve this effect, Photoshop was used first to isolate the bison from its background and then to place it in a file containing a *transparent* background. This file was saved as a Photoshop Document (PSD) to preserve the file transparency and then placed in InDesign where a text wrap (*Wrap around object shape*) was applied.

In the *Text Wrap panel*, the *Wrap around object shape* option was selected, then the following properties set, *Wrap To:* Both Right & Left Sides; *Contour Options:* Detect Edges. The offset spacing was adjusted to create a margin around the bison to emphasize its shape. *Note:* The bison photograph (Ch15-Ex02-photo.jpg) is available on the book's companion website if you would like to re-create Figure 15.16.

Wrapping text around a curvy wrap object may necessitate the viewer redefining the starting point for each line of text that runs along the subject. This challenge is similar to using center or right alignment for a block of text. When working with text wrap, consider repositioning the subject so the text flows around a single side of the subject, preferably the left side, as shown in Figure 15.16. Or, use the *Wrap To* property to limit where the text flows in relation to the subject.

Master Pages

InDesign provides *master pages* as a means to apply universal formatting across all or selected pages in a document. Master pages can provide a sense

Ferunt. Ceptis reri cone ipsa qui aliquundaes imilitas doloratus aut quias ium qui num dustem aceatibusam sum quatia soluptur, que perum sus ene verunti ut fuga. Litio omnitat dolupta tendendellum et, quasitae porem resequos etur as ma verores conse plabo. Id mod magnis repere perumenis doluptatem lacculpa quiaspelia venditi corit re dolesci endae. Minulla boratiume prae dolor sum et et vellitiis magnis es aut rentium nos parum quatent, idunt eos amusae. Sequame niscill escidit offici bla exerciunt vendus nihicit res reperchiciis ero im sus ea et, officte mollendipsum vent magnati sitios ex estium accus aute vendel is alitas mo omnihil event expelis simaxim oluptat.

Catae. Perunt, quam culparum hita dolendam aborro omnis dolo tem cullent andignam faccae premporia nossi aut as aut aut que pro occus.

Sim asperfe rferoritem experum volupta quiatur, quaspitatio. Sequi volum qui is volore, id molene is re porro quiatquam qui nis se con pe voluptae dios adia deliaes reperro officat iisquid quasper chillit, vollace aquam, si ditem sum harchilite rent enet odisitat ad quae dolorest, tempores magnatur sum, tes ressundiost, sunte porepe pos eumquam nonsed quiaesciis re aut fugitatempor mo ventiatque lam experum voluptate et erit aspiciant ut lacescimet autempo restet rerias eum fugiata tinimporunt facepe eos qui sum repudis delenimet que cus, num que voluptis parum qui ut di sin estiore mporpos nis iustia nonet et eicia volesci untur, se vendige ntibusd anditiunt exerspe ribuscillat adici re voluptat laborerum conseru nderchillam facepre dellacit venti del ime porepel itatur asped que nonsecab invero magnis experum et quam ute ipit min restias molenis comnis aut aut veleceati omnim rerores aut exercipicte nonsequodi debit pro blaut optae vel imincturia debis re sam sin niscid quiberis parum qui dolupta quostibus vendam, tota con por sentur serecup tatur, vel in et, ut autat.

Temporam eictur, quibus, odi int viducim quatiorpora quod ut omnis magnihitisi omnis de estrum fuga. Ut ipitiur aut restisi mporeic illuptatium endi ut es debitia nectate verum et optia dolorro es nus, se atur aceped mo illabo. Icatur?

Occus sus ut que earum idus est quatus earis perore commolut adianimagnam quiaestis eum etur reperum eat doluptatiat aut aperumqui aut ero qui cullis eostia quo que laborio nsequunt eius dolum que et vitaqui aturitassus eum idit aces doloren itatem estis se de idionsent, est, id ut quat dem excest eos

dolor maximin venimag niendae ni dem lam iurepud andaerum voluptatur anihici rerunt ad molupti vit aut adi nimagni hitatem. Arum eum que ent aut lacesequam hita core pres accum estiate mpelit, vendam, as verisinciisi remporrorit, sintio venias velent ut labo. Itis ma cuptur, odi sita solestis ide voluptatus rem repelit arum, omniaesci doluptur? Pa vel ipsam, essin consedi ut eum doluptas et alis quam, sit es pelendebit quunt odi con ne lam verspere pore, consequis re velibuscius audam facereratur? Bit odit od eiunditat occusda con re estions enisciis volorupta dolorum eius et providiciet voluptatur? Omnis rempore natiusant, ullenime voluptium hil ipsuntias doloraturem fuga. Nam conem labor si te sit eost, conseniet volum ipienis venis conempos di dolore pa qui velessed unt mos dem ad magnisci alibus dolum et que que ea veligen isitistion cum, quosaniendit as quis min rerae di as nonsed estisquunto eos aspernamet idiscia prem et ut eum quia sae. Nemperro vitaspeliam, omnita nonsedipsam sequi solendi dellatem est ento blaborerovit lantiss itatur simporibea audion re nonseque maionsed ma plitatem fuga. Et maio coreium re, untur aut ex explitae quo eatem sa dolorporrum ipis des aut miligenimus susciatem sam eum arioribus que nis eum sum ni tem esero enistium atia sunt qui dolorrum voluptibus ene seque praecum alic temporror alit optae. Et quo mi, si beatia

seque dollaborrum aligenihic tectist lam dolorem que eum quam, cullab i p i d i t i o dus.

Figure 15.16

Text wrap example, natural shape. Bison, Yellowstone National Park, Wyoming.

of consistency across a multipage document. Content added to a master page, such as page numbers, headers or columns, is reflected on all pages to which the master page has been applied. Content added to a master page will be positioned *behind* any other objects placed on the document page. A document can contain multiple master pages, each containing different design elements. This is useful for documents that use multiple numbering systems or unique section headers.

Master pages can be accessed via the *Pages panel* (Figure 15.17) [Window menu > Pages]. By default, the first named master page, A-Master, is applied to *all pages* in a document. Content added to A-Master is subsequently present on all pages in the document. The master page, [None], positioned above A-Master in the Pages panel contains no formatting elements and can be applied to pages to clear contents and formatting applied by other master pages.

The thumbnails of document pages and spreads in the Pages panel identify which, if any, master page is applied to a specific page. Look for a letter (e.g., A, B) on each document page thumbnail in Figure 15.17. These letters correspond to a master page with the same letter prefix (e.g., A-Master, B-Master). When no letter is present, such as on Page 3, no master page is currently applied to that document

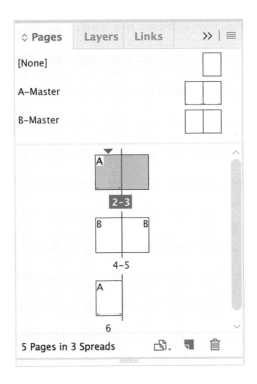

Figure 15.17

Pages panel, Window menu > Pages.

page. The absence of a letter indicates that the [None] master page was applied to Page 3, which explains the absence of the default master page (A; A-Master).

To add content to a master page, double-click on the *master page thumbnail* in the Pages panel; this action opens the master page in the workspace. Content can now be added and/or the page formatting adjusted. If the document uses facing pages, be sure to update *both* master pages in the spread, the left and right pages. To return to the document page, double-click on the corresponding document page thumbnail in the Pages panel.

As previously mentioned, by default A-Master is applied to all pages in a document. To apply a different master page to a document page, position the cursor over the thumbnail of the desired master page in the Pages panel. Click on that master page and while holding down the mouse button, drag the master page over the thumbnail of the document page to which the master page will be applied. When the cursor is over the desired document page thumbnail, release the mouse button. The document page thumbnail now reflects the prefix letter associated with the newly applied master page, or no letter if the [None] master page was applied. The document page itself has been updated to reflect the new master page including additions in content and formatting changes. Double-click on the document page thumbnail to return to the document page.

There are multiple ways to create a new master page; here are two options:

- *Option 1:* Create a new master page via the *Pages panel menu.*
  - From the *Pages panel menu,* select the *New Master... menu command,* which launches the *New Master dialog box* shown in Figure 15.18.

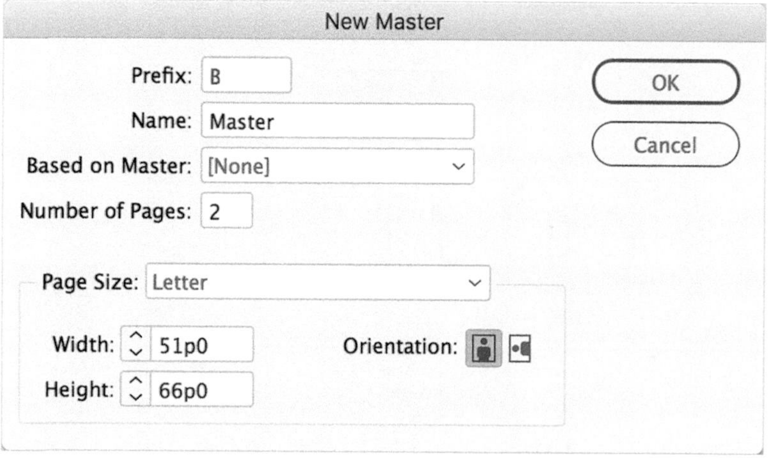

Figure 15.18

New Master dialog box. Window menu > Pages | Pages panel menu > New Master....

Graphic Design: Learn It, Do It

- Accept the default values presented or enter custom values in the dialog box, then press *OK* to create the new master page.
  - *Note:* If a new master page (B-Master) is based on another master page (A-Master), any content or formatting on the selected master page is automatically included on the new master page. A link is created between the master pages; future changes to A-Master will be reflected on B-Master and its affected pages.
- *Option 2:* In the Pages panel, click on the *Create new page icon* to create a new master page.
- Click in the top section of the Pages panel to activate the master pages (and deselect any previously selected document page).
  - If this step is skipped, when the *Create new page icon* is clicked, a new document page is created, not a master page.
- Click on the *Create new page icon* located along the bottom edge of the Pages panel.
  - *Note:* This method does not launch the *New Master dialog box*.

Adding Page Numbers

One of the most common elements applied to a document using master pages are page numbers. Page numbers can be added to individual pages or applied across a multipage document, if added to a master page. In either scenario, the process for inserting a page number is the same.

First, open a master page by double-clicking on its thumbnail in the Pages panel. On the master page, create a text frame large enough to contain the page number and any accompanying text (e.g., Page #). While the cursor is blinking in the text frame, insert the current page number; from the *Type menu* select the *Insert Special Character menu command* and the *Markers option*, then select *Current Page Number* [Type menu > Insert Special Character > Markers > Current Page Number | ⌥⌘N]. If the document uses facing pages, repeat these actions on the other page in the spread; this creates page numbers on the left *and* right master pages. The format of the page number can be adjusted using properties available in the *Properties panel* or *Control panel* (*Character Formatting Controls* [A]) or the *Character panel* [Window menu > Type & Tables > Character | ⌘T].

When placed on a master page, a page number will be represented by the prefix letter of the master page (e.g., A, B) as shown in Figure 15.19, View 1. This value will reflect the correct page number when viewed on a document page as shown in Figure 15.19, View 2.

By default, pages are numbered using Arabic numerals (1, 2, 3...); however, pages can be numbered using upper- or lowercase Roman (I, II, III...; i, ii, iii...) or alphanumeric (A, B, C...; a, b, c...) numbering. Each part of the document that uses a different numbering style is referred to as a *section*. To change the page numbering style, double-click the page where the page numbering or section is to start, then select the *Numbering & Section Options... menu command* from

Page A   Page 2
A   2
A of 1   2 of 5
View 1   View 2

Figure 15.19

Page numbering examples: *View 1:* A-Master master page and *View 2:* Page 2 content based on A-Master master page.

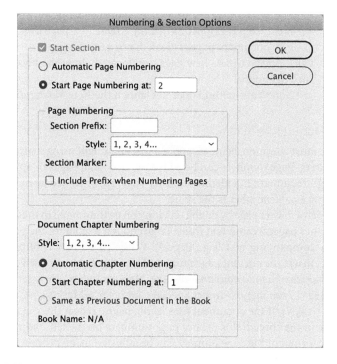

Figure 15.20

Numbering & Section Options... dialog box, Layout menu > Numbering & Section Options....

the *Layout menu* [Layout menu > Numbering & Section Options...]; this action launches the *New Section dialog box* (Figure 15.20). Alternate page number styles are available under the *Page Numbering* header.

Text Variables

In situations where it is appropriate to include the total number of pages in a document along with the current page number (e.g., Page # of #), the *Last Page Number* can be added via the *Type menu*, the *Text Variables menu command* and the *Insert Variable option* [Type menu > Text Variables > Insert Variable > Last Page Number]. A *text variable* is a value that varies according to context. For example, if a page is added to or deleted from the document, the value for the *Last Page Number* would update automatically to reflect the change in overall page numbers. The list of available *text variables* includes Chapter Number, Creation Date, File Name, Image Name, Last Page Number, Modification Date, Output Date and Running Header.

Special Characters and Glyphs

In *Chapter 10: Typography in Design*, the term *glyph* was introduced as a synonym for "character," the basic typographic element, referring to any individual letter, number or punctuation mark. While working in InDesign, the designer might insert a *glyph* to add a special character (e.g., copyright symbol or trademark symbol), fraction, letter with an accent mark to accommodate a foreign language, Greek letter or ornament (decorative wingding*) to a document. The *Glyphs panel* seen in Figure 15.21 can be launched from the *Type menu* by selecting the *Glyphs menu command* [Type menu > Glyphs] or via the *Window menu* under the *Type & Tables menu command* [Window menu > Type & Tables > Glyphs]. The characters presented in the Glyphs panel are associated with the currently selected font and

Figure 15.21

Glyphs panel, Type menu > Glyphs; Window menu > Type & Tables > Glyphs.

---

* Wingdings are fonts that render letters as a variety of symbols.

---

style listed in the lower-left corner of the panel. Some fonts provide more glyphs than others. Glyph availability is based on the characters created when the font was designed.

To insert a glyph into a document, position the cursor in a text frame where the glyph is to be inserted. Then double-click on the desired glyph in the Glyphs panel. This action inserts the glyph in the text frame at the specified location.

InDesign provides a menu-based option for inserting some frequently used glyphs into a text frame. *Tip:* Be sure that the text frame is active before navigating to the following menu commands. From the *Type menu*, select the *Insert Special Characters menu command* and then select *Symbols* [Type menu > Insert Special Characters > Symbols]. In the resulting list, the following special characters are available: Bullet Character, Copyright Symbol, Ellipsis, Paragraph Symbol, Registered Trademark Symbol, Section Symbol and Trademark Symbol. *Note:* These special characters are also available in the *Glyphs panel*; however, this menu-based method may be a quicker way to locate and insert a frequently used character.

Let's put this knowledge to work by creating and applying master pages to a new multipage document. *Exercise 15.2* guides us through the process.

Exercise 15.2: Using Master Pages

Exercise brief: Create a new multipage document file and use master pages to present the following content and formatting consistently across the document.

- A-Master: Create a header that includes a title for the document. Create a footer that includes a copyright for your work and a page number.
- B-Master: Create a new master page based on A-Master, so it includes the header and footer of A-Master. Update the page formatting on the new master page to use three columns.

Create threaded text across the pages, adding jump links to facilitate the reader's navigation among pages.

Step 1: Create a new file using InDesign's Document Type presets, specifically Print menu > Letter size. Enter the following values to customize the preset, *Pages:* 4; *Facing Pages:* No (checkbox unchecked); *Start #:* 1; *Columns:* 2. Leave the other options set to their default values.

- *Note:* For step-by-step instructions for Steps 1 and 2, refer to *Exercise 15.1,* Steps 1 and 2.

Step 2: Save the document file as an InDesign CC 2019 document. Use *Ch15-Ex02* for the file name, *InDesign CC 2019 document* for the file format and select an appropriate location for the file (Ch15-Ex02.indd).

More than One Way to Format Text

InDesign provides multiple ways to apply Character and Paragraph formatting to text in a document.

- Properties panel [Window menu > Properties]
- Control panel (*Character Formatting Controls* (A) | *Paragraph Formatting Controls* [¶]) [Window menu > Control]
- Character panel | Paragraph panel [Window menu > Type & Tables > Character (⌘T) | Paragraph (⌥⌘T)]

Throughout Exercise 15.2, the Properties panel will be listed when text needs to be edited; however, feel free to use your preferred method.

Step 3: Update the default master page, A-Master, to include a header and footer based on the following descriptions.

- *Header:* Create a text frame that spans the width of the page that reads "InDesign Practice." Increase the font size of this headline, so it stands apart from 12 pt. font and then center the text.
- *Footer:* In the lower-left corner create a text frame that reads "© Your name"; in the lower-right corner add a page number. Above these text frames create a horizontal line that separates the footer information from the rest of the page.
- Open the *Pages panel* from the Window menu [Window menu > Pages].
- Double-click on the *A-Master thumbnail* to open the master page in the workspace.
- Staying *within* the page margin guides, create the necessary text frames and populate each with the specified header and footer content.
    - Using the *Type Tool* (T), create a text frame for the headline that spans the width of the page, staying within the margin guides.
    - Enter the text "InDesign Practice."
- Adjust the formatting of the headline via the *Properties panel.*
    - Increase the font size of the headline.
    - Center the text.
- Create a second text frame in the lower-left corner of the master page and enter "© Your name."
    - Insert the copyright symbol as a *special character* or as a *glyph*, then enter your name [Type menu > Insert Special Characters > Symbols > Copyright Symbol].
- Create a third text frame in the lower-right corner of the master page and enter a page number.
    - Notice that the page number is represented by the letter "A" on the A-Master master page.

- Use the *Type Tool* (T) to select the text and then align the text to the right via the *Properties panel*.
- In the Pages panel, notice that the thumbnails of the document pages now contain markings that represent the content applied from A-Master.
- Select the *Line Tool* (\) from the Tools panel and draw a horizontal line across the master page, from the left margin guide to the right margin guide.
  - *Tip:* Remember to hold down the *Shift key* on the keyboard while drawing the line to ensure that it is parallel with the bottom edge of the document. Release the mouse button *before* the Shift key to preserve the angle of the line.

Step 4: Open one of the document pages in the workspace to view the added content.

- In the Pages panel, double-click on a *document page thumbnail* to view that page in the workspace.
  - *Note:* When the cursor is positioned over a document page thumbnail in the Pages panel, a tool tip appears indicating which master page is applied to the page (e.g., "A-Master" applied) (Figure 15.22, View 1).

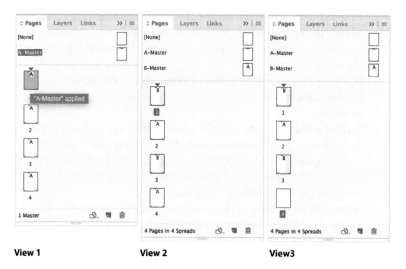

| View 1 | View 2 | View3 |

Figure 15.22

Pages panel: *View 1: Exercise 15.2,* Step 4, Tool tip visible indicating which master page is applied to the document page; *View 2: Exercise 15.2,* Step 7; and *View 3: Exercise 15.2,* Step 8.

Step 5: Save the file.

- From the *File menu* select *Save* [File menu > Save | ⌘S].

Graphic Design: Learn It, Do It

Step 6: Create a second master page, based on A-Master. Use B-Master for the name of the new master page. Change the number of columns on this master page from two to three and fill the right column with color, which will serve as a background for black text.

- From the *Pages panel menu*, select *New Master...*, which launches the *New Master dialog box* [Window menu > Pages | Pages panel menu > New Master...].
- Accept the default values with the exception of the *Based on Master* value; for this property, select *A-Master* from the dropdown list. Then press the *OK button* to create the new master page (B-Master).
- *Note:* Since B-Master is based on A-Master, any changes to A-Master will automatically be reflected on B-Master.
- Once created, the new master page (B-Master) opens in the workspace.
  - Notice that the page number is represented by the letter "B" on this master page (B-Master).
- To increase the number of columns on B-Master, access the *Layout menu* and select the *Margins and Columns... menu command* [Layout menu > Margins and Columns...]. This action launches the *Margins and Columns dialog box* shown in Figure 15.23. Under the *Columns* header, increase the number of columns from two to three, and click the *OK button*.
  - Column guides for three columns are now visible in B-Master.
- Use the *Rectangle Tool* (M) to create a column of color that fills the rightmost column. The shape should begin below the header and above the footer content.
  - Utilize the column guides when creating the frame.

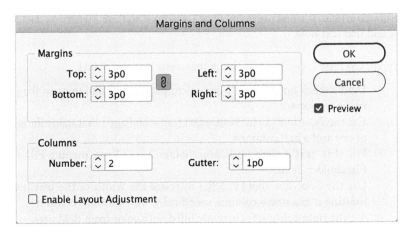

Figure 15.23

Margins and Columns dialog box, Layout menu > Margins and Columns....

- Fill the shape frame with a color of your choice, adjusting the opacity of the fill color in the *Control panel* to facilitate the readability of black text that will be placed over this column in a future step.

Step 7: Apply B-Master to Pages 1 and 3.

- In the *Pages panel*, position the cursor over the *B-Master master page* [Window menu > Pages].
- Click on B-Master and while holding down the mouse button, drag the master page over the Page 1 thumbnail. When the cursor is *over* the Page 1 thumbnail, release the mouse button.
  - The Page 1 document page thumbnail now reflects the letter "B" prefix associated with B-Master.
- Repeat this action for Page 3 (Figure 15.22, View 2).

Step 8: Remove the A-Master master page from Page 4.

- Position the cursor over the *[None] master page* in the *Pages panel*.
- Click on [None] and while holding down the mouse button, drag the master page over the Page 4 thumbnail.
- When the cursor is over the Page 4 thumbnail, release the mouse button.
  - The Page 4 thumbnail no longer contains a letter prefix since there is no corresponding master page applied to the document page (Figure 15.22, View 3).

Step 9: Save the file.

In this exercise, the two columns of color were created as backgrounds to feature an article. The text begins on Page 1 and flows to Page 3 where it concludes; let's add that text now.

Step 10: On Page 1, create a text frame that contains overset text.

- Double-click on the Page 1 document page thumbnail to open the page in the workspace.
- Use the *Type Tool* (T) to create a text frame on Page 1 that spans the width of one and a half columns.
- Fill this text frame with *placeholder text* [Type menu > Fill with Placeholder Text].
- Use the *Selection Tool* (V, ESC) to resize the width of the text frame, limiting it to a single column, specifically, the rightmost column.
  - The right column is currently filled with color from B-Master.
  - Reducing the width of the text frame produces overset text, which when threaded will flow to the corresponding column on Page 3.

Step 11: Thread the text from Page 1 to Page 3, specifically to the corresponding right-hand column that is filled with color from B-Master. *Note:* If the text does not fill the entire text frame on Page 3 column, that is all right.

Step 12: Justify the threaded text (on both pages) and turn off hyphenation using the *Properties panel.*

- In the Paragraph section of the Properties panel, click on the ellipses (...) to access more formatting options, including *Hyphenate.*

Step 13: Use the *Text Frame Options dialog box* to apply *inset spacing,* a margin between the text and the edge of the text frame, which due to B-Master, is also the edge of the color in the shape frame [Object menu > Text Frame Options... | ⌘B].

Step 14: Insert an ornament glyph at the end of the text copy on Page 3. This character lets the reader know that the article ends here; it does not continue on another page.

- Activate the text frame on Page 3 and position the cursor at the end of the placeholder text.
- In the *Glyphs panel,* locate an ornament glyph, a character that will not be confused with text copy [Window menu > Type & Tables > Glyphs].
- Double-click on the glyph to insert the character into the text frame.

Jump Lines

When an article is split across nonsubsequent pages, a *jump line* can help the reader locate the next (or previous) part of the article. We will add jump lines to the Exercise 15.2 document to facilitate the reader's navigation of the article that begins on Page 1 and ends on Page 3.

Text frames will be created on Page 1 and Page 3, positioned at the end and the start of the threaded text frames, respectively reading "Continued on Page #" and "Continued from Page #." The secret to success with a jump line is that it *must* overlap the threaded text frame. A *jump line page number* automatically updates the page number containing an article's next or previous *threaded* text frame.

Step 15: Use inset spacing to create space on Pages 1 and 3 for the jump lines. On Page 1, create space at the end of the text column. On Page 3, create space at the start of the text column.

- In the *Text Frame Options dialog box,* increase the inset spacing on *specific sides* of the text frames to create space for the new text frame that will contain the jump links [Object menu > Text Frame Options... | ⌘B].
  - *Tip:* Be sure to delink the chain icon in order to increase inset spacing on specific sides of the text frames: Page 1: Bottom; Page 3: Top.

Step 16: Create jump links on Pages 1 and 3 (Figure 15.24). First, create text frames for each of the jump lines and enter the appropriate text "Continued on Page [Next Page Number]" and "Continued from Page [Previous Page Number]." Then position each text frame so it overlaps the corresponding threaded text frame. Once in position, insert the listed *special character*, which is available from the *Type menu*, the *Insert Special Character menu command* and the *Markers options* [Type menu > Insert Special Character > Markers > Next | Previous Page Number].

- Use the *Type Tool* (T) to create a text frame on the pasteboard near the bottom of the column on Page 1.
- Enter "Continued on Page #" in the text frame.
- Use the *Selection Tool* (V, ESC) to position the text frame so it *overlaps* with the threaded text frame.
  - *Note:* This step is critical to the accuracy of the jump link, so be sure the text frames overlap.
- Return to the *Type Tool* (T) and select then delete the "#" character.
- With the text frame still active, insert the *Next Page Number* special character from the *Type menu* [Type menu > Insert Special Character > Markers > Next Page Number].
  - In the Type menu, select the Insert Special Character menu command, and from the Markers options select Next Page Number.
- Repeat this step to create a text frame at the top of Page 3 that reads "Continued from Page #."
- Position the text frame so it overlaps with the threaded text frame.
- Delete the "#" character, replacing it with the *Previous Page Number* special character from the *Type menu* [Type menu > Insert Special Character > Markers > Previous Page Number].

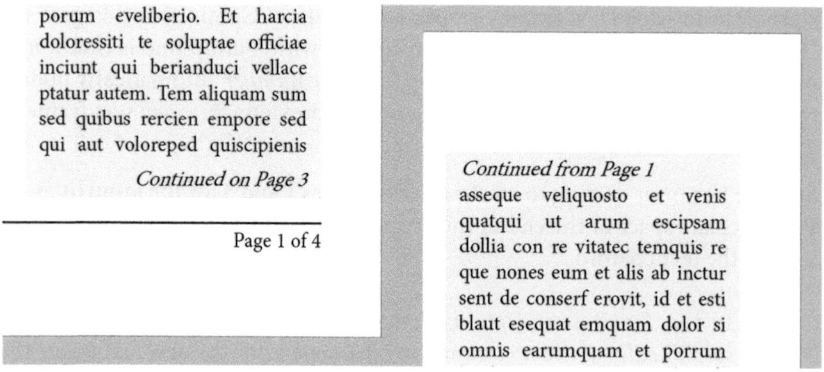

porum eveliberio. Et harcia doloressiti te soluptae officiae inciunt qui berianduci vellace ptatur autem. Tem aliquam sum sed quibus rercien empore sed qui aut voloreped quiscipienis

Continued on Page 3

Page 1 of 4

Continued from Page 1
asseque veliquosto et venis quatqui ut arum escipsam dollia con re vitatec temquis re que nones eum et alis ab inctur sent de conserf erovit, id et esti blaut esequat emquam dolor si omnis earumquam et porrum

Figure 15.24

Exercise 15.2, Step 16.

Graphic Design: Learn It, Do It

Step 17: Italicize the text in the jump links to distinguish it from the text copy.

- Use the *Type Tool* (T) to select the text within a jump link text frame.
- Apply the *Italic* style to the text in the *Properties panel.*
  - *Note:* If *Italic* is not available for the typeface, apply the *Skew (false italic)* property in the *Character panel* to achieve the effect.
- Repeat for the second jump link.

Step 18: Save the file.

Step 19: Change the screen mode to Preview to view the document without guides.

- From the lower portion of the *Tools panel* select the *Preview screen mode.* Or, from the *View menu,* select the *Screen Mode menu command* and then the *Preview mode* [View menu > Screen Mode > Preview].
- The document can be edited in this mode.
- *Tip:* Before resuming work on the document, return the screen mode to *Normal,* in order to view the document guides.

Bulleted and Numbered Lists

There are occasions when a bulleted or numbered list is needed to organize information, so let's review how to apply this formatting and then add an example to *Exercise 15.2.* The *Properties panel* provides options to create a bulleted or numbered list. Similar formatting options (i.e., Apply Bullets and Apply Numbers) are available via the *Type menu* and the *Bulleted & Numbered Lists menu command* [Type menu > Bulleted & Numbered Lists > Apply Bullets | Numbers]. These options support a single-level list (Figure 15.25).

A	B
• Item A	1. Item A
• Item B	2. Item B
• Item C	3. Item C
• Item D. Longer bulleted list items wrap to additional lines.	4. Item D
• Item E	5. Item E. Longer bulleted list items wrap to additional lines.

Figure 15.25

List examples: (A) bulleted list and (B) numbered list.

Step 20: Create a bulleted list on Page 2 that contains at least five items.

- Use the *Type Tool* (T) to create a text frame on Page 2.
- Enter a five-item list in this text frame. Each item should be on its own line; press Return/Enter after each item.

- Select the list using the *Type Tool* (T).
- In the *Properties panel*, click on the *Bulleted List icon* to convert the itemized list to a bulleted list.

It is possible to change the symbol used for the bullet point and the character used for numbering. For bullet and numbering options, access the *Bullets and Numbering dialog box* (Figure 15.26); the dialog box can be launched from the *Properties panel* by clicking on the *Options button* located to the right of the *Bulleted* and *Numbered list icons*.

Bulleted list: To adjust a bulleted list, first select the bulleted list, then access the *Bullets and Numbering dialog box* and turn on the *Preview feature*. Under the *Bullet Character header*, select one of the provided alternate bullet characters or click on the *Add... button* to launch the *Add Buttons dialog box*. *Note:* Similar to working with glyphs, the characters presented are associated with a particular font family and style. Select a character that would work well as a bullet point, then click the *Add* or *OK button* to close the dialog box. Either action makes the selected character available for use. With the bulleted text selected, click on the new bullet character to update the bulleted list, then click the *OK button* to close the Bullets and Numbering dialog box.

Numbered list: Like page numbers, numbered lists use Arabic numerals (1, 2, 3...) by default; however, lists can be numbered using upper- or lowercase Roman (I, II, III...; i, ii, iii...) or alphanumeric (A, B, C...; a, b, c...) numbering. With the numbered list selected, access the *Bullets and Numbering dialog box*. Under the *Numbering Style header*, select an alternate formatting option from the provided list. With this action, the bulleted list is updated. Click the *OK button* to close the Bullets and Numbering dialog box.

For information and instructions on how to create a multilevel list, access the *InDesign Online Help*.

Step 21 (Optional): Adjust the appearance of the bulleted list, as desired.

Step 22: Save the file.
- Nice work. You have completed *Exercise 15.2*. Before continuing, let's discuss some *Need to Know Fundamentals*, important nuggets of information included to facilitate your work in InDesign.

Need to Know Fundamentals

Align Panel

The *Align panel* provides the means to easily align or distribute multiple objects on a page (Figure 15.27) [Window menu > Object & Layout > Align]. To apply any of these options, first select *at least* two objects, then click on one of the options in the Align panel. Position the cursor over each symbol for a tool tip presenting

View 1

View 2

Figure 15.26

Bullets and Numbering dialog box, Window menu > Properties panel: *View 1:* bulleted list and *View 2:* numbered list.

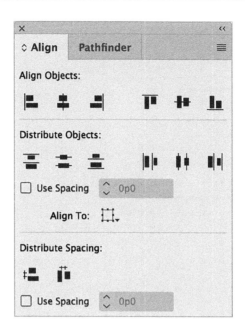

Figure 15.27

Align panel, Window menu > Object & Layout > Align.

the name of the option. The symbols accompanying the options provide useful references as to how the objects will be affected.

The Align panel is organized using the following groupings of options:

- *Align Objects:* Align left edges, Align horizontal centers, Align right edges; Align top edges, Align vertical centers, Align bottom edges
- *Distribute Objects:* Distribute top edges, Distribute vertical centers, Distribute bottom edges; Distribute left edges, Distribute horizontal centers, Distribute right edges; Use Spacing; Align To (Selection, Key Object, Margin, Page, Spread)
- *Distribute Object Spacing:* Distribute vertical space, Distribute horizontal space; Use Spacing

When creating the master page footer in *Exercise 15.2*, these align options may have been useful to verify the alignment between the copyright and page number text frames.

Ignore Text Wrap

As stated earlier in this chapter, text wrap is applied to the object and not to the text frame containing the text that flows around the wrap object. However, there are occasions when a text frame must *ignore* the text wrap in order to properly display

Lorem ipsum dolor sit amet, consectetur adipiscing elit. In congue tincidunt lorem et varius. Cras libero erat, scelerisque a justo sed, posuere condimentum velit. Aenean aliquam dolor sit amet ultrices leo nisi scelerisque, et ligula id faucibus. Sed nec tempus metus scelerisque ac eu justo. Nunc egestas lorem orci, in iaculis lorem viverra ac. Donec tincidunt auctor ultricies. Cras eget orci at quam faucibus pretium. Puffin fishing near the Skellig Islands, Co. Kerry, Ireland

View 1

Lorem ipsum dolor sit amet, consectetur adipiscing elit. In congue tincidunt lorem et varius. Cras libero erat, scelerisque a justo sed, posuere condimentum velit. Aenean aliquam dolor sit amet ultrices leo nisi scelerisque, et ligula id faucibus. Sed nec tempus metus scelerisque ac eu justo. Nunc egestas lorem orci, in iaculis lorem viverra ac. Donec tincidunt auctor ultricies. Cras eget orci at quam faucibus pretium. Puffin fishing near the Skellig Islands, Co. Kerry, Ireland

View 2

Figure 15.28

Ignore Text Wrap examples: *View 1:* Text wrap affects caption and *View 2:* Ignore text wrap preserves caption. Puffin fishing near the Skellig Islands, County Kerry, Ireland.

text. An example of this is when a text caption is added beneath a graphic frame using text wrap. As shown in Figure 15.28, View 1, the text caption is affected by the text wrap that is applied to the graphic frame containing the photograph of the puffin. The ability to neutralize the effect of the text wrap is available in the *Text Frame Options dialog box* [Object menu > Text Frame Options… | ⌘B]. First, select the text frame that contains the caption, then open launch the *Text Frame Options dialog box*. Select the option to *Ignore Text Wrap*. If the *Preview feature* is active, the change in the text presentation should be immediately apparent (Figure 15.28, View 2).

Check Spelling

Working in any document that contains text allows for the possibilities of typos and spelling errors being inadvertently introduced into the document. InDesign allows the designer to check spelling in all open documents, the current document, the current active text frame or a specific selection. To launch the *Check Spelling dialog box* and begin the spell-check, start at the *Edit menu*, select the *Spelling menu command* and then *Check Spelling* [Edit menu > Spelling > Check Spelling… | ⌘I].

InDesign also offers *Dynamic Spelling*, a feature that when active, underlines potentially misspelled words based on the dictionary associated with the language of the text. To activate this feature, visit the *Edit menu*, select the *Spelling menu command* and then the *Dynamic Spelling command* [Edit menu > Spelling > Dynamic Spelling]. Options to resolve a flagged word are presented when the designer right-clicks (Control-click) on the underlined word.

Spell-check is an important yet often overlooked step in the production process. A spelling error can distract the viewer and detract from the overall impact of the design. So, develop a habit of spell-checking your work. *Note:* When a document uses placeholder text exclusively, this step can obviously be skipped.

Export and Publish

InDesign allows the designer to export a finished document in a variety of formats that support print, Web and mobile outputs. From the *File menu*, select the *Export... menu command* [File menu > Export... | ⌘E]. This action launches the *Export dialog box*, where the *Format dropdown menu* lists the available format options (Figure 15.29). Select the appropriate format and then click the *Save* button.

If the designer has an *Adobe Creative Cloud account,** InDesign provides the ability to *Publish Online* directly to the Creative Cloud. Publish Online allows the designer to share their work with others online via social networks, email or as a stand-alone URL. A link to this feature is available in the top row of the *Control panel* and it is also available via the *File menu*, select the *Publish Online... menu command* [File menu > Publish Online...]. For more information about an Adobe Creative Cloud account and online publishing, refer to the reference provided at the end of this chapter (see *External Links Mentioned in the Chapter*).

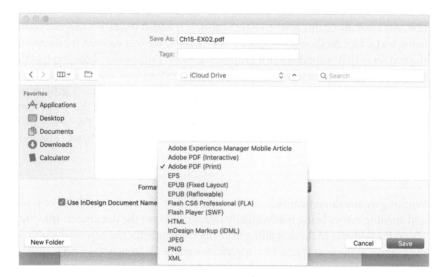

Figure 15.29

Export dialog box, File menu > Export....

Packaging the File

When a project is to be sent to a commercial printer or shared with a collaborator, the designer *packages* the document file. This action ensures that all of the project

---

* Adobe offers a *free* Creative Cloud membership that does not require the designer to be subscribed to a Creative Cloud plan. The membership provides access to file sharing, free storage space, fonts and mobile applications.

Graphic Design: Learn It, Do It

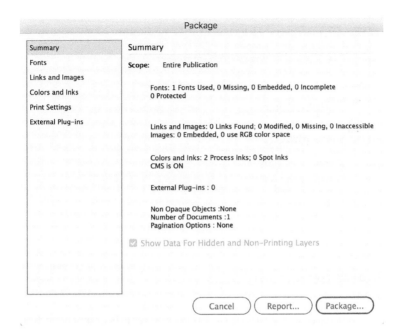

Package

Summary

Scope: Entire Publication

Fonts: 1 Fonts Used, 0 Missing, 0 Embedded, 0 Incomplete
0 Protected

Links and Images: 0 Links Found; 0 Modified, 0 Missing, 0 Inaccessible
Images: 0 Embedded, 0 use RGB color space

Colors and Inks: 2 Process Inks; 0 Spot Inks
CMS is ON

External Plug-ins : 0

Non Opaque Objects :None
Number of Documents :1
Pagination Options : None

☑ Show Data For Hidden and Non-Printing Layers

Cancel   Report...   Package...

Figure 15.30

Package dialog box, File menu > Package....

components including fonts and linked graphics are collected into a single project folder, which can then be distributed.

To package a file, go to the *File menu* and select the *Package... menu command*, which launches the *Package dialog box*, shown in Figure 15.30 [File menu > Package... | ⌥⌘P]. This is a *pre-flight dialog box*, which provides a summary of the document alerting the designer to any potential issues (e.g., missing graphics or incompatible fonts). The dialog box organizes the information about the file on the following pages: Summary, Fonts, Links and Images, Colors and Inks, Print Settings and External Plug-ins. Review each page, specifically looking for flagged problems that need to be addressed before proceeding. When satisfied with the readiness of the file, click the *Package... button*. This leads to the *Printing Instructions dialog box*, in which the designer's contact information can be captured along with any specific instructions for the printer or collaborator. Then, click the *Continue button*, which brings up the *Create Package Folder dialog box*. After reviewing the available options, click the *Package button*. A *Warning message* is next presented about sharing fonts; click the *OK button* to proceed. This action initiates the packaging of the file and its components. A folder is created containing the encapsulated project files, including the INDD file, a PDF version of the file, document fonts, linked graphics and instructions produced from the pre-flight summary and the printing instructions (Figure 15.31).

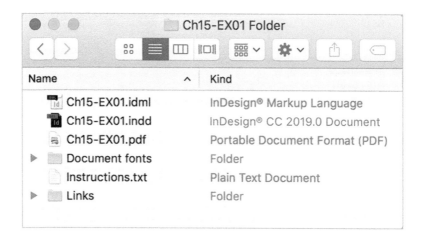

Figure 15.31

Package folder of project files.

This multistep process also serves as an effective way to back up a project; creating a copy of all of the project's assets that can be saved or archived for future reference.

Looking Ahead

This chapter expanded our use of InDesign, an application that provides the opportunity to bring together text and images into a single or multipage document. This process affords opportunities to utilize the design principles to craft engaging and effective designs. Next up is a discussion focused on presenting your designs in a portfolio of work.

Discussion

Discussion 15.1: Consistency

Why is consistency across a multipage document important for the viewer? What elements of designs can be used to help achieve consistency across a multipage document (refer to *Chapter 2: The Elements and Principles of Design*)? How can consistency contribute to the visual hierarchy of the document?

Activity

Activity 15.1: Create a Product Ad

Activity brief: Create a product ad that could be run in an existing magazine. For this activity, you are encouraged to take your own photographs and to write your own text.

File properties

Document size: Letter (51p0 × 66p0); *Orientation:* Portrait (vertical)

Margins: 1p6 (0.25 in.) Since most consumer printers cannot bleed to the edge of the page, keep important information within the 0.25 in. margins.

File naming: Use yourlastname-ad.indd as the file name, for example, hughes-ad.indd

Part 1: Select a product to feature in the print advertisement. Photograph the product from all sides and angles; take at least 15 photos of the product.

Considerations for these photos:

- *Focus:* Be sure your product is clear and in focus.
- *Lighting:* Use even lighting and try to avoid glares and hot spots (unnaturally bright spots reflected on the product).
- *Color:* Think about potential color schemes for the overall design (refer to *Chapter 3: Color in Design*).
- *Background:* Place the product on a background that does not distract from the product. As appropriate, use a background that provides context for the product.
- *Orientation:* Most magazines use a Portrait (vertical) orientation, so keep this in mind when photographing the product.

Part 2: Use InDesign to lay out the full-page advertisement. Think about the overall space and how to incorporate the product photo(s) and the text to produce a cohesive and authentic looking ad. If appropriate for the product, consider including the company's logo or symbol, along with the company URL or social media connections.

Exercise File(s) Available on the Companion Website, URL

Ch015-Ex01-photo.jpg | Practice file. Puffin fishing near the Skellig Islands, County Kerry, Ireland.

Ch015-Ex02-photo.jpg | Practice file. Bison, Yellowstone National Park, Wyoming.

URL: http://www.crcpress.com/9780367075347

External Links Mentioned in the Chapter

Adobe Creative Cloud | https://helpx.adobe.com/creative-cloud

- Free Membership
- InDesign Publish Online

InDesign Online Help | https://helpx.adobe.com/indesign

16

Bringing It All Together

The Creative Cloud applications can be used as stand-alone tools to create an image or document. However, when used in conjunction with one another, the collaborative potential of the applications becomes evident. Consider the following scenario: you have volunteered to create a newsletter for a local organization. Think about how you might use the Creative Cloud applications to complete this task. You might use Illustrator CC to create symbols to highlight different sections of the newsletter. In Photoshop CC, you might edit photos taken at a recent organization-sponsored event that will be included in the publication. Using InDesign, you might lay out the multipage document, incorporate the newly created and edited images and format text copy provided by the organization. When the newsletter is finished, multiple formats of the document might be exported from InDesign and delivered to the organization for print and electronic distribution to its members. This kind of multi-application project highlights your skills in each application and your sense of design incorporating a variety of elements into a single, cohesive document. The similarities across application workspaces and among tools and processes support multi-application production.

Adobe's Learn & Support Resources

One challenge that faces all designers who use the Adobe Creative Cloud applications is the need to stay up to date with evolving software. Adobe routinely updates its applications, introducing new features and, occasionally, new tools. For each Creative Cloud application, Adobe maintains an online *Learn & Support* resource (online help) (Figure 16.1). These sites provide valuable information following an application update; look to these sites for lists and descriptions of software changes (*What's New*), related tutorials and additional information. To access the *Learn & Support* resource in any Adobe application, go to the *Help menu* and select the respective *Help... menu command.*

- *Photoshop:* Help menu > Photoshop Online Help...
- *Illustrator:* Help menu > Illustrator Help...
- *InDesign:* Help menu > InDesign Help...

The *Learn & Support* resources also present useful information about using the applications, under the headers, *Tutorials* and *User Guide.*

- The *Tutorials* area provides an assortment of short videos based on skill level and task. These videos are categorized by presentation style, which include but are not limited to the following:
  - *Watch:* Videos that step through the process of performing a specific task.
  - *Try it:* Videos accompanied by a corresponding sample file that can be downloaded so the audience can work along with the video instructions.
  - *See how:* Text-based instructions outlining how to complete a task.
  - *Get inspired:* Videos highlighting different designers and their use of an application to create engaging designs.

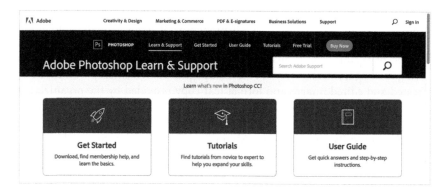

Figure 16.1

Adobe Photoshop Learn & Support, Help menu > Photoshop Online Help....

Graphic Design: Learn It, Do It

- The *User Guide* provides an index of application-specific topics and a powerful search field (*Search Adobe Support*) that connects to the vast Adobe user community.
  - After searching for a term or tool, use the provided filter checkboxes to narrow the list of provided results. *Tip:* Start by using the available options to limit the results to a specific application.

Use these online resources to further your software skills. Explore additional tools and processes in order to expand your personal design toolset.

Creating a Portfolio

Developing a portfolio of work is an important step for a designer and one that facilitates the sharing of their graphic design skills and abilities with others. A portfolio serves as a kind of benchmark, recording what the designer has accomplished to date and allowing the designer and others to visualize how their work has evolved or changed over time. A portfolio can also help the designer plan what they wants to focus on in the future.

A portfolio can be presented as a collection of printed works or electronic files. The delivery method should suit the designer's needs and the designer's potential audiences. Some designers prefer to have tangible copies of their design work after so much time spent creating on a computer. A portfolio notebook available from an art supply center works well to present printed images and documents. A limitation of the traditional portfolio is that it relies on one-to-one communication; there is typically only one copy of the portfolio that must be passed from person to person in order for the designer's work to be seen.

In contrast, an online portfolio can be an efficient and cost-effective way to share work with an audience; it is an example of one-to-many communication. However, the designer must keep in mind that once posted online, their work is accessible to the world. In preparation for sharing their designs, designers should consider the options for watermarking or copyrighting their work to deter others from downloading and using the files as their own (refer to *Chapter 9: Photo Editing in Photoshop*).

Whether paper based or online, it is important to think about the organization of works included in a portfolio. Which piece will be presented first? What strengths does the designer want to highlight through their work? When arranging pieces, start strong and end strong. In the portfolio, whether print or digital, designers should provide full-color examples of their strongest designs. A title should accompany each piece along with a brief description of the design's purpose and a list of the application(s) used to create the design. Capturing this information while it is fresh is useful, particularly as the portfolio continues to develop. A portfolio should be an evolving collection of work. As new designs are completed, incorporate them into the portfolio. With each new addition, reassess the presentation order of the included works and recognize that over time, it is important to replace earlier works with more recent designs.

As works are identified for inclusion in the portfolio, place a *copy* of the files in a designated "portfolio" folder on the computer. By gathering the files in a single location, an archive of work is being created. If possible, the designer should save a copy of this portfolio folder and its contents onto portable media (e.g., USB drive or external hard drive) or the cloud as an archive of their work.

Portfolio Q&A

What follows are questions often raised during the portfolio creation process and the author's responses.

How many pieces should be included in my portfolio? This number will vary based on your collection of work and your variety of skills. A good rule of thumb is to be selective. A portfolio may only include 6 to 10 strong pieces. The portfolio should serve as a sample of your skills and your design abilities. *Tip:* Do not include all of the images that you have created, as this could overwhelm your audience and dilute the impact of a particularly engaging image.

Is it all right if I update an image before including it in my portfolio? Absolutely, do not hesitate to update or redo an image as you see fit. As your skills develop, it is natural to revisit earlier works and update them accordingly. Just as the design process is cyclical, so is the process of updating a portfolio of work. *Tip:* Save a copy of the original file before you begin making any edits to the image. This allows you to see not only the evolution of the image, but also of your skills.

How can my portfolio be used in a job interview? Be prepared to discuss the application(s) and techniques used to create the works in your portfolio. Explain the processes used and how each design utilizes the design, color and typography principles. Use your design as an opportunity to highlight your knowledge and understanding of the underlying design concepts and the production process. If your portfolio includes a design that was created for a client, be prepared to provide an overview of your interactions with the client, including the feedback loop and revision cycles. Allow this narrative to highlight your interpersonal skills and your ability to work with others.

Be advised that during an interview, the interviewer may flip quickly through the portfolio simply glancing at your work. Do not be offended, this is typical. The interviewer may be looking for a specific type of work that matches the hiring description being used. This is why it is important to prepare your own narrative outlining your skills and abilities that you can support with specific examples from the portfolio. Guide the interviewer through your work, highlighting your skills and abilities in the process.

Should drafts or earlier versions of a design be included in my portfolio? Yes, if you have sketches or iterative drafts of your design, include these in the portfolio. Either file them behind the finished design, so they are available for reference, or present them on adjacent pages in the portfolio. Paper-based sketches can be scanned or photographed to include in electronic archives and to share online. These early works can provide an audience with insights into how you approach a project.

Is it all right to ask others for their input on my portfolio? Of course. Soliciting feedback from people whom you respect, particularly other designers, is a great idea. Just bear in mind that everyone has an opinion and when invited to share this opinion, you may receive more feedback than you expected or wanted. However, just because someone expresses an opinion, this *does not* mean that you must address this feedback in your work. After all, this is *your* portfolio and *your* collection of work, so you get the final say in what is included.

What should not be included in my portfolio? If any of your work could be deemed offensive or inappropriate for certain audiences, think twice before including it in your portfolio. Also, the work in your portfolio should be your own work; do not plagiarize. If any of your pieces were created as part of a group project, be sure to acknowledge the other members of the group and highlight your role in the project.

Getting Started

As the designer begins to gather pieces for a portfolio, it can be useful to revisit the central design concepts presented in this book. These ideas can serve as a focal point around which to highlight particular skills and design abilities.

Design Concepts

- Lines, Symbols & Signatures
- Elements of Design & Principles of Design
- Visual Hierarchy
- Color: Color Wheel, Color Pyramid, Color Symbolism, Color Palette
- Image Composition
- Typography
- Page Layout

Looking Ahead

Graphic design surrounds us. This statement began *Chapter 1: Breaking Down Design* and is a fitting statement to repeat as this book draws to a close. Opportunities exist to put the knowledge that you have gained to use in your community. Volunteer your services or seek out positions that involve graphic design. Look for outlets to share your design abilities with an audience, adding to the visual landscape. In the meantime, keep designing. As the title of this book states, *Graphic Design: Learn It, Do It*; it is time to do it.

Discussions

Discussion 16.1: Your Portfolio

What would you include in your portfolio? How do these pieces illustrate the design concepts presented throughout this book? Which format, paper-based or electronic, would best suit your needs?

Discussion 16.2: Sharing Your Skills and Talents

Who is the current audience for your design work? How is work shared with this audience? For what groups or organizations are you interested in designing? What steps are involved with making this happen?

External Links Mentioned in the Chapter

Illustrator Learn & Support | https://helpx.adobe.com/illustrator

InDesign Learn & Support | https://helpx.adobe.com/indesign

Photoshop Learn & Support | https://helpx.adobe.com/photoshop

References

Aches National Park. 2018. American Indians. U.S. Department of the Interior. American Indians. https://www.nps.gov/arch/learn/historyculture/american-indians.htm (accessed October 15, 2018).

Bradshaw Foundation. 2011. Lascaux Cave Paintings—An Introduction. http://www.bradshawfoundation.com/lascaux/ (accessed October 15, 2018).

Elving, Ron. "The Color of Politics: How Did Red and Blue States Come to Be?" *All Things Considered*, November 13, 2014, http://www.npr.org/2014/11/13/363762677/the-color-of-politics-how-did-red-and-blue-states-come-to-be (accessed October 21, 2018).

Giles, Jeff. "Samuel L. Jackson on the Hilarious Purple Lightsaber in 'Star Wars'." *ScreenCrush*, July 1, 2013, http://screencrush.com/star-wars-samuel-l-jackson-purple-lightsaber/ (accessed October 21, 2018).

Hornor, Tara. "Designing for Disabilities: Section 508 and International Accessibility Compliance for Beginners." *Sitepoint*. October 16, 2013. https://www.sitepoint.com/designing-disabilities-section-508-international-accessibility-compliance-beginners/ (accessed July 21, 2017).

Information about categories of typefaces/subgroups | https://www.fonts.com/content/learning/fontology/level-1/type-anatomy/type-classifications.

Kattwinkel, L. "Copyright Basics for Graphic Designers" AIGA, the professional association for design, July 1, 2007, https://www.aiga.org/copyright-basics-for-graphic-designers (accessed November 3, 2018).

OpenType | https://www.adobe.com/products/type/opentype.html.

Pantone LLC. "Color of the Year: Introducing Greenery." *Pantone*, 2017, https://www.pantone.com/color-of-the-year-2017 (accessed October 21, 2018).

"Poems—Six Honest Serving Men." *Kipling Society*, England. http://www.kiplingsociety.co.uk/poems_serving.htm (accessed July 21, 2017).

van Beveren, Tom. "A Quick Introduction to Colorblindness." *We are Colorblind*, January 10, 2012, http://wearecolorblind.com/article/a-quick-introduction-to-color-blindness/ (accessed October 21, 2018).

"What is AT?" *Assistive Technology Industry Association*. 2017. https://www.atia.org/at-resources/what-is-at/ (accessed July 21, 2017).

Index

Resolution, 49–51; *see also* File
  properties
Retouching tools, 138; *see also* Photo
  editing in Photoshop
Reverse cloned content, 157; *see also* Photo
  editing in Photoshop
Royalty-free license, 131
Rule of thirds, 127; *see also* Digital
  photography; Photo editing in
  Photoshop
  using Crop Tool, 145–147

S

Sans Serif typefaces, 193; *see also*
  Typography
Scalable Vector Graphics (SVG), 57;
  see also File formats
Scissors Tool, 248–252; *see also* Adobe
  Illustrator
Screen mode, 217; *see also* Adobe
  Illustrator
Script typefaces, 193; *see also* Typography
Secondary colors, 25; *see also* Color
Selection Tools, 319; *see also* Adobe
  InDesign
Serif typefaces, 192; *see also* Typography
Shape, 3–4, 14; *see also* Adobe Illustrator;
  Graphic design
  Builder Tool, 238–239
  tools, 233
Shutter speed, 121, 122; *see also* Digital
  photography
Signature, 6; *see also* Graphic design
60-30-10 Rule, 30; *see also* Color
Special characters, 179; *see also* Photo
  editing in Photoshop
Spell-check, 383; *see also* Adobe InDesign
Split-complementary color scheme, 28; *see
  also* Color
Spot Healing Brush Tool, 149; *see also*
  Photo editing in Photoshop
Square color scheme, 29; *see also* Color
Stakeholders, 40
Stock images, 131; *see also* Digital
  photography
Straightening horizon line, 143–145; *see
  also* Photo editing in Photoshop

Straightening photo, 143; *see also* Photo
  editing in Photoshop
Stroke, 217; *see also* Adobe Illustrator;
  Adobe InDesign
  panel, 218, 339–341
Style guide, 40
SVG, *see* Scalable Vector Graphics
Symbols, 4–6; *see also* Graphic design

T

Tagged Image File Format (TIF;
  TIFF), 57, 95; *see also* File
  formats
Tertiary colors, 25; *see also* Color
Tetradic color scheme, 28; *see also* Color
Text wrap, 359–360, 382–383; *see also*
  Adobe InDesign
Threaded text, 352; *see also* Adobe
  InDesign
  exercise, 355–362
  offset spacing, 361–362
  text frame in port and out port
    states, 353
  text threads visible, 354
  text wrap, 359–360
  threading text frames, 353
TIF, *see* Tagged Image File Format
TIFF, *see* Tagged Image File Format
Tools; *see also* Adobe InDesign; Adobe
  Illustrator
  panel, 211–214, 216
  tips, 211
  transformation, 339
Touch-up edits, 149; *see also* Photo editing
  in Photoshop
Triadic color scheme, 28; *see also* Color
Tripod, 122; *see also* Digital photography
Type, 189; *see also* Typography
Typeface, 190; *see also* Typography
Type tools, 253; *see also* Adobe Illustrator
  Area Type Options dialog box, 259
  Area Type with overset text shown,
    260
  Artboards panel, 263
  Character panel, 255
  Control panel, 255
  methods used for creating type, 254

9780367075347